233

D1065200

In This Most
Perfect Paradise

In This Most Perfect Paradise

Alberti, Nicholas V,
and the Invention of
Conscious Urban Planning
in Rome, 1447–55

Carroll William Westfall

The Pennsylvania State University Press
University Park and London

Library of Congress Cataloging in Publication Data
Westfall, Carroll William.
  In this most perfect paradise.

  Bibliography: p. 185
  1. Alberti, Leone Battista, 1404–1472. 2. Nicholas V, Pope, d. 1455. 3. Cities and towns—Planning—Rome (City) I. Title.
NA9204.R7W47   711'.4'0945632   73-3352
ISBN 0-271-01175-0

Contents

Preface

The history of the city is an immature field of scholarship. It lacks the definitions and methodological procedures that promote scholarly discourse, and it has few established means of drawing from and contributing to other fields of historical inquiry. It therefore seems appropriate to provide some definitions and explanations that may orient the reader as he traverses this *selva purtroppo oscura*.

In antiquity, and again from the Renaissance on, the physical city, more than any other instrument of man, has been the locus for activity in the many areas in which men choose to act. Men may, as Aristotle said, unite several villages into a community in order to sustain their lives and promote the good life. Or, as more recent views suggest, men may be unconcerned about promoting the good life in a civic community. They may desire simply to participate in a variety of activities in a relatively large, dense, permanent, safe, and socially heterogeneous settlement. Either way, cities have been the instruments that men have built to achieve the good life and to participate in diverse activities. Yet men's cities have remained imperfect—at times lacking in the good, at other times simply being dull. Something has always been missing. Leon Battista Alberti agreed with those who taught that "human affairs are never perfectly secure, though laid in the lap of Jupiter himself," and he chose a good authority to instruct him about how men might order their affairs. As James Leoni's eighteenth-century version of Alberti's *De re aedificatoria* puts it, "we may not improperly make use of the same answer that Plato made when he was asked where that perfect commonwealth was to be found which he had made so fine a description of; that, says he, was not the thing that I troubled myself about; all I studied was how to frame the best that possibly could be, and that which deviates least from resemblance of this ought to be preferred above all the rest." Alberti was practical, but not entirely so; he was thoughtful, but not impractically so. His was a persuasive view during the quattrocento, and it is the intention of this study to recover what men in mid-quattrocento Rome thought was the best city that possibly could be, how they hoped to build it, and why.

For the historian to describe that city he must consider the energy and thought devoted to it, but these qualities are difficult to pin down. They can only be incompletely defined by the available materials, and these cannot be interpreted with the precision possible in other subjects of historical inquiry. Many of the usual boundaries that guide historians within their discipline seem inappropriate when the city is the subject; but because the energy and thought of a citizen are directed into diverse fields of activity, the historian can achieve some order in his inquiry. The citizen makes works of art, he participates in institutionalized political and religious activities, and he speculates about the nature and character of art, institutions, politics, and religion. In the city art, activities, and speculation mingle with one another and assume a character that no one of them would have in isolation. The city is lost sight of when art is separated from events and activities, when these are separated from the institutional structures that give them form, and when the ideological content of art, activity, and institutions is ignored. The city can be seen when these elements are believed to interpenetrate.

The history of the city is a distinct area of historical inquiry. When interpreting any piece of evidence, one hopes to discover what it reveals about the city. Each element must be considered as if it were a part of a larger whole, and a definition of that larger whole must stand as the goal of the study. When the city is subjected to the scrutiny of the art historian, he must consider it to be both cause and effect of conceptions about it and its buildings. It is more than all the buildings within its bounds, and it is less than all the ideas generated in and about it. Here, when dealing with a quattrocento city, the verbal material was used as a gloss on the visual, and the visual material was accepted as a gloss on the verbal, as well as an independent bearer of meaning. This meant that the traditional approach and interpretative emphasis used for some of the verbal and visual material had to be altered and willful distortions avoided. Contemporaries said that Nicholas V's rebuilding project embraced the entire city. In assessing the evidence in order to confirm and to understand that sentiment, aspects of buildings that are seemingly unimportant when considered from the point of view of the artistic achievement they represent become significant. Stylistic criteria commonly employed by art historians seem largely irrelevant because they reveal little about the character of the project Nicholas undertook. In the history of the city, unlike the history of architecture, the designer may be less important than the patron, whose role as patron may be less important than his other activities, and the building may assume significance within the city through the patron's other activities or because of different, nonvisual criteria. But concern for formal qualities and the assessment of artistic achievement are still required for understanding the history of the city and for evaluating the accomplishment of builders. The history of the city is an important part of the history of art, but the emphasis of the historian of the city must be different from that of the historian of architecture or of the other arts.

Unlike the art historian, the historian of the city is concerned with the art object within a larger whole made up of other art objects and of objects that have nothing to do with art. He must therefore be more interested in formal qualities that allow him to gain an understanding of the contemporary meaning and significance of the object than he is in formal qualities that are assessed according to modern, historical critical standards. Such an approach would be difficult, if not impossible, when dealing with a period poor in nonvisual material; it is particularly appropriate for the quattrocento, however, because of the nature of quattrocento demands on objects of visual interest. The meaning and significance these objects had were conveyed by formal qualities, and the meaning, significance, and desired formal qualities were the subject of closely related literary material. The quattrocento in Italy was the last time in the past when such a close bond would exist between the verbal and the visual. Men then could profit from the older idea that the painter, the sculptor, and the builder made products that were to convey some significant content and that they were to choose forms that would add impact to that content. By the end of the century the first chink in that formidable structure of post-classical belief would be apparent, and the present notion about art—that the forms that convey whatever they convey are more important than whatever it might be that they convey—could begin to be formulated. The content quattrocento artists conveyed was related directly to political and religious events, institutional structures, and ideas, each of which may be known through investigating nonvisual and even nonartistic sources. The quattrocento city was simply an aggregate of such content.

This had not been the case earlier, and herein lies the significance of the quattrocento city. Not before the middle years of the quattrocento was the city thought of as yet another physical object that could convey content through the conscious effort of an individual who used his intelligence to design its facilities. Among the group who controlled the papacy from 1447 to 1455, the content was political, institutional, and doctrinal, and the purpose of the political and institutional structures, as well as that of the architectural ones, was to protect and propagate Christian doctrine. The modern conception of the city and of urban planning appeared when the notion was invented that buildings throughout the city, and the entire city that was composed of all those buildings, should be subjected to conscious design to reveal some ideological point.

It was not Nicholas V's intention to invent the modern city; he simply wanted to make Rome into something different from what it was when he ascended the pontifical throne. He died prematurely, with his project only barely begun, but beyond his fondest dreams he was successful in accomplishing his intention, not only in Rome but elsewhere. The Rome that popes attempted to build for the next several centuries, and that unknowingly haunted Mussolini, was largely Nicholas's conceptual invention. It might be said that the journey on the number 64 bus in present-day Rome traverses Nicholas's city. It is his legacy more than that of any other planner, and it is a modern testimony to the grandeur of his vision and the significance of his achievement. It begins at the railway and airline terminals at the Stazione di Termini, within the walls but in the midst of ancient ruins, and proceeds down the via Nazionale and through the Piazza Venezia, with its successive views: down the via del Corso to the Porta del Popolo, of the Palazzo Venezia, and of the Capitol. Continuing along traces of the via Papalis and avoiding the Campo de' Fiori, but crossing the Tiber near the Ponte Sant'Angelo, it circles near the Castel Sant'Angelo and moves in a stately fashion through the Borgo to the Basilica of St. Peter. There it turns and twists and then comes to rest just short of the Vatican Palace. That ride describes Rome; it is Nicholas's Rome, and that Rome continues to shape one's understanding of the Alma Urbis, incessantly dominates Italy, and unremittingly gives coherence to Roman Catholicism. It is perhaps a touching irony that modern Rome has resulted from what Nicholas considered ephemeral rather than permanent. He wished to use buildings to transmit doctrine to posterity, because they alone leave a lasting testimony and impression; but he either did not complete them, or they survive only in fragments. The buildings of modern Rome resulted from actions that were stimulated by reports and then by traditions that Nicholas had considered incapable of effecting the grand purposes he had in mind.

Nicholas's Rome was the mother of modern Rome; it was also the midwife of the modern city—midwife, not mother, because that distinction must belong to Florence, where Nicholas and his friends had grown to intellectual maturity. There for the first time the city came to be much the same thing it is today, an arena wherein men could follow their vocations to achieve their fame. The city had a purpose, and through civic activity which promoted that purpose men could gain tangible rewards or suffer disappointments at the hand of Fortune. In the city they could exert their wills and overcome adversities to achieve goals and rewards which were partly there, in the city. During the quattrocento the city existed for a different purpose from any we believe in, and men had different goals from our own, but for the first time men accepted the city as the place where they might attain their ends, as we often do today.

An equally important offspring of the conception of the city invented in the quattrocento is the modern belief that the city does indeed contain nearly all that is physically present within its boundaries. Not until the quattrocento did men think of—and actually see—the city as a collection of visible, tangible, physical objects: churches, palaces, houses, shops, works of art, festivals, fellow citizens, etc. These certainly existed in earlier cities, but during the previous centuries there is no indication that each of them was either looked at or valued both for its own distinct quality and as a part of a city that would have been incomplete without it. A medieval description of a city might emphasize the vast number of its houses and the grandeur of its palaces to indicate its magnificence, but absent are references to the architectural quality of the houses or of individual palaces, which demonstrated the virtue, fame, and individuality of the palaces' builders or architects. Similarly, a visual representation of a city, even well into the quattrocento, stressed only its important monuments; other parts—particularly humble houses and open spaces—were excluded, in order that they not detract from the important or the significant. Superfluity vitiates the essential; to reveal civic magnificence by stressing the important (in part by keeping the inferior subordinate), by illustrating and building a diversity of clearly structured types of buildings, by devoting attention to unique detail, and by arranging grand open spaces is an early Renaissance invention that survives in present belief and practice.

The belief that the physical fabric of the city reveals the purpose of the city, that it is the place wherein men may best act, and that it contains nearly all that is physically present within it allowed cities to be built that are now admired. The Rome of Nicholas V, Julius II, and Sixtus V, the Paris of Henry IV, Louis XIV, Napoleon I, and Napoleon III, and the Vienna of Franz Joseph have appeal because they are grand, orderly, and purposive. The grandeur and order derives from the subjection of the physical elements of cities to a purpose that likewise determines the hierarchical social and political structures housed with grandeur and order. But behind the grandeur and within the interstices of the order are qualities of human concern that we would consider unconscionably inhumane. The same structured hierarchy that saw to it that St. Peter's dominated Rome assured that a cardinal's palace would be grand and his cobbler's residence a hovel. This is ignored when modern eyes are dazzled by early modern cities; unthinking tourists, junketing city planners, and all too many architects see only the forms and miss the content. Although they eschew hierarchies and believe that humanity, or at least some of humanity, has freed itself of inherited and external constraints on human liberty, freedom, and dignity, they admire the products of past hierarchical structures and attempt to transpose their glories to an alien arena.

The deception that blinds one while visiting the past guides one in the present as well. Today, the quality of human concern and physical accommodation that many people and activities receive in our own cities reveals a continued attachment to hierarchical structures, even though we decry hierarchies of human concern. From the middle of the quattrocento on, an intelligently designed urban fabric was to make clear the existence of a carefully contrived and protected hierarchical order. But is the same not the case today? Is it not true that intelligent design is reserved for those on top? The hierarchy of wealth and power, and consequently the hierarchy of human concern, can be read in the physical facilities of any present American or European city or town. We still value intelligent design, but the standards we use to assess it, and the categories in which we choose to apply it, derive from a structure that survives from the past. The belief that intelligent design is to be put to the service of some problems but not of others must be the least beneficent element from the early Renaissance to survive today. Perhaps an understanding of how the grip of this belief was first imposed may help to loosen its hold, if we now see that it is inappropriate. Perhaps a realization of how broad and perspicacious was the thought that went into its invention will suggest the clarity of insight needed to dismember it and replace it. Perhaps a knowledge of how different the past was from the present—and how much the same—will point up the urgency of the task. If history teaches, its lessons must have to do with how to separate the historical from the past and the past from the present, as Burckhardt said. It may teach what should be salvaged or scrapped from the past, but more importantly, it can suggest standards for achievement to which we may justly aspire in the present. Historical study allows men to grapple with their fellows across time, to measure themselves against the achievements of more than merely their contemporaries, and to be moved by the example of past—but presently inappropriate—standards of excellence.

Acknowledgments

My debts are numerous; my execution of expectations is inadequate.

With deep respect I acknowledge the instruction and assistance of the late Professor Rudolf Wittkower and of Professor Paul Oskar Kristeller of Columbia University. In addition, reference must be made to scholars who have worked their way through a far vaster mass of material than is found here. The historiographical tradition established by scholars from Burckhardt through Baron, Garin through Trinkaus, Pastor through Jedin, and many others is demanding and rewarding. That tradition has been relatively free of the religious polemic that sometimes surrounds the history of papal policy. I trust that my own persuasion will be as inconspicuous as is the deeply held belief of Roman Catholic scholars who have contributed to our understanding of many of the questions handled in this study. Something should also be said about the ideas of those who have worked on the specific question treated here. It has not always been possible to cite them, but anyone familiar with this topic must acknowledge the works of Dehio (1880), Magnuson (1958), MacDougall (1962), and Battisti (1958; Rome, 1960).

Summer explorations in 1968 were made possible through the assistance of the National Endowment for the Humanities and the American Council of Learned Societies; in 1969 the Samuel H. Kress Foundation came to my rescue; in 1971 a Ford Foundation Humanities Summer Grant administered by Amherst College enabled me to complete the work. The bulk of the research and writing was done in Rome during the academic year 1969–70 through the generous support of a Trustee-Faculty Fellowship awarded by President Plimpton and the trustees of Amherst College.

Many institutions and individuals assisted me. In Rome, the generosity and hospitality of the director and staff of the Bibliotheca Hertziana were crucial. With pleasure I acknowledge the courtesy of the Biblioteca Nazionale Vittorio Emanuele II and the Archivio Capitolino. The Biblioteca Vaticana, Fototeca Vaticana, and Archivio Segreto Vaticano also deserve my warmest recognition. Important and stimulating assistance was freely given by Professors Charles Trinkaus of the University of Michigan, James Ackerman of Harvard University, Mark Weil of Washington University in St. Louis, Ronald Malmstrom of Williams College, and Peter Marshall of Amherst College, and by Drs. Ursula Nilgen of the Bibliotheca Hertziana and Julian Gardner of the Courtauld Institute. Deoclecio Redig de Campos, Direttore Generale dei Monumenti Musei e Gallerie Pontificie, deserves my warm thanks. Special and ultimate recognition must be reserved for the late Professor Anne Lebeck of

Amherst College. Her assistance with the intricacies of Latin clarified, stimulated, and purified my own inclinations; her Greeks did not write like Nicholas's Italians, and all lapses in interpreting what quattrocento Latinists were trying to say represent my persuasion.

Rome and Amherst

A Bibliographical Note on the Ideal City

This study should not be considered a contribution to that genre of literature that deals with the ideal city during the Renaissance. It did not exist, or, as Alberti put it, attributing the idea to Socrates, "whatever cannot be altered but for the worse, is really best." I have, however, profited from the literature and have thought it proper to acknowledge my debt by listing several studies here. The list may be convenient for those who wish to pursue the ideological elements of Nicholas's project within the context suggested by these works. They appear here in approximate chronological order. Only a few call for comment; the full citations appear in the bibliography.

Münter, 1929

Lavedan, 1941; a general review which turns more heavily on ideal concepts in Renaissance cities than is now thought to be appropriate.

Blunt, 1940; chapter I; and,

Eden, 1943; together, these contain the best short review of Alberti's so-called ideal city as presented in *De re aedificatoria*.

Lang, 1952

Firpo, 1954

Braunfels, 1966; first edition, 1953. This is a classic that deserves close study; although it does not deal with the ideal city or with utopian thought, it does deserve mention in any bibliography on the city.

Rosenau, 1959

Eimer, 1961

Garin, 1961

Klein, 1961

Bauer, 1965

Argan, 1969. His brief review opens with a reference to Lewis Mumford's statement: "The Renaissance city does not exist, or rather... in the fifteenth and sixteenth centuries there were no cities which may be called Renaissance in the same way that Siena may be classed as Medieval or Rome as Baroque"; this allows the book to ally itself to the useful concept which has long provided the context for Argan's approach to Renaissance art. Thus, it reports that the humanistic culture of the Renaissance "was the first to take a conscientious view of the city as the heart of an organized society and as the *visible* expression of the functions of that society. It was, in fact, the first time since the decline of the classical world—with the rise of this new humanistic culture—that a theory, or science, of the city was created" (my italics).

xvi   In This Most Perfect Paradise

Dates of Popes

Although it is easier for the writer to follow the tradition and the material that dates activity in Rome according to pontificates, the dates of the popes are not always the data which are most familiar to the reader. Therefore, a list of those who are important in one way or another in this study may prove useful.

Innocent III, Conte, Anagni, 1198–1216
Nicholas III, Orsini, Rome, 1277–80
Boniface VIII, Caetani, Anagni, 1294–1303
Boniface IX, Tomacelli, Naples, 1389–1404
Martin V, Colonna, Rome, 1417–31
Eugenius IV, Condulmero, Venice, 1431–47
NICHOLAS V, Parentucello, Tuscany, 1447–55
Calixtus III, Borgia, Valencia, 1455–58
Pius II, Piccolomini, Siena, 1458–64
Paul II, Barbo, Venice, 1464–71
Sixtus IV, della Rovere, Liguria, 1471–84
Innocent VIII, Cibo, Genoa, 1484–92
Alexander VI, Borgia, Valencia, 1492–1503
Pius III, Piccolomini, Siena, 1503
Julius II, della Rovere, Liguria, 1503–13

1   The Quattrocento Papacy
Before Nicholas V

The pontificate of Nicholas V (1447–55) marked one of the most important turning points in the history of the papacy. Some popes have been considered more important than Nicholas primarily because, at the time they occupied the Throne of Peter, their actions had an important bearing on European history. Boniface VIII, for example, exaggerated the temporal pretensions available to the papacy; Martin V was elected to govern a reunited Church and returned its head to Rome; Leo X showed how incompetence could rend the seamless tunic of the Church; and Clement VII demonstrated how vacillation could turn brothers in Christ against one another. Other popes have commanded attention due to their quite personal execution of their office as head of the Church. Sixtus IV, for example, is known as a patron, an administrator, and a nepotist. His nephew Julius II is remembered as a man cut from the same cloth and seemingly inspired more by his namesake, Julius Caesar, than by his predecessor, Peter the fisherman. Alexander VI is a reminder of the dangers inherent in a dynastic and bellicose papal policy stemming from an emulation of his namesake. The policies and actions of these men took decades to change, amend, or negate. Alone among the Renaissance popes stands Nicholas V. He presided when a new conception of the papacy was formulated; his actions bore consequences throughout Europe, even though he viewed Europe from an exclusively papal point of view.

When he ascended the pontifical throne, Nicholas knew the problems the Church faced because he had been active in the ecclesiastical hierarchy throughout his adult life. But unlike his two immediate predecessors, he resolved to address these problems within a broad historical and theological perspective that stressed the role of the Church in the sacred affairs of men. He turned his energies to two tasks: one was to restore the order of the Church; the other was to implement a new conception of the papacy within a Church which existed in a world that was changing and that was therefore changing the Church. To be successful in one, he had to be successful in both; and he was successful. He outlined the order the Church might attain and defined the role of the papacy within the Church. Nicholas's predecessors had defended the primacy of the papacy within the Church and of the Church in both sacred and temporal affairs of men, and they had indulged in open, willing, and indiscriminate use of secular and sacred prerogatives; but the most adroit among his successors would steer the Church along the tack he had set for them. They would concentrate on their responsibilities for the sacred affairs of men. The doctrine defined at the Council of Trent derives in large part from a definition of the papacy that Nicholas had first used to guide his actions as pope, and after Trent, these actions guided popes for centuries.

One means Nicholas used to implement his conception in practice was to rebuild the city of Rome. Both his city-building program and his building activity in Rome are the subjects of this study. As he set about rebuilding Rome, he considered the city to be the total collection of its institutional and physical structures. He designed each of the elements in that collection as parts of a whole. And he designed in such a way that the parts and the whole might make their order conspicuous and reveal his role in establishing and maintaining that order. What he did in Rome, others soon did elsewhere. They altered their understanding of the city, imitated his program, and emulated his accomplishment. The conception of the city that Nicholas first articulated physically in Rome became the conception of the city that would prevail until the concept of order on which it was based became debased centuries later.

The conception of the papacy that Nicholas implemented was made both necessary and possible by the actions of his two immediate predecessors. Neither Martin V (1417–31) nor Eugenius IV (1431–47) had recognized the opportunity available to them for a complete renovation of the papacy. Most of their actions had been determined by circumstances, particularly those which stemmed from the healing of the Great Schism at the Council of Constance (1414–18). One issue there was schism, another was reform, and a third was the contest between conciliarism and papal primacy. Schism was healed with the balm of conciliarism, but the traditional idea of papal primacy triumphed on the issue of reform, when the council itself recognized the pope's superiority over it by accepting Martin's prohibition of appeals in matters of faith to tribunals other than the pope's.[1]

A fourth issue was the conflict between the traditional claims for universal jurisdiction put forth by the pope and the emperor-elect and the actual system used for conducting the council, which was formed around national jurisdictions. It made for an ill-formed structure at the council, but no one seems to have been disturbed by the possible ramifications it could have on future political events, as it had allowed the council to operate. A pope had been elected to preside over subjects whose sacred allegiance was to a universal body and whose secular allegiance was to various national corporations. That the pope might therefore concern himself exclusively with sacred affairs was not immediately recognized. A divided allegiance for Christians was instituted because this allowed a single pope acclaimed by all to be elected; it allowed the schism to be healed and a triumphant Church to return to Rome. In that context it made little difference that the pope was both prince and priest.

Reform was now the most important unresolved problem. Martin supported a council at Pavia and Siena (1423–24), which had been called during the closing days of the Council of Constance. It accomplished nothing—which, from Martin's point of view, made it a success. At its happy dissolution he scheduled another to be held at Basel, but he died just as it was being assembled. Eugenius immediately sought to establish his control over the new council. It grew irritated at this, however, and turned itself into a conciliarists' reforming council, which sought to dismantle the monarchical structure of the Church and to establish an assembly of some sort in the place of the pope as the head of the Church. Eugenius had inherited this troublesome council from Martin, but another legacy had been the nearly mature fruit of continuous negotiations with the Greeks, which sought to unify the Latin and

---

[1]Jedin, 1957, I, p. 16; see also Jacob, "Conciliar Thought," 1963, pp. 4 ff.

Greek Churches.[2] Eugenius seized the opportunity for union as a lever to pry the conciliarists away from the dangerous question of reform. From the point of view of the Latins, and particularly from that of the Italians, here was an opportunity to resolve theological problems within the Church universal and to temporize on many intractable political problems within the west. In the next few years both the council at Basel and the pope wooed the Greeks; the pope's suit was more appealing, and he opened the Council of Union in Ferrara in 1437.

After its translation to Florence early in 1439, negotiations with the Greeks resulted in acceptance of terms for union. These defined the papacy within the Church and in spiritual terms, but said nothing about its temporal powers. The key document is the bull *Laetentur Coeli*, promulgated July 6, 1439. It refuted the conciliarists' proposition that "the General Council is above the pope" and became, in Hubert Jedin's words, the "Magna Carta of the papal restoration."[3]

> We define the See of the Holy Apostle and the Roman pope to hold primacy in all the world, and the pope to be the successor of St. Peter the Prince of the Apostles and the true Vicar of Christ and head of the universal Church and father and teacher of all Christians, and that in the person of Peter full power was conferred on him by our Lord Jesus Christ for caring for, reigning over, and governing according to the acts of ecumenical councils and sacred canons.[4]

Laetentur Coeli suggested a completely new interpretation of the office of pope. Like Martin at Constance, Eugenius was given the opportunity to define the pope's role as a spiritual one within the Church and to subordinate his temporal role in the affairs of states to his sacred office. The bull did not, as it could not, contradict earlier ones. Its novelty was in its emphasis, and its emphasis corresponded to the circumstances that had brought it into existence. In contrast to its most important predecessor, *Unam Sanctam*, promulgated by Boniface VIII in 1302, it stressed the spiritual and made no reference to the temporal. There was no need to discuss the relationship between temporal and spiritual in *Laetentur Coeli*, and in temporal affairs Eugenius, like his predecessors, followed the definition of papal prerogatives contained in *Unam Sanctam*. He did not refashion his actions in accordance with *Laetentur Coeli*. It represented only a welcome weapon against the conciliarists and a positive recognition of papal primacy within the universal Church. It did not affect his conception of his office or his program of activity. He did not consider it the most important definition of his office, and it would not be clear that the bull could play such a role until after his successor had demonstrated its potential through practice.

The councils were concerned with matters of general Church policy, and both Martin and Eugenius were constrained in their dealings with them by what might be called their domestic policies. Both were temporally minded, as *Unam Sanctam* and tradition told them they could and should be. When Martin returned the papacy to Rome, he must have considered its constitution and prerogatives to have been un-

---

[2]For the negotiations that had begun even before the Council of Constance, see Gill, 1959, pp. 20 ff., 43 ff. For a supplication for a council of union made at Constance in the name of the eastern Churches, see Fillastre, 1961, pp. 434 ff., and for another, see Richental, 1961, p. 176. For Urban V's program in 1365, see Mollat, 1963, pp. 156–157.

[3]Jedin, 1957, I, pp. 18–20; see also Gill, 1959, p. 313

[4]*Bull. Rom. noviss.*, I, pp. 266–267; also Gill, 1959, appendix, pp. 412–415. For the background of its drafting, ibid., ch. VIII.

changed during its century of exile and schism. Most of his actions seem to be con-
tinuations of thirteenth-century factionalism, with his family, the Colonna, now in
ascendancy over the Orsini.[5] Eugenius belonged to no Roman faction, but even after
his return to Rome from the Council of Union, there was no discernible change in the
Venetian's conception of his office. Eugenius was perhaps too bound by the older
conceptions of his role as both head of the Church and as temporal ruler of a large
part of Italy to profit from the interpretations that had been formulated in Florence.
Alternatively, perhaps he did not consider it necessary to change; perhaps he was less
skilled in constructing conceptual structures; or perhaps he was simply less concerned
with using literary and visual forms to show that the office of pope had been rede-
fined. Nicholas's hands were much less tied; the redefinition had been worked out by
his predecessor, who had too much at stake to change his policies abruptly in mid-
stream. Unlike Martin and Eugenius, Nicholas did not belong to a strong family. He
had risen to the top of the hierarchy quickly and without the assistance of factions
and allies who had vested interests in maintaining the old system. In addition, he
had come to maturity after the Council of Constance; he had made his reputation as a
secretary to a conciliator of factional disputes rather than as a sponsor of one or
another party, and he had won early renown through his contribution to the Council
of Union. Thus, although Eugenius had presided when the papacy triumphed and
in large part had made it possible to institute a restored papacy on a new conceptual
foundation, Nicholas was the first to use that success to display the new eminence of
his office.

One important sign that Martin and Eugenius were of a like mind and that Nicholas was of a different one is in the attitudes they held about the place from which
the Church was governed. On this issue both Martin and Eugenius showed that they
sought to restore and not to change recent connotations and conceptions. When
their attitude is understood, the significance of Nicholas's program can be appreciated.

San Giovanni in Laterano was the cathedral church of Rome. Through his taking
possession of it and his presiding over the Church from it, the pope could stress
that he had succeeded to the office of Peter, the first Bishop of Rome, and, additionally, that the Bishop of Rome had succeeded to the imperial dignity of the ancient
emperors. The Lateran Basilica and its attached papal palace had strong imperial
connotations because they were believed to have been built on the site of Constantine's palace, which the emperor himself had given to Sylvester, the bishop of Rome.
According to the Donation of Constantine, the emperor had given it to the bishop in
recognition of the superiority of the papacy over the empire. The authenticity of the
Donation had often been challenged. In 1440 Lorenzo Valla, the Roman-born
humanist who would later espouse Nicholas's program, had hurled an attack against
it in conjunction with a campaign against Eugenius from Naples, but not even his
argument, valued as it was by the humanists, caused Eugenius to doubt the document's continued force. The early medieval forgery was part of canon law as codified
in Gratian's *Decretum,* and its declaration of Rome's supremacy over the sees of
Alexandria, Antioch, Jerusalem, and Constantinople was cited by Eugenius at the
council that issued *Laetentur Coeli.*[6] Its granting of the use of the tiara and of other
signs of superiority of the papal dignity over the imperial dignity, its gift of "the
city of Rome, and all the provinces, places, and cities of Italy and the western

[5]See Partner, 1958, and compare the discussion of Boniface VIII's policy by Boase, 1933,
pp. 159 ff.
[6]Coleman, in Valla, 1922, p. 4; also Fois, 1969, pp. 296–300, 324–345, esp. p. 343.

regions," and its promise that the emperor would hold these statutes inviolate were elements in papal tradition that Eugenius could hardly overlook and was loath to forego.[7]

Against this background it is hardly surprising that when Eugenius transferred the Council of Ferrara and Florence to Rome in 1443, he transferred it to the Lateran.[8] The pope was addressed in *Laetentur Coeli* as "the successor of St. Peter, the Prince of the Apostles." It was the "See of the Holy Apostle and the Roman pope" that was defined as holding "primacy in all the world," and the Lateran best represented the position within the Church universal that Eugenius believed belonged to the bishop of Rome. But in his own mind this still meant that he was as much the successor to Constantine and Sylvester as he was to Peter. He was still primarily preoccupied with domestic affairs, and in domestic policy the Lateran held a strong edge over any other place that might be considered important.

This was because many connotations had accrued to the Lateran in the course of time that tended to stress the office of pope as the possessor of the temporal prerogatives the papacy had assumed from the empire. Boniface VIII had resided there rather than at the basilica of the Prince of the Apostles in the Vatican during the last years of his pontificate; he held his abortive council there, and he had used its imperial connotations in his political actions.[9] Dante recognized this and decried Boniface and the temporally powerful papacy; he referred to the worldly preoccupation of the Church of Rome by naming the Lateran when he stood in Paradise and contemplated the Rose that was the Church.[10]

During the long residence of the papacy in Avignon, a theory was developed that allowed the pope to be considered the universal governor precisely because he was attached to no particular see—or, it was once suggested, if attached to a see, it was to that of New Rome, which was located in Avignon.[11] Such ideas were novel, if even received and understood, in Italy. When Urban V did manage to return to Rome from Avignon in 1368, Coluccio Salutati, who from 1375 until his death in 1406 would be chancellor of Florence, wrote to Petrarch: "If you were at Rome you would ... rejoice. Your piety of soul would bless him who had rebuilt the Lateran, restored St. Peter's, and roused the whole city." [12] The implicit ambiguity here between the rival status of the Lateran and St. Peter's was addressed directly by the Avignonese pope, Gregory XI, in 1372. In a bull which referred to the Donation, he declared:

> We, therefore, wishing to put an end to doubt and, in addition to that, to remove reason for hesitation, declare by the apostolic authority of those present and decree and indeed define that the sacrosanct Lateran Church, our special seat, holds the supreme place among all the other churches of the city and of the world and [among all] basilicas and is even above the church and basilica of the Prince of the Apostles in the city and that it is by right

[7]The Donation is given in Valla, 1922, pp. 11–18, in Latin and English.

[8]For the transfer, see below p. 15. The council was dissolved sometime between 1445 and 1447; Gill, 1959, pp. 337–338.

[9]Platina, p. 338 (Life of Boniface VIII), mentions the Lateran "portico...sù'l quale... si publicano le scummuniche"; for it, see Mitchell, 1951, passim. Boniface promulgated *Unam Sanctam* from the Lateran. For the Lateran and its monarchical connotations, see Ullmann, 1955, pp. 325 ff.

[10]*Divina Commedia, Par.* XXXI, lines 34–36.

[11]Wilks, 1963, pp. 400–407.

[12]Quoted in Mollat, 1963, p. 159.

greater than all the other churches and basilicas mentioned above and that it rejoices in the honor of priority, dignity, and preeminence beyond all the individual churches aforesaid and [beyond all] basilicas.[13]

This represented the policy of Martin V after the schism was healed. He declared that the Lateran, "among all the churches of the world, [is] the one most worthy of devotion and faith."[14] In the list of churches in Rome compiled for Martin V by Niccolò Signorili, the *scribasenatus* (chancellor) of the Roman commune, San Giovanni was placed first and, uniquely in this list, it was commented upon. "The sacred church of the Lateran," Niccolò said, "which is the head of all the churches of the city and of the world, as is explained in letters sculpted in marble above the columns of the entrance portico of the said church, which say the following . . . ." They say, in short, all that the Donation of Constantine and the 1372 bull had said about the church's primacy in imperial and papal doctrine.[15] Martin chose to have his tomb at the Lateran, the church on which he had spent the major part of the building funds he devoted to restorations and repairs.[16]

Despite its strong connotations, residence at the Lateran was not required of a pope. Before 1447, the place of residence seems to have been less important as a display of doctrine than it was after that date. During more than a century and a half before the Captivity, the popes were peripatetic; when they did reside in Rome, they generally stayed at the Lateran, although some stayed at one or another of the palaces attached to various basilicas in Rome. The Lateran at that time was the best equipped to house the pope and his curia, and that would have been an important consideration when there were no obstacles to prevent his residence there. Among the least well equipped was the Vatican. The first pope to have built anything that survives there was Eugenius III (1145–53), while Innocent III (1198–1216) was the first to live there for any length of time, although for only about twenty months of his eighteen years as pope, and he made no elaborate claims for what he had built there.[17] He stated simply that it was necessary "not so much for honor as for utility."[18] No pope before Nicholas did much about the physical facilities at the Vatican.

The Lateran was important, but residence there was not—not even after Martin returned the papacy in 1420. He lived for the most part at the Colonna family palace

[13]*Super universas orbis*, 23 January 1372, in *Coll. Bull. Vat.*, II, pp. 20–21; among the sources given by the editor of the collection is a marble tablet posted at the Lateran. See also Ehrle and Egger, 1935, pp. 25 ff. and 49–50.

[14]The phrase occurs in a letter allowing the despoliation of disused churches for the ornamentation of the Lateran; dated 1 July 1425, in Müntz, *ACP*, I, p. 4, n. 1.

[15]The list appears in Armellini, 1942, I, pp. 73–79; this quotation, p. 74. See also the appearance of the Lateran at the head of Signorili's list of patriarchical basilicas in Signorili, 1953, p. 170. For the inscription he cites, which is twelfth-century in origin, see Armellini, 1942, I, p. 124.

[16]Accounts in Müntz, *ACP*, I, pp. 9 ff. As Julian Gardner has pointed out to me, Martin's actions were quite understandable in that the Colonna had always had a strong interest in the Lateran, while the Orsini prevailed at St. Peter's and at Santa Maria Maggiore. After 1435, such considerations would have much less meaning, due to Vitelleschi's slaughter of members of both factions and their changed attitude about where they might find advancement; for which, see below, chapter 4.

[17]See Redig de Campos, 1960, pp. 235–236, and below, chapter 7, for this and later work. A sense, by no means precise, of the place of residence of popes may be gained from the registration of bulls collected by Jaffé, 1885, through Celestine III, and Potthast, 1874, Innocent III through Boniface VIII.

[18]Quoted in Ullmann, 1955, p. 326, n. 3.

at SS. Apostoli.[19] Eugenius had no fixed residence in Rome during the few years before he went to Florence;[20] upon his return to Rome, he went to the Vatican for nineteen days, then went to the Lateran where he attended to the business of the council, and subsequently returned to the Vatican, where he apparently stayed. While he was in Florence repairs had been undertaken at the Vatican, and both Martin and Eugenius housed their curia there, but each favored the associations the Lateran had for the papacy.[21] The Lateran was, as Eugenius could read in Flavio Biondo's *Roma instaurata,* composed between 1444 and 1446,[22] "the most superb of all the celebrated buildings and basilicas of all the world" that Constantine had given to Sylvester; "it is the first seat of the Roman popes, and in the past was usually lived in." Today, Biondo continued, it is in ruinous condition.[23] Eugenius himself had said in 1432 that it was more important to repair the pontifical palace at the Lateran than anything else.[24] He did nothing to diminish the stature of the Lateran. The last act of his pontificate to be recorded by the Roman diarist Stefano Infessura was to receive the tiara from Avignon and install it at the Lateran. Infessura reported that this was the tiara given Sylvester by Constantine.[25]

Neither Martin nor Eugenius had ignored St. Peter's, but neither of them considered it as important as the Lateran. Each took an interest in its repair and restoration, but neither undertook a concentrated campaign to make its contiguous palace an important residence for the papacy. Instead, each concentrated on making the basilica fit for worship, and each spent as liberally on the mosaics on the basilica's portico façade within the atrium as he did on the interior.[26] One of the most expensive projects Eugenius undertook must have been the addition of new doors to the basilica's central portal, the Porta Argentea, a commission that probably slightly postdates his departure from Rome in 1434 (fig. 1). Here he provided a clear state-

[19]Between 1421 and 1423 he lived at Santa Maria Maggiore; Magnuson, 1958, p. 224. Diener, 1967, p. 46, shows that he lived at SS. Apostoli continuously after May, 1424, except for ten weeks in the spring of 1426 when he was at St. Peter's. For biographical reports about his attention to SS. Apostoli's precinct, see Ptolemy of Lucca, *Vita,* col. 867 (also in *Liber Pontificalis,* II, p. 522); Müntz, *ACP,* I, pp. 5–6, for notes; and Platina, pp. 400–401 (Life of Martin V).

[20]He resided at the Vatican, at the Castel Sant'Angelo, and at the palaces at San Lorenzo in Damaso, San Crisogono, and Santa Maria in Trastevere; Diener, 1967, pp. 54–55. For the palace at Santa Maria in Trastevere, see Golzio and Zander, 1968, pp. 109, 110; for the palace at San Lorenzo in Damaso, which preceded the Cancelleria and was used by Vitelleschi and then by Lodovico Scarampo, see Golzio and Zander, 1968, p. 376, where older literature is cited, and Diener, 1967, p. 51, s.d. 24 September 1433. Infessura, pp. 42–43; also in Platina, p. 412 (Life of Eugenius IV); Gill, 1959, p. 334.

[21]For evidence of Eugenius's favoring of the Lateran, see his bull *Quamquam in omnibus orbis,* 30 March 1436, Theiner, *Cod. dip.,* II, no. 271, p. 338; his grouping of St. Peter's, the Lateran, and San Paolo fuori le mura in his concession of some hearth taxes, 12 November 1432, *Coll. Bull. Vat.,* II, pp. 85–86, and related documents, pp. 87 and 87–88; and his continuation of Martin's priorities in the construction projects he undertook as documented in Müntz, *ACP,* I, pp. 32–67; idem, 1885, pp. 321–328.

[22]For the date and background see Weiss, 1969, esp. p. 68.

[23]Biondo, 1953, I, lxxxiiii, p. 279.

[24]Müntz, 1885, p. 322, in a letter soliciting support from the barons. For Aeneas Sylvius's report on what he accomplished there, see Pius II, "De morte Eugenii IV," col. 897. See also Platina, p. 414 (Life of Eugenius IV); Armellini, 1942, I, p. 126.

[25]Infessura, p. 44.

[26]Müntz, *ACP,* I, p. 10, for Martin; p. 38 for Eugenius. The restoration of the mosaics was completed by Nicholas, probably in 1449; ibid., p. 120, n. 3.

ment about his conception of the papacy, and once again he showed that he belonged to the world of his predecessors.

The great bronze doors were made by Antonio Averlino, called Filarete, a Florentine who had been associated with Donatello and Michelozzo; he had possibly cast and chased Martin V's tomb.[27] There were two separate stages in the evolution of the doors' program. In the original design, each valve had three large panels surrounded by frames with elaborate foliage running between mythological scenes and characters, putti, and profile portraits, everywhere studded with enamel adornment.[28] Prominent in this program on the left valve in the top panel is Christ upon a throne, with the text EGO SUM LUX MUNDI ET VIE VERITATIS visible in the book open on his knee. Below him and of equal scale stands Paul, holding a sword and a book. Below Paul in a square panel is his condemnation and execution. In the border at the top of this valve, putti hold Eugenius's arms surrounded by a shell. On the right valve, at the top, appear putti who hold the papacy's arms surrounded by an oak wreath. In the top panel appears Mary with the subscription AVE GRATIA PLENA D TECUM, which supplements Christ's title SALVATOR MVNDI on the left valve. Below Mary and opposite Paul is Peter, with the figure of Eugenius kneeling before him and holding the keys (fig. 2). Below Peter is the scene of his condemnation and crucifixion (fig. 3).[29]

The program stresses the traditional Church. It had been founded by Christ, Mary was its figure, and it was constituted by Peter and Paul. The program shows that the papacy is the legitimate successor to the apostolic dignity of Peter and of Paul. This program is appropriate for the Basilica of St. Peter because the church housed important relics of both apostolic saints. The decision to invest resources in this commission and this program, with this display of papal doctrine, even before the Council of Union had been convoked, may correspond to an attempt to emphasize the apostolic role of the pope, along with his role as bishop of Rome; but commissioning doors with this program does not represent a drastic revision in the conception of the papacy. An analogous action was Eugenius's introduction of a new coin type for the popular silver *grosso* issued by the Roman papal mint. The older coin had perhaps been first minted by John XXII (1316–34); it showed the pope seated on a chair supported by lions, wearing a mitre and cope and giving the sign of benediction.[30] The type had originated perhaps as much as a hundred years earlier in coins of the same denomination minted by the Roman senate and showing a seated figure of Roma.[31] Both Martin and Eugenius minted the *grosso* introduced by John XXII.[32] Early in his pontificate, however, Eugenius issued a new silver *grosso*. It showed the standing figures of Peter and Paul, Peter with the keys and a book, and Paul with the

[27]For the date of the commission and Filarete's background, see Seymour, 1966, pp. 115 ff.; also below, pp. 14–15. Eugenius reportedly made another set of doors, which were in wood. See Müntz, *ACP*, I, pp. 44–45, who supposes their commission to have been in 1444 and their completion before 1447, and Cerulli, 1933, pp. 362–363. The report refers to the bronze doors. Eugenius made no wooden doors. The assistance of Dr. Ursula Nilgen, who is preparing a study of the Filarete doors, is gratefully acknowledged. For the repair of the older doors, see Alberti, *De re aed.*, II, vi, p. 123; Alberti: Leoni, p. 29.

[28]See Roeder, 1947, for the borders.

[29]For an interpretation of the topography shown in this last scene, see Huskinson, 1969.

[30]Serafini, 1910, I, p. 67, nos. 1–3, pl. XI, 4. They were minted at Ponte della Sorga.

[31]Ibid., I, p. 33, no. 29, pl. VI, 8, is perhaps the earliest example.

[32]Ibid., I, pp. 100–102, nos. 2–44, pl. XV, 22–25, pl. XVI, 1–8, for Martin; pp. 107–108, nos. 5–21, pl. XVII, 3–6, for Eugenius.

sword.[33] The doors, however, show that while the pope would display himself as apostolic successor, he is still the governor of a Church that is formal, hieratic, aloof, Lateran-based, and Constantinian.

The forms as well as the traditional program make this point. Old forms are used to show old figures. Mary appears as an enthroned and archaic relative of the domestic Virgin appearing in Florence by the time Filarete had left. The facial types used for Peter and Paul are emphatically those that had been used on pontifical bulls with almost no change for several centuries.[34] Filarete's handling of them recalls the heavily geometric forms of these conservative representations of papal authority, rather than the roundness and fidelity to observation that is already evident in the bronze tomb effigy of Martin V. His handling of Eugenius's image, deriving from the marble relief of Boniface VIII at the Lateran from 1295–99,[35] is especially revealing. The prototype for the Boniface image had been Arnolfo di Cambio's statue of Charles of Anjou, and the image had been part of a series of representations of the Caetani pope that had included references to Frederick II's gate at the Castello at Capua. The series had been produced with the intention of stressing papal power in furthering Boniface's temporal and political aims.[36] At some point the coat of arms of the relief at the Lateran had been converted from that of Boniface VIII to that of Boniface IX, but the pope's image had originally been in the same relationship to SS. Peter and Paul as the one shown by Filarete, i.e., kneeling between them and facing toward Peter.[37] It has been proposed that Filarete's program, forms, and manner of execution must have been deliberate reinterpretations of an earlier medieval style.[38] He probably drew on outdated models because they still best conveyed the traditional ideas Eugenius wanted prominently displayed on the new doors for the Basilica of St. Peter.

At some point, while manufacturing the doors, Filarete added four small narrative panels containing scenes from the events of Eugenius's pontificate (figs. 4–8).[39] Their formal treatment is closer to the new Florentine practice, with which Filarete was well acquainted, than is that of the original program. In changing the form, Filarete was able to show that the content of these additions was of a different character from that of the original panels, and in adopting this particular new form, he was able to present these scenes as vivid historical events; meanwhile, through inserting them within the interstices of the original design, he was able to subordinate them to the original program and allow them to serve as glosses on the main content in much the same way that illuminations and illustrations served as commentaries on the texts of manuscripts. His additions were anything but haphazard; each of the four panels was carefully related to both the file and rank in which it was placed.

---

[33] Ibid., I, p. 108, nos. 22–31, pl. XVII, 7–11. This was the type used by Nicholas; see I, pp. 111–113, nos. 13–29, pl. XVII, 26, pl. XVIII, 1–6.

[34] The type of bull appears continuously from Pasqual II (1099–1118) until a dramatic change occurs with Paul II, and the type then reappears, although in drastically revised form, with Sixtus IV. It then survives well into the sixteenth century. See Serafini, 1910, I, pl. M, 4, for Paul II, and pls. H through N for the continuity. Compare, for example, Masaccio's looser use of the type in the frescoes in the Brancacci Chapel.

[35] Seymour, 1966, p. 118; Gardner, 1969, pp. 117–120, who has recently dated the relief to 1295–99, and has shown that Boniface originally appeared in a different setting, for which, see below.

[36] Gardner, 1969, pp. 120–121.

[37] Ibid., pp. 117–120.

[38] See Seymour, 1966, p. 118.

[39] Ibid., pp. 116–118, for observations about the manufacture of the doors.

The two doors together show the foundation of the Church and its dual constitution in Peter and Paul. The supplement shows that the pope was fulfilling his office; additionally, it shows that Eugenius had amplified Rome as the legitimate seat of the papacy and that he had reaffirmed papal primacy within both the spiritual and secular realms.

The spiritual office of the pope demanded that he tend to the continued health of the Church. Eugenius had healed the Church by negotiating the union of its Greek and Latin branches, and the rank below Christ and Mary portrays the Council of Union (figs. 4,5). Below Christ is the departure of the eastern emperor from Constantinople and his arrival in Ferrara, where he is seen kneeling before the seated pope (fig. 4).[40] This last scene is fictitious; both the pope and the emperor had stood when they met.[41] Filarete's intention was to report the event from a retrospective and papal point of view, which suggested that the eastern emperor rather than the patriarch, who had also come, was the proper person to show as the pope's counterpart in the eastern delegation. The emperor was the "convener of the synod" and the effective director of the Greek contingent. His tenacity of purpose kept the Greeks and the Latins on the course that led to union, and after the patriarch's death (June 10, 1439), several weeks before *Laetentur Coeli* was promulgated, he had actually assumed direct guidance of the Greek delegation.[42] *Laetentur Coeli* meant recognition of the pope in Rome as the head of the Church universal, and the emperor of the east would, of course, kneel upon being received by the seated head of the Church, even before the sessions had begun.

On the same rank and below Mary, the council is seen in assembly (fig. 5). The setting is probably Ferrara, where the sessions were public. The pope sits on one side; on the other, the eastern emperor sits, lower, with the patriarch standing. They listen to two debaters in a pulpit set up above the notaries and clerics.[43] On the far right part of the panel the emperor is seen approaching his boat and embarking for Constantinople. The Church is whole, union is all but effected, and the emperor, who had come to the pope, may return to the second Rome now that he has recognized the primacy of the first Rome. Eugenius, through his careful guidance of the council, has restored the health of the Church, the heavenly bride of Christ and the earthly issue of Mary.

In the lower rank Filarete showed two other events from Eugenius's governing of the Church. Below Paul he indicated that the temporal primacy of the Church had been confirmed through the coronation of the emperor Sigismund at St. Peter's on May 31, 1433 (figs. 6,7).[44] Filarete carefully included three distinct events here,

[40]John VIII Palaeologus had left Constantinople on 27 November 1437; Gill, 1959, p. 88. He met the pope on 4 March 1438; ibid., p. 104. For the dress of the several Greeks, see Vespasiano, 1963, p. 25; Gill, 1959, p. 109, 184; Krautheimer, 1970, pp. 180–184.

[41]Gill, 1959, p. 104.

[42]Ibid., pp. 237–238, 244, 253–254, and esp. 270.

[43]For the seating arrangements, ibid., pp. 107, 143. In the earlier arrangement there was to be an empty throne for the western emperor corresponding to that of the eastern emperor, but the uncertainty of the final arrangements makes it unclear how faithful Filarete was to the actual scene.

[44]The caption in the plate in Seymour, 1966, pl. 55(a), identifies two of the three scenes in the panel as "the entry of the pope and patriarch into Rome." He does not illustrate the coronation scene on the far right. This appears in Barraclough, 1968, fig. 89, p. 183, with the caption "Sigismund receives the imperial crown from Eugenius IV (1433)." Neither author discusses the panel in his text, and no other text worth mentioning attempts to identify the events in the scene. The early seventeenth century report of F.M. Torrigio quoted in Müntz, *ACP*, I, pp. 44–45 (from Torrigio's *Le Sacre grotte vaticane*, 2nd ed., Rome, 1639, p. 156), describes the doors in this way: "L'incoronatione di Sigismondo imperatore in S. Pietro nel 1433 per mano di detto Eugenio,

making explicit the identities of the persons and places. On the far right is the coronation, in the center is the departure of the emperor from the Borgo, and on the left is the emperor's reception by a papal official. The emperor appears twice with the same garb and beard, first at the coronation where he is accompanied by the legend INCORONATIO/IMP SVGISMVNDI, and again on a horse in the central section. There, next to him and on a mount whose bridle is held by a courtier, is the pope, labeled EVGENIVS P̄P̄/IIII. The pope indicates that the emperor is to be received by the man on horseback awaiting him and labeled ANTONIVS DEᴿ/IDDO·C, or Antonio di Rido (fig. 7).

Filarete, like other reporters of the event, has stressed the lack of jurisdiction the emperor now had in Rome. The reporters made it clear that the emperor departed from the Borgo, where the pope stayed, and that he then went to reside at the Lateran for the duration of his short stay.[45] Filarete used many devices to make the same point. The emperor is shown being taken toward gates that are festooned with coats of arms. Those on the left belong to the canons of St. Peter's,[46] and the two on the right are the arms of Eugenius surmounted by the tiara but without the crossed keys, and the arms of the papacy with both the crossed keys and the tiara. Both the emperor and the pope are within the Borgo, and the point of view for this scene is from within the Borgo looking toward Rome. Here the pope as presiding officer over the canons of St. Peter's enjoyed absolute temporal authority, which he administered through the castellan of the Castel Sant'Angelo, in order that, as Eugenius had put it, the inhabitants of the Borgo might not be without laws and honest customs and be subject to no justice at all.[47]

The man awaiting the emperor and who will conduct him across Rome is Antonio di Rido (or di Rio, da Riddo, and variations), a Paduan who was the castellan of Sant'Angelo when Filarete made the panel, but not when the coronation had actually taken place.[48] Filarete has not allowed any ambiguity to exist about his identity or his office; a retainer holds di Rido's shield with his coat of arms and wears the castellan's helmet, and di Rido himself holds his scepter of command with a banner that seems to be attached to it.[49] By the time Filarete made this panel, di Rido may

e vi si vede il prefetto di Roma, tenendo avanti lui lo stocco; la loro cavalcata per Roma; l'unione della chiesa greca con la latina; l'entrata dell'ambasciatore del Rè dell'Ethiopia, ed altre historie di quel tempo.'' In addition to wrongly saying that these scenes were on the wooden doors Eugenius had installed, Torrigio is inaccurate in other ways, as will be shown in the discussion that follows.

[45]See Infessura, p. 30, and Tommasini's note 2 on the same page. Platina, p. 404 (Life of Eugenius IV), also reports this detail, although he seems to have taken it from Infessura.

[46]For their distinction from the arms of the papacy, see Galbreath, 1930, pp. 6–16.

[47]In *Romanus Pontifex licet*, 12 September 1437; *Coll. Bull. Vat.*, II, pp. 92–94. This is a confirmation of the ordinances promulgated on 6 April 1437 by Vitelleschi in an attempt to encourage people to reside in the Borgo. For the precedent established in 1421, see Partner, 1958, doc. 11, pp. 219–220.

[48]The castellan had been Giacomino Badoer; di Rido was appointed in May, 1434, and served until Nicholas V replaced him. Pagliucchi, 1906, pp. 86–87, 94.

[49]His coat of arms and the helmet appear on the monument to him, which includes a high-relief equestrian statue above a basement with the inscription B M/ ANTONIO RIDO PATAVINO SVB/ EVGENIO PONT MAX ARCIS RO/ PRAEFECTO AC NICOLAI V COPIARV̄/ DVCI IOANNES FRANCISCVS FILIVS/ EX TESTAMENTO F C; it stands in Santa Francesca Romana (Santa Maria Nova) in Rome. The banner on the door has the crossed-keys arms of the papacy without the tiara, as was common on the flags that the pope entrusted at this time to his special representatives in temporal affairs; Galbreath, 1930, pp. 59–60. With the arms on the monument are those of Eugenius without papal emblemata, indicating that di Rido was also a personal representative of the pope.

well have established himself as the most trusted soldier in Eugenius's entourage and would therefore have been a much more important figure to represent than the actual castellan at the coronation.[50]

That the papal castellan rather than a communal official was shown as the emperor's guide rankled Stefano Infessura, a zealous republican; although nothing of the sort appears, he cited the evidence of the doors to claim that the castellan had been accompanied by "Mancino." That would have been Laurentio Petri Omnisancti, called "lo Mancino," one of the three *conservatori* of the Roman commune at the time of the coronation.[51] Infessura's fabrication is perhaps explicable by the fact that the event had occurred as much as seven years before his birth; what he was reporting was rooted in local pride, for both he and "lo Mancino" were from the rione Trevi. Infessura's report could not be based on fact. According to the laws of the commune, the senator, not one or more of the *conservatori*, would have represented the commune if the commune were represented; if there were no senator, the three *conservatori* would substitute.[52] But there was a senator, who had been reappointed only a few weeks earlier,[53] even though such a reappointment was against the communal statutes. To have included the senator in the ceremony may have been dangerous because it might have enflamed old associations between the senatorial dignity and the emperor's office.[54] But Infessura was unhappy to leave the commune unrepresented, so he inserted a *conservatore*, who he might have believed would have remained inconspicuous enough to be allowed to remain in the panel.

It is, however, the castellan alone who will take Sigismund, the temporal lieutenant of the Church, across Rome to the Lateran, where he will reside as the pope's guest. In Rome he will enjoy as little temporal authority as he did in the Borgo. The scene below Paul, then, shows the pope establishing the emperor in his temporal office as protector of the Church, while making it clear to his lieutenant that the imperial office has no authority within jurisdictions reserved to the papacy. It reinforces in visual imagery the substance of the oath from Gratian's *Decretum* that Sigismund had sworn to Martin V at Constance in 1417, when the new pope had confirmed the election of the King of the Romans:

> Whenever, by God's permission, I come to Rome, I will exalt the Holy

---

[50]For di Rido's involvement in Vitelleschi's death in 1440, see Pastor, 1938, I, pp. 299–301, 398–400 (docs. 20, 21); additional information in Pagliucchi, 1906, pp. 100–110, 157–163. Eugenius outlined his duties and heaped praise on him in a bull granting him a fief in 1445; see Moroni, XII, pp. 314 ff.; Pagliucchi, 1906, pp. 106–110; *Coll. Bull. Vat.*, II, pp. 105–107. For its confirmation and for further dealings between di Rido and Nicholas—who had him replaced as castellan, as was traditional, but who still entrusted him with important tasks—see *Coll. Bull. Vat.*, II, pp. 110–111, 117–123, 125–129, and 129, for documents from 1447 and 1448. Müntz, *ACP*, I, p. 162, published two documents which show that di Rido was paid for construction on the fortress at Orvieto in 1450; in 1451 another man was paid for similar work. Di Rido died late in 1450 (Pagliucchi, 1906, p. 109), although one finds other dates in undocumented literature, including Forcella, II, p. 11, no. 30, who gives the date 1475 next to the monument's inscription, which has apparently served in later studies as the source for the date for di Rido's death and for the monument's erection.

[51]Infessura, p. 30. For the identity of "lo Mancino," Tommasini's note 3 on the same page; for Infessura's birth date as about 1440, Tommasini's preface, pp. xiii ff.

[52]For the communal statutes, see below, chapter 4. Compare also the reception of Frederick III, discussed below, chapter 4, and Epilogue.

[53]Salimei, 1935, p. 179.

[54]Compare the careful provisions Nicholas made in 1452 for the visit of Frederick III, which included the senator in his proper role, discussed below, chapter 4 and Epilogue.

Roman Church and you, its governor, to the utmost of my power. Never by my will or consent, my counsel or desire, shall it lose life or member or honor. While in Rome, I will issue no edict or ordinance affecting anything that belongs to you or to the Romans without your counsel. The territory of St. Peter that lies within our authority I will restore to you. To whomever I may commit the kingdom of Italy, I will require him to swear to be your aid in defending the territory of St. Peter to the utmost of my ability.[55]

The basis for the oath, like the ceremony and its representation, was the Donation of Constantine; Valla's observation in his challenge to the Donation's authenticity in 1440 reveals a distinct attitude toward the event that Eugenius had so carefully negotiated and Filarete so clearly represented: "What more contradictory than for him to be crowned Roman Emperor who had renounced Rome itself, and to be crowned by the man whom he both acknowledges and, so far as he can, makes master of the Roman Empire!"[56]

But for Eugenius there was no contradiction; indeed, the scene was probably chosen for representation on the left valve because it gave a thematic unity to that valve. The emperors of both the east and the west are shown kneeling before the pope, and between them stands Paul with his sword. The pope directs the sword of empire in the secular realm in the service of the Church; he governs with the arms of empire.

He also governs with intellect; that is, he tends to spiritual affairs with reason or deliberation, as Filarete made clear on the right valve. The doors present the common *topos,* or conventional and traditional framework for organizing material, that saw activity exerted through arms and letters.[57] The panel below Peter again shows the pope presiding over a council (figs. 8–11). Here, the setting of the scene on the left is Florence (fig. 9). John the Baptist appears in the lunette and FLORENTIE appears on the jamb of a carefully designed, carefully articulated doorway that resembles the type being used at this time for niches and doorways in Florence.[58] Eugenius is seen before a cloth-draped wall. He is seated on a high dais and is wearing the tiara and a cope; next to him are two bishops in mitres, and below him is a monk, who is probably meant to be a theologian, conferring with a cardinal. Facing the pope is a nine-man delegation, the members of which are variously dressed and in discussion among themselves. No one here wears a tall hat like those worn by the Greek emperor's attendants; the crucifix in the hand of the amply corporeal man in front indicates that these are clerics. They are receiving a document from the pope, which the dangling seal identifies as a bull. In part of the panel Filarete shows the same group as a caval-cade entering a gate clearly labeled ROMA (figs. 10,11).

It is difficult to know exactly what this panel represents, although it is clearly the continuation of the Council of Union, and some elements in it can be interpreted with precision. The bull cannot be *Laetentur Coeli.* It was promulgated in a joint ceremony with the Greeks and Latins, and no Greeks are shown here; additionally, the ceremony had been held in a setting considerably different from the one Filarete shows. Furthermore, the Greeks had not visited Rome. Wearied by the deliberations, they had immediately left for Venice and had set sail for Constantinople on October

[55]Fillastre, 1961, pp. 433–434.

[56]Valla, 1922, p. 159.

[57]This subject will be discussed again, below, chapter 2.

[58]See, for example, the portal to the Strozzi Chapel, S. Trinita, Florence; Krautheimer, 1970, fig. 93, discussed p. 261, dated between 1418 and 1423.

14, 1439. There were other bulls connected with union, but none would obviously call for a representation of Florentine events in conjunction with an entry into Rome. After the Greeks had ratified, deliberations with other branches of the Church were held. Preliminary negotiations with the Armenians, who arrived in Florence soon after the Greeks had departed, had been underway for some time. They agreed to union on November 22, 1439, and set sail for home as soon as possible, leaving from Genoa at the end of the year. Negotiations with other groups of Christians proceeded on the basis of information that had only recently become available from travelers into Muslim countries, information either solicited by the pope or ventured as a consequence of the excitement that surrounded the council.[59] The Egyptian Copts arrived in Florence on August 26, 1441; they negotiated with the Latins and visited Rome briefly in October, returned to Florence, and ratified union with the Latins on February 4, 1442. They then left for the east as soon as possible.[60] They had been accompanied on their journey to Florence and Rome by a group of Ethiopian monks who were normally resident in Jerusalem but who, upon arriving from the east, presented a letter to the pope which explained that they did not have the authority to speak for their Church. They did, however, encourage the pope to send envoys to Ethiopia. The panel might be interpreted as representing the union of the Coptic Church and the visit of that delegation with the Ethiopian monks to Rome, as was suggested in the seventeenth century. The left part of the scene might, on the other hand, show the pope delivering a copy of the Bull of Union with the Greeks to the Ethiopian monks, which they were then to transmit to their Church, as has been suggested more recently.[61] But something larger and more important would seem to be more suitable as a part of the program as a whole.

Its content might be interpreted in conjunction with the date of completion of the doors, which are inscribed "1445" and which were inaugurated on the Feast of the Assumption of that year (15 August), as well as in conjunction with the content of the inscriptions that appear in the frames below the feet of the two apostles. Below Paul appears: VT GRAECI: ARMENI: AETHIOPES: HIC ASPICE: VT IPSA ROMANAM AMPLEXA EST GENS IACOBINA FIDEM; below Peter and, appropriately, Eugenius, is: SVNT HAEC EVGENI MONIMENTA ILLVSTRIA QVARTI EXCELSI HAEC ANIMI SVNT MONIMENTA SVI.[62] The Jacobites were the Copts,[63] and the Ethiopians are included because on February 1, 1444, the

---

[59]Rogers, 1962, pp. 39–48.

[60]Gill, 1959, pp. 325–326; Rogers, 1962, pp. 40–43.

[61]See Cerulli, 1933, pp. 354, 356–357, 368, who reports the interpretation given by Muñoz and Lazzaroni, who followed Torrigio. Cerulli's interpretation depends upon three suppositions (for information given below, see Cerulli, 1933, passim). One, that the Ethiopians were important enough to merit so much space on the doors. This is possible to believe if one assumes that the pope believed that the Ethiopian emperor had the armed strength the monks claimed and that he believed that the emperor would assist him in fighting the Turks. This in turn demands that one believe that Eugenius was more concerned about the Turkish threat to the Greeks than he was about the health and unity of the Church. Two, that Filarete mistakenly combined the Coptic and Ethiopian delegations in the scene showing the receipt of the decree and that he showed them correctly in the Roman scene. Filarete was working in Rome, but was the confusion that great? And, three, that Filarete represented the scene that occurred earlier (October, 1441, and February, 1442) on the right rather than on the left, contrary to the direction of the figures' movement but analogous to the temporal sequence on the lower left panel, showing the coronation of Sigismund.

[62]For the suggestion that Maffeo Vegio was involved in these inscriptions and in the program for the doors, see Huskinson, 1969, pp. 156–157; for his association with the curia, p. 139.

[63]Their bull of union with the papacy was titled *Decretum Unionis Jacobinorum cum Sancta Romana Ecclesia;* Cerulli, 1933, p. 354. For the confusion which led to that identification, see Rogers, 1962, pp. 19–29, 81–82.

pope had received a report from Jerusalem indicating that the ecclesiastical and civil authorities of the Ethiopians, whose head was believed to be Prester John, had received the Bull of Union between the Latin and the Greek Churches and had accepted it with great joy.[64] In Rome at that moment this was considered tantamount to ratification. Excluded from the inscription are the Syrians, the Chaldeans, and the Maronites. The Syrians of Mesopotamia had ratified union on September 30, 1444; the Chaldeans (formerly Nestorians) and the Maronites of Cyprus had ratified on August 7, 1445.[65] They had not visited Florence, and their incorporation into the Latin Church must have occurred at too late a date to be included in the inscription. They had attended the council after its translation to the Lateran; the translation bull was promulgated in Florence on February 24, 1443, and the council was formally reopened at the Lateran on October 14, 1443. The earlier date would be about the last possible moment to add to or to revise the program for the four narrative panels. To represent the transfer of the council to Rome, where the pope could continue to preside over it, would fit the larger program of the doors.

The panel, therefore, possibly shows in general terms the continued attention to the problems of union and to the spiritual affairs of the Church that Eugenius intended to undertake through continuing the council in Rome; it was to work not only for union but also for the eradication of heresy, for reform, and for peace throughout the Church.[66] The group in Florence is receiving the translation bull, and the same group entering Rome is composed of representatives of the disparate branches of the Church that were still to recognize the primacy of the Latin Church, as is indicated by their strange dress,[67] and, probably, others interested in reform of the members by the attention of the head.

The original program, then, was supplemented by historical scenes that would show Eugenius's governing of the Church. Along the top rank he is shown healing the schism between the Greek and Latin Churches; along the lower rank he is shown using Rome as the seat of his authority by crowning the emperor and moving the council there; on the left valve he appears as governing through arms; and on the right valve he appears as governing through letters.

These panels, however, only supplement the original program that had been formulated before the Council of Union; this indicates that the events portrayed in them did not produce a fundamental reformulation of Eugenius's conception of the papacy. Two different references to the doors by contemporaries make this clear. Flavio Biondo said that the doors showed the union of the Greeks, Armenians, Ethiopians, Jacobites, and other peoples whom Eugenius had reconciled to the Church.[68] Biondo had, in other words, read the inscription on the Paul valve and had indicated that negotiations postdating the inscription had proved successful. His emphasis was on the restored health of the Church, and he found it unnecessary to point out that Eugenius had been involved in achieving it. Maffeo Vegio, a minor humanist active in the curia, read the inscription under Peter and said only that the subject of the doors was the great and outstanding deeds and actions of Eugenius.[69] Vegio emphasized the personal achievement of the pope; he knew that the union and

---

[64]See Gill, 1959, pp. 322–327.

[65]Ibid., pp. 335–337.

[66]Ibid., pp. 333 ff.

[67]See the notice quoted in Gill, 1959, p. 324, n. 4.

[68]For the quotation from *Roma instaurata*, I, lviii, see Huskinson, 1969, appendix I, p. 158.

[69]Quoted in Huskinson, 1969, appendix II, p. 159, where an improved text of the relevant passage from *De rebus antiquis memorabilibus Basilicae Sancti Petri Romae*, II, iii, is given.

the council had been interpreted by Eugenius's successor as a mandate for a new formulation of papal government and policy, and he attributed to Eugenius the responsibility for establishing the basis for that new formulation through his deeds and actions. This would not have been obvious to Biondo, writing during Eugenius's pontificate, but it would have been to Vegio, who wrote his report in 1455, after the death of Eugenius's successor, Nicholas V.[70] Not until Nicholas's ascension to the Throne of Peter were the Petrine implications of the council's definitions made central in the conception of the papacy. Eugenius's program for the doors, like his entire program of papal government, was traditional; but on the foundation laid by events sponsored in the name of tradition, Nicholas was able to build a new papacy.

[70]For the date of Vegio's work, see Weiss, 1969, p. 72, n. 5.

2 Nicholas V—
Governor, Priest,
and Builder

When Tommaso Parentucello (b. 1397) emerged from the conclave at Santa Maria sopra Minerva as Nicholas V on March 6, 1447, the opportunity for instituting a new conception of the papacy was at hand. The major issues that had filled the first half of Eugenius's pontificate with turmoil had been subjected to patient negotiation throughout its second half and had been brought to a stalemate. Although a state of torpor seemed to prevail, old issues were ripe for resolution, and no new ones with similar dangers were apparent. Conciliarism was all but vanquished. The concordats between the papacy and the princes of Europe, which had been disrupted through conciliarists' machinations, needed only their final negotiation. Peace among the factions of Italy was yet to be established, and the papacy had yet to consolidate its sway over the Patrimonium of Peter and secure its position in Rome, but the necessary conditions had been achieved. The union the Greeks arranged in Florence had to be consummated through ratification in Constantinople. And the Turkish threat to that beleaguered city had to be turned back. Vigorous action promised success.

Nicholas's accomplishments during his eight years on the Throne of Peter fulfilled the hopes stimulated by the universal rejoicing at his election. Germany (early 1448) and then France (1448) established their concord with the papacy, and in 1452 Frederick III was crowned emperor at St. Peter's. The conciliarists disbanded, their anti-pope Felix V abdicated (1449), and Nicholas created him cardinal as an act of charity. Bologna (August, 1447), other divisions of the Patrimonium, and Rome reconciled themselves to papal government. A great Jubilee was celebrated in 1450. The states of Italy moved toward peace by forming the Lega Italica. And on December 12, 1452, the hierarchy of the eastern Church, with the approval of the eastern emperor and the ratification of the eastern government, celebrated the final union of the two Churches in Santa Sophia in Constantinople.[1] These were stunning successes, but Nicholas was soon cast into a gloom from which it was said he never recovered, for on July 8, 1453, he learned that Constantinople had been stormed by the Turks and terrible ravages committed against its citizens.

That defeat was far in the distance when Nicholas set out to formulate his program for papal government, but it haunted him on March 24, 1455, when he lay on his deathbed. With the cardinals gathered around, he delivered his testament *viva voce*, as his secretary, Giannozzo Manetti, reported. The testament survives as the major portion of the third of three books in Manetti's *Life and Deeds of Pope Nicholas V*,

---

[1] See Gill, 1959, pp. 384–387.

the most important biography of the pope.[2] The testament contains the only direct statements attributable to Nicholas concerning his conception of the papacy and his program for papal government. It is, therefore, a very important document and must be treated with care. It is presented implicitly, not as a summarization of events, but as a review of principles that Nicholas had formulated in 1447 and later executed. There is no reason to doubt its authenticity, except to allow for some alterations in its rhetoric, or to question the early date for the conception of its content. Manetti and Nicholas had known one another since their youth; Manetti had been in contact with the pope throughout his pontificate; and the Florentine humanist had been the pope's secretary since 1453. He wrote the *Vita* within a year of the pope's death, and the content of it and of the testament are in close agreement with what can be known from other sources.[3] Unlike what one might expect if the testament were the invention of a sympathetic biographer composing an apology, it does not obscure the single conspicuous reversal of Nicholas's pontificate, the loss of Constantinople and the pope's inability to give aid. That subject is introduced as a digression and is explained as an unexpected event. It was unexpected because it did not follow from what Nicholas believed was the natural and God-ordained course of events. He had believed that if the Greeks followed the will of God and accepted union with the Latins, their city would be spared.[4] The Greeks ratified the agreement, and the Turks conquered their city. Although unexpected, it was an event of such importance that it had to be included in the résumé of his pontificate, but it found its way into the testament as a digression within the context of his principles of government and their execution.

Another catastrophe was included in a similar manner. During the closing days of the Jubilee of 1450, as the pilgrims were returning at dusk from St. Peter's to their lodgings in Rome, the Ponte Sant'Angelo became obstructed. The crowds in the back continued to push forward, and scores of pilgrims on the bridge were trampled and squeezed by the pressure of those behind or were pushed into the river, where they drowned. To commemorate this sad event, Nicholas ordered the construction of two memorial chapels beside the bridge in a piazza cleared at its landing in Rome.[5] Nicholas mentioned this in the context of the Jubilee in the section dealing with the great events he supervised and administered as pope, not in the section that dealt with the other buildings he projected or built. Similarly, in the second book, which is devoted to Nicholas as pope, Manetti mentioned the catastrophe and the construction of the piazza and memorial chapels as parts of his description of the Jubilee, not in his lengthy description of the building program Nicholas sponsored in Rome. Like the fall of Constantinople, it was an unexpected event; that these events were incorporated in the way they were adds credibility to Manetti's claim that he had written the life of Nicholas as Nicholas lived it,

---

[2]The only other one to survive is that of Michele Canensi; it has recently been discovered and published by Miglio, 1971, pp. 501–524. For lost biographies, see Miglio, 1971, pp. 481–483.

[3]Vespasiano, 1963, p. 57, states that Manetti wrote down the words as Nicholas delivered them; Vespasiano drew on Manetti's transcript for his own reduced version of the testament as it appears in his life of Nicholas (Vespasiano, 1963, pp. 57–58). Pagnotti, 1891, p. 411, n. 3, states that one manuscript copy has a note which says that the testament section of the *Vita* was written the same year in which Nicholas died. Pastor, 1949, II, p. 166, n. 2, states: "That this speech has been very considerably touched up and embellished by the biographer is highly probable, but there is no reason to doubt its essential accuracy." For a more recent assessment that comes to the same conclusions, see Miglio, 1971, pp. 491–492.

[4]Gill, 1959, pp. 378–379.

[5]For details, see Pastor, 1949, pp. 96 ff.

not as Manetti invented it, and that he had merely reported the pope's last words to the cardinals. It also supports Nicholas's implicit claim that the content of the testament derives from the principles he had formulated in 1447.

In his testament Nicholas stated that he had worked steadfastly on three principal duties—to preserve the sacraments, to restore the buildings of the Church, and to govern the Church in order to put down all that would deflect him from properly administering his office.[6] Either Martin or Eugenius would have been pleased to have accomplished only the third part of this program, and having done that much, each would have considered his duty to have been fulfilled. But Nicholas had a completely different conception of the papacy; he considered himself to be priest, builder, and governor, not merely governor. He considered these to be three distinct but coordinated duties; each reinforced the others. Additionally, he understood his duty as priest to be above the other two; as builder and governor, he was to amplify and strengthen the sacraments. This clear emphasis on the purely priestly or sacred role of his office emerged more clearly through his actions than through his statements, and, as had been the case with his predecessors, his actions were the most important means for interpreting the content of his statements. In his statements, but more profoundly through his vigorous and conspicuous actions, he established the papacy on a new foundation, which his successors honored, respected, and strengthened. In putting a clear emphasis on the priestly duty of the pope, Nicholas changed the character of the papacy.

His most conspicuous action was to make the Vatican into the accepted and expected permanent residence of the pope. Although this does not seem to have been an officially stated policy, it was done nonetheless, and it shook a long tradition and implicitly negated recent formulations about the Lateran. In 1447 Nicholas had been presented with a properly arranged list of churches whose first two items he simply reversed in practice. It began with the patriarchical basilicas, indicating whether they were under the jurisdiction of religious orders, presbyters, or cardinals; it then listed the titulary cardinalate churches in order of dignity; next it listed the episcopate churches in the States of the Church that were directly under the jurisdiction of the pope; and, finally, it listed all the archbishoprics with the bishoprics subordinate to them throughout Christendom. In agreement with the Donation of Constantine and recent policy, but without mentioning anything about the bishopric of Rome, it began: "In the city of Rome are these patriarchal churches, and they are: the Church of San Giovanni in Laterano," which was followed by St. Peter's, then San Paolo fuori le mura, Santa Maria Maggiore, and San Lorenzo fuori le mura.[7] Nicholas never considered his cathedral church as bishop of Rome superior to his seat as head of the apostolic Church, the basilica of St. Peter, the Prince of the Apostles.

One of the clearest reasons he gave for St. Peter's superiority occurs in a letter meant to clarify the order of march in an important procession; its most probable date is July, 1448. Nicholas called the basilica of the Prince of the Apostles the "holder of the keys to the kingdom of heaven" and said that it "excels in the privilege of special dignity among all the churches of the city and of the world." It is "the chief and mother church and the seat of our apostolic dignity."[8] In a letter from December 18, 1447, he had used similar language and had added the explanation that it is not without merit that, of all the churches of the world, all

[6]Manetti, *RIS*, col. 947.

[7]Archivio Segreto Vaticano, Armadeo XXXIX, vol. 6, fols. 19ʳ-25ʳ.   In future references the abbreviation ASV will be used.

[8]In *Coll. Bull. Vat.*, II, pp. 123–124, where the problem of the date is discussed.

eyes are directed to St. Peter's, which constitutes the chief defense of Rome and the principal base of the Christian Church.[9]

For Nicholas to establish himself principally and clearly at the Vatican rather than at the Lateran was not to turn away from a Constantinian basilica, because it was believed that St. Peter's had also been founded by Constantine. At this time, St. Peter's seems to have been less important as a continuous Petrine shrine than it was as the shrine of Peter built by Constantine. Vegio, who was the best informed of the mid-quattrocento reporters on the subject, said that the emperor had built a basilica in the Vatican in conjunction with the site of St. Peter's martyrdom, and that he had translated the body of the saint from the catacombs where he had been interred to the basilica that Sylvester had consecrated.[10] Nicholas's settling into the Vatican represented the pope's turning from the temporally oriented Church that Dante had excoriated; St. Peter's was just as Constantinian as the Lateran, but its authority was Petrine and apostolic rather than imperial and associated with the bishopric of Rome.

In an action that was equally conspicuous and that also emphasized the Petrine and priestly conception of the papacy, Nicholas renounced his family coat of arms and took those of Peter, the crossed keys.[11] The keys at this moment were the subject of intense controversy. In taking them as his own, he served potent notice that he would give no hearing to conciliarist doctrines and that he possessed the full plenitude of power as pope to bind and loose souls, a power he believed Christ had given Peter, not the Church. He therefore showed that the keys were held by the pope, not by a council.

Early in the century the conciliarists had based their claim to legitimacy on the old and controversial thesis that the keys had been transmitted by Christ to Peter for the Church; they claimed that they, the hierarchy assembled in a general council, had primacy above the pope in handling them. The reverse of the bull used by the Council of Constance during the *sede vacante* showed the crossed keys in place of the usual content, the name and number of the pope.[12] The Council of Basel took the usual conciliarist position, and even during the last years of Eugenius's pontificate, supporters of papal supremacy were unwilling to challenge the conciliarists unequivocally.[13] The Dominican theologian, active participant in the Council of Union and champion of papal primacy, Cardinal Juan de Torquemada, was less reserved, and during Nicholas's pontificate he supported papal primacy on the basis of traditional theology. His *Summa de ecclesia*, which he finished assembling when Nicholas was pope, "became the arsenal of the defenders of papal primacy right up to the Council

[9]In a letter to a papal collector, in *Coll. Bull. Vat.*, II, pp. 115–116. For similar letters with closely related language, see II, pp. 116–117 (11 July 1448), p. 132 (16 July 1450), pp. 117–123, 125–129, 129, 141–142, and 142–146, for negotiations carried on from 1448 through 1453; ibid., p. 137, for the extension of the Jubilee indulgence to the French, 12 June 1451. See also the charge to the vicar of St. Peter's, 4 June 1447, pp. 111–113, in comparison to that of Martin V, 30 December 1421, p. 80.

[10]Vegio, in Huskinson, 1969, appendix II, p. 160, giving the text from *De rebus ... Basilicae*, II, i–ii; for earlier opinions on the original location of Peter's body before Constantine's work, see Huskinson, 1969, pp. 136–137, esp. n. 7, which may be supplemented by the varying accounts in the *Liber Pontificalis:* I, p. 118 (Peter), p. 125 (Anaclitus), p. 150 (Cornelius, for a translation of the body), and p. 176 (Sylvester, for the building of St. Peter's and the "replacement" of the body there). See also Toynbee and Ward Perkins, 1956, pp. 169 ff. and passim; Robathan, 1970, p. 211.

[11]For his family coat of arms, Galbreath, 1930, p. 83.

[12]Sella, 1937, no. 707, pl. XXIX, 707.

[13]Jedin, 1957, I, p. 26.

of Trent."[14] In two other works, which must certainly have been written at Nicholas's request, Torquemada developed his ideas about the primacy of the pope and stressed the pope's spiritual role in the Church. One of these was the *Commentary on Penance*, where he stated unequivocally that the pope held the keys, that he got them directly from Peter, and that he alone had jurisdiction over them.[15]

For Torquemada, and therefore for Nicholas, the keys represented the spiritual power of the pope. Citing Thomas Aquinas, Torquemada distinguished between the pope and bishops, and therefore between the pope as successor to Peter and Vicar of Christ and the pope as head of the Church through his office as bishop of Rome: "The pope has the plenitude of pontifical power like the king in his kingdom, but the bishops assume the part of solicitor like judges hearing individual cases of citizens."[16] The kingdom is that of heaven, and the pope's keys have two uses, that of binding and that of loosing souls.[17] They also have two names, that of rational knowledge and that of power of authority in deciding in judgments of the soul.[18] These two designations are related; one key is useless without the other, and both are necessary to unlock the treasury of the Church.

Nicholas had unlocked the treasury when he issued a plenary indulgence for the Jubilee of 1450; Torquemada's *Commentary on Penance* is the Jubilee's theological explication. "The indulgence is granted as an assistance for man's infirmity," stated the Dominican. The pope as Vicar of Christ draws on this treasury, which is "instituted by the reverent saving up of and devotion to the Apostolic See that was founded in this city [Rome], which is mother and head of all churches and teacher of all the faithful."[19] Continuing directly, Torquemada then pleads the Petrine foundation of papal power: "Whence Christ said to Peter, you I call *cephas*, which means head. To you I give the keys of the kingdom of heaven"; this is so not because of the efforts Peter and Paul lavished on the Church for the honor of the faithful, but because the Apostolic See at St. Peter's itself contains the overflowing treasury on which the indulgence is drawn.

The Jubilee was the great event of Nicholas's pontificate, and the first that had been celebrated in a moment of peace and unity. The first Jubilee had been instituted by Boniface VIII in 1300, and it had served as the precedent for those that followed. The Jubilees of 1300, 1350, and 1375 were referred to in Nicholas's Jubilee bull, which ignored the ones held in 1400 and 1423. Boniface's bull had been quite simple; it stated that "the trustworthy account of the ancients" sanctioned the remission of sins to all those who, "being truly penitent," visit "the venerable basilica of the Prince of the Apostles in Rome," and that in order to satisfy the amplified devotion of the faithful, the basilicas of both Peter and Paul are to be the goal of

---

[14]Ibid., I, p. 27; see also Gill, 1959, pp. 313 ff., who discusses the work under the title *Oratio synodaldis de primato*. A copy was in Eugenius's possession in 1443; Müntz and Fabre, 1887, p. 19.

[15]The other work is the *Commentary on Consecration*. The *incipit* and *explicit* of each commentary state that the commentary was done during Nicholas's pontificate. A statement in *Poenitentia*, fol. 42[v], mentions, possibly as an interpolation, the crusade indulgence that Nicholas issued in 1453 (for the date and the bull, see Pastor, 1949, pp. 275 ff.); this indicates a late date for the completion of the commentaries, but the substance of the discussion is based on the indulgence that Nicholas issued in 1449 for the Jubilee (for which, see below).

[16]*Poenitentia*, fol. 40[r].

[17]*Poenitentia*, fol. 18[r].

[18]"Scientie ratione, potestis, authoritas discernendi in iudicio anime"; *Poenitentia*, fol. 18[v]. For the paternity of these assertions, see Tierney, 1955, pp. 25–36.

[19]*Poenitentia*, fol. 43[r].

their spiritual attentions.[20]   His theologians expanded the brief declarations of his bull, erecting a theological justification for the indulgence it granted, but they did not grasp the full implications of Boniface's promises. Crusade indulgences, pilgrimage indulgences, and the sacrament of penance defined by Innocent III had provided the foundation for his Jubilee indulgence, but a penitent spirit was apparently considered to exist in the pilgrim if he simply got to Rome and attended to his devotions at the basilicas for a sufficient length of time.[21]

Unlike earlier Jubilee bulls, Nicholas's touched on a great number of issues, some doctrinal, some more immediate, but all connected directly to his new conception of the papacy, which stressed the priestly role of the pope in the affairs of the Church, located the papacy at the Vatican with its Petrine shrine, and, using a traditional theology, viewed the pope as the holder of the keys because in him resided knowledge and the power to judge matters of the soul. Careful attention to the bull also reveals a new evaluation of the sacraments and their role in salvation.

The bull opened with a recitation of the means God had used to bring salvation to man. These were great blessings:

> The blessings of divine mercy, which language seems rather to demean than to reveal, are immense and innumerable. Through these blessings the ineffable clemency of God the Father and our lord Jesus Christ worked and always is working for the salvation of the human race, because to give life to the human race and to free it from everlasting death the everlasting Father sent his Son, coeternal with himself; because the Son of God, so that he might make men the sons of God, was willing to be a son of man; because he humbled himself so that he might lift up the prostrate; because he took on[22] a servile body so that he might free those subjected to servitude; and because he endured death so that he might show immortality to mortals. Wondrous and ineffable are these things, but how wonderful and great is his divine clemency!

It then moved immediately to a reference to the sacraments, necessary because of the nature of man.

> This clemency as redemption took forethought for man through salvation, such that even if after the regeneration of baptism [lit.: the baptism of salvation] man, in accordance with his fragility and weakness, should commit new sins, he should still find healthful remedies for curing and healing his wounds.

Following a reference to the praise of God given by David, it then addressed the position of Peter within the Church established by Christ and included the Church's foundation as a blessing like the others, which are immense, innumerable, and ineffable.

---

[20] *Antiquorum habet fida*, 22 February 1300; in *Bull. Rom. noviss.*, I, p. 159.

[21] Thurston, 1900, pp. 12–23; Boase, 1933, pp. 231–327; Fedele, in Bandini, et al., 1934, pp. 7–25; Frugoni, 1950. Boniface's bull was promulgated on the Feast of the Cathedra Petri and was originally dated from the Lateran, although Boniface changed this to read St. Peter's. Clement VI and Gregory XI added Santa Maria Maggiore and San Giovanni in Laterano to make the complete list of basilicas that appeared in Nicholas's bull.

[22] At this point read *induit* rather than *indicit*, as it appears in the source cited in note 23.

Amongst these beneficent blessings, this also must be numbered, namely, that our Lord *himself*, full of mercy and merciful, who was made for us by God as wisdom (*sapientia*), justice, redemption, and sanctification, when he was about to leave his disciples in his bodily presence and was about to ascend to his Father, to the apostle Peter, whom he wished to be his vicar in lordship *(dominicus vicarius)* over his flock, and his pastor, he conferred full power for binding and loosing . . . .

After explaining this power, it moves on to the place of Peter and his successors in the scheme of salvation outlined in the bull.

That power and fullness of power he wanted to remain for all the successors of Peter, in order that through his ministry the bonds of sinners should be loosed and in order that for the souls of the faithful there should be open an easier entrance into the kingdom of Heaven. Moreover, this too we believe should be reckoned amongst the gifts of heaven, namely, that it pleased the Holy Spirit, which governs, teaches, and protects its Church, that of the apostle Peter, whom the universal Catholic Church throughout the whole world reads of and sings of as custodian of heaven and key-bearer of eternal life, that several successors, our predecessors,[23] Roman pontiffs, ministers of Christ and dispensers of the mysteries of God, chose certain times in which the streams of divine mercy should flow more plentifully for faithful peoples, knowing that omnipotent God had renewed for the better at certain periods of time the pristine state of fallen man, now by the Flood, now by circumcision, now by the Law, now by other means, but finally by the mystery of the Incarnate Word. By the illumination of the Holy Spirit they understood that what pertained to the Old Testament according to the letter pertained in the New according to the Spirit; thus, the mystery of the Jubilee year, which of old saw the remission of the world, the freeing of slaves, and the restitution of properties that had been bought for a price, they took care to show to the Christian people in a spiritual manner so that on every fiftieth [*sic]* year all people guilty even of the most serious sins, *truly repentant and having confessed,* and all people who have visited the churches of the apostle Peter and of the apostle Paul and the Lateran and Santa Maria Maggiore in the city in certain manners and forms that are contained in their apostolic letters and especially those of Clement VI and Gregory XI our predecessors . . . should receive a plenary indulgence for their sins.[24]

The bull makes it clear that the popes are responsible for the institution of the Jubilee and that these popes are to be understood as *Laetentur Coeli* had defined them. Indeed, the Jubilee emerges as the celebration of *Laetentur Coeli*'s promulgation. Also clear is the emphasis that the penitent spirit of the faithful pilgrim is the basis

[23]From this point on the bull is transcribed in Raynaldus, ad anno 1449, no. 15, with the following change: Raynaldus begins, "Nonnulli praedecessores nostri," while the bull itself reads, ". . . ecclesia nonnulli successores predecessores [*sic*] . . . ." Raynaldus's alteration was necessary to obscure the deletion of the earlier section. The part given above derives from a sixteenth-century copy, ASV, Armadeo XXXI, vol. 56, fols. 95ʳ–99ʳ (120ʳ–124ʳ), a source not included in Pastor, 1949, p. 75, n. 2. The title in ASV is *Immensa et innumerabilia*, dated 19 January 1449, St. Peter's.

[24]Emphasis added; the phrase appears first in Boniface VIII's bull and is repeated in the concluding lines of that of Nicholas. Both Clement's and Gregory's bulls are repeated here.

for his reception of the gift of the indulgence. One must conclude that Nicholas's new conception of the papacy arose not only from certain historical circumstances such as the pacification of the political arena and an opportunity to claim papal primacy, but that it was also developed directly from a new belief about the role of the sacraments in general and of the sacrament of penance in particular in the divinely instituted apparatus of salvation.

Earlier Jubilees, to be sure, had linked the indulgence with penance and with the prescribed "manners and forms," but now even Torquemada explained that the indulgence cannot be drawn like a sum from a bank account; to be efficacious, it must be received after penance. The justice of God is effective through the "remission of sins, which is the principal work of God"; "penance is the primary foundation."[25] Penance must be accompanied by contrition and confession, each of which the Dominican treated extensively. Penance makes the soul of the faithful receptive for the gift of grace.[26]

This was more than mere rhetoric and theology that passed between clerics in the curia. It was understood and practiced by at least one pilgrim to Rome in 1450, Giovanni Rucellai, the rich Florentine merchant and patron of Leon Battista Alberti. In a description he left of his visit, he explained in the first two paragraphs that the "Jubilee was ordered by God the Father, as one finds in the Bible," and he then repeated the Old Testament precedent in Law that dealt with slaves, possessions, and property. He had already pointed out that through confession, contrition, and satisfaction for the sin, and through having "true sadness and true penitence and true displeasure of all the sins that you have ever made, and with having made the penance which the confessor imposes on you, that is, that of the visitation" which had been outlined in the Jubilee bull, "the above-mentioned *confession* liberates you from the pain of hell but not from that of purgatory, except that the plenary remission which one acquires through the said Jubilee allows you to have freedom from the pain of purgatory, about which it is said that for every mortal sin one must stay there for ten years."[27] Rucellai had understood what Torquemada and the Jubilee bull were explaining: that the plenary indulgence, which was given by the power of the pope to bind and loose souls, in no way replaced the sacraments as signs of grace.

The Jubilee was only a sign for part of the full gift of grace, which was available through the Church to all who were genuinely repentant; it resembled the Law of the Old Testament, which had been a sign for the gift of grace offered in the New Testament. The Jubilee dealt with purgatory through the satisfaction of one's sin through a sign of contrition, while the five personal sacraments dealt with hell and demanded confession and true inner contrition. The sacrament of penance was given a prominent position among the other sacraments, and with the emphasis on confession and contrition within the sacrament of penance, a voluntarist theology was broached. This interpretation of salvation corresponded to the explanation of the sacraments that Nicholas gave to the cardinals in his testament.

After he apologized for the brevity that his failing strength required him to find while explaining each of the three parts of his program, Nicholas immediately turned to his beliefs about the sacraments. His explanation was personal rather than doctrinal or dogmatic, and it forms a distinct contrast to the statement on the sacraments that had been taken directly from Aquinas and issued at the Council of Union

---

[25] *Poenitentia*, fol. 82ʳ.

[26] *Poenitentia*, fol. 43ʳ, on the justification of the indulgence.

[27] Rucellai, 1960, p. 67; see also p. 52, and below, Epilogue. Emphasis added.

shortly after the promulgation of *Laetentur Coeli*.[28] Nicholas, of course, said nothing to dispute it; his statement recognizes that the sacraments fulfill the old Law and that they do not confer grace but make it possible for God to grant it as a gift. He found it unnecessary to discuss the matter and the form of the individual sacraments, which was the principal content of the bull. And he did not retain the emphasis of the bull on the primacy of the institutional Church as possessor of the sacraments; this was in the bull to confound the conciliarists at Basel. Because that battle had been won by 1455, Nicholas did not need to belabor the point that the sacraments are administered by the Church to the sinner for purposes that relate directly to the integrity of the Church. Such an emphasis had already appeared in his Jubilee bull. It had suited the purpose of the council's bull to list baptism as the first sacrament, its traditional place. "Holding first place among the sacraments is holy baptism because it is the door to spiritual life, by means of which one becomes a member of Christ and is incorporated into the Church." The next are confirmation, eucharist, penance, and extreme unction. The list concludes with the two dealing with the institutional relationship between the Christian and the Church, ordination and matrimony. Penance is different from the others only because its matter is its form; as an act it is defined as having three parts: contrition, confession, and "satisfaction for the sin according to the will of the priest," which may be through prayers, fasting, or the giving of alms. Its effect is simply the "absolution of sin." It is not presented in any special relationship to the other sacraments, and its definition is entirely traditional.

Nicholas's emphasis was quite different. He wasted no time on ordination and matrimony; he simply said that they are voluntary and renovative. The other five, he said, "are necessary for health because of human nature." Among these five, baptism and confirmation need little explanation; baptism is the remission of sin through the gift of the Holy Spirit, and confirmation conserves and perfects that remission. The remaining three deserve special attention because they deal with man's salvation from damnation through voluntary sin. The first of the three is penance; just as baptism absolves man from involuntary sin arising from the sin of Adam, penance absolves him from voluntary sin to which all of Adam's sons succumb as they are buffeted by the storms of life. Nicholas added that the sacrament of penance needs special attention because it has many distinctions, questions, and ambiguities, but rather than linger on those problems, he went on to define its place within the sacramental machinery God established to save men. Only through penance can we find health and tranquility; without penance, he said, God's grace cannot be bestowed. Eucharist confirms the faithful who seek penance with true contrition and strengthens their resolve to seek the good. Extreme unction completes the renewal; through it, divine grace may flow to the individual. The five sacraments from baptism through extreme unction allow the faithful to join the Father, Son, and Holy Ghost in the celestial realm.[29]

The most important element in this formulation is its distinction between voluntary and involuntary sin. Men would sin willfully; they could willfully seek the gift

---

[28]This bull is usually referred to as the *Decretum pro Armenis* although its title is *Exultate Deo* (22 November 1439). It established the union between the Latin and Armenian churches; it defined doctrinal orthodoxy in much the same way and for much the same reason that *Laetentur Coeli*, whose text was included in it, had defined the position of the pope in the Church. See Gill, 1959, pp. 307–308; *Dict. Théo. Cath.*, XII, i, cols. 1046–1048; XIV, i, cols. 594 ff. The bull is published in *Bull. Rom. noviss.*, I, pp. 268–270.

[29]Manetti, *RIS*, cols. 947–949.

of grace. Nicholas believed that penance addressed itself to the will; one had so to love God that he would recognize his sin, be contrite, act on his contrition through confession, and through satisfaction give a sign that he willed to do the good. This schema, although outwardly traditional, derived from a new formulation of the role of the will in the actions of men; the new formulation not only evoked from Nicholas a place within the doctrine of the sacraments for a means to deal directly with voluntary sin, but it also served as the thread which connected his conception of the means God had established for saving men with the means he would use to govern the Church as priest, builder, and governor.

Nicholas was not the only person at this time to concern himself with voluntarism and its implications, and he was not alone in investigating the implications of considering sin a willful act which could be expiated willfully. St. Antoninus (1389–1459), the learned and respected Dominican theologian and archbishop of Florence, had broached it.[30] Others developed it. Sicco Polenton (1376–1447), chancellor of the commune of Padua, believed that all sins were voluntary and, as was common, that *superbia* was the worst of the mortal sins. He reiterated the older, scholastic thesis about sin and the sacraments, but his emphasis on penance and its relationship to the will set his interpretation apart from that of his predecessors.[31] Bartolomeo della Fonte, in a dialogue with Donato Acciaiuoli, the Florentine, gave will and penance the central position in man's relationship to God within the sacramental system. Indeed, his stress on the will allowed him nearly, if not actually, to remove penance from among the sacraments and to use it instead as the matrix that gave order to the system of the three theological and four cardinal virtues.[32] Significantly, Polenton's position, which approaches that of Nicholas, was worked out in 1435–36, and della Fonte's, which far exceeds that of the pope and perhaps approaches unorthodoxy, was first articulated in about 1468.[33] Nicholas's testamentary statement fits within this context of thought; casual as it may have sounded, it was rich with connotations that suggested a new belief about the relationship between man and God.

Nicholas had treated the sacraments not as a dogmatic system but as a set of signs that pass between the Christian and God within the Church; he turned a dry and institutionalized system into a vivid exchange and broke with the emphasis on form that had been instilled by the scholastics, in favor of an emphasis on belief and the acts it motivates through the will. He recognized something that his predecessors had obscured—that the voluntarism of Pelagius and Augustine was a more important legacy for the Christian seeking salvation than was the doctrine found in the books Torquemada read. But his formulation was not Pelagian;[34] rather, it was Augustinian. In *On Christian Doctrine*, written before the system of the sacraments had become canonic, the Early Christian father had explained why the keys had been given to the Church; it was "so that whoever in His Church did not believe his sins to be forgiven should not have them forgiven, but whoever believed and in correction turned himself from them, having placed himself in the bosom of His Church, should be healed by that faith and correction"; he followed this directly with the statement that "...the soul after penance, by means of which it puts aside its former evil

[30]*See Dict. Théo. Cath.*, XII, i, cols. 1010–1014.

[31]Trinkaus, 1970, pp. 616–626, 632–633.

[32]Ibid., pp. 626–633.

[33]For the dates, ibid., pp. 616 and 627, respectively, with notes.

[34]On the potential or incipient Pelagianism of the group to be discussed below, see Garin, 1964, p. 65 (for Valla); Trinkaus, 1970, esp. pp. 633 and 649.

habits, is reformed for the better...."[35] The emphasis was on belief; to penance, Nicholas could add eucharist to fortify the repentant sinner in his resolve to seek virtue, and he could also promise that through extreme unction the gift of grace would be available to allow the Christian admission to the heavenly kingdom. In building and governing, Nicholas would provide a setting for the actions of the men who sought God.

Nicholas's formulation of his belief about the sacraments belonged to a new and larger outlook on the world. To the extent that this new outlook turned to questions of the doctrine of the Church, Augustine was its father, Francesco Petrarch was its midwife, and the quattrocento humanists were its offspring. Petrarch grappled anew with the classics—Greek, Latin, and Christian—and, as Professor Paul Oskar Kristeller has put it, "like most philosophical (and political) prophets, he was one of those who foresaw the future because they helped to make it."[36] Of the many aspects of the future that Petrarch prepared, the theological, the Christian, has been the least emphasized and studied.[37] This aspect was naturally the most important for Nicholas and for those around him in Rome, and the most important for understanding Nicholas's program for governing and for building. To understand Nicholas, one must understand Petrarch and his legacy.

Petrarch's major contribution was to give body and voice to three distinct beliefs. One was that faith gave man nobility, that faith in God's gift of grace and love for God can move man to seek virtue and to shun vice. While Truth presides, Augustine constantly admonishes Petrarch in his *Secret* that love for God must direct all of his operations; it depends entirely upon the individual whether his love is the vilest passion or the noblest action of the soul, a sentiment that Petrarch himself utters but that Augustine had to clarify for him.[38]

Concomitant with this outlook was Petrarch's understanding of a belief circulated by Duns Scotus, Bonaventura, and many Ockhamists, which also had the support of Franciscans, although Petrarch cited Augustine when he discussed it. He believed that the will was superior to the intellect; the will, driven by love, would have the intellect train the mind, which has the ability to reason. As he put it, "the object of the will, as it please the wise, is to be good; that of the intellect is truth. It is better to will the good than to know the truth."[39]

Petrarch's third important belief arose from his knowledge of the earthly accomplishments of pagans who seemed to exhibit Christian virtues and from his wondering why it is that a person is not to enjoy fame on earth as a sign of his desire for heavenly glory. Petrarch finally reasoned that pagans could be considered *exempla* for Christians, and Augustine explained to him that glory and fame were not incompatible. If, driven by love for God, we seek heavenly glory, earthly fame will follow, but if we seek only earthly fame, we will lose both glory and fame.[40]

One group of Petrarch's successors, the group in Florence with which Tommaso Parentucello associated, sought to transform Petrarch's program from a weapon forged for personal study and eloquent discourse into one that was also honed for

[35]Augustine, *On Christian Doctrine*, 1958, I, xviii, 17–xix, 18.
[36]Kristeller, 1964, p. 18.
[37]See Kristeller's balanced view, 1964, pp. 1–18 (Petrarch), pp. 19–36 (Valla), and passim; also Jacob, 1965; Trinkaus, 1970, passim, esp. pp. 651–654, 683, 761–774.
[38]*Secret*, 1911, p. 110. See below, chapter 3.
[39]Petrarch, *Ignorance*, 1948, p. 105.
[40]Petrarch, *Secret*, 1911, pp. 182–183.

active engagement in the affairs of the world.   Additionally, as Professor Charles Trinkaus has said, the group that flourished then saw mankind as "alive, actively assertive, cunningly designing, storming the gates of heaven."[41]   When Nicholas became pope, he enjoyed the services of members of this assertive group.

They were assertive and expected their rewards, because they believed that to be active and to receive rewards were complementary aspects of the divine love they felt. As Alberti put it in the 1430s or 1440s:

> This intellect, this knowledge and reason and memory so infinite and immortal, how do they come into me if not from him who is infinite and immortal.... Am I perhaps only to use them to serve this body of mine and these weary and troublesome limbs? Will I not delight myself more in adapting this intellect, this knowing things and reason and memory, to the glory and immortality of my name, fame, and dignity, of my family and of my country?[42]

By his country, as a Florentine writing in Florence, he meant the city of Florence; here he was speaking as a person at home in the climate of thought that had developed during the previous generation, when Florentines had made the active life in the republic a moral necessity for the citizen.[43] But Alberti did not limit himself to such a parochial view. He continued directly:

> Am I seriously to consider myself to have been born not only, as Anaxagoras claimed, for contemplating the heavens, the stars, and the universe of nature, but also and primarily, as Lactantius affirmed, for recognizing and serving God, when serving God is nothing other than giving myself to promoting the good and maintaining justice?

A person so constructed must be the friend of every justice and the enemy of every injustice. Alberti continued:

> Consequently we dedicate our soul to be void of every injustice and filled with goodness. Hence we are well composed in every task of humanity and in our cultivation of our ability and render good service to natural society and to true religion, and place the highest premium in all of our life on being resolute and free.

If an individual was resolute and free he was to be active and use his divine gifts. As Lorenzo Valla explained, a man should conduct himself with strength of spirit and an undeviating drive toward his goal; to do so was to exhibit his *virtù* when his goal was that of loving God.[44] Alberti explained that one's *virtù* must be carefully cultivated from among the innate gifts he had been given by God. *Virtù* allowed a

---

[41]Trinkaus, 1970, p. xxi.

[42]*Profugiorum ab aerumna*, p. 122; see also ibid., p. 137, and *Theogenius*, p. 100 and passim.

[43]See Baron, 1938, passim; idem, 1966, passim; Garin, 1964, pp. 38–42, 47–51, who discusses the positions of the will and intellect as a confrontation between Salutati, sympathetic to a Franciscan position, and Giovanni Dominici, a Dominican Thomist (for example, Salutati, "To ... Dominici," p. 349); Seigel, 1968, passim; who (p. 43) points out that Petrarch realized, on the model of Cicero, that the orator's proper place was in the city; and Bouwsma, 1968, p. 9, who has stressed the importance of the superiority of the will in republican thought.

[44]See Trinkaus, 1970, pp. 160–168.

man to assist his fellow men; in using his God-given gifts he could oppose vice, overcome fortune, and properly love God.[45]

Petrarch's successors were active; because there were a number of different fields open to them, they had little problem in choosing a field of activity in which to engage. They favored the rhetorical or persuasive arts rather than the intellectual or teaching ones. They often organized their discussions of fields of activity within the broad *topos* of arms and letters because it was flexible and implied that arms and letters were used for some purpose. Arms were for the young and the warlike; letters were for the mature and the scholarly; each was related to the other, so that neither was independent of the other. Alberti developed his theory of art partly on the basis of inserting painting and architecture into the letters part of the *topos*, infusing what had been crafts with the prerequisites of knowledge and thereby raising painting and architecture to the level of poetry, history, and other humanist liberal arts.[46] The moving biography that Vespasiano da Bisticci (1421–1498), the Florentine book dealer and biographer, left of Federigo da Montefeltro, duke of Urbino, stayed closer to the *topos:* Federigo exerted himself in governing, in letters, and in arms; in governing and in wielding arms he was guided by his study of letters. The *topos* had also given structure to the additions Filarete made to the bronze doors. He showed arms on the left valve and letters on the right, thus indicating the two means Eugenius had used to govern the Church. In addition, the *topos* was used to organize a fresco cycle that showed men active in Florentine affairs.

Andrea del Castagno painted the cycle in the Villa Pandolfini-Carducci at Legnaia, near Florence, between 1449 and 1451 (figs. 12–16).[47] On one end of the long wall are men of letters—Dante, Boccaccio, and Petrarch, Florentines who had contributed to their city through their eloquence. Just as books identify this group as poets, martial implements identify another group of three men as warriors. Brief inscriptions specify the deeds of Farinata degli Uberti, Niccolò Acciaiuoli, and Filippo Scolari. Commentaries, histories, and biographies familiar to Florentines would have made clear their contributions to Florence.

The rest of the cycle reinforces points made in other material available in Florence from the pens of humanists: the actions of Florentines belonged not only to the particular history of their city but to universal history as well, and virtuous individuals of other ages could be *exempla* for Florentines. This was shown by the insertion of three heroines into the space between the poets and warriors; they also fall within the arms-letters *topos*. Queen Tomyris, a female warrior, had killed King Cyrus, which vindicated the death of her son and liberated her country. The virtuous Cumaean sibyl, a woman of letters who had prophesied Christ to the Romans, had "received the light of prophecy" from "that true Sun which lightens every man who comes into this world."[48] The Jewish Queen Esther had saved her people when they were in bondage. The three heroines represent three pre-Christian ages in universal history, and like the poets and warriors, they serve as *exempla* for Christian action.

The cycle also makes another favorite point among the humanists: the rewards for

[45]See particularly *Della famiglia*, p. 63 (Alberti: Watkins, p. 76); ibid., pp. 132–133 (Alberti: Watkins, pp. 134–135); *Theogenius*, p. 223; *Profugiorum ab aerumna*, passim, esp. pp. 124, 160–161, and 173–174. A good definition of Alberti's meaning of *virtù* is in Mancini, 1911, pp. 184–185.

[46]See Westfall, *JHI*, 1969, and *SR*, 1969.

[47]For the date, see Fortuna, 1957, pp. 57–60; Hartt and Corti, 1966, pp. 232–234. For the cycle, see Horster, 1955, with a useful list of previous examples of the type. Schlosser (1895) 1965, p. 36, cites this as an "echo" of the Nine Worthies cycle (for which, see below, chapter 7); if so, the original tune is nearly inaudible.

[48]Boccaccio, *Concerning Famous Women*, p. 51.

those who act virtuously for the city are available to them because they are virtuous Christians. On one of the surviving end walls are Adam and Eve and Christ and Mary; to the history of states is added the history of salvation, or, to say the same thing, the history of states takes place within the history of salvation (figs. 14,15). But virtuous activity in itself is not enough to assure salvation; that is available only through the grace of Christ and the intercession of the saints. That would have been clear by the representation on the other end wall, now lost, which showed a Crucifixion and Saints Jerome and Mary.[49]

That immortal glory and mortal fame are rewards for actively exercising one's *virtù*, one of the major themes of the cycle, is a common topic in humanist literature. Petrarch had learned from Augustine that fame followed in the wake of glory, and he also wrote: "Our life will be judged by our conversation; when the proof of our actions is gone, only the evidence of our speech will remain."[50] His successors spoke more bluntly. "Oh sweet thing, that glory we acquire through our endeavors," Alberti declared. More than an inscribed slab of stone should remind those who follow us that we have grown old here among men. "Said the poet Ennius: do not cry after me, do not make obsequies; I wish only to live through the words of learned men."[51] Valla was more outspoken. He found joy in a great many activities because such activities were directed at loving God. He looked forward to enjoying God, and it was this anticipation of future joy that he believed moved men to use their *virtù* in the first place.[52] Manetti also accepted the thesis and added that to work in this world according to one's talents in order to leave memorials to one's name was a human manifestation of one's love of God and an earthly equivalent to celestial happiness that men should seek.[53] None of these men left any doubt that love drove men and that properly directed love manifested through vigorous activity merited glory and immortality.

Manetti believed with the others that knowledge is to be sought not for its own sake but for the guidance it gives one as he exerts himself in arms and arts, and that there was a proper reward for such exertion.[54] It would be expected, then, that when writing a biography he would present his subject within this context, as he did in his *Life of Nicholas V*. This was not a disservice to his subject. It is consonant with what one would expect of Nicholas, who had grown to intellectual maturity among the group that had developed these ideas, and who had patronized their advocates when he became pope. And, more importantly, Manetti's use of these ideas to describe Nicholas is consonant with Nicholas's own explanations in the testament, especially when dealing with the sacraments, and with his actions as known from other sources. Thus it seems clear that, for the most part, what Manetti reported

---

[49]"Libro di Antonio Billi," Fabriczy, 1891, p. 328; also published with other reports in Fortuna, 1957, p. 94. Salmi's objection (1950, p. 301) to this subject because it would have been interfered with by the doorway lacks conviction; Castagno could certainly have solved such a problem.

[50]Petrarch, *Solitude*, 1924, p. 100.

[51]*Profugiorum ab aerumna*, pp. 124, 131–132.   See also *Della famiglia*, p. 145 (Alberti: Watkins, p. 145).

[52]Garin, 1964, pp. 64–69; Trinkaus, 1970, pp. 133 ff., 163, 167–169.

[53]See Trinkaus, 1970, pp. 240–241, for the passage from Manetti's *De dignitate et excellentia hominis;* the phrase that Manetti uses for talents is "varia diversorum hominum ingenia." The work was written about 1452 or early 1453, although earlier versions possibly existed before September, 1449. See Trinkaus, 1970, p. 231, and n. 3, pp. 413–414. For man's office as governor and administrator in this world, ibid., p. 250.

[54]"Vita et moribus trium . . . poetarum," p. 111; also the material cited above, note 53.

closely resembles what Nicholas himself did and believed. It is now possible to turn to Manetti's biography of Nicholas.

Tommaso Parentucello, Manetti explained, had been specially made by God to be pope;[55] after he was elected "against his own desire," he turned his full energies to three primary tasks: establishing peace throughout the temporal and sacred realms of the papacy, rebuilding the city of Rome, and building a library for the papacy that could guide him in his exertions.[56] In the first book, Manetti explained how Nicholas had prepared himself for his future success. As a young scholar he had shown early promise and had mastered the seven liberal arts as well as history, philosophy, natural law, and the writings of the canonists, theologians, and doctors of the Church. He avidly acquired books and established a library for Cosimo de' Medici that would serve as a model for others, including the one he would later build at the Vatican. He also received education in practical affairs, particularly in the arts of governing. While on leave as a student from the university in Bologna, he served as the tutor to the children of two Florentine knights; Manetti does not name them, but Vespasiano points out that they were Rinaldo degli Albizzi and Palla Strozzi, the two key figures in the Florentine government at the time.[57] He served his apprenticeship with a papal legate to temporal princes, Cardinal Niccolò Albergati, who was also the early patron of Parentucello's fellow student, Alberti, although there was no reason for Manetti to mention this.[58] Manetti's *Life* is structured in order to show how the young man had been properly prepared to be the great pope he was, but, unlike Vespasiano, he does not make the point that at an early age Parentucello had shown a passion for building buildings.[59] As pope he built a great library that was "of utility to the prelates of the Roman Church and a perpetual and eternal ornament to the sacred palace" in which it was housed. It was stocked with a wide variety of authors; canonists, theologians, and doctors were side by side with as many pagan authors as Nicholas could acquire. His earlier experience had been put to good use; he now modeled his efforts after those of Ptolemy Philadelphias, king of Egypt.[60] He also had success in governing the Church; using his special and God-given abilities, he established peace, finding that knowledge was more useful than arms and therefore putting into practice the belief that not to resort to arms was to prove one's ability at their portage. The purpose of arms was to establish peace, and whatever established peace could be called the exercise of arms.[61] Manetti stated clearly that vigorous activity in governing, building the library, and rebuilding the city of Rome allowed Nicholas to demonstrate his love for God and to acquire the earthly fame and immortal glory he sought.[62]

Manetti's life corresponds closely, but not exactly, to the statements Nicholas had

[55]See the extensive analysis of this theme in Manetti's biography as given in Miglio, 1971, pp. 486–494.

[56]See esp. *RIS*, col. 940, where Manetti recapitulates the major themes of book II before dealing briefly with specific events during the pontificate. Peace and strength are developed in cols. 921–925 and again, 940–945/946; the building program is outlined in cols. 929–940, and the library is discussed in cols. 925–928.

[57]*RIS*, col. 912; Vespasiano, 1963, p. 32.

[58]See Mancini, 1911, pp. 59 ff.

[59]Vespasiano, 1963, p. 37.

[60]Manetti, *RIS*, col. 926.

[61]See also, for example, Alberti, in *De re aed.*, preface, p. 11; Alberti: Leoni, p. x; and Alberti, *Theogenius*, p. 70. For a general review, see Hale, 1960, passim.

[62]*RIS*, col. 925.

made in his testament; Manetti was still a Florentine, and Nicholas was the head of the Church. As pope, he could not transport Florentine ideas to the Vatican without translating them as well. Manetti wrote of governing, building the library, and rebuilding the city of Rome; Nicholas spoke of protecting and amplifying the dignity of the sacraments and of doing so by building and governing. Nicholas's reference to the library and to the translations he sponsored occurred when discussing the beautiful things—including gems, stones, gold and silver vessels, tapestries, and buildings—that he had acquired and constructed for the Church, and when citing the treasures that, like the translations from Greek and Latin authors, he could acquire because he had governed the Church well and had brought it peace.[63] Nicholas did not seek fame and glory for his actions the way a Florentine did. Although Castagno's cycle shows better than the treatises of the humanists that what Florentines sought through activity should be understood in a Christian context and that their immortal glory amounted to entrance to Paradise, Nicholas could not be so evasively classical and seemingly pagan in his discussion of rewards. He said that the Christian achieved the gift of grace and admission to the celestial kingdom through the sacraments. His emphasis on penance showed that one had to be as vigorously assertive to receive the gift of grace as any Florentine was when he sought immortal glory, but it also showed that Nicholas was operating in a different context from that which prevailed in Florence. Castagno's cycle and its surrounding Florentine rhetoric also showed that a Florentine invested his energies in his republic; Florentines praised their republic because, as Coluccio Salutati had put it, "the foundation of our government is the parity and equality of all the citizens."[64]   To this Leonardo Bruni, the great humanist and chancellor of Florence in 1410–11 and again from 1427 to his death in 1444, added in 1428, "the hope of winning public honors and ascending is the same for all, provided they possess industry and natural gifts and lead a serious-minded and respected way of life; for our commonwealth requires *virtus* and *probitas* in its citizens. Whoever has these qualifications is thought to be of sufficiently noble birth to participate in the government of the republic."[65]   The government of the Church was hardly republican; its structure was like that of a principality, the character of which was justified by a north Italian humanist, Giovanni Conversino, in a polemic aimed at Florence:

> The more similar the creature's condition is to that of its creator, the more beautiful, orderly, and perfect the creature is in his life. Consequently, since the creator and ruler of all things is one, government by one man is, in my opinion, preferable, because of the greater conformity with the universe than with any other form of government.[66]

Nicholas's Church had such a structure; his officers were members of an orderly hierarchy. The head is superior to the members; it directs, and they execute. Just as the soul is superior to the body, so is the ecclesiastical order superior to the lay order: *coelestia regunt terrena.*[67]   Nicholas could not address the members as if they were republicans, much as he might conduct himself as a Florentine. Thus he could not claim, as Manetti had, that he had demonstrated his love for God and through

---

[63] Manetti, *RIS*, col. 956.

[64] Quoted in Garin, 1959, p. 200.

[65] Transl. in Baron, 1966, p. 419; quoted p. 556, n. 21.

[66] Transl. ibid., p. 144; quoted p. 496, n. 53.

[67] See Ullmann, 1949, chapter IV, esp. pp. 159 ff.; idem, 1955, pp. 437–446.

his activity acquired the earthly fame and immortal glory he *sought*. He had governed the Church with vigor because it was God's will that he be pope; he could love God and desire the bliss of Paradise, but he could not believe that he might deserve that which was God's alone to give. Nicholas could not be a Florentine republican on the Throne of Peter, but he could make a Florentine point in another way, and did.

Nicholas explained to the cardinals that he had devoted his energies to rebuilding the buildings of the Church for two purposes. He used a *topos* which would have made it clear to his audience that he was denying that he sought the fruits of the *superbia vitae* which Satan had offered Christ from a high tower, the fruits of pride of life or knowledge of the world and of its dignity, pomp, and power.[68] He said:

> Not for ambition, nor pomp, nor vainglory, nor fame, nor the eternal per-
> petuation of my name, but for the greater authority of the Roman Church
> and the greater dignity of the Apostolic Seat among all Christian peoples and
> the more certain avoidance of the usual persecutions we conceived such
> buildings in mind and spirit (*mens et animus*).[69]

The justification for the project given in the testament had been associated with Nicholas earlier; Michele Canensi, a papal biographer who wrote a brief eulogy of the pope in late 1451 or early 1452, had used almost the same terminology to refer to the motivations that had always stirred Parentucello.[70] Nicholas's own stated purposes in building were to amplify devotion and to protect the Church. He realized that buildings could achieve his purpose, and he believed that he must "conceive such buildings in mind and spirit." Nicholas was able to rebuild the city of Rome be-cause he understood that the buildings which could serve his purposes had to be designed. He gave a lengthy explanation to the cardinals in order that the point be absolutely clear:

> We want your graces to know and to understand that there were two main
> reasons for our buildings. Only those who come to understand the Church's
> origin and growth from their knowledge of letters realize that the authority
> of the Roman Church is greatest and highest. The throngs of all other
> peoples, ignorant of letters and wholly untouched by them, although they
> often seem to hear the greatness of these things from learned and erudite
> men and seem to assent to them as to truths and certainties, their assent,
> supported as it is on a weak foundation, gradually collapses in the course of
> time, until it falls back to nothing, unless they are moved by certain extra-
> ordinary sights. But when that vulgar belief founded on doctrines of learned
> men is continually confirmed and daily corroborated by great buildings,
> which are perpetual monuments and eternal testimonies seemingly made by
> God, it is forever conveyed to those, both present and future, who behold
> these admirable constructions. In this way belief is preserved and aug-
> mented, and in this way it is laid down and held fast by a certain admirable
> devotion.[71]

To build was a part of Nicholas's coordinated program. He established the ac-

---

[68]See Howard, 1966, pp. 44–56.

[69]Manetti, *RIS*, col. 950; for the usual persecutions, see below, chapter 7.

[70]Miglio, 1971, p. 493 and p. 513 (fol. 18ᵛ).

[71]Manetti, *RIS*, cols. 949–950.

cepted residence of the pope at his apostolic seat at the tomb of Peter; he elevated the Vatican to a new level of dignity through rhetoric and through his residence there; when he took the arms of Peter as his own, he showed that the pope is the repository of knowledge, the final judge on earth in matters of the soul as well as the head of the Church; he stressed the protection of the sacraments as his most important duty as pope; and he administered the Jubilee. These actions would amplify devotion, and so, too, would his building program. In each of these actions his purpose was to make clear in visible form the definition of the papacy that had been spelled out in *Laetentur Coeli:*

> We define the See of the Holy Apostle and the Roman pope to hold primacy in all the world, and the pope to be the successor of St. Peter the Prince of the Apostles and the true Vicar of Christ and head of the universal Church and father and teacher of all Christians.

In addition, his buildings would move men to love God.

3 The Theoretical Background for Nicholas V's Urban Program

Nicholas stated that he would use buildings throughout Rome to represent his position in the Church and to make Church doctrine clear. This was a novel approach to city building, but in using it, Nicholas was carefully adapting the latest available thought about architecture and cities to the tradition-bound seat of the papacy. The means of representation he would call into play was novel only because it applied ideas that had been common in other contexts to one in which they had not been applied before. The pope knew that Rome and the papacy were hardly proper places to experiment. Unlike a humanist developing an idea with a group of intimates, or a state chancellor or secretary hurling a polemic at a particular rival state, or a theorist working out the implications of an argument as it applied to a special theoretical problem, the doctrine to which he wished to give form in Rome was meant for a universal audience. It applied to all men and to the activities of each individual. It therefore had to refer to a wide range of arguments and to be recognizable by all individuals. There could be no esoterica, no particularism, no favoritism, and no obscurity. Traditional and well-known ideas had to be stressed, themes that had become familiar through long use had to be conspicuous, and still, through their use, the doctrinal point that the pope was now firmly established on the rock of Peter as the head of the universal Church was to be represented.

Nicholas had novel theories about art and architecture available for use, and he depended heavily upon them, as will be made clear in the sequel. But when he put them into service, he depended equally heavily upon traditional means of making his point. In building, as in formulating and executing his office as priest, he erected on old foundations in order to make the new structure clear. In order to understand how he used new ideas, it will be necessary to examine the old foundations that allowed art to represent doctrine, a subject that has been lamentably neglected.

This neglect is explicable. Previous interpretations of the theories and ideas of those associated with Nicholas have concentrated on their relationship to Renaissance and humanist concerns, particularly those which excited Florence; such studies have not had to take into account the differences between Florence and papal Rome. Furthermore, studies of Renaissance architecture and its theory and interpretations of Nicholas's program for rebuilding Rome have sought to define the place Nicholas's works occupied in Renaissance art. In this approach the desire to distinguish between non-Renaissance and Renaissance works on the basis of formal qualities led to an overemphasis on discontinuity; it also obscured the continuity in meaning conveyed by the forms and the continuity in the intention in producing those forms. During the period under review here—roughly from Petrarch through Alberti—there is a continuity of meaning and intention that is based on ideas the introduction of which preceded the invention of new visual forms that represented them. The precocity of ideas relative to these forms has not been noticed in previous studies, because they have been too narrow in focus. Earlier scholars believed that directly following a dramatic event in the history of the Church—for example, the healing of the Great Schism at the Council of Constance—major doctrinal and conceptual modifications were inevitable; thus, studies of a "Renaissance" papacy begin with Martin V. Other scholars have awaited a dramatic change in forms before they would declare that a major change in ideas had occurred; the result has been that Rome has been largely ignored by art historians until the pontificate of Julius II, who employed Bramante, Raphael, and Michelangelo, or at best until that of Sixtus IV, who built and first decorated the Sistine Chapel.

The intention here is to inquire into both elements of historical study—that is, into the political, institutional, and conceptual structures on the one hand and the visual monuments and verbal documents that gave them form and substance on the other. When all these elements are accounted for, a relationship less dependent upon political upheavals or dramatic formal change becomes possible, and a simple sequence appropriate to an inquiry into the history of the city emerges. It appears that first the ideas that defined the meaning and intention of works of art and architecture changed, then the forms changed, and then the theory that explained the new art was written. The architectural forms changed less dramatically and more slowly than the forms used by painters and sculptors, and Nicholas depended upon architecture for his public displays almost to the total exclusion of painting and sculpture. The result is that it is even more necessary to pay careful attention to what occurred in the arts other than architecture and to what was said and written than would be the case if there were dramatic formal changes in architecture to account for. Fortunately, we are rather well supplied with written evidence of what was intended and why; Manetti's account is crucial but not unique. And, like Nicholas, we have available the theories of Alberti and others. These theories were eagerly pressed into service in Rome by a pope anxious to show in new ways what the nature of the Church and of the papacy was. In order to follow Nicholas's program, it seems necessary to review the larger and quite traditional beliefs about how art served doctrine, then to examine quattrocento art and its theories, and lastly to turn to a more detailed investigation of the theories Nicholas used.

Whether in its traditional or in its quattrocento formulation, the means Nicholas used to reveal doctrine can be simply stated: the invisible was to be shown in the visible. The ability of something visible to reveal something invisible is the basis of all representations or presentations of doctrine in visual or literary forms; all theories of artistic representation dealing with Church art, from the Early Christian period until well past the Renaissance, are simply glosses on this basic conception. The conception was as common and as sound as Pauline and Augustinian doctrine, and it was supported by texts of unassailable authority. In the Wisdom of Solomon, a book dear to Nicholas, one reads: "For the greatness and beauty of created things give us a corresponding idea of their Creator."[1] St. Paul's gloss was: "For all that may be known of God by men lies plain before their eyes; indeed, God himself has disclosed it to them. His invisible attributes, that is to say his everlasting

---

[1]Wisdom of Solomon 13:5.

power and deity, have been visible, ever since the world began, to the eye of reason, in the things he has made."[2]

St. Augustine elaborated this into a method of exegesis and of allegorical interpretation that was to become canonic. "All doctrine," he explained in *On Christian Doctrine*, "concerns either things or signs, but things are learned by signs."[3] In books II and III he dealt with the interpretation of signs, but first he distinguished between things. "Some things are to be enjoyed, others to be used, and there are others which are to be enjoyed and used" (I, iii, 3). Concerning the first category, he said: "The things which are to be enjoyed are the Father, Son, and the Holy Spirit, a single Trinity...";   these are the things that make us blessed (I,v,5).   About the second category, he said: "Those things which are to be used help us and, as it were, sustain us as we move toward blessedness in order that we may gain and cling to those things which make us blessed" (I,iii,3).   The things that are to be used are the things that are also signs. They are not to be enjoyed for their own sake but are to be used because they signify that which is to be enjoyed. We have been placed in the midst of things that are to be used; if we are "shackled by an inferior love," we will pervert our love for God by enjoying things given to us for use (I,iii,3).   In the third category was a single thing that was to be both enjoyed for its divinity and used for its signification of divinity, that is, man: "a great thing,...made in the image and likeness of God." Man is to be enjoyed and used when men are united with one another in charity, which is love of one's neighbor as oneself.[4]

Augustine outlined this scheme when he was explaining the uses of literature and rhetoric, but eventually his doctrine of signs was applied to allegorical interpretation and representation in visual art. The only way art could convey doctrine was through the means Solomon, Paul, and Augustine had explained, and the only art that would be useful to Nicholas would have been art that conveyed doctrine. Sanction for the Church's use of doctrinal art had been given by Gregory the Great, who had defined two types of art that were useful for the Church—the *istoria* and the iconic cult image—and these, along with the private devotional image that had developed later, were still serving devotion during the quattrocento.[5] Each of the three types of art presented a thing or things that signified, and these things appeared as figurative representations or figures, or they formed parts of figures that in turn appeared within larger figurative structures.[6] For example, grapes signified the wine that Christ had used at the last supper to signify the blood he would shed at his Passion, which would assure man's salvation. In Masaccio's majestic Pisa Altarpiece (1426; main panel, National Gallery, London), the Christ Child plays with grapes and a grape pip; here the Child appears with the Madonna surrounded by saints and angels, which form a

---

[2]Romans 1:19–20.

[3]Augustine, *On Christian Doctrine*, 1958, I, ii, 2. References in the text are to this work.

[4]I, iii, 3; xxii, 20, which contains the reference to Genesis 1:26.

[5]See Ringbom, 1965, ch. I, sections 1–3, and passim. In his detailed analysis, he has shown that during the fifteenth century psychological responses to art that formerly had been peculiar to one type or another became confused with one another, and the forms of the three types also became confused with one another and underwent a drastic overhaul. Nonetheless, art was still allegorical, and the object still served devotion.   For an older treatment of north Europe alone, see Huizinga, 1956, esp. chs. XIX and XX, and p. 266.

[6]The art historical term "program" is often used mistakenly to refer to a figure; "program" should be reserved for a collection of figures into a cycle. An "iconographic type" is also simply a figure. It might be mentioned also that the term "symbol" is often used in place of the term "sign" or Augustinian "thing which signifies"; the term "symbol" has its own dangers. In patristic writings, "figure" and "allegory" are synonymous in some uses.

larger figurative structure. Predella panels with *istorie* (now dispersed) that appeared below added content to the main figure, as did the great Crucifixion (now in Naples) above. In the altar the grapes appear in a larger figurative structure signifying that through Christ's passion and the saints' intercession, the gift of grace can be dispensed to the faithful, so that they might join Christ and his mother with the saints in paradise. The invisible doctrine of salvation was made visible by presenting things (figures) that signified. Christ as Redeemer, here shown as a child with the grapes, was the central figure, and the material that was added to form the larger figurative structure gave it greater content and additional meaning. The figures used in visual representations often had a supplement or an equivalent in verbal presentations, such as commentaries and sermons. These literary productions were constructed in much the same way that a complex work of art was; to a standard and recurrent topic or theme, or *topos*, would be added a gloss to serve as a supplement and as an interpretation of the invisible doctrine.

Things had significance in less elaborate or in mundane contexts as well, and they could include significant or meaningful actions as well as visual things or verbal *topoi*. For example, Nicholas found that much was signified by the crossed keys of Peter. Similarly, in his abortive plot for revolt in Rome, Stefano Porcari included images, actions, and cries that he hoped would stir the people to move against the papal tyranny that he believed existed.[7] Probably none of these things that signified was independent of the others, and probably none was new; Porcari seems to have had a program and to have modeled it on the events that had attended the revolts and governments of Cola di Rienzo and others who created chaos as a concomitant to their republican aspirations.

Another example is the way a person could be responded to as if he were a sign. It would appear that the response was to the man as an officer rather than as an individual and that he was merely a figure for the office, which was itself loaded with meaning. Vespasiano said of Eugenius IV that "the air of devotion that hung around him was such that few who looked on him could retain their tears"; and "indeed, it was as if the people felt they looked upon the Divinity as well as upon the Vicar of Christ."[8] So, too, a final example concerns those who flocked to St. Peter's in 1450 to view the precious relic of Veronica's veil on the fateful day when the Ponte Sant'Angelo became choked; the veil at the Vatican was an iconic sign of Christ's divinity, and it had become a popular image familiar to visitors because it was the model for paintings and crude woodblocks used in many parts of Europe as devotional images.[9]

These things, when used as signs—whether singly or within a larger structure, and whether presented verbally or visually—received much of their impact from their traditional use, and the traditions attached to them continued to have force throughout the quattrocento. St. Bernardino of Siena early in the century and Savonarola at its end employed rhetorical forms untouched by the new demands for a humanist eloquence; their sermons were framed primarily to evoke a hearty response to significant things presented in traditional and accepted figures and other allegorical structures. The inscription of the former in the book of saints and the violent destruction of the latter attest to their abilities to evoke responses.

Most of this is well understood by art historians adept at iconographic analysis of allegorical art. But ignored in iconographic studies is an understanding of how

[8]Vespasiano, 1963, p. 27.   [7]See below, chapter 4.

[9]Ringbom, 1965, pp. 23–30.

allegorical art that conveyed doctrine worked—that is, what mechanism was called into play in order that the art could serve its purpose and teach doctrine. By the late middle ages, the means by which a person was expected to respond to an allegorical presentation of doctrine was clearly understood because it was coordinated with an anthropology or a belief about how man was constituted. He possessed, it was believed, an intellect that was the guide, reins, and prod for the will, which in turn directed passion and love. Paul's eye of reason examined the visible to learn the invisible, which was God's love; through rational examination of the doctrinal presentation, the intellect led men to participation in that love. Allegories, such as Dante's *Divina Commedia* or Andrea da Firenze's Spanish Chapel frescoes in the cloister at Santa Maria Novella in Florence (ca. 1366–68), were constructed to present doctrine that, through study, could lead one to love God. Similarly, other things, real things in the world, were considered as signs immersed within larger figurative structures, and they, too, taught how to love God. These things, whether figures, *topoi*, or real and significant things in the world, were approached in a standard method that Augustine had outlined as a psychology of sin. *Suggestio,* the appearance of the thing, was followed by *delectio* (sometimes *delecatio*), or reflection about the thing and its possible use or abuse, which led to *consensus,* in which one consented to achieve that which had been preferred, whether for use or for abuse. Petrarch knew the system well; he had Augustine lead him through it in his *Secret,* written in 1342–43 and revised before its final copy was made in 1358.[10]

But Petrarch was dissatisfied and impatient with this traditional psychology, and in his impatience he laid down a serious challenge to all that he could learn about significant things, men, and sin from those who had written since Augustine. He believed that the then-current psychology of sin depended too much on the intellect and not enough on the will, and that it failed to give proper recognition to the role of love in approaching God. Petrarch believed that to desire to possess God is to enter into a reciprocal relationship with God, who is love. This willful love, not a love trained by the intellect, is the one to be cultivated. This is a strong love; Petrarch had Augustine remind him that Cicero, who knew Plato's doctrine, "was right when he wrote that 'of all the passions of the soul, assuredly the most violent is love'."[11]

But love of what? Certainly not love for those things that were to be used and not enjoyed. Together with Augustine, Petrarch dealt with this problem within the *topos* of the three lusts Satan had presented to Christ, which we encountered earlier in Nicholas V's testament. After examining the lusts, he was able to convert each one from something the world offered for abuse of love into something in the world that could be used to love God. His doing so contributed to the active, worldly, and assertive program that his humanist successors would construct in the quattrocento. What flowed from his examination and from the conclusions of his followers were the new ideas that defined the meaning and intention that artists and architects would eventually convey through new forms.

Petrarch examined the three lusts under the figures of Laura, learning, and fame.

---

[10]Petrarch, *Secret,* 1911, pp. 131–132. For a review of the three-step process, see Howard, 1966, pp. 56–65; for the larger context, see the important studies on allegory by Robertson, 1962, ch. II, 1 and 2, and pp. 295–300; also the review by Kaske, 1963; see also, for revisions and new directions, the studies by Hollander, 1969, introduction and ch. I; Allen, 1971, ch. I. See also Mazzeo, 1956, passim. Trinkaus, 1970, pp. 568–571, 621, 688, 702–703, 704–711, and 726–734, gives a discussion of its use and interpretation during the Renaissance.

[11]Ibid., p. 132; see also p. 44. Note that love is a passion of the soul, while the senses belong to the body.

Augustine persuaded Petrarch that the poet had erred in loving Laura; his love for her could not be an earthly sign of the love he should have had for God. Petrarch's love for Laura was only a more extreme case, Augustine argued, of his having confused the love of the creature with the love of its Creator.[12] He had sought to enjoy his love for Laura and not Laura herself; having loved Laura only in this way, he had been unable to allow her to serve as a sign that enabled him to love God.

Laura, the lust of the flesh, was related to her namesake, the laurel, the lust of dominion or of knowledge. "Discovering that the laurel of empire was beyond your reach, you have, with as little self-restraint as you showed in the case of your beloved herself, now coveted the laurel of Poetry, of which the merit of your works seemed to give more promise," Augustine said sternly to Petrarch. Forget it; put away the childish things of your youth; abandon your *Africa*, he continues, and reflect on the ill-health of your soul.[13] Petrarch did not put away his *Africa* but remained frustrated with it; meanwhile he developed the theme of the utility of letters in a number of different works. "It is one thing to know, another to love; one thing to understand, another to will."[14] Loving and willing are superior to knowing and understanding; those who are great in letters sting and set their hearers afire and urge them toward love of virtue and hatred of vice.[15] Put away vanity and seek *virtù* through letters, he concluded.

But letters must not be pursued in order to satisfy the last lust, that of pride of life, the sin of *superbia*, the most heinous abuse of love. Augustine disabused Petrarch of the notion that it was proper for mortal man to seek mortal things like glory as a sign of his desire to enjoy things immortal.[16] Seek—that is, desire, or love—immortal virtue and you will attain mortal glory in its wake.[17]

With the Father's continued assistance, Petrarch was now able to argue persuasively for an active involvement in affairs of the soul. The spiritual guide in the *Secret* explained to the poet that virtue is a sign of a healthy soul and that "desire of virtue is itself a greater part of virtue."[18] In harboring this desire, Petrarch set himself apart from those who stood between himself and Augustine. They had not been sufficiently inflamed with the love of God; they had wanted to know the truth, but they hardly seemed to will the good. Although they might know, they might not love. For them, the world was veiled in useful signs; but for Petrarch, while the world was filled with useful signs, it was also filled with things of great beauty that referred to the beauty of their Creator, and it was also a world in which men lived and in which men sought God. He considered the appeal to the intellect that was fundamental in the allegorical system then prevalent to be insufficient; with Dante, Petrarch's predecessors knew that intellectual illumination allowed the pilgrim to understand how:

[12]*Secret*, 1911, p. 124.   The position Petrarch is arguing against was made legitimate by Gregory the Great; see Robertson, 1962, pp. 28 ff., and passim. The route to Petrarch's position had been plotted earlier in the century and uniquely in Italy; see Freyhan, 1948, pp. 75–79.

[13]*Secret*, 1911, pp. 135, 159–166.   For the *Africa* and the identity in Petrarch's mind of the *Africa*, Laura, and the laurel, see Bernardo, 1962, pp. 1 ff. and 47 ff., 64–65.

[14]Petrarch, *Ignorance*, 1948, p. 103.

[15]Ibid., referring to Cicero and Seneca and refuting claims for the superiority of Aristotle.

[16]Petrarch, *Secret*, 1911, pp. 176 ff.

[17]See chapter 2 above; for the three temptations in this context, too briefly sketched, see Howard, 1966, pp. 70–75.

[18]*Secret*, 1911, pp. 24, 192.   See also Augustine, *City of God*, XV, xxii.   In a passage that defines *virtus* Augustine moves from love as *amare* to the definition of *virtus* as "ordo est amaris" and on to "'Ordinate in me caritatem.'"

già volgeva il mio disiò e 'l velle
si come rota ch' igualmente è mossa
l'amor che move il sole e l'altre stelle.
                    (*Par.* XXXIII, 143–145)

But only too rarely could they have that vision by themselves and for themselves. Petrarch wanted something more direct, immediate, and active; as a man of letters concerned about his soul, he examined the potential of persuasive eloquence as an antidote to complex argument, because from Augustine he had learned that men were to be moved by rhetoric. Rhetoric would still involve things that signified, and it would still use the psychology of sin that moved from suggestion to delectation to consent, but it would depend upon a different anthropology in which the will would be superior to the intellect. Therefore, a man would aim his rhetorical appeal to the will of another man, and a different relationship would be established between men when the issue was the love of each for God.

Petrarch learned about rhetoric and the will from Augustine. He must have noticed that in *On Christian Doctrine,* after having explained what things are and how to interpret things that signify, Augustine had moved on to the topic of teaching. In book IV he explained that classical rhetoric should be used by the ecclesiastical preacher. He had three tasks—to teach, delight, and move— and, in quoting Cicero, he explained what each amounted to: "'To teach is a necessity, to please is a sweetness, to persuade is a victory.'" Teaching and pleasing play a subordinate role to that of moving the listener. Only when a listener is moved will he be persuaded to act, to live good habits, to avoid evil, and to love God and his neighbor as himself.[19] Eloquence is directed at the will; rhetoric may now replace demonstration and argumentation in moving men to love God.

In the same book Petrarch could also learn how to act in his vocation, that is, how to accommodate his own love for God and his desire for virtue to the vocation of preacher, as Augustine called the Christian orator, or poet, as Petrarch called himself. When attempting to move men to love God, the poet was binding himself to other men in charity, and he was serving God. The teacher "chooses a good life in such a way that he does not also neglect good fame, but provides 'what may be good not only before God, but also before men', insofar as he is able, by fearing God and caring for men."[20] Indeed, his life itself may be so ordered "that he not only prepares a reward for himself, but also so that he offers an example to others, and his way of living may be, as it were, an eloquent speech."[21]

To pursue eloquence was to serve God and one's soul by serving men; such service would have its reward. To seek immortal virtue through acting in one's vocation is to show one's love for God and to attain mortal glory as well. To pursue eloquence was to enter into a demanding service; it required the direct involvement of one man in the affairs of another, and these affairs were as often carried out in the arena of worldly activity as they were in the recesses of religious service and personal devotion. Petrarch had outlined the program that made direct action in the world possible, but he had engaged in affairs of the world only reluctantly and only when his autonomy and independence were assured, preferring instead to devote himself to letters. His successors were less secluded; they made a rather different use of the program he had

---

[19]*On Christian Doctrine,* 1958, IV, xii, 27 ff.; also xxv, 55.

[20]Ibid., IV, xxviii, 61, quoting 2 Corinthians 8: 21.

[21]Ibid., IV, xxviii, 61.

initiated. Many of them called themselves his disciples; they cultivated the program of classical and liberal studies he had formulated, but they were more directly engaged in activities. After two generations of humanists who were active mainly in Florence had developed Petrarch's thoughts, they were transported to Rome where Nicholas put them into service. While the intellect could still persuade men to love God, among this group it was more important to have eloquence move men to act for the good. As Augustine had said, "... persuasion is victory, for people may be taught and be pleased and still not consent. And of what use are the first two [i.e., teaching and pleasing] if the third does not follow?"[22] Men who love God can call on the intellect to serve as a tool to teach them about the God they love. The humanists sought words that had sting and figures and other structures that had force and gave new insight. They reexamined old signs and figures, and they discovered, as Petrarch had, that pagan antiquity and ancient rhetorical eloquence contained the richest fund of material adaptable for use by the Christian.

They also found things that could be used in the world around them. Petrarch had had qualms about using things of the world, but the men with whom Nicholas associated had resolved Petrarch's problems with worldly things and could enjoy them. Valla, for example, was able to identify pleasure with love. He explained that "the joy which I take in seeing brightness, or hearing a mellow voice, is not the same as the brightness or the voice, but these things offered to my senses bring it about that I enjoy." He thereby receives a vision and knowledge of God, and "from the vision and knowledge of God beatitude itself is generated." He loves not the pleasure, but God: "Pleasure itself is love, but what makes pleasure is God. The recipient loves, the received is loved; loving [*amatio*] is delight itself, or pleasure, or beatitude, or happiness, or charity, which is the ultimate end and on account of which all other things are made."[23]

Meanwhile, Alberti defended riches. He explained that while riches were not a sign of virtue and were not to be displayed and flouted, a virtuous man was naturally blessed with the goods of fortune that in turn assisted him in his *virtù*.[24] And Nicholas himself was lavish in patronage, in spending, in acquiring beautiful things, and in financing architectural works. Poverty had no place in his scheme of virtue,[25] although he said that he acquired things for the use of the Church and never left himself open to the charge of having abused things by saying that he enjoyed them as things.[26] It seems unlikely that he would have responded to preachers such as Savonarola; the friar stimulated the people to destroy things because they were vanities, the enjoyment of which was a form of abuse rather than one of use. But not everyone in the quattrocento would be expected to consign expensive garments and "lewd" paintings to the flames; some men of the period considered the use or abuse of things in the world to be less the issue than the use or abuse of their love and will in operating actively in the world.

These humanist ideas opened up new and rich opportunities for painters and architects, because now patrons could justify expenditures for undertakings that had

[22]Ibid., IV, xii, 28.

[23]From *De vero bono*, quoted and discussed in Trinkaus, 1970, p. 138.

[24]See *Theogenius*, pp. 65–73; *Della famiglia*, pp. 76 ff., 143 ff., and the first pages of book III. For Florence and Alberti, see Martines, 1963, p. 25. For Poggio, see "De avaricia," p. 266; Doren, 1922–23, pp. 111 ff., 132–133. For Filelfo, see *De paupertate*, pp. 498 and 512.

[25]See the parts of virtue in his decorative scheme, to be discussed below, chapter 7; none of the sources listed there includes poverty or denial under the parts of Temperance, although Temperance in Nicholas's scheme has not survived to confirm this point.

[26]See Manetti, *RIS*, col. 956.

formerly been of questionable value to the Christian, and because they now could ask for a broader range of subjects to be depicted or projects to be built. Again, literary explorations of these opportunities preceded visual ones. Petrarch, for example, believed that in the lives of men he had found examples of stinging rhetoric that he could use to move men to love. When he explored the classical past, he studied and wrote about ancient heroes, men who had made history, controlled fortune, and achieved glory.[27] These were men worth being remembered and imitated, as he said when he introduced them in his *De viris illustribus:* "It is the fruitful task of the historian to make known that which the reader should imitate or that which he should avoid, so that of these two a number of illustrious examples are available here."[28] Petrarch's successors followed his program; they were historians like himself, but because they were more engaged in the present than he had been, they were more convinced than he had been that their own activities should be *exempla* for others. This attitude made possible the vigorous activity of those around Nicholas in Rome. It also introduced a new attitude about how heroes could be used as subjects in a rhetorical art, and it wrought an important change in the forms used to represent them.

The effect the new humanist ideas about heroes had on their representation in art will be examined in a moment to illustrate a more general and important point: The artists who matured during the first decades of the quattrocento invented a new art, in part to respond to new demands and expectations of their public. Petrarch's new anthropology and his reorientation of attitudes toward the will and the intellect, toward loving and knowing, and his and his followers' subsequent reexamination of material that could serve the eloquent poet who attempted to move men to love God had already had its impact on literature. Petrarch's own activity and that of his successors had produced a form of eloquence that was calculated to move men, and apparently the men they addressed became accustomed to hearing stinging rhetoric that treated topics from their daily lives. Painters would now have to find an equivalent in the subjects they painted and in the forms they chose to show them. They would now paint *istorie* that treated events as familiar activities that the citizen might encounter and render them in forms that duplicated in one way or another the daily visual experience of those who were meant to look at their works. Thus, in response to the new meaning and intention for works addressed to men that the humanists had worked out, artists abandoned familiar paths. The content of figures and figurative structures that painters used changed; abstract notions of virtue and of typical actions undertaken within a preordained scheme of history gave way to the presentation of personal exertions by unique individuals at particular moments in history. Similarly, images rich in iconic character gave way to supple representations of aggressive individuals engaged in vigorous activity. This new art could appeal to men who through their *virtù* manifested love for God; it differed from the earlier art, which presented a complex system that was primarily intellectual and which presented to an intellect for consideration things that signified within the traditional and intellectually based psychology of sin. In literary terms, the older art would have been considered ineloquent. Worse, it did not refer to the world men now lived in.

The shift to the equivalent of eloquent rhetoric occurred in architecture as well as in the representational arts of painting and sculpture, although it developed more slowly in architecture. The first conscious exploitation of the new attitude in architecture on a comprehensive scale was undertaken in Rome during Nicholas's pontificate. His

[27]Nolhac, 1907, II, pp. 8–9.
[28]Quoted in Mommsen, 1959, p. 173; see also pp. 173 ff.

architectural program was the product of a careful extrapolation into architectural theory and practice of the precepts developed in sculpture and particularly in painting. To understand the new architecture, it will be necessary to consider the changes that occurred in representational art.

Briefly put, the old art had stressed traditional figures that had recognizable significance because they were directly related to external sources and traditional meanings. While the content conveyed by external and traditional sources remained more or less constant through the continued use of many of the same figures, three changes occurred. One was that artists began to present a more lively representation of the persons involved in the traditional figurative action; thus the persons involved in the action began to assume significance. Another was that they began to place their subjects in a grander framework, which allowed for the representation of an interaction between persons, and to show this interaction as one that took place in this world. Finally, they began to show the interaction and its setting as subjects that in themselves conveyed meaning and that supplemented the traditional figure.

The changes in representation may be illustrated by concentrating mainly on the handling of images of exemplary individuals. A statement by Petrus Berchorius, the precocious French humanist and mythographer, explains the role of such representations. In his *Repertorium morale*, compiled in the later fourteenth century, he stated: "For just as statues are set up in public and not in private places in order that by sight of them men be drawn toward devotion, so good men are set forth as an *exemplum* for others in order that by seeing them, through their teaching and their example, men be aroused toward the better."[29] The contemporaneous visual evidence suggests that what one saw in such an image of the *exemplum* was qualities not necessarily innate in its forms. The six major panels in Filarete's doors at St. Peter's differ little in formal content from what one would have found in Berchorius's lifetime (figs. 1–3). Although they are consciously archaizing—and they are not statues—the panels illustrate what Berchorius had in mind in the first part of his definition. The design of each of the panels is calculated to convey the figurative content of the subject as it is known through sources external to the images themselves. Christ and Mary are hieratic figures. Paul and Peter, with Eugenius, are officers rather than men; they appear more as stern representatives of their offices than as men whose activities should be emulated in order to arouse other men toward the better. And their martyrdoms, while *istorie* and not personifications, are nonetheless given a similar treatment. These important events are shown as collections of actions that led to the saints' deaths rather than as sequences of actions that had dramatic unity at the time and that occurred in a place that was a recognizable extension of the viewer's world. In these panels Filarete included nothing that detracted from the traditional, figurative content. This encouraged intellectual contemplation of these *exempla* of God-directed activity, but it hardly allowed the character or the *virtù* of the individuals represented to move the viewer.

Berchorius, who had been in touch with Petrarch, had said that the actions of living men may provide stirring incentives to others. Petrarch's *De viris illustribus* had been based on the notion that the lives of men who had lived could move others to virtuous activity. His book had provided the conceptual basis and much of the program for a cycle of exemplary figures in the Sala Virorum in the Carrara Palace in Padua, done between 1367 and 1379.[30] That gallery of ancient ducal heroes then served as the conceptual foundation for a civic cycle painted in 1413–14 in the Palazzo Pub-

[29]Quoted in Heckscher, 1955, p. 41, n. 67; from 1631 ed., s.v. "imago."
[30]See Mommsen, 1959.

blico in Siena by Taddeo di Bartolo.[31] In each of these cycles the program was far in advance of what later painters would show to be the appropriate form for the representation of heroes; thus the written program, but not the painted forms, presents persons whom the humanists are already able to see as individuals. The new meaning and intention of works of art has emerged in the program, but the forms remain old.

The Siena program illustrates qualities that should guide the actions of the governors of the republic of Siena in the form of personifications of the Christian virtues, of Romans who represent those virtues, and of Aristotle, who appears as a guide to orderly government (figs. 17–19). Aristotle's concept of government dominates the cycle, but the way in which he plays his role is typical of that of the other figures. What he can teach is made clear not through any intrinsic characteristic of his formal representation, but through a long inscription he holds: "I am the great Aristotle, and I tell you in hexameters about the men whose virtue made Rome so great that her power reached to the sky."[32] The program is clearly a Renaissance one. It emphasizes the virtue that accrues to the state through the virtue of its individual citizens; Romans occupy a central position as *exempla* for viewers, and great care is lavished on the literary form and on the structure of the program. But the forms used by the painter have been left untouched by the new ideas that they present to the viewer and that had allowed the elements to be selected for the program. New forms apparently had to await a clearer and broader understanding of what these new programs were to convey.

This clearer understanding was presented visually by Masaccio and Donatello in their earliest mature works, and during the second quarter of the quattrocento it began to emerge in discussions about art. Bartholomaeus Facius (d. 1457) explained what should be stressed to evoke a response in keeping with the new humanist anthropology. The humanist historian and secretary of Alfonso of Naples presented his ideas in a treatise written in 1456, but it probably contained few ideas postdating his residence in Florence before 1444.[33] He began by stating that "a painting is indeed nothing else but a wordless poem," a phrase that he took directly from Plutarch and that shows his affinity with the Florentine humanists who developed Boccaccio's and Salutati's theory of poetry. He explained that "no painter is accounted excellent who has not distinguished himself in representing the properties of his subjects as they exist in themselves." That is, the painter is not merely to produce images that depend upon external material for their impact; what he represents must be content that actually exists in his subjects. He therefore distinguished between two things, that of representing a man who personifies a virtue or a vice, and that of representing the external characteristics which indicate that a man is internally filled with qualities associated with virtue or vice. Using the example of *superbia*, he states: "For it is one thing to paint a proud man (*superbum*), but quite another to paint a mean or fawning or improvident one, and so forth." Both the poet and the painter, he continues, are "to represent these properties of their subjects," but only a very foolish man would represent avarice as a lion or an eagle, or liberality as a wolf or a kite because "the nature of things thus likened to each other should be similar." That is, the painter is addressing himself to men; therefore, men with these qualities, not animals that represent them, are to serve as *exempla* for other men. This makes it possible to address the representation to that part of man which is responsible for

---

[31] Rubinstein, 1958; Symeonides, 1965, pp. 138 ff.

[32] Rubinstein's paraphrase, 1958, p. 193. The *titulus* is given there in note 93. For all the *tituli*, see Symeonides, 1965, p. 168, n. 34.

[33] Baxandall, 1964, p. 90. The text of *De pictoribus* is given there, p. 99, translation, p. 98. See also Baxandall, 1971, pp. 83, 99 ff.; also, note 3 to chapter 6, below.

his actions, a part that Petrarch had raised to an important position in his program for caring for his soul. As Facius put it:

> Painting requires the representation not only of the face or the countenance and the lineaments of the whole body, but also, and far more, of its interior feelings and emotions, so that the picture may seem to be alive and sentient and somehow move and have action. Otherwise it would be like the sort of poem that is beautiful, indeed, and tasteful, but languid and unmoving. Truly, as Horace says, "it is not enough for poetry to be beautiful, it must also be pleasing—such as to move the hearts and feelings of men in whatever direction it wishes."

The inner feelings and emotions must be stung so that the love will seek God. Facius is seeking an equivalent in the visual arts to the grand style in rhetoric that, as Augustine had had Cicero explain, achieves victory through persuasion.

The obvious immediate source for Facius's aesthetics as represented here is Alberti's *Della pittura* (Latin edition, 1435), which systematically outlined what the painter should do and what a painting should accomplish. When discussing *istorie,* Alberti had dealt with the representation of individuals in paintings. He said, "Painting has contributed considerably toward the piety that binds us to the gods and toward filling our souls with sound religious beliefs."[34] The greatest work of the painter is the *istoria:*

> An *istoria* you can justifiably praise and admire will be one that reveals itself to be so charming and attractive as to hold the eye of the learned and unlearned spectator for a long while, with a certain sense of pleasure and emotion (*animi motu,* i.e., movement of the soul).[35]

It is the movements of the body that reveal the movements of the soul.[36]

This passage corresponds to something Augustine had said. The Father had explained that the preacher could assess the effect of his oratory on his audience by observing their actions. Frequent and vigorous applause may accompany any of the three styles—the subdued, the moderate, or the grand—but when listeners have been affected by the grand style, the one that persuades rather than teaches and delights, they "do not show it through applause but rather through their groans, sometimes even through tears, and finally through a change of their way of life."[37] Later Alberti, in his explanation of what would make an effective statue of a hero or a saint in a church, said that in them the "sculptor should endeavor as much as possible to express both by the deportment and bearing (*habitu et gestu*) of the figure the life and character (*vitam et mores*) of the person."[38] The visual eloquence of such a figure, a figure that presented an individual who had lived in the world and whose life had represented his *virtù* through his actions, could persuade the viewer to change his

---

[34] Alberti, *De pictura*, II, 25. See also *Della pittura*, p. 76; Alberti: Spencer, p. 63. For observations and emendations to Mallè's text, see Grayson, 1953, II: "Appunti sul testo *della Pittura.*" References to Spencer's text are included for convenience. I have substituted "souls" for Grayson's "minds" in accordance with Alberti's meaning as represented in *De re aed.,* for which see below, note 101.

[35] Alberti, *De pictura*, II, 40; *Della pittura*, p. 91; Alberti: Spencer, p. 75. See also below, note 101.

[36] See esp. Alberti, *De pictura*, II, 40–44; *Della pittura*, pp. 95 ff.; Alberti: Spencer, pp. 76 ff.

[37] Augustine, *On Christian Doctrine*, 1958, IV, xxiv, 53.

[38] *De re aed.,* VII, xvii, p. 663; Alberti: Leoni, p. 161.

way of life for the better. Now there is little or no need for material external to the representation to explain what moral lesson it is presenting.

This is a point a viewer could see when examining Castagno's fresco cycle at Legnaia (figs. 12,13,15). The representation derives directly from the formal inventions of Masaccio and Donatello, and the program is an adaptation of the one that had appeared in the Sala Virorum in Padua and in the Palazzo Pubblico in Siena. The cycle illustrates all three characteristics that set the new art apart from the old, and it reveals how the new art could make an appeal to the observer. Castagno's figures are persons, not personifications. They are alive and filled with character; they are conspicuously fuller of the movements of the soul than are the heroes in Siena, and they therefore have no need to speak with hexameters when they can speak with their bodies (figs. 17–19). They were therefore given the simplest labels. Rather than respond to mere figurative images, the observer was now expected to imitate in his own *virtù* the *virtù* of whole people who were moved, as Petrarch had explained, by their love for God and their will for Him. Castagno's images are images with sting.

In order to understand the other two characteristics of the new art—how the depicted persons interact with one another and with the viewer, and how their interaction and setting have their own content and meaning—we must go beyond the point to which Facius takes us. His remarks show how the demands for an eloquence that moves the hearer could be related to images that move the viewer, but they only hint at the possibilities of combining such images into a composition to produce an *istoria* that shows the interactions of individuals in a setting. He stated that "... truly almost equal attention is given by both [the painter and the poet] to the invention and the arrangement of their work,"[39] and he believed that painting is the origin of sculpture and of architecture, but he took these statements from Alberti without fully understanding them. By invention and arrangement Facius means simply that the painter adds a certain vigor and liveliness to the representation of the persons being depicted;[40] he left his remarks about the primacy of painting among the other two visual arts undeveloped.

Alberti's earlier treatise had made a more fundamental contribution, and Facius's hesitant comprehension of its content shows how truly innovative it was and therefore how difficult it was to profit from all that it contained. But his work did not go unnoticed. Archbishop Antoninus complained that painters "are at fault when they make images that provoke to desire, not because of their beauty (*pulchritudine*) but because of their arrangement (*dispositione*), such as naked women and the like."[41] Creighton Gilbert is surely correct when he translates *dispositione* as arrangement and suggests that the term has the same meaning as Alberti's term "composition." Alberti—and the attentive archbishop—understood that the form of a painting is intimately bound up with the action being depicted, that a painting is successful when the two are congruent, and that it is unsuccessful if deficient in one or the other element.[42] Even a painting of a nude woman could teach doctrine if the nude was a

---

[39]Baxandall, 1964, p. 98.   Invention and arrangement are the rhetorical terms *inventio* and *dispositio*; ibid., p. 93; Spencer, 1957.

[40]The last phrase "enlivened by a certain vigor" is Baxandall's rendering of Facius's "figura," for the significance of which see his discussion, 1964, pp. 95 ff.   Facius's reformulation of its meaning to agree with Quintilian's "figuratus" as discussed by Baxandall corresponds precisely to the changes in form and purpose being discussed here.

[41]Quoted in Gilbert, 1959, p. 76.

[42]Ibid., pp. 78–80.

proper part of a composition, that is, of an *istoria*. This was the point Antoninus was making, and, as Gilbert has shown, he was making it on the basis of works produced by the innovative artists of the early quattrocento. In preparing *Della pittura*, Alberti had collected the most important principles explored by that new breed of artists, had subjected them to critical scrutiny from the point of view of his humanist culture, and had transformed them into a coherent humanist treatise. The result was a book that served as the point of departure for the theory and criticism of art for the next several centuries.[43] With *Della pittura*, we are at the third stage of the sequence outlined at the introduction to this chapter. Petrarch and his successors had defined the new meaning and intention of works of art; Masaccio and Donatello—here illustrated by Castagno's later frescoes at Legnaia—revealed the new forms that corresponded to the new stinging eloquence in rhetoric; and Alberti's treatise on painting broached the theory that explained what these artists were doing and how their products were to be connected with the new rhetoric. Clearly, the sequence is more easily marked by the succession of ideas than by that of years, as Fustel de Coulanges put it when studying the city in antiquity (*The Ancient City*, III, ii); but such an approach to the sequence is appropriate to this study because the material of interest profited from the fully developed integration of the new theory and practice, and a detailed investigation of the sequence would here be irrelevant and superfluous.

In *Della pittura*, Alberti's overriding concern was the *istoria*, because it was not enough to represent the movements of the soul by showing the movements of the body; the figures also had to be composed as if they were participating in a unified action, thus producing the *istoria*, and the painter had to place the *istoria* within an ordered space. Alberti suggested some *istorie* that would have been familiar only to the few who were as fully endowed with a knowledge of the classics as he was, but most subjects painted by his intended readers would have been traditional ones with a standard figurative content and form. They would have been as well known through their use as literary figures as they were as traditional visual figures, and Alberti was attempting to explain how these familiar subjects could be given new life and sting. The painter was to concentrate on rendering the relationships that would exist between the figures when they were doing what the painter was showing them do and when they were in a space like that inhabited by the viewer. Alberti's intention was to find a means by which the painter could make a presentation to the viewer that could only be made by a visual figure, no matter how familiar the subject might have been as a literary figure. Painting could be independently eloquent and moving.

The means available to the painter had been demonstrated by Masaccio, Donatello, and the others who appear in the dedication of the Italian *Della pittura* (1436), and they had been explained by Alberti. These means may be said to devolve from four points of style, although this is not the way Alberti explained it. One was the careful manipulation of a coherent spatial structure that simulated the one familiar to the eyes of the viewer through his everyday contact with the world. Another was the illumination of the objects in the painting from a uniform source, which was itself somehow coordinated with the structure of the spatial setting. Another was the depiction of the material qualities of things, such that they were understood to be-

---

[43]For the content and impact of Alberti's criticism of art, see Vesco, 1919, which is filled with felicitous observations; for a general discussion, see Clark, 1944. See also Baxandall, 1971, and note to that book, below, chapter 6, note 3. For two contrasting views about Alberti, his treatise, and art in 1435, see Krautheimer, 1970, chapters XVI, XIX, and XXI, and Gombrich, "Artistic Progress," 1966. For the interpretation of Alberti's theory of painting in the sections that follow, including evidence and a fuller bibliography, see Westfall, *JHI*, 1969.

long to the same world as that inhabited by the viewer rather than one which is distant and inaccessible to him. The final point was the representation of actions that involve individuals acting in coordination with one another, within the spatial structure and its coherent illumination and in response to the same earthly powers of gravity, material stress on garments when pulled aside by vigorous action, and twist and pull on anatomy that one may observe daily in the piazza and palace.

In one way or another, each of these four stylistic innovations allowed the painter to respond to the new demands made by his viewers. The personality of the subject and the importance of his actions, as well as his interaction with others and his occupation of a definite setting, would be stressed by manipulating the spatial structure, light, material qualities, and actions to show something that could be duplicated in the observer's everyday experience. If the same artist were to handle these four elements of style in two markedly different ways in the same work, he would be able to convey two different meanings and intentions in it, as Filarete did in the doors at St. Peter's. The four small narrative panels display a unity and a continuity of action that is lacking in the images of the four main panels and in the two larger martyrdom panels (figs. 1–3, 4–6, 8). The new style allowed Filarete to show that the actions of the pope that occur in this world at this time continue to augment the traditional power and dignity of the papacy, which is represented in the conspicuously different six major panels. Filarete avoided diluting this emphasis—and shielded himself from obvious compositional difficulties and hazards—by concentrating on the dramatic actions transpiring among the participants while rendering the setting in a very abbreviated fashion. The newer panels supplement the content of the doors as a whole primarily by the narrative unity of the actions, rather than by the clear representation of a space that is a similitude of that inhabited by the viewer.

Just the opposite emphasis occurs in Castagno's cycle at Legnaia, which forms a marked contrast to the earlier cycle in Siena. Traditionally, cycles of heroes had been shown simply as images of men not engaged in actions; traditionally, the heroes had been placed within a fictive architectural setting that had little if any relationship to the space in which the observer moved and that, furthermore, had at best only a vague relationship to the painted figures.[44] A traditional setting holds the ancient heroes in the Palazzo Pubblico in Siena (figs. 17–19). They are shown in a variety of sizes and enframements that belong to a decorative architectural scheme. Some figures are seen in full length and standing within a fictive arcade; others are seen only in half-length and are smaller in scale;[45] and yet others are forced into small roundels within the decorative architectural scheme. The personifications of the virtues are again different; they are seen seated and holding their attributes, a pose shared by Aristotle, who holds his hexameters and points to them. Personifications of the ancient gods, which also appear in the cycle, are shown in yet another scale and setting. Taddeo had a purpose in using this arrangement; the variety clarifies the connections to the literary, external content of the cycle by separating one element from another, thus allowing each element to be studied in turn according to the type of meaning each might convey. The cycle could teach and its lessons could delight the viewer, but its forms and the interpretation those forms revealed about the men they displayed would hardly move a viewer. Although its intellectual content was

[44]See the list given by Horster, 1955; examples will be given below, chapter 7.

[45]For these figures, see Symeonides, 1965, pls. LXX b, LXXI b; Rubinstein, 1958, pl. 19 b,d. For the Virtues, see Symeonides, 1965, pls. LXIX a, LXXII a–d. For the ancient gods, ibid., pls. LXX a, LXXI b. For the overall arrangement, ibid., facing p. 146.

carefully contrived, the variety lacks appeal and the cycle has no coherent spatial structure. The fresco therefore is deprived of a visual content that reinforces or supplements the content of the figures it contains.

Castagno's fresco seems to be the earliest surviving example of this type of cycle—one which presents heroes and *exempla* for emulation—which attempts primarily to move the will rather than to present a demonstration to the intellect (figs. 12–16). Castagno did this not only by presenting persons filled with their own personalities, but by producing a composition filled with interactions. One interaction is between the figures and the viewer (in an *istoria*, the interaction between the figures themselves would be more emphatic than would be the interaction between the figures and the viewer), while another takes place between the figures and their setting. These interactions are important to the content of the cycle, as is the design of the setting in which the figures appear.

The viewer can interact with the figures because Castagno presented the figures in a forthright, direct way; they stand and gesture with set, distinct features and unique outward appearances that reveal their inner characters. They draw the eye of the observer and move his soul. They therefore allow the observer to recognize that these are individuals whose actions are to be emulated here, in this world. Castagno heightened this suggestion by showing no detail or narrative to detract from the character of each individual, and by placing them all in a setting that in its spatial quality, its illumination, its depiction of material qualities, and its scale is a fictive extension of the viewer's environment.

The long wall was originally illuminated with light that flowed in from an arcade opening to the outside, and the features of the figures are shown as if they were molded by that same source of light.[46] The niches that hold the figures form part of an architectural scheme that belongs to the space of the room itself (figs. 13,14). The dado is the fictive decoration of the wall of the loggia in which the observer stands, and it supports the niches and figures, some of whose feet, weapons, and other elements overlap the foremost plane of the fictive architecture. The roof trusses foot on two of the piers that frame the niches, and intruding into the rhythm of the trusses are putti holding wreaths, standing in the clerestory and above the other piers (fig. 16).[47] The design of the setting, like the forms used to render the figures, makes it clear that these *exempla* had lived actively in a world like the observer's own; the latter would understand that his actions must take place in the world in which they all lived.

Subtleties in the design of the surviving end wall enrich this theme. Because Adam's and Eve's role in the history of salvation had been superseded by that of Christ and Mary, and because their role as *exempla* for virtuous activity for the Christian was unlike that of the nine figures from more recent history, Castagno

[46]This is more conspicuous on the end wall (for which, see below, p. 51), which receives raking light, than on the frontally illuminated long wall. The original loggia was walled up; recent restorations, visible at the villa, have revealed a fourteenth-century pier at the corner of the surviving end wall. A strip of very recent restorer's paint on the end wall, perpendicular to the face of the pier and the thickness of a plaster coat, is deceptive; it obscures the fact that the plaster on the end wall (for which, see below) originally returned around the corner, covering the pier. This would indicate that the wall was rebuilt, probably as an arcade and probably when the frescoes were done. Later, in the sixteenth century, the arcade was destroyed and a wall with two windows and a door which are clearly sixteenth-century in form were installed. According to a verbal report of the workmen, these openings have been replaced in a new wall; the sixteenth-century wall was investigated for traces of fifteenth-century work, but only the fourteenth-century pier emerged.

[47]These features are quite clear in the sinopia at the villa but have been obscured by restorations to the detached intonaco where spurious piers have been added in the attic.

showed the First Parents as statues set on low pedestals,[48] rendered them in subdued tones, and placed them well back in the space of the niches (figs. 14–15). The Madonna and Child, however, are set off from the First Parents and are represented as a small statue group. The Savior and his mother are centered in the wall and placed on the now damaged fictive cornice of a doorway entering the room. The trappings of their elaborate setting, with angels drawing aside the curtains of a baldachino to reveal them, intercept light from the same source as that which illuminates all the other figures (even casting deep shadows to emphasize the light's careful manipulation), and the figures and their setting are rendered as parts of the same space as that of all the other figures. The setting therefore allows one to understand that events in the history of salvation were real events enacted in the same world as the one inhabited by the heroes, heroines, and viewer.

The setting adds to the cycle's content by showing that the cycle belongs to the viewer's environment. But it also does more. Both the setting and the relationship between the figures that it establishes has content independent of that discussed up to this point. That is, the cycle presents not only thirteen figures who are to move the viewer, but it also presents a setting that would teach. The fictive architectural surrounding in which the figures appear derives from the traditional one that placed heroes in niches and other enframements, but this is the oldest surviving example of this type of setting, designed to have a content supplementing the content of that which it contains. The surrounding of the figures in Siena clarified the relationships between the figures, but when deprived of its figures, it became only meaningless decoration. Here, if the setting were viewed purely intellectually and independently of the character of the figures it contains, its empty niches and two empty pedestals would demonstrate that nine of the figures are related to one another in one way, that these as a group are related to the First Parents and are quite distinct from them, and that these eleven figures have a relationship to the Madonna and Child that is again similar but again different. And the setting would also explain the relationship of all those figures to the space in which the viewer moved (see esp. fig. 15). The setting would not move the viewer, but it would teach him. And it would be essential that the viewer comprehend the setting's lesson. He could not fully understand the cycle if he simply identified the figures and related them individually to what was said about them in external sources and in Castagno's interpretation of their individual personalities. To understand the full implications of the cycle he must also contemplate the setting in which the figures appear, and he must ponder the relationship between it and himself that is suggested by the setting's architectural structure.

To suggest that the viewer would have looked at the cycle in this way—and, it would seem, to suggest that Castagno knowingly constructed it to respond to this form of viewing—is to suggest that it fitted into the larger framework of humanist thought that had been developed from Petrarch's original notions. Art had content, both before and after Petrarch's activity, and that content could be known by referring to standard, outside sources, such as the biographies of heroes and explanations of the eschatological significance of heroic actions. But when that content was presented to a viewer, it had to move him by addressing itself to his will, and it had to persuade him to exercise his *virtù* to love God. In the process of making a moving presentation, the quattrocento artist would study new ways to present traditional figures. Castagno revised the traditional figurative structure that had shown semi-

---

[48]The pedestal under Eve is clear; that area of Adam's representation is badly damaged, but visible in the villa is both the base and a fragment of the hoe overlapping the base, which shows that the figures were both set back in the space, unlike the figures on the long wall, who overlap their settings because they are set well forward in their niches.

iconic heroes in architectural enframements; he emphasized the individual personalities of the figures, the interactions between them and between them and the viewer, and the content of the interactions and the setting in which the figures were placed. Much of what he showed conveyed information that could not be learned from non-visual sources, or at least was not so vividly portrayed there, and all of what he showed was clearly the result of his own interpretation of his sources and of his understanding of the cycle's subject. He could be identified as the author of this unique cycle because it was unique.

Alberti had discussed each of these points in *Della pittura*. In book II he outlined the means the artist could use to combine individuals into an action in a setting in an *istoria*, while in book I he gave the theoretical principles pertaining to the setting's construction. The treatise as a whole made the point that the painter was to operate with a sure intellectual method that derives from nature, and that, like the poet, the artist's purpose was to move men from vice to virtue. In book III Alberti explained why the artist should operate in this way; like any man who exercises his *virtù*, the successful painter deserves the rewards of immortal glory and earthly fame. Augustine's and Petrarch's teaching can be seen behind these principles; the orator or poet must teach and please, but, most important, he must move; in so doing, he lives charitably through seeking immortal virtue, with earthly fame following in his wake. For Alberti, as with the painter, so too the architect; Alberti's theory of architecture grew directly from his theory of painting, and it was this theory that Nicholas pressed into service in Rome.

Alberti developed, and Nicholas used, three central principles in rebuilding Rome. The buildings were to be intelligently designed to have a particular content; they were to house or contain significant actions; and the intelligence of the designer was to be conspicuous, in order to serve as evidence of the designer's *virtù*. The first would be analogous to the Legnaia setting, the second to the figures in it, and the third to the humanist ideas about the role of the painter and his rewards, which Alberti had transposed from theories about poetry into his new ideas about art in *Della pittura*. That an intelligently designed building can have content, the first of these points that connects architectural activity to other humanist concerns, is usually overlooked. At Legnaia, Castagno was working within a tradition that prescribed certain visual and literary conventions for his presentation of the figures; an architect would also work within a tradition that would suggest, if not dictate, certain conventional elements that had to be present in an architectural design and that carried with them certain connotations or a certain content.[49] Buildings, in other words, were things or figures that signified, in the Augustinian sense; the architect was to make them clear, visible representations of things invisible. Alberti went further; he explained how to design buildings that were apt settings for actions the outward forms of which served as evidence of an inner character possessed by the actors.

Architecture, especially Renaissance architecture, is too seldom considered by historians as the representation in material form of significant content, of the invisible made visible, even though this was the most common way buildings were perceived until an independent system of aesthetic and visual analysis was developed.[50] Archi-

---

[49]The content contained in the format of presentation used by Castagno will be introduced, but not developed, below, chapter 7; for the purposes of this study, Castagno's transformation of that convention is not a relevant consideration.

[50]For introductions to and remarks about this problem see, for the medieval period, Krautheimer, 1942 (1969), passim, esp. p. 130; for the Gothic, Simson, 1962, passim; and for the Renaissance, Wittkower, 1962, part I.

tecture had diverse kinds of content. Petrarch's *Secret* contains an example of architecture as a figure when Augustine says:

> When your eyes behold some ancient building, let your first thought be,
> Where are those who wrought it with their hands? and when you see new
> ones, ask, Where, soon, the builders of them will be also? If you chance to
> see the trees of some orchard, remember how often it falls out that one plants
> it and another plucks the fruit.[51]

Petrarch grouped buildings and trees together and treated them in the same manner;
that is, he used them as illustrations of the same idea rather than as things whose
individual qualities were interesting. They were to remind men that a man may be
more mortal than the buildings he builds or the tree he plants. The mind of Poggio,
viewing Rome from the Capitol, and that of Alberti, in the famous passage describing
the sorrow he felt when gazing upon Rome's physical decay, were constrained
by the same *topos* that had bound Petrarch's mind; in the crumbling ruins of ancient
Rome they saw little except the moral lesson *sic transit gloria mundi*.[52] Even Giovanni
Rucellai, when visiting the Pantheon—the best preserved of ancient buildings—did
not fail to see it as a monument that referred to something else, in this case to the
fame of the "private citizen who was called Marco Agrippa," who had built it.[53]

Rucellai's references to the loggia he had Alberti build (which survives today along
with the related palace façade that forms a pleasant piazza in Florence[54]) reveal
another kind of content in a building. He says nothing that allows one to know what
the building looks like, because that was less important than its connotations; he
describes the loggia as a figure that represents attributes he values. Rucellai explained
that he built it "for the honor of our family, for using it for celebrating happy and
sad events," and as an example of what some Rucellai could do for the entire Rucellai
family.[55] In 1466 Rucellai held a great celebration in the piazza and loggia in honor
of the marriage of his son to a daughter of Pier di Cosimo de' Medici, and a reference to the loggia is included in the description Giovanni left of the festival.[56] The
honor of the family was enhanced not only by the marriage to a member of the Medici family but also by Rucellai's ability to lavish money on the festivities and to hold
them in a noble building.[57] We are nowhere told what the building looked like, but
we are told what we would see if we looked at it as Rucellai did, that is, figuratively.

Much the same point was made later by the more sophisticated dilettante Antonio
di Tuccio Manetti, when discussing Brunelleschi's contribution to the Palazzo di
Parte Guelfa in Florence. If one wishes to judge the beauty of it, he may go look
at what was built; "and he who truly wishes to judge well the *virtù*" of the architect,

---

[51]*Secret*, 1911, p. 186. Compare Augustine, as quoted and discussed in Storoni-Mazzolani, 1970,
p. 250. The *topos* had a continual life; for Rome as the place for such buildings, see Lenkeith,
1952, pp. 14 ff.

[52]Poggio, "Var. fortu.," 1953, pp. 233–234 and notes; Alberti, *De re aed.*, VI, i; see also
his history of architecture, ibid., VI, iii.

[53]Rucellai, 1960, p. 72. See also below, Epilogue.

[54]Rucellai began the palace façade, to Alberti's design, in 1446. He acquired the land for the
loggia in 1456; construction took place after 1461 and was completed by 1466. See Perosa's notes
to Rucellai, 1960, pp. 143–144, nn. 1 and 2, p. 145, n. 1. See also Thiem and Thiem, 1964,
cat. 23.

[55]Rucellai, 1960, p. 20.

[56]Ibid., p. 28.

[57]See Martines, 1963, pp. 18 ff.

he added, should compare Filippo's inexpensive work for the Guelf party with the rooms serving a similar purpose in the Palazzo Vecchio, where no expense was spared.[58] Manetti bemoans the contumacy of those who spoiled parts of Brunelleschi's design and then, citing neutral facts rather than forceful opinions, he states that the Palazzo di Parte Guelfa "remained incomplete, the governors of the city considering it proper that, for this organization, it would be better to have something of its reputation taken away than added."[59] To those who know how to look, the building reveals the ability of Brunelleschi to make a beautiful thing; it shows the inability of others to follow or to accept Brunelleschi's superior abilities. It demonstrates the architect's ability to relate his work for the Guelf party to the priors' chambers, which serve the same purpose, and it makes explicit the attitude of the Signoria toward the Guelf party. It was much more than a mere building; in the Florence of the 1480s when Manetti wrote, it was a visible figure for many ideas that agitated the citizens.[60]

The reverse of this Florentine approach was common in literature; an action that was the primary part of the narrative was given an architectural setting that was figurative, the elements of which served as glosses on the action being performed. Federico Frezzi, Bishop of Foligno, described a tour he took in about 1400 through the Realm of the Virtues, the fourth and last book of his Dantesque *Quadriregio*. The tour consists of movement through paradise settings and the encountering of the various virtues, often within figurative architecture. St. Paul is the guide in the domain of Faith, the first of those presided over by the three theological virtues; he conducts a lecture on the articles of faith in a church:

> Paul led me then into the sacred temple,
> made of the blood and made of the strength
> of saints, dead through bitter and sharp duels.
>
> It seemed to go to the heavens in its height,
> built on twelve columns,
> and four miles or nearly in its amplitude.
>
> . . . .
>
> Thousands of lights shone in every part,
> indeed as the light of the sun at noon.
>
> . . . .
>
> The chapels seemed like rows of gold,
> and their redness had the appearance of corals,
> and purple were the slits of the windows.
>
> The meat and the bones were more clear than crystals,
> all set with the most precious gemstones,
> loaded with hyacinth and precious stones.[61]

Architecturally, the figure makes little sense, but figuratively, it serves Frezzi's purpose. The pilgrim is in a setting resembling paradise, which is filled with elements that serve to illustrate doctrine through their signification.

---

[58]Manetti, 1970, lines 1122–24; 1124–32 (my translation).

[59]Ibid., lines 1151–1154 (my translation).

[60]For similar examples from earlier in the century, see Bruni and Dati, to be cited below, pp. 58. See also Manetti, 1970, p. 123, for the motivation of the "cittadinj, massime di quelli del quartierj," in undertaking the construction of Santo Spirito.

[61]Frezzi, 1914, IV, xv, lines 1–6, 11–12, 16–22.

Frezzi's figures resemble those of Juan de Torquemada in their lack of architectural coherence, but Frezzi's fellow Dominican theologian was able to produce a richer figurative meaning when using them. Torquemada employed figures for precisely the purpose Augustine had in mind—to make visible some invisible points of doctrine concerning the Christian faith. He introduced buildings into his argument in order that through reference to familiar visual images the invisible meaning might be clarified. The sacraments, he said, display the rational dignity and eminence of the law, by which he meant the new law Christ vouchsafed to the Apostles. They protect and therefore cure the soul, and as such they are the arms of the king of heaven; they expel tyrants from the precincts of holy knights; and they make inexpugnable the cities that defend the Church. They may therefore be likened to a tower.[62] He transferred the connotations of towers—which, as all knew, protect knights and cities in everyday life—to the sacraments. In the same passage Torquemada said that the sacraments and the Church are interchangeable. He now speaks in unequivocal Augustinian language: the Church may be compared to a tower that can be viewed by the minds of men; their minds are beshrouded by sin, but vision through the reason established by the holy doctors of the Church—or those who continued to expound Paul's "eye of reason"—allows a clear view to be obtained. The rational dignity and the eminence of the new law invested in the Church in the form of the sacraments may be perceived by a pre-Petrarchan man whose intellect will spur his love for God.

In another, more elaborate literary figure, Torquemada said the Church is a mystical body and a church building is a physical body with spiritual significance. There are, he reported, fifteen parts of the material church, each of which "signifies and represents the principal parts of the Church militant." The walls are faith made up of stones that are squared and solid and cemented by charity; the length of the church is magnanimity, its breadth is charity, its height is hope. The columns are the doctors of the Church, who teach and sustain the entire Church, and so on.[63] By the standards prevalent among the humanists at mid-century, Torquemada's language is as archaic as the major panels on Filarete's doors or as the setting of the Siena cycle—the character of the representation does not supplement the content. The reader must already be familiar with the characteristics of the physical church to understand the relationship between the things the church building, used figuratively, is to make visible. And the church used figuratively is abstract; the selection of elements used to conjure up a building is based primarily on sources external to their place in an architectonic or visual structure in a building. The observer already knows that faith and charity, and that magnanimity, faith, and hope, go together just as stones and mortar do and as length, breadth, and height do. There is no indication that he will learn more about the invisible Church by inquiring more deeply into the actual stones and mortar or the peculiar relationship between the three dimensions of space. The viewer is not expected to learn anything by studying the relationship of the parts of the building to one another as they exist in themselves; indeed, it seems unlikely that Torquemada understood that a purely architectonic structure that held the parts of a material church together was other than the result of the application of experience to the craft of construction as practiced by workmen.

Finally, a church building itself could be considered an example of the most profound mystical doctrines. When pondered, a building could be considered as something different from a collection of elements that could be rearranged and used to

[62] *Consecratione*, proem, fols. 2^{r-v}.
[63] Ibid., fols. 5^{r-v}.

suit the demands of a literary figure. A building could reveal proportions and a quality of light that permeated it; one could contemplate these and learn about God. Proportions and light were thought to refer anagogically to the Godhead in a theological system steeped in Neoplatonism. Within a doctrine that was as indebted to pseudo-Denis the Areopagite as it was to Augustine and that was more prevalent in the north of Europe than it was in Italy, the church building was used to represent something invisible. But the means of transmission was indirect; the building conveyed qualities such as proportionality and light, which were the attributes of the Godhead and of the Heavenly Jerusalem. They were more readily accessible as qualities than as quantities; they were more easily perceptible through commentaries about the building than through examination of its physical fabric; and they were made available to the viewer through the physical fabric of the church and were not firmly linked to or perceptible within the architectonic structure itself. The church was indeed a building, but it served more persuasively as a sign (in the Augustinian sense) than as an earthly building, because its material was nearly—if not completely—lost sight of in the overwhelming heavenly splendor to which it referred. Again, the buildings that were the subject of this sort of contemplation were the product of largely anonymous interpreters of doctrine, of nameless craftsmen, and of writers with only the fuzziest grasp of architectural terminology, who happened to write descriptions of churches; they were not the product of learned patrons or skilled and intelligent architects.[64]

The attitude that saw in things some sort of spiritual significance was not suddenly swept aside by a frame of mind that valued the earthly value of earthly things; at mid century it was possible to value both the earthly and the spiritual significance of things, and there is little room for doubt that Nicholas's buildings could be seen in each of the ways indicated by these authors. Petrarch would have—and Poggio, Alberti, and Rucellai may have—considered them lasting monuments to the pope's earthly fame. Rucellai and all those with whom he was in contact may have viewed them as lasting testimonies to the character of the pope who had built them. Torquemada may have considered them collections of figures—of individual elements—that conveyed spiritual significance. And Aeneas Sylvius, the Sienese humanist and future pope Pius II, who reveled in figurative contemplation of churches as proportionality and light, may have been blind to the architecture as he contemplated the splendor of God in them, although it is more likely that he was able to perceive both splendor and architecture, as were his friends and acquaintances Alberti, Manetti, and Nicholas.[65] But there is a considerable difference between architecture that appears as a literary figure for literary purposes and architecture that is a building, built to convey some particular doctrine through figurative representation. In Nicholas's program, this difference was understood. Nicholas believed that his program for governing could be made evident through the buildings he would build, and he exploited three different means to accomplish that end. First, as will be seen later when his buildings are examined in detail, he believed that certain elements represent certain things and that these elements should be used with care. Second, and more important as an indication of his program as a whole, he believed that the means used to assemble these

[64]For investigations of medieval architecture that illustrate the lack of consciousness of a coherent architectonic structure in churches, see Krautheimer, 1942 (1969), passim, esp. pp. 120–130; Ackerman, 1949, passim; Simson, 1962, passim, esp. part I, ch. 2, and pp. 125 ff., 192 ff.; and Boskovits, 1962–63, 1963, pp. 152–155. This list is by no means complete. For a general treatment of figures in literature, see Cornelius, 1930, introduction; for examples of the genre of mystical description, see Suger, 1946, and *De claustro animae*, passim, esp. III, chs. xi–xxix, which deals with Solomon's temple.

[65]See Pius II, 1959, pp. 286–289, for his description of the cathedral he built in Pienza.

elements was important and significant; not only were the individual parts to have significance, but the means by which they were assembled, or the architectonic structure that held them in place, was itself to have content. Finally, he believed that the activities within the structure were to be meaningful *exempla* of *virtù*, and that the effectiveness of these activities would be amplified by the support given them by the place in which they were performed. That Nicholas's buildings were intelligently designed to have a particular content in their architectonic structure, and that they were to house significant actions, derives from Alberti's theory of architecture.

Alberti had outlined his theory of architecture in *De re aedificatoria*, which he had largely completed by mid century.[66] Here he extended the principles that had appeared in his theory of painting in the direction suggested by the humanist culture Petrarch had launched and the humanists had developed in Florence. The architectural treatise contains an extremely advanced consciousness of activity as a positive virtue, and it is permeated with the belief that civic activity which involves all citizens in the actions of the city brings order to the city. Alberti acquired this belief in Florence. The individual, the city, and virtue were among the main issues under discussion among the humanists in Florence when he arrived for his first extended residence in his *patria* in 1434. During the two decades that followed he argued that the individual must actively use his talents and that the city should be his arena.

In *Della famiglia*, begun in Rome in 1432–34 and polished in Florence before its publication in 1443, he had an old member of the Alberti family, Giannozzo, rehearse the two sides of the question that had agitated Petrarch. Giannozzo is asked, should one live a secluded life in a villa? "Oh, God, yes, a proper paradise," Giannozzo said of a villa. The city is corrupt; in a villa one may enjoy his escape from "the violence, the tumult, the storm of the city, of the piazza, of the town hall.... What a blessing it would be to live in a villa, an unknown happiness."[67] Because it is free of vice, one indeed should live there. But, Giannozzo is asked, should a man raise his children there? No, he replied, because there they are unlikely to be exposed to vice. "He who has not heard the sound of the bagpipe cannot judge whether the instrument is good or not good."[68] Lionardo, one of the young disputants who did not believe that the city was corrupt, reminds the old man that "in the city one learns to be a citizen, acquires *buone arti*, sees many *exempla* to teach him to flee vices...." There he learns that honor is the most beautiful thing, that fame is comely, that glory is divine; "there he tastes the sweets of praise, of being named and esteemed and admired. By these wondrous things a youth is awakened to the pursuit of *virtù* and comes to devote himself to attempting arduous things worthy of immortality." But Giannozzo is not quite persuaded and strikes a median position. Each man should choose, but he should understand that "in the city are the workshops of the greatest dreams, governments, constitutions, and fame, while in the villa one finds quiet, contentment of soul, liberty of living, and robustness of health."[69] For the man whom nature made to overcome fortune and to acquire immortality, fame, and glory through the diligent practice of any of the *buone arti* of citizenship, the uncorrupt city must be his jousting ground. Even Giannozzo must recognize that when such a city exists, Petrarchan seclusion is no longer tenable.[70]

[66] The date of the treatise will be discussed below, Epilogue.

[67] *Della famiglia*, pp. 200–201; Alberti: Watkins, p. 193. Compare Petrarch's description of Avignon, *Secret*, 1911, p. 97.

[68] *Della famiglia*, p. 201; Alberti: Watkins, p. 193.

[69] *Della famiglia*, pp. 201–202; Alberti: Watkins, p. 194.

[70] Other works that developed these themes during this period were: *Fatum et Fortuna* (ca. 1439), *Theogenius* (ca. 1436–39), *Profugiorum ab aerumna* (1435–42), and *Momus* (begun 1443; known by 1451); dates from Mancini, 1911.

Painting and architecture were *buone arti* of citizenship; those who were naturally endowed with the requisite talents for their practice would operate in the city. They, like the statesman, contribute to the order of the city. In *De re aedificatoria* the city is the place in which all citizens pursue virtuous activities; more than that, for the first time, the city is considered to be a collection of buildings and of open spaces consciously designed and related to one another, a collection that allows citizens to bring order to their society through their participation in its affairs.

Alberti's conception of the city was unprecedented. Sources such as Plato's *Critias, Laws,* and *Republic,* Aristotle's *Politics,* Cicero's *Dream of Scipio,* and Augustine's *City of God* described cities or states and discussed constitutions and order, but the physical elements in the cities were not the result of some person's conscious application of design to the requirements of the particular city under review. Vitruvius's treatise, while replete with buildings for many civil functions, did not examine the political structure of the city. The Roman theorist did not consider it the business of an architect to inquire into the principles that defined the relationship between the form of a political structure and the design of buildings to serve it. Medieval treatises and descriptions of cities would have been even less useful; they simply enumerated things, whether they were buildings, mills, or magistrates, and remained mute about any theoretical unity between the things [71] Still, these sources served Alberti well.

More useful to Alberti was the consciousness of the city that had been developed in Florence soon after 1400. Leonardo Bruni described Florence as ordered; he saw the city as a unified physical structure related to abstract geometric forms, and he believed that this physical harmony was analogous to the harmony of the carefully constituted political institutions of the city.[72] But Bruni lacked the sense that individual buildings were parts of that harmonic order; the buildings made the city, the city described a circle, but the circle was not made of buildings. Nevertheless, it was an important first step, and Bruni's understanding was widely and quickly diffused. In 1423 Goro Dati described the city of Florence as a combination of history, institutions, and buildings, each one of which reflected the other and each of which was subject to the thought of active individuals.[73] From this background, which included ancient, medieval, and recent thought, Alberti was able to articulate a fully developed conception of the city. He understood the city to be a unique combination of physical and political forms, and he believed that the activity of individuals produced and maintained the order of the city.

When he discussed a building in his architectural treatise, Alberti never failed to account for its relationship to the city as a whole.[74] He stated that a building must satisfy the demands of beauty and the demands of ornament. The architect cannot satisfy either demand unless he understands that a city is a place where citizens act to produce order. Because the demands for each building in the city are different, each building would be unique. When the architect has satisfied the demands of beauty and of ornament, he has helped make visible the invisible quality of the city's order.

---

[71]See, for example, Bonvicinus de Rippa, 1898, from 1288 in Milan. A study of this literature would pay a handsome reward.

[72]Bruni, "Laudatio," 1968; see Baron, 1966, pp. 199 ff.

[73]See the text and discussion, Dati: Gilbert, 1969. See also Whitfield, 1965, p. 158; his claims concerning Alberti's debt to Palmieri are exaggerated, but his attempt to place Alberti in a Florentine and Petrarchan context and his remarks about the nature of the city Alberti described are instructive and useful.

[74]As a supplement to what follows, see Westfall, *SR,* 1969. In addition, see Mühlmann, 1969; Klotz, 1969.

Beauty and ornament are different, but related. Ornament is subordinate to beauty; ornament is a luster added onto—indeed, worked into—a beautiful design. Beauty can exist without ornament, but ornament cannot redeem a design that is not beautiful. Although beauty is essential, it does not follow that ornament is superfluous; it is simply added enrichment.[75]

When the architect designs, he involves himself first and fundamentally in the problem of beauty. Beauty resides in the architectonic structure and results from having designed properly. When the architect designs he uses what Alberti calls "an admirable and intelligent theory and method." He combines design (*lineamenta*) with construction (*structura*); that is, the architect combines perfect forms, which are modified as required by circumstances, with material taken from nature.[76] The forms are modified in response to the demands, or criteria, of beauty; these are structural stability, visual pleasantness, and social usefulness. In designing, the architect is imitating the process God uses as he creates in nature. He must comprehend how God creates, and he therefore must study both nature herself and other proper forms of God's revelation. Because a beautiful building is produced by imitating God, a beautiful building is a figure for the Creator.[77] As Alberti put it elsewhere when referring to the Duomo in Florence, "we enter here to greet the name and figure of God."[78]

Buildings had been considered figures for the Creator before Alberti had developed his theory, but a building considered in that way was not the unique product of an individual architect; additionally, it lacked architectonic substance, and only a sacred building could qualify for such consideration. Albert added not only secular buildings to the ranks, but he also, and more importantly, added all the buildings in the city, including the spaces left between buildings—streets, piazzas, bridges, open spaces of every sort.[79] He considered a city to be a big house and a house to be a little city; this was common enough in discussions of states and families. He also proposed that both a city and a house were to be subject to the same criteria of beauty and ornament; they were to be the products of the same theory of architectural design.[80] This was an innovation.[81] And both a house and a city held a society.

Both buildings and societies began as products of nature and had been given order through the operations of intelligent men. To guide himself when designing, the architect must study nature and other sources of God's revelation, and he must study ancient buildings.[82] To understand societies, nature and revelation are supplemented

---

[75]The definition of ornament is introduced in *De re aed.*, VI, i, and developed in subsequent books.

[76]*De re aed.*, preface, pp. 7–9; Alberti: Leoni, p. ix. Compare Alberti's belief about the proper means of acting in guiding the state; he requires that "disegno e proponimento" be used when reins are imposed on a citizenry: "Adunque, se le cose di noi uomini conseguono contro a nostra voluntà, elle succedono secondo el volere di chi così le guida. E certo sarebbe intollerabile arroganza la mia, se io pur volessi ch'ogni cosa isse a mio arbitrio, e nulla uscisse del mio disegno e proponimento. Tante nostre volontà adempiemmo altrove; ora lasciamo che altri ancora in qualcuna sua voglia si contenti." *Profugiorum ab aerumna*, p. 157.

[77]See Gadol, 1969, pp. 100–108.

[78]*Profugiorum ab aerumna*, p. 157; the passage follows directly upon the one quoted in note 76 above and reads: "Ma poi che giugnemmo a questo religiosissimo tempio, entriamo a salutare el nome e figura di Dio."

[79]See *De re aed.*, IV, passim; VII, i; VIII, i; VIII, vi; X, i.

[80]Ibid., I, ix; V, xiv.

[81]See, for example, *De re aed.*, V, ii.

[82]For the ancient buildings, see the striking introductory paragraph in Alberti, *To Matteo de' Pasti*, p. 17.

by history, which shows the operations of men. In developing this belief, Alberti analyzed and discussed societies following the same method he had used for buildings, but because this was an architectural rather than a political treatise, he gave only the most meager treatment to societies.[83] Their beauty resides in their order; nature and revelation taught him that men, like animals, are to be divided into various sorts. History is a record of men's activities. It confirms that the division of men is natural, and it reveals various distinctions, demonstrating that societies are to be divided into two types and men into several classes. One type of society is the republic; there, among the highest class of citizens, some men are superior in wisdom, some in knowledge of the useful arts, and some in their abundance of the goods of fortune.[84] The other type is the kingdom or principality in the broadest sense, where there are only two classes of citizens; one is the prince, the other his subjects. Princes are to be distinguished from one another by their desire to act only for their own good or for the good of themselves and of their subjects.[85] The order of a society provides its beauty, and the activities of the citizens enhance that beauty, add luster to it, and are therefore to be considered ornaments. Among useful and ornamental actions in a republic are public festivals and spectacles in which all the people participate. Alberti bemoaned their paucity and encouraged their revival.[86]

A different form of building is required for each of the two different types of society, and each class of citizen and each activity requires its particular accommodation;[87] when each is properly housed, the order of the political structure will be conspicuous in the physical facilities of the city. In prescribing the buildings appropriate for cities, Alberti establishes a hierarchical order. Buildings serving religion and justice, the two highest values of a society, occupy the place of primacy.[88] He divides buildings into sacred and profane, and then into public and private;[89] sacred and public dominate profane and private. A building for religious concerns always dominates a building for secular affairs at the same level, because justice between man and God is superior to justice between men and men; thus a church dominates a "basilica," and a "priest's curia" dominates a senate house.[90] Similarly, a theater or an amphitheater, where ornamental festivals and spectacles teach citizens through the display of letters and of arms, are related to basilicas but are one step inferior to them, because in the basilica justice is acted out in practice while in the theater and amphitheater it is only acted out in fiction.[91] Although Alberti discussed the classification most systematically as it applied to republics, he was also explicit about its application to principalities. In the republic the hierarchy began with the major temple and descended through the senate house, where the patricians met to promulgate laws, and the basilica, where civil justice was administered. In the principality these last two buildings were combined in the prince's palace, where the prince himself established and administered justice. Next in the republic was the reproduction at district level of the central civic facilities—the parish church and the palace of the

[83]See esp. *De re aed.*, IV, i; V, vi.

[84]Ibid., VI, i.

[85]Ibid., V, i. The distinction had been developed by Salutati in *De tyranno*.

[86]*De re aed.*, VIII, vii.

[87]See *De re aed.*, passim, and especially IV, i; V, i.

[88]See in particular *De re aed.*, VII, i, where religion and justice as well as the classification of buildings are discussed. See also Michel, 1930, pp. 275–276; Wittkower, 1962, I, preface, p. 1; I, i, pp. 6–7.

[89]*De re aed.*, preface; I and IV–IX, passim.

[90]Ibid., VIII, ix.

[91]Ibid., VII, vi; VIII, vii–viii.

principal patrician. The palace combined the functions of establishing and administering justice, as if the patrician were a prince in his district, and where he does act as the district's magistrate. The district, as well as the city, is then rounded out with the houses of middling citizens or those competent in the arts and blessed by fortune, and by the rude houses of tradesmen.

The architect may make these classifications and hierarchical distinctions visible in the city, through attention to the situation, manner, use, and quality of each building.[92] The first three of these concern beauty. By "situation" Alberti meant placement. The architect must give the more important buildings and the more important parts of buildings the more important sites; he determines this when he first starts to design. He should recall that the temple dominates the city and that the public parts of a district patrician's palace, the place in which he administers justice between citizens in the area, dominates the piazza of the district and his palace. By "manner" Alberti meant care in design. The higher in the hierarchy, the greater the care in producing beauty.[93] Temples demand the greatest care and best materials; the architect should devote greater care in designing the urban palace of a patrician than in designing his villa outside town, where he—or the patrician—may indulge his fantasy and whimsy. By "use" Alberti meant satisfying the functional requirements of the activities the building accommodates.[94] Magistrates' palaces are to have public parts for the administration of justice and private parts for repose and for the activities that concern only the family. "Quality," finally, relates to ornament. The architect must reveal the quality of a building by using forms that embellish and enhance the beautiful design, and he must make certain that there is no ambiguity about a building's place and the place of its inhabitant and function in the ordered structure of the city.[95]

A city filled with beautiful and properly ornamented buildings would reveal the existence of order, but it would also do more; it would facilitate that order by providing places for conspicuous participation in the activities that make order in the city. This in turn would serve as a didactic or rhetorical means to move men to undertake virtuous activities. Alberti made certain that wherever a virtuous act was to take place, it would be conspicuous. Citizens going about their business in the senate house and in the loggia would serve as *exempla*, persuading others to contribute to order. The facilities for festivals would be public facilities, because festivals teach;[96] preaching orders would be located near theaters, amphitheaters, and piazzas where the preachers could exhort the concourse of people to forsake vice for virtue.[97] And just as the protective city walls, by their rugged beauty, would prevent enemies from wishing to do them and the city damage,[98] so too would the dominating church of the city persuade men to seek religion.

The central temple renders the most important service of all the city's buildings because religion is the most pleasing activity to the Creator. It is to entice the visitor and hold his attention.[99] Inside, its single altar would be in the place of

---

[92] Ibid., I, vii; Alberti's words are "situs," "modus," "usus," and "ratio."

[93] Book V presents the principal argument.

[94] Books I and V present the principal argument.

[95] Books VI–IX present the principal argument.

[96] *De re aed.*, VIII, vii.

[97] Ibid., V, vii; Alberti sees this location as one that would supplement the activities of the theater and amphitheater, rather than as one that would deter men from seeking luxurious vices there.

[98] Ibid., V, iv; VI, ii. See Białostocki, 1964, passim.

[99] *De re aed.*, V, vi; VII, iii.

maximum dignity and solemnity, and it would be well illuminated within the dimly lit interior. Candelabra and the instruments used in the sacrifice are worthy ornaments and would be placed in order to be seen with admiration and respect.[100] There would be nothing to give pleasure to the senses at the expense of religious devotion, and the decorations in the building would be of the noblest and most durable materials. Some decorations would be sentences filled with philosophical sagacity; others would be lines and figures from music and geometry in the pavement. From every part of the temple the soul would be excited toward the development of the spirit.[101]

This represents a direct extension of Petrarch's beliefs about the power of eloquence and about the will into problems of architectural design. The design must allow the inner feelings and emotions to be stung so that love will seek God. But Alberti does not say that men, prodded by their love, will go into the church in order to learn about God, although it is clear that, once they are inside, Alberti's church would teach men about the God they love. The church must draw men into it, but not by offering a gaudy spectacle. Rather, it is a figure for God, and therefore beautiful and appealing to men, whose greatest gift from God is the power to love him. Alberti always shows human understanding and never becomes doctrinaire. He wants the church to be a place in which men may worship. And he wants the city to be an ordered place in which men may live. The city is to be dominated by the church, and it is to move men to act for the good. As he put it in *Profugiorum ab aerumna*, the designer's is the skill that allows men "to flee the bad, and desire and consign himself to the good, and hate the vicious, and beg for and love *virtù*."[102] *Virtù* means that vigorous action based on love with the hope of reward which Petrarch had broached and which Valla, Alberti, Manetti, and Nicholas had elaborated in their individual ways.

Here Alberti's theory of architecture and Nicholas's program for papal government flow together. In his testament the pope outlined a purpose for buildings, and in his treatise the architect described the principles of design for such buildings. Buildings that were perpetual monuments to doctrine would also be architectonic structures conjoined into a city that would facilitate the activity of citizens whose love for God moves them to strive for the good through *virtù*. The pope, while governing the Church, would be a stinging *exemplum* of *virtù*, moving the lower members of the hierarchy to seek God actively. Rome and its buildings would be proper settings for Nicholas's exemplary actions.[103]

---

[100]Ibid., VII, xii–xiii.

[101]Ibid., VII, x, p. 611; see also VII, xvii, for limiting the number of statues, and *Profugiorum ab aerumna*, pp. 109–110, for the soul, music, philosophy, and religious devotion. Alberti's statement in *De re aed.* (p. 611) is, "ut ex omni parte ad animi cultum excitemur." Wittkower's translation (1962, I, i, p. 9) is, "so that everywhere the education of the mind is stimulated." The mind here must be understood as more than merely the intellectual faculty that seeks additional knowledge of God, prodded as it is by love for God. See Wittkower's statements (1962, I, i, p. 7): "Alberti is explicit about the character of the ideal church.... Its beauty should surpass imagination. It is this staggering beauty which awakens sublime sensations and arouses piety in the people. It has a purifying effect and produces the state of innocence which is pleasing to God." Here he cites *De re aed.*, VII, iii, early sections, and refers to Michel, 1930. Alberti had used the term "anima" in the same sense in *Della pittura* in the passages cited above, notes 34 and 35. "Anima" is best rendered as "soul."

[102]*Profugiorum ab aerumna*, p. 161; see also the scene-setting in the introduction to the first book, pp. 107–108, and the conclusion to book II, p. 157, quoted above, note 78.

[103]See Krautheimer, 1970, p. 271: "To his [Alberti's] humanist thinking architecture is aimed at creating dignified backgrounds for dignified actions of dignified people."

4 Rome under the Early Quattrocento Popes— Its Condition and Its Laws

Rome became a Renaissance city during the pontificate of Nicholas V. During the Captivity and Schism it was the papal city without a pope and then the battleground for members of one faction of the Church. During the first two decades of the quattrocento it sank more deeply into the mire of disorder, as the Schism widened and central Italian politics became more turbulent. After Martin V returned the papacy to Rome in 1420, the city became the subject of the Colonna pope's ducal pretensions; after a Venetian became pope, it subjected itself to its own form of disorder until it was finally beaten into submission by the iron hand of Vitelleschi's tyranny. By the time Vitelleschi met his own violent destruction in 1440, a modicum of order had been established and the papacy gradually secured its position. During the half decade before Nicholas's ascension to the pontificate a semblance of stability began to be accepted as the expected condition in Rome. Nicholas V could treat Rome as a normal city, and during his pontificate the city was able to enjoy the fruits of its pacification.

It was not circumstance alone that allowed Rome to become a Renaissance city; Nicholas's carefully conceived program for governing it should be given at least equal credit. For the first time the city came to be considered a place in which people pursued their individual goals within a setting that promoted their activities, as well as a place the visible character of which revealed the intention that directed these activities. Nicholas was the first pope to manipulate Rome consciously, thoughtfully, and purposefully, both politically and physically, as a city that served men. Unlike his predecessors, he understood that Romans lived in Rome; it was a place in which people worked and went about their business, and one in which they built and destroyed in the process. He realized that these activities had an effect on the physical fabric of the city and that special measures not contained in existing legal codes were required to assure that the physical elements in the city would facilitate them. He considered it to be the responsibility of his office to watch over and care for the Romans, but not to control and manipulate them exclusively to his own ends. It was their city; although they could not do with it as they wished, within limits what they did do with it was up to them.

In 1420 the population was at its nadir of about 17,000 people.[1] The walls of Rome, whose gates had small suburbs with warders and toll collectors, were far in the

---

[1]For general information and further bibliography on what follows, see Paschini, 1940, parts I and II; Magnuson, 1958, part I; and Golzio and Zander, 1968, ch. VI.

Porta del
Popolo

Mausoleum
of Augustus

VIA DEL CORSO or LATA

S. Lorenzo
in Lucina

Trevi
Fountain

Porta di S. Pietro

Castel Sant'Angelo

Ponte Sant'Angelo

SS. Apostoli

Vatican
Palace

BORGO

VIA RECTA or DEI CORONARI

6

St. Peter's

18

16

Piazza
Navona

9

7

5

17

8

Pantheon

4

VIA PAPALIS

12

10

VIA DEL PELLEGRINO

Campo
de' Fiori

11

Palazzo
Venezia

CAPITOL

3

2

1

Theater of
Marcellus

A.   Map of Rome at the middle of the fifteenth century, indicating
the major streets, palaces, and places of interest in Nicholas V's
program, and other items of importance (after Touring Club Italiano
and Magnuson)

Santa Maria
in Trastevere

13

1 Palazzo del Senatore
2 Palazzo dei Conservatori
3 Santa Maria in Aracoeli
4 Colonna palace at SS. Apostoli
5 Santa Maria sopra Minerva
6 Collegio Capranica, blocking the via dei Coronari
7 Palazzo Domenico Capranica
8 Sant' Eustachio
9 Palazzo d'Estouteville at Sant'Apollonia
10 Palazzo Condulmero, later replaced by the Cancelleria, with
    San Lorenzo in Damaso
11 Palazzo Pio, formerly Francesco Condulmero
12 Palazzo Roderigo Borgia, later Sforza-Cesarini
13 papal palace at Santa Maria in Trastevere
14 papal palace at Santa Maria Maggiore
15 *vigna* of Cardinal Bessarion
16 Palazzo Orsini on Monte Giordano
17 Palazzo Orsini on via Papalis
18 Piazza S. Celso

TESTACCIO

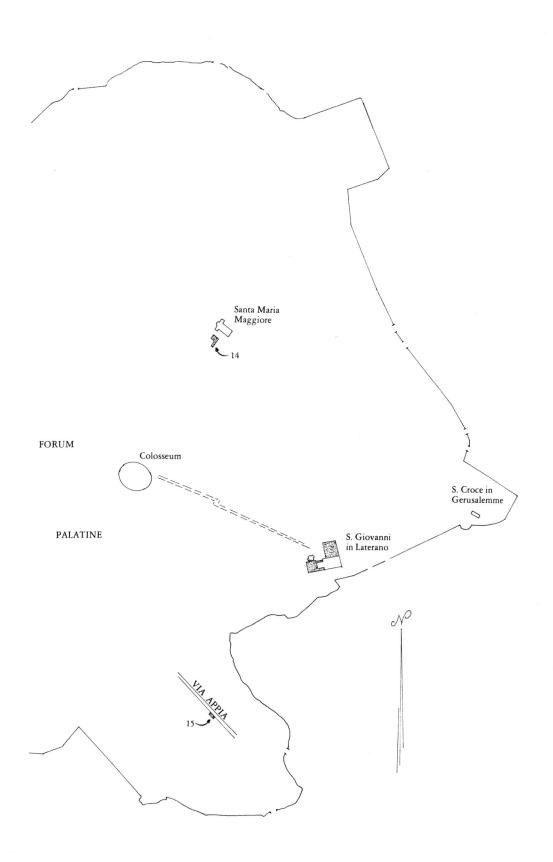

Santa Maria
Maggiore

14

FORUM

Colosseum

S. Croce in
Gerusalemme

PALATINE

S. Giovanni
in Laterano

VIA APPIA

15

distance from the inhabited districts. The Romans huddled for the most part either in Trastevere or in an area within the bend in the Tiber. The outer limit of the area described a nearly regular crescent that ran from the Theater of Marcellus over to the Capitol, behind the Colonna complex at SS. Apostoli, along the base of the Quirinale to the Trevi fountain, and back to the Tiber somewhere between the Column of Antoninus Pius and San Lorenzo in Lucina (fig. A).

By mid century the population had grown to perhaps 40,000. The new residents filled abandoned pockets, reinhabited long-abandoned buildings, and extended the edge of the built-up area around the repaired Trevi fountain and along the main roads leading in from the walls. One of these main roads was the via Flaminia's extension inside Rome, the via Lata, renamed the via del Corso after Paul II moved the carnival races to it. It ran from the Porta del Popolo straight to a piazza near the base of the Capitol; Flavio Biondo lived somewhere just off its northern section. Another main road on the outskirts was the section of the via Papalis that crossed the Forum and ran from the Colosseum to San Giovanni in Laterano. The area along this road attracted fewer inhabitants because it was ill-supplied with water.

Near the walls, and distant from the built-up areas, were several of the seven major and minor basilicas—San Lorenzo fuori le mura, Santa Croce in Gerusalemme, and San Giovanni in Laterano—with their small suburban communities. San Paolo fuori le mura was some distance away but was easily accessible from the Tiber. San Sebastiano fuori le mura was less accessible. Santa Maria Maggiore was between the walls and the inhabited portion, and it too had its own suburban community. These basilicas, along with St. Peter's, were the goals of visitors to Rome; the pilgrim found them by following paths around ancient ruins, across farms, and near ecclesiastical buildings that were scattered around the outskirts. An isolated monastery or church that somehow had managed to remain in repair might be the base of a national church in Rome and even include a hospice for pilgrims.

Rome's principal economic base was provided by the pilgrims and by the papacy and the curia. The city had no share in the international trade or specialized industries that had brought riches to Florence, Milan, and Venice; Pier Paolo Vergerio, a north Italian humanist and disciple of Salutati, cynically observed in 1398 that the two arts in which the Romans excelled were those of selling pictures of Christ to pilgrims and making lime from ancient buildings.[2] As the papacy became more stable, so, too, could the economic condition in Rome. At the end of the quattrocento, when economic stagnation afflicted Europe, Rome became a strong magnet, drawing people and their talents to the ambience of the rich papal court and making possible the splendor of the early sixteenth century papacy. That, however, was in the unknown future during the early quattrocento. At that time the papal banking accounts were still handled by branch offices of the larger Tuscan family banks, mostly Florentine. Cosimo de' Medici was central in the banking of Martin V, the Medici remained active in papal accounts, and other firms shared in the transactions. The only wealthy lay Romans not attached to the papacy were the Roman barons who derived their revenues from feudal estates that they held in fief from the pope. A Roman either worked for his equally poor neighbor, for the baron in whose area of the city he lived, or for a cleric who could be a cardinal or a poor priest. The revenues of the city treasury were based primarily on the taxes collected on wine and other goods brought into the city through the gates or through the two major ports, the Ripa downstream or the Ripetta upstream, or on the transhumance taxes levied on the barons' flocks of sheep, which were driven in the fall from the mountains in the Abruzzi to the plains and hills of the Campagna and back again in the spring.

[2]Vergerio, 1953, p. 97.

The communal treasury always showed a loss that the popes made up. After the Church had returned to Rome and its finances had again become organized, money flowing to Rome could circulate among the citizens after members of the curia and others who had access to the papal treasury had first spent it.

Before 1420 the Romans were primarily preoccupied, as they had been for a generation, in factional disputes centering around the barons. The latter vied for control in Rome when they were not challenged by more powerful forces, such as those of the King of Naples or of the pope and his allies and *condottieri*. Martin V subdued factional disputes by allowing only the Colonna to hold sway. Eugenius IV allowed the Orsini to get the upper hand over the Colonna, but he then had Vitelleschi bleed the Orsini, the Colonna, and all the allies of each faction. His ruthlessness persuaded the barons to seek advancement and power through the Church, rather than in competition with the Church through continual strife in Rome and its territory. Vitelleschi's bloodletting and the establishment of orderly, centralized strength in a unified papacy in Rome made it possible for Nicholas V to establish political clarity and order in the city.

Political order was required before there could be physical order. If Vergerio could write in 1398, ''Rome, which was host of every virtue, master of just arms and sacred laws, now is a den of bad thieves; now rules not discipline, not reason, but vice,''[3] it is clear that a Roman had to look out for his own safety. Buildings had first to be strong, and then they could possibly be pleasant. As the century progressed Rome became more secure and Romans could build places to pursue pleasure. Tommaso Spinelli, a Florentine banker and treasurer to the city of Rome at the time, had a ''casa'' outside the Porta di S. Pietro near Monte Mario, where in 1452 he entertained Frederick III.[4] By that time Cardinal Bessarion had probably begun to frequent his *vigna* in the countryside on the via Appia within the walls of Rome.[5] In 1472 Cardinal d'Estouteville entertained associates from the curia in his *vigna*.[6] But more important than villas were the urban palaces. Even in the middle of the century, when Florence could be seen as a Renaissance city, Rome must have had the appearance of a battleground with occasional ruins, fortresses, and outbuildings. By the end of the century, however, it had changed. As in Florence, it had become possible to see in the appearance of its physical facilities that political order existed, even if, from time to time—as, for example, during the Borgia pontificate—appearances were deceiving.

During the second half of the century the appearance of Rome changed, not only because the political and economic situation had become more stable and because the population had increased, but also because a new conception of architecture had been imposed on construction in Rome. It derived from Nicholas's project, and it was

[3]Ibid., p. 89.

[4]Infessura, p. 51, calls it the Porta Viridaria; this was the Porta di S. Pietro. For it, see below, chapters 6 and 7.

[5]It was later (1468?) refurbished and decorated by Paul II's nephew, Cardinal Zeno. Pernièr, 1934, pp. 6–7, discusses Bessarion's dwelling, which was part of the property of the Church of San Cesario (S. Cesarii in Turri tituli Tusculani). Bessarion (d. 1472) was given title to Tusculani on 23 April 1449 and transferred to Sabinensis in 1468. See also Tomei, 1942, p. 93; Maccari, 1873, pl. 25; Pernièr, 1929; Gnoli, 1938, p. 53; G(iovannoni), 1937; and Biolchi, 1954, p. 8.

[6]See Eubel, II, n. 318, p. 38. Its location is only vaguely defined: Roderigo Borgia ''recessit de palatio associatus per omnes card. ad pontem s. Mariae apud vineam domini Rothomagensis.'' The Ponte Santa Maria was below the Tiber island and led to Trastevere; it is labeled on the Urbino, Paris, and Strozzi views, for which see below, chapter 5. Scaglia, 1964, p. 152, discusses it. D'Estouteville's villa was probably south of Rome, but could well have been within the walls or even between the Borgo and Trastevere.

uniquely suited to Rome. Florence was not transported to Rome; instead, Rome was rebuilt.

Florence and Rome were different in many important ways. These had a direct influence on their physical differences. One distinction was in the distribution of wealth. In Florence, there was a greater proportion of rich families and more security in wealth at all levels; in Rome, wealth was neither so broadly nor so consistently distributed, which meant that there were many poor and very few rich. Another distinction was in the quality a builder would want to make evident in his palace. A Florentine would wish to appear grave and serious, to indicate his distinctiveness, and to show that he was a faithful republican citizen contributing to the honor of the city.[7] A Roman who built a palace was a prince of one sort or another; to show that status required a different type of palace from that which a Florentine would build. During the first half of the century in Rome strength and protection still had to be more highly prized than beauty and the clear display of quality. A third distinction was in the traditional prototypes out of which the prevalent palace types of the two cities were developed. In Florence, Cosimo de' Medici's palace combines the most conspicuous elements of the Palazzo Vecchio and the traditional blocklike Tuscan palace type; in a broad way, its design corresponds to the principles Alberti would outline in *De re aedificatoria*, although it did not use the forms Alberti had prescribed. But in Rome, what was there that might be worth using as a prototype for a cardinal's palace, or for the palaces of other important residents?

Another significant difference was in the cumulative effect on the appearance of the city as a whole that could occur through a little construction done here and there over a period of years. In Florence, dozens of lesser patricians built palaces that emphasized decorum rather than distinctiveness. They often incorporated the old fabric of tower-houses, with their rough stone walls, into a "new" palace that emphasized a smoother, more regular and horizontal pattern. The changes required in the fabric were minor in proportion to the major visual change to the palace, and entire streets lined with orderly palace façades resembling Cosimo's were altered in this way. Rome, however, was quite different.[8] The city had few if any large, recent buildings with a fabric sturdy enough to remodel, and there was no accepted and active formal tradition that could be altered slightly to produce the effect of a major formal change in either large palaces or smaller buildings. In Rome there was simply no possibility for a visual continuity such as that which exists between the Bargello, the Palazzo Vecchio, the Palazzo Davanzati, the Medici palace, and the dozens of derivations from Cosimo's great model.

The situation could hardly have been helped by the appearance of the Roman streets.[9] Few streets in the inhabited quarters had a façade that approached regularity. The substantial buildings serving as smaller residences were sometimes simply square, high towers with crenellations on top and porticoes opening into shops at the bottom.[10] More common, however, was a street made up of a series of buildings

---

[7]See Vespasiano's biography of Cosimo de' Medici (1963, pp. 213–234; e.g., p. 223), with Bruni's definition of the qualifications for office in Florence, quoted above, chapter 2.

[8]See the review of the Roman pattern in Golzio and Zander, 1968, ch. VII, and the literature cited on pp. 373–384.

[9]For the following remarks about Roman buildings, see Giovannoni, "Case," 1935; Tomei, 1938; idem, 1939; Apollonj, 1937; Giovannoni, 1946, pp. 31 ff.; Magnuson, 1958, part I; Boethius, 1960, pp. 129 ff.; Golzio and Zander, 1968, ch. VII, esp. pp. 79–93.

[10]The crenellations would eventually be replaced by loggias or belvederes, and the structures beside the towers would perhaps receive an additional story or two, thus increasing the evident size of the original structures and defortifying many of Rome's buildings. This does not seem to have been the general case until late in the century, however; see Elling, 1950, pp. 23 ff. See also Amadei, 1969, passim, and pp. 9–14, for a brief history of Roman towers.

seldom having more than three low stories. They often rested on ancient foundations and were usually built of stucco over rubble walls. They commonly had shops in front with stairs opening behind them to the rooms above. There might be a *loggia* on top and a garden behind, and usually one stood between others like it.[11] Also common were blocky apartment buildings, often with shops on the ground floor and with entrances to stairs between alternate shops. Such a structure was simply a row of the basic house type run together and standing side by side, perhaps curving and jogging to follow the irregularities of the street line. A street of these buildings would not have a high profile and would be made of a number of small vertical units; there would not be a continuous plane along the street, and the windows might appear at uncoordinated levels along the block. Balconies, porticoes, shop benches, and pieces of wall projecting into the street would add to the visual confusion.

Furthermore, Rome was more spread out, less dense and less compact. It had a lower population than Florence or any other major Italian city. It had not expanded outward from an old nucleus but had contracted from a vast area and shifted away from its former monumental center, which now lay in ruins. Rome was not concentrated, as was Florence, into two or three nearby places, such as the Piazza del Duomo, Piazza della Signoria, and Mercato Vecchio (expanded in the nineteenth century into the present Piazza della Repubblica). Instead, it had condensed into clusters that were dominated by baronial strongholds—such as the Scavelli headquarters at the Theater of Marcellus, the Colonna complex, or the Orsini compound at Monte Giordano—or into districts dwarfed by ancient monuments such as the Pantheon. During the quattrocento a Roman district might also have been dominated by a palace attached to a cardinal's titular church, such as the one Vitelleschi and members of Eugenius's family had built at San Lorenzo in Damaso (it preceded the Cancelleria) or the one built by Cardinal Jean de la Rochetaillé at San Lorenzo in Lucina. Or it might have been overawed by new but rough palaces, such as those of the prefect of Rome at the head of the Piazza Navona or of prelates and nephews at the Campo de' Fiori. In Rome one saw great contrasts in scale and a clear juxtaposition of those who were important and those who were not, but it was size, not design, that formed the contrast. By Florentine standards, none of it would have looked very important.

And, finally, Rome lacked a clear visual structure as a city. Florence was dominated by the cathedral and the Palazzo Vecchio; each had a piazza that provided space for important civic activities, and the two buildings themselves served as symbols of Florence. Brunelleschi demonstrated perspective by representing the baptistry from just inside the doors of the cathedral, and by showing the Palazzo Vecchio as it appeared from across the Piazza della Signoria. The cathedral and the Palazzo Vecchio, which had dominated fourteenth-century representations of Florence, still loom larger than they actually were in the carefully constructed *View of Florence with a Chain* (Berlin) from the 1480s (fig. 24). The street that connected these two poles of the city was also important and was given added significance by its embellishment. In the late fourteenth century its appearance had been the subject of ordinances that regulated the façades of the buildings facing it.[12] But in Rome the conceptual

[11]See, for example, the description of a rather elaborate house, "quandam domum terrineam solaratam tegulatam cum sex cameris in ea existentibus, cum duabus salis, cum cellariis, cum tinellis, cum coquina, cum reclaustro et puteo, cum porticali reclauso intus eam, cum furno et aliis suis membris," given by the widow of Giacomo Orsini to Santa Maria Nuova in 1466 (Dengel, 1913, doc. 22, pp. 8–9), and a smaller house bought for demolition for expanding the Palazzo Venezia, "unam domum dictorum domini Jheronimi et fratrum terraneam et solaratam cum cameris, sala, coguina, reclaustro, porticali coperto columnato ante eam," in 1466 (ibid., doc. 23, p. 9).

[12]See Braunfels, 1966, pp. 119–120; see also pp. 101–104, 115–116.

center of the city did not have a commensurate physical importance. The Capitol was the symbol of Rome, but it was on the edge of the built-up area; it was largely in ruins, and major streets went near it but not to it. More important than the Capitol as a place where Romans met was the Campo de' Fiori, but it was a mere market and a place for executions and assemblies not held on the Capitol, and it was crossed by one of the three major streets, the via del Pellegrino. This street wandered vaguely through the southern part of Rome from the Ponte Sant'Angelo to the Theater of Marcellus.

The other two major streets were more important; each also departed from the Ponte Sant'Angelo. The via Papalis was the processional route from the Vatican to the Lateran. It touched Monte Giordano, approached the southern end of the Piazza Navona, wound along to brush against the Capitol, and then crossed the Forum to connect the Colosseum and the Lateran. The via dei Coronari was the main processional route from the Vatican to the via Lata and from there to the Porta del Popolo, the main entrance to Rome for important visitors from the north. It ran in a more or less straight line, first between the Tiber and Monte Giordano, next near the northern end of the Piazza Navona, where it swayed a bit, and then along the edge of Monte Citorio to the open space around the Column of Antoninus Pius. Processions were among the most important civic events in Rome, and it is doubtful if these streets would have received any attention from the popes or the people had they not been processional routes. Still, they were not safe from acts of civic vandalism. The ability of a cardinal to act without civic consciousness is illustrated by the way Cardinal Angelo Capranica violated the character of the via dei Coronari. In about 1460 he built the Collegio Capranica with the bequest of his brother, Cardinal Domenico Capranica, as an extension to the palace that his brother had built. He attached it as an ell on the back of the palace, running it directly across the via dei Coronari and thus forcing traffic to pass in front of rather than behind his palace. Now processions could admire his palace rather than ignore it. Florentines had opened and regularized streets for public benefit a hundred years before Romans had quit blocking them for private gain.

The physical appearance of each city at the middle of the century revealed its political and social structure. Florence was tightly clustered around the two poles of civic order, the cathedral and the Palazzo Vecchio; many families were important, and they vied with one another in contributing to the physical order of the city. The other citizens considered themselves primarily Florentines rather than clients of powerful families. Although a Florentine's representation to the central government was seldom direct, but was instead channeled through his guild or through the patrician in his neighborhood, the patricians who dominated the offices of the commune and who in effect were the *signoria* shared a commitment to Florence that could put the public interest of the many above the private interest of the few. On the other hand, Rome was diffuse, physically and politically. Its communal government was the single available instrument that might promote the public good of the many, even if it meant curtailing the private gain of a few. It was the single legal source of political power for Romans as political beings, but it was weak; it was at the mercy of the superior power of the papacy, and it was not alone in its claim to legitimacy. The papacy could also make a legitimate claim to absolute temporal jurisdiction in Rome, which theoretically the pope would administer through the officers of the curia. But actually the power that had long been exercised by the barons, first in the name of the papacy and then in its absence, was beginning to be exercised during the quattrocento by the cardinals, who acted as princes of the Church rather than as curial officials. In practice, then, a Roman baron or cardinal was a prince, and as such he was the patron of his clients and the police chief in his district. His clients gave him their respect and service, and in return the baron, and later the cardinal, offered vicarious honor and real protection. During the span of the quattrocento the city passed from the hands of medieval barons claiming ancient Roman lineage into those of Renaissance princes claiming descent from the Apostles of Christ,[13] and it was in the brief period between the hegemony of the barons and that of the cardinals that Nicholas attempted to give dignity to the commune of Rome.

Nicholas was more Florentine than Roman in his attitude toward the city. He knew that its physical and political order were intimately bound together, that each had an important effect on the other, and that each required clarity of definition. He clarified each, but to understand the character of his architectural program, it will be necessary to review his program for political clarification in the affairs of Rome and of the Romans.

The legal structure of the city of Rome and its statutory relationship with the papacy fitted within the larger framework of Italian political theory and practice, but the Roman situation was always a little different from that which prevailed elsewhere. The local government was both like and unlike any other in Italy, whether a republic or a principality. The strongest power in Rome, the papacy, was like and unlike that in any Italian principality. The governments of cities with strong princely rulers during the quattrocento have not been adequately investigated, but even without the control and insight such studies would allow, it does seem possible to draw some conclusions about Nicholas's treatment of Rome.[14]

The local government in Rome was organized as a republic. The political structure that was supposed to guide the policies of the communal government and its relations with the papacy during the quattrocento had been established during the fourteenth century. In 1363, following the upheavals that attended Cola di Rienzo's ambitious programs, with the pope and emperor both quite uninterested in anything other than peace, economy, and stability in their Italian territories, Rome had been granted independence from papal and imperial control. The statutes that defined the government the Romans could conduct on the Capitol provided for a senator, a *giunta* to control him, and a bureaucracy of fiscal, administrative, and judicial officers. The senator was to be a non-Roman, serve six months, represent the commune, and be responsible to the *giunta;* the *giunta* was to be composed of democratically selected Romans; and all officers were to be independent of outside control.[15] The senator could be considered a *podestà* and *gonfaloniere della giustizia,* and the *giunta* could be thought of as a *signoria.* By the time Martin V returned to Rome in 1420, the senator was a papal appointee; the *giunta* was reduced to three *conservatori* serving three-month terms of office (as the statutes of 1363 prescribed), who were also papal appointees (contrary to the statutes). Other officials had also long been under the control either of the papacy or of the pope's chief administrative officer, the *camerarius,* or of his lieutenant, the *vicecamerarius.* Martin respected the

[13]Machiavelli was "the first to observe [that] aristocracy and monarchy went together. Identifying republics with social equality and lordships with inequality, he remarked that a prince, without a nobility, could not administer government, and that where no nobility existed, it would have to be created." Jones, 1965, p. 93.

[14]For tentative studies and details see Ercole, 1929; Cusin, 1936; Jones, 1952 (particularly useful); idem, 1960; idem, 1965 (with extensive bibliography); Bueno de Musquita, 1960; idem, 1965, pp. 317–331.

[15]The statutes were published by Re, 1880; see also Rodocanachi, 1901; Partner, 1958, ch. I.

statutes as amended through decree or practice, but, as has been observed, he used them as a means to rule the city.[16]

Martin considered Rome his to rule; he possessed it through the Donation of Constantine, and his family was one of the Roman baronial powers. He had no sympathy for any Roman republican sentiments. Before arriving in the city he appointed a senator in language that baldly revealed his attitude about the city:

> To the city of Rome, in which the Omnipotent established the head of the Church Militant, as well as to those people belonging to that Church, bearing the affection of paternal love, we desire that the city and its people, whose condition of peace and tranquility it is known depends on good government, be ruled usefully and governed advantageously (*salubriter gubernantur*).

Ranuccio Farnese, the letter of appointment continues, will serve as senator at the pleasure of the apostolic authority and is to do all that is necessary for the city's regulation and government "to our honor and to that of the Roman Church," because events in the city will redound to the glory of the Apostolic See.[17] Rome was Martin's responsibility; this was explained to him in 1431 by Niccolò Signorili, the *scribasenatus*, who was one of Martin's appointees to the Capitol and whose task was similar to that of the chancellor of Florence.[18] Signorili explained that the city of Rome is legitimately governed by the Church, because the Church has succeeded to the offices of the empire and continues to administer to the needs of the residents of Rome in succession to the empire. To this historical argument he added a sacramental one common in late-medieval thought: the pope is the "father and spouse" of the Romans, tied to them by inseparable bonds of matrimony. This "beautiful union," he continues, is decorated by the duality of the pope, who is head of the faith and head of the world; the pope is to use the strength of his arms made invincible by the power of God to defend Rome and to bring it honor.[19]

Martin's successor, Eugenius IV, at first introduced no changes into the relations between the legally independent commune and the actually dominant papacy, except perhaps a lesser degree of adroitness in operating Martin's system. He surely offended the Romans when, in 1432, he addressed two letters to the *conservatori* reminding them that it was his prerogative to appoint officials in the Roman government and that they were to honor the oath they swore to the *camerarius*.[20] The *camerarius* was Eugenius's nephew, Francesco Condulmero, whom Eugenius had made a cardinal in his first promotion (September 19, 1431) and *camerarius* soon after (January 13, 1432).[21] The new *camerarius* enjoyed using power more nakedly than had Martin's officers. Eugenius also treated his senators in a more high-handed

[16]Rodocanachi, 1901, p. 143; see also Partner, 1958, p. 169. Compare the Malatesta's treatment of their cities, as described by Jones, 1960, esp. p. 225. Jones, 1952, p. 328 and 328, n. 1, shows that in his relationship with cities throughout the Patrimonium, Martin attempted to adhere to pre-Schism, i.e., Albernozian, institutions and administration. See also ibid., p. 339, n. 4, and pp. 349–351.

[17]Theiner, *Cod. Dip.*, III, no. 165, p. 236: *Ad urbem Romanam*, 27 April 1419. For Martin's earlier appointees, see Salimei, 1935, pp. 163–165. Although the senator served at the pope's pleasure, that actually meant for the six-month term prescribed in the statutes; he was to work with the *conservatori* and other communal officials and did not necessarily have absolute authority.

[18]See Tommasini, 1887, pp. 174 f., for this office.

[19]Signorili, 1953, pp. 162–165.

[20]Tommasini, 1887, pp. 178–182, discusses and publishes these letters (p. 182, n. 1).

[21]Re, 1952.

fashion than had his predecessor; he appointed them with less regard for statutory restraints on their power, and he used them more fully for his own purposes.[22] Relations between the pope and the commune soured, and soon after Sigismund's coronation on May 31, 1433, the Romans began to respond to pressures from supporters of the conciliarists and to brood on their own grievances. They finally assaulted a vacillating pope disguised as a monk and crouched in the bottom of a boat, driving him from Rome under a hail of stones, arrows, spears, and epithets. From June 4, 1434, until his return on September 28, 1443, Rome remained the seat of the papacy, but the pope remained elsewhere.

The Romans put together a popular government based on some archaic provisions of the 1363 statutes that had not been exercised for decades, but it collapsed within a few months. By October the city was again under the control of the pope. Eugenius was represented by the soldier-bishop Vitelleschi, who had the help of the *condottieri* bands led by Francesco Sforza and Francesco Orsini. Vitelleschi's measures were cruel, but they established a numbed tranquility to which the Romans responded favorably. In 1436 they voted to erect on the Capitol a marble equestrian statue of him as the "third father after Romulus" of the city of Rome, but the project predictably came to nothing.[23] Within four years Vitelleschi had been made a cardinal and had become the victim of a fatal plot, perhaps initiated by, and certainly sanctioned by, Eugenius. The city had also been subjected to changes in the structural relationships between the commune and the papacy, which were to have long-lasting effects. Eugenius reduced the position of the barons and made possible the ascendancy of the cardinals. It was in this context, after the decline of the barons and before the rise of the cardinals, that Nicholas introduced his reforms.

The pope had at his disposal a prefecture of Rome, a baronial office that, it was believed, had been established by Romulus. He could use it for any number of purposes.[24] The office had long been held by the di Vico family and had been effective under Martin in policing the territory of Rome. In 1435 Vitelleschi beheaded the last of the di Vico prefects; Francesco Orsini was made prefect, but the office was made purely honorific.[25] It would remain one of trappings without real power until the della Rovere assumed interest and power in Rome, and even then the prefect would be relatively unimportant. Eugenius gave additional responsibility for temporal affairs in Rome to the *vicecamerarius*, at this time usually a bishop. That officer's title now began to carry the new and additional designation of governor of the city of Rome. At first the two titles occur separately on occasion; not until the pontificate of Paul II, or perhaps that of Sixtus IV, do they become indissolubly linked together, with the office given to a metropolitan bishop or, more commonly, to a cardinal who exercised real power and authority.[26] Either office, and especially all the duties of

---

[22]See, for example, ASV, Reg. Vat. 381, fol. lxxx[r-v], the appointment of Rinaldo degli Albizzi, who served as senator from 1 January to 30 June 1432. See also Salimei, 1930–32, doc. XXX, and docs. XLV, LXXV, LXXXVI, and CXXXVII.

[23]Gregorovius, 1900, VII, i, p. 58.

[24]See in general Moroni, XCIX, pp. 118 ff. (s.v., *vicecamerlengo di Santa Romana Chiesa*), which augments XXXII, pp. 5 ff. (s.v., *governatore di Roma*).

[25]See Calisse, 1887, pp. 410–425; Rodocanachi, 1901, pp. 158–159, and 193, n.1; ASV, Reg. Vat. 381, fol. cclxi[r], for Orsini's appointment, 9 January 1436.

[26]Partner's assertion (1958, pp. 181–182) concerning the office of governor is too general. For the appointment on 17 January 1435 of Giuliano de' Ricci, bishop of Pisa since 1418 (d. 1461), as governor of Rome in addition to *vicecamerarius*, see Theiner, *Cod. Dip.*, III, no. 279, p. 336. See also ASV, Reg. Vat. 381, fols. cclxvi[r-v], for an apparently unique senatorial appointment that tells the senator to follow the commands of the governor and the *conservatori*; it is dated 5 February 1435. Nicholas occupied the office of *vicecamerarius* in 1443, apparently until his appointment as bishop of

both combined into one curial officer, could be used to strengthen the hand of the pope at the expense of the commune's senator, marshals, and other officers. Eugenius did not use them for that purpose, but popes from Pius II onward would, and they would enjoy superiority over the prefect.

These arrangements suggest that Eugenius had learned something about Romans through his exile. In his first years he had acted as Martin had, but after 1440 he apparently was not intent on augmenting the power of curial officials in Roman affairs. After he had lost Rome in 1434, he naturally wanted to regain possession of it and impose order on it. He got possession through Vitelleschi's strength, but to impose order he resisted strengthening curial officers and instead turned to counsel and patience. He believed that greater clarity in relations between the papacy and the commune could prevent another collapse into exile and anarchy. Beginning in 1439 or, more likely, 1440, and proceeding irregularly for the next six or seven years, the *camerarius*, the *vicecamerarius* (who in 1443 was Tommaso Parentucello), and representatives of the commune worked at establishing a concordat that would resolve ambiguities in the interpretation of the statutes and introduce whatever necessary revisions they could agree upon.[27]

In a concordat effective August 30, 1446, the pope and the Romans established a broad field of agreement.[28] They recognized the desire of the Romans to have greater control over the senator and to introduce certain ceremonial, fiscal, and financial changes that would allow him to represent the commune with greater dignity; they regularized the system of legal appeals in order that the communal prerogative could be more easily exercised; and they introduced other modifications that strengthened the process by which the commune could keep order in Rome. But they did not challenge the right of the pope through his officers to exercise final authority. Although far from granting the autonomy the commune had enjoyed in 1363, this concordat was an important reform. It had the effect of affirming the illegality of the high-handed treatment that Martin had used and that Eugenius himself had claimed as his right in the letters of 1432.

Eugenius died too soon after the concordat had been signed for it to be known how faithfully he would have honored it, but Nicholas's actions indicate that the new pope seized upon it as a means to initiate a new relationship between the commune and the papacy. Six weeks after his elevation to the office in 1447 he issued a bull

---

Bologna on 27 November 1444, a seat he occupied also as a cardinal and until he became pope. According to the statement published by Pastor, 1949, p. 17, n. 2, "in quo officio ac dignitate quid diligentiae atque solicitudinis praestiteris quisque Romanus civis magno mihi testimonio esse potest." Nicholas was apparently not governor of Rome; that title belonged to Astorgio Agnese, archbishop of Benevento, who had been appointed governor of Rome *in temporalibus* in March, 1442 (ASV, Reg. Vat. 382, fol. cl^r–cli^r), the same day as his appointment as vicar *in spiritualibus* of Rome and its district (loc. cit., fol. cliiij^{r-v}; published in Theiner, *Cod. Dip.*, III, no. 296, pp. 349–350). After Nicholas was elevated to the position of bishop of Bologna, Agnese apparently dropped the title governor of Rome and assumed that of *vicecamerarius*, the title he used in the records of the concordat of 1446 to be discussed below, where he appears as an adjunct of the *camerarius* throughout the proceedings. It was he who kept Porcari at bay during the *sede vacante* of 1447. Nicholas created him cardinal (20 December 1448); in 1449 he was *camerarius;* he died on 10 October 1451. See also below, note 33.

[27]For the date of the beginning of these sessions, see Rodocanachi, 1901, p. 155, n. 2, who disputes an earlier date suggested by Re, 1880, pp. civ ff. The argument of neither author is persuasive; after Vitelleschi's death would be more reasonable than before that time.

[28]The best copy is a vellum manuscript from 1486 of the statutes of Rome as revised in 1469, Archivio Storico Capitolino, Rome, Cred. IV, tom. 88, fols. 138^r–143^v; another version, marred by inaccuracies, is a hurriedly prepared incunabulum, for which see Rodocanachi, 1901, pp. 154 ff.

that established and extended the spirit of autonomy agreed upon nine months earlier.[29]

Nicholas restored direction of the communal treasury to the *conservatori*, with only limited restrictions that were themselves in harmony with the 1446 concordat.[30] He also implicitly recognized the revival of *imbossulatura*, or election by drawing names from a pouch, for selecting communal officers, including the *conservatori;* even though the names in bags would be approved by the pope, there would be more than one name for each office in the bag, the Romans themselves would draw them to select their officers, and the officers would act in the roles specified in the statutes.[31] Throughout his pontificate, in a marked departure from the practice of either of his predecessors, Nicholas allowed the Romans to select their officers from the *conservatori* on down, with some exceptions.[32] Finally, Nicholas guaranteed that all offices in the communal government except that of senator would be staffed by Romans, and he promised that, insofar as possible, all benefices in the city would be given to Romans. His purpose was tranquility, and he believed this would come through clarity rather than through interference or through complete autonomy. He seems not to have appointed a person with the permanent office of governor of Rome or to have given to others in the curia any powers that would allow them to meddle.[33] Orsini, meanwhile, remained a powerless prefect. Nicholas restored very little of the independence that the Romans had lost since 1363; what he gave them he gave "by

[29]Theiner, *Cod. Dip.*, III, no. 314, pp. 367–368; *Licet es domito debito;* 1 May 1447, see Rodocanachi, 1901, pp. 150ff.

[30]Revenues from tolls collected at bridges and gates were to be used for the university, for maintaining the walls of the city, and for other things of public utility, in that order. Compare rubric xix of the 1446 concordat, and the "Littera Apostolica pro studio generali in urbe," rubric lxxv, fol. 158^v–160^v; a copy of this second document is in ASV, Reg. Vat. 381, fols. lxvii^r–lxviiij^r, dated 11 October 1431.

[31]The revival of *imbossulatura* was contained in a revision of the statutes of the college of notaries, who were to maintain the current lists; this revision, which is included in Archivio Storico Capitolino, Cred. IV, tom. 88, was approved along with the concordat; see also Tommasini, 1887, p. 176, n. 6, and p. 185.

[32]See Tommasini, 1887, passim, which was apparently misunderstood by Partner, 1958, p. 164. Gregorovius's statement (1900, VII, i, p. 132), "The magistrates on the Capitol were no longer elected by the community, but were appointed by the pope. Nicholas V transformed the city into a papal fortress," cannot be sustained, much as its rhetoric can be appreciated. The officials whom the pope continued to appoint were mostly tax officials (whose offices were farmed), judges, and marshals, although this last category was limited to special occasions and to special functions. See, for the most part, ASV, Reg. Vat. 432, 433, and 434, passim.

[33]The titles governor of Rome and *vicecamerarius* did not always coincide during Nicholas's pontificate, and the office of governor was, apparently, not always filled; it seems to have been honorific or to have been conferred under extraordinary circumstances. The *vicecamerarius*, apparently after Agnese was created cardinal (20 December 1448), was Niccolò Amidano, bishop of Piacenza from 15 January 1448 and archbishop of Milan from 19 March 1453 until his death 24 March 1454. His term as *vicecamerarius* is uncertain; both Moroni, XXXII, p. 37, and Pastor, 1949, p. 227, name him as *vicecamerarius* in January, 1453, on the basis of de Godis's report on the Porcari affair, for which see below, p. 76. In early May, 1449, he was named governor *in temporalibus* "in nostri absentia," a title added to that of *vicecamerarius* in the appointment, ASV, Reg. Vat. 433, fols. xii^r–xiij^r. The occasion of the appointment may have been Nicholas's preparations to depart from Rome due to the plague; on 6 June he was in Spoleto to escape it; Pastor, 1949, p. 86, n. 1. Before Amidano was given the title with its restricted application, it had been conferred on Giovanni Poggio, a canon of Bologna cathedral whom Nicholas had appointed to the Bolognese bishopric, which he himself had vacated to become pope. Shortly thereafter Poggio was named governor of Rome; Pastor, 1949, p. 68. He died on 13 December 1447; he was never *vicecamerarius*. It is not known whether or not there was a governor of Rome between his death and Amidano's appointment more than a year later.

virtue of apostolic authority," not by virtue of any recognition of rights. What he established on the Capitol was a government that was at the same time subordinate to the papacy and a dignified, respectable, and ordered representative of the interests of the Romans.

Nicholas continued to respect the spirit of the 1447 bull. The negative evaluations commonly made about his government have always been based on the attitude Stefano Porcari took toward it. Porcari was highly respected by the humanists and has suffered from unfortunate neglect by serious scholars because a century ago he was given undeserved fame as a republican revolutionary, but there are several reasons to discount Porcari as a responsible critic of Nicholas's government. One is the extremely cool response of the Romans to Porcari's exhortations in 1450, largely a repeat of his call for liberty made shortly before the assembly of the conclave which elected Nicholas. Another is their continued coolness in response to his abortive coup in January, 1453.[34] Indeed, it was the quick action of the *vicecamerarius* acting in concert with communal officials that had stopped Porcari and his small band of conspirators before they had had a chance to course through the streets with their republican banners, costumes, and appeals in an attempt to call the people to rebellion.[35] The unanimous judgment of those who wrote on the subject afterward was that Porcari had acted from personal *superbia*, a judgment that is supported by Nicholas's failure to exact reprisals from the Romans and by his limiting his punishment to the conspirators alone.[36]

Although Gregorovius saw Porcari's conspiracy as the natural result of Nicholas's tyranny,[37] there is no evidence to support the judgment. Nevertheless, there were several important actions that Nicholas had taken by 1453 which Porcari could have misinterpreted and which could have driven him to act at the moment he did. Nicholas's building program was sufficiently advanced to be visible, and it could be interpreted by a republican zealot who refused to sanction any papal intrusion into communal prerogatives as a threat to the future of the republic.[38] In 1452 Nicholas had reinforced the police powers of the senator; but he had also admonished the *conservatori* to be equally vigorous in suppressing homicide, robbery, and general rapine, and he had allowed them to use in full vigor whatever recent amendments

[34]For the attribution of the trouble to outside, non-Roman forces rather than to any grievances of the Romans themselves, see the report of the ambassador of Francesco Sforza in Fumi, 1910.

[35]Nicholas's use of the regular police apparatus, in which he apparently had faith when faced with a threat of sedition, is stressed by de Godis, Vat. Lat. 3619, fol. 2ʳ. There it is reported that after the plot had been made known in Rome to the curia, the *vicecamerarius* called out the senator, *conservatori, caporioni,* and marshals. The evidence is confirmed by the arch-republican, Infessura, p. 53, who reports: "The senator went ... together with the *vicecamerarius* and with many infantry to the house of master Stefano...." The most extensive, if overdrawn, recent review of the conspiracy is Rodocanachi, 1922, pp. 250–262, for Porcari's illustrious and meritorious early career, and pp. 289–299, for his end. See also Pastor, 1949, pp. 215–239, and Porcari's confession, appendix 14, pp. 516–517; and Mancini, 1911, pp. 357 ff., which contains information not found in other secondary sources.

[36]Pastor, 1949, p. 230, states that the death sentence against Porcari was passed by the senator, although the location of the trial is given as the Vatican Palace in the sources quoted (ibid., p. 501, n. 1). Porcari was hanged from the Castel Sant'Angelo. For the judgment that *superbia* motivated him, see Alberti, "Porcari," esp. pp. 264–265; Manetti, *RIS*, col. 943; de Godis, Vat. Lat. 3619, fol. 7ʳ; Brippi, Vat. Lat. 3618, lines 81 ff. For Nicholas's limitation of reprisals, in addition to Pastor, see the pardon issued in July, 1455, by Calixtus III, Archivio Storico Capitolino, Arm. VI, tom. 51, fols. 1ʳ–2ᵛ. According to Infessura (p. 57), Nicholas did cancel the Testacchio games "per questa cascione."

[37]Gregorovius, 1900, VII, i, pp. 132–133. See also Pastor, 1949, pp. 215 ff.

[38]The dates and possible interpretations of the conspicuous elements will be discussed in various later chapters. Porcari, one of the most interesting Romans of the period, still awaits a proper biography.

and apostolic letters were relevant and to use full apostolic authority in facilitating their task.[39]   This action was congruent with the spirit of the preamble to the 1363 statutes,[40] with the concordat of 1446 and the bull of 1447, with the appointment of extra marshals for a short term in conjunction with the coronation of Frederick III earlier in the year, and with the general attitude prevailing at this time about the rights of a *signore* in the communal affairs of his city.[41]   Not even Infessura objected to the appointment of the marshals; they strengthened the city, he said, and he was satisfied—or reported that he was satisfied—that the senator, the representative of the city of Rome, enjoyed precedence over these specially appointed papal officers.[42]

Nicholas made another administrative adjustment in Rome; it should not be attributed to a desire to depart from his intentions of 1447, even though it could be wrongly interpreted as one.   In April, 1453, after long deliberation, he combined the communal treasury with that of the papacy, reestablishing the situation that had existed during Eugenius's pontificate.[43]   The change was necessitated by actions of the treasurer himself, Tommaso Spinelli, a Florentine, who had been investing the funds of citizens, courtiers, cardinals, and perhaps of the city itself in the Florentine Monte, from which they were having trouble retrieving them.[44]   What had begun as a good idea had apparently gone bad, and a return to the older administrative form was the only way to resolve the problems introduced, perhaps by the innovation of 1447, but possibly by Spinelli's own malfeasance.   What Nicholas sought was clarity and order, and in pursuing those goals he treated the Romans with respect, leaving to them as much management of their own affairs as possible.[45]

Nicholas's desire for administrative clarity and his wish to invest responsibility for Rome in the Romans themselves is nowhere more obvious than in an administrative action he took in 1452.   It was to have a long-lasting effect on the physical

[39]ASV, Reg. Vat. 421, fols. cclxxviiij^r–cclxxx^r, dated 4 August 1452; it has been misinterpreted by Re, 1954, p. 27, following Rodocanachi, 1901, p. 157, who did not mention the admonition to the *conservatori.*

[40]See Re, 1880, preamble to the statutes of the city of Rome.

[41]See Bueno de Mesquita, 1965, pp. 316–317.

[42]Infessura, p. 51.   Pastor's comments on this episode (1949, pp. 147–149) seem groundless; for Pastor's attitude toward republicans, see his attack on what he considers Tommasini's too-liberal republicanism, as Pastor believes it appears in his editing of Infessura's diary; Pastor, 1925, p. 614, n. 6.

[43]Nicholas informed Tommaso Spinelli, whom he had appointed as communal treasurer on 1 April 1447 (ASV, Reg. Vat. 432, fol. vi^r–v), that he was henceforth to hold the office of depositor to the apostolic treasury and that he was to follow the form of office established by Eugenius; ASV, Reg. Vat. 404, fols. ccxxviiij^v–ccxxx^v.   Spinelli, a Florentine, died in 1453 and was replaced by Jacobo Radolphi di Mozzo, another Florentine; ASV, Reg. Vat. 434, fols. xviiij^v–xx^r. Spinelli had been active as a private banker in Rome since at least 1438 and had advanced the money for Nicholas's coronation.   See Müntz, *ACP*, I, p. 65; idem, 1885, pp. 325, 331; idem, 1889, pp. 153 ff.   For the apostolic office, see Partner, 1958, pp. 136–138, and idem, 1960, where older, standard literature is cited.

[44]The situation had been brewing since 1 November 1451, according to the letters of the Florentine ambassador, Donato Donati; see Archivio di Stato, Florence, Dieci di Balia, carteggio responsivo, 22, fols. 83^r, 84^r, 87^r, and 88^r; these indicate that the situation was cleared up by late November, 1451.   The last states that funds formerly invested in the Monte would then go to the building funds for the monastery of San Paolo fuori le mura.

[45]An additional indication of continued respect for the Romans' independence is an action of unspecified date in 1452, in which Nicholas informed Cardinal Torquemada that he was no longer to receive the heads of oversized fish landed at the Tiber port.   These had traditionally gone to the *conservatori;* Martin V had directed that they be given to the cardinal of Santa Maria in Trastevere (Torquemada's *titulus*), but the old custom was to be restored.   ASV, Arm. XXXI, vol. 56, fols. 208^r–209^v.

character of the city of Rome and on the role of the papacy in its relations with the commune. In that year he promulgated a new code for the Romans' magistrates of buildings and streets. It partakes of the same spirit as his other actions in the city, both conceptual and administrative. The new code was to provide the model for the better-known reforms of Sixtus IV, which continued to define the administrative apparatus for papal and private intervention in the physical fabric of Rome until the present Italian state was established.[46]

Special magistrates and legal devices to tend to the physical condition of the city had long been present in Rome and elsewhere in Italy.[47] The Roman statutes of 1363 contained certain provisions for policing the physical facilities of the city, which fell into four general categories. Some were intended to supervise new construction,[48] some sought to protect extant buildings,[49] some sought to assure that the city did not become clogged with refuse,[50] and some sought to assure that streets and bridges remained viable.[51] Responsibility for enforcing these provisions was left vague; usually the task was simply given to the senator because he was the officer in charge of public order. Most of these statutes were intended to prevent the city from becoming a fortress or its facilities from harboring bandits and malcontents. The only hint that the buildings themselves had any value, significance, or importance that transcended their purely utilitarian purposes is given in the article that forbade destruction of ancient monuments; these need to be preserved because they decorate the city.[52] The statutes specified that two street magistrates, who would serve for two months, would be selected along with other lesser officials through *imbossulatura*, but there is no reference to a code to guide their operations.[53]

The earliest surviving magistrates' code to supplement the communal statutes has a preamble dated 1410,[54] but that is surely only the date of the reenactment of the edition of the code that has the dated preamble. Indeed, the circumstances surrounding the code's issuance in that year suggest that only the preamble, which carries the date, was drafted in 1410. The curia that issued the code had been formed in Pisa the year before, and Rome had been occupied by Ladislaw of Naples since the previous spring; this hardly suggests that the code was drafted in 1410 or in the years immediately before 1410. The articles of the code mesh nicely with the 1363 statutes of the city. They state that the magistrates are to operate "for the honor of public things of Romans and of the streets of the city according to the form of the ancient and modern statutes of the city";[55] the code itself emphasizes order, preservation, justice, and cleanliness, attributes that correspond to the desires of the

[46]For the period after Nicholas, see Bardus, 1565; Fenzonio, 1636; Scaccia-Scarafoni, 1927; and Scavizzi, 1969.

[47]For Rome, see Schiaparelli, 1902, passim; Magnuson, 1958, p. 35; see also Braunfels, 1966, pp. 88 ff., 95 f.; and *Statuti di Lucca*, 1960.

[48]Re, 1880, I, article c, ci; II, lxxxvi, lxxxvii.

[49]Ibid., I, xcii, xciii; II, xvi, xxiv, cli, cxci, cxcvi.

[50]Ibid., II, clxxviii–cxc, cxciv, and cxcv.

[51]Ibid., II, cxxxv, which attempted to ensure that no street be narrower than four *palmi* (less than a meter), and cxcii.

[52]Ibid., II, cxci; this goes farther than any of the fourteenth-century documents published by Schiaparelli, 1902; those are concerned exclusively with health and viability. See esp. docs. x–xiii, pp. 50–59.

[53]Re, 1880, III, xxxv, cxxxiv; see also Rodocanachi, 1901, pp. 92–97.

[54]Published by Scaccia-Scarafoni, 1927, appendix.

[55]Scaccia-Scarafoni, 1927, article 1; compare the *Statuti di Lucca*, 1960, p. 11, for 1342, and p. 22, for 1379.

legal statutes of 1363, the preamble to which speaks of the repression of vice and brazenness.

The 1410 preamble, on the other hand, has a different tone. It states that the code was decreed and authorized by the Sacred Senate. That body was composed of the Pisa cardinals controlling Alexander V, and the phrase itself indicates the strong conciliarist spirit of that assembly. The preamble also clearly identifies the city of Rome with the papacy. It states that the magistrates' code is given force in order to bring honor to the Holy Mother Church and to the dominion of the pope; it is for the utility of public things that old things must be preserved, it continues, and it is more important to preserve old things than to invent new ones for beauty and order.[56] This attitude corresponds to the one prevailing ten days earlier when Alexander V had accepted dominion of the city of Rome from the Roman people and had confirmed the 1363 statutes—with alterations in his favor.[57] The Pisa pope was supported by Florence, and Florentines were among his curia; it seems likely that within that group the confirmation of an extant magistrates' code would be considered a natural adjunct to the confirmation of the purely political and legal statutes. It appears, then, that an older code had been brought forth and confirmed because it was part of the political machinery of the moment, not because any new attitude about the city was about to be launched in Rome.[58]

This code invested powers in the magistrates to adjudicate property disputes, to supervise the physical facilities (including ancient monuments, streets, fountains, and public buildings), to undertake amelioration of the city through the building of drains, and to levy fines against those who impeded public things or fouled the city with detritus. The magistrates were public officials responsible to the Romans; at the end of their tenure, syndics reviewed their actions and the records they were required to keep. As communal officials, they had the power to be assisted in their actions by the marshals and other armed officers of the commune.[59] If they were to perform their tasks effectively, the office would have to be attached to a powerful and orderly organ of government. From the period of Pius II onward, and in the statutes promulgated by Sixtus IV, the papacy provided that power and order. During the pontificates of Martin V and Eugenius IV, however, the magistrates enjoyed no access to power and the commune was not orderly; therefore, the city of Rome deteriorated as it revived.

Nicholas's two immediate predecessors treated the magistrates in a manner that was consistent with their policies in other fields. When the magistrates could be useful, they were used; but usually, because they were communal officials, they were ignored and others were given their duties. In 1423 Martin empowered a curial official to police his strictures against the destruction of churches;[60] this was not an infringement on the magistrates' prerogatives, because they were not responsible for eccle-

---

[56]Scaccia-Scarafoni, 1927, preamble.

[57]See the concordat in Theiner, *Cod. Dip.*, III, no. 109, pp. 172–174. It included two magistrates of streets among those listed as recognized communal officers.

[58]Schiaparelli, 1902, attempted to move the magistrates' code dated 1410 back to 1363 and to see it as a supplement to the general communal statutes, but he based his supposition on insufficient information and a bad text, as has been demonstrated by Scaccia-Scarafoni, 1927. Scaccia-Scarafoni's belief that 1410 is the date of its drafting cannot be sustained. Thus, although it is clear that the code postdates 1363 and predates 1410, there is no evidence concerning what its date might be.

[59]Like the marshals, they and their officials were allowed to carry arms; Scaccia-Scarafoni, 1927, article 16.

[60]Theiner, *Cod. Dip.*, III, no. 220, pp. 284–285, *Quia mundo posito*, 14 June 1423.

siastical property. But sometime during his pontificate Martin appointed a man to act as "custodian of walls and of certain other public buildings," who was empowered to invoke the assistance of the senator, the *conservatori,* and the communal treasury; this was an intrusion into the magistrates' duties.[61] Eugenius made other appointments of a similar nature,[62] and when the magistrates did function, they appear as adjuncts of the *camerarius* rather than as communal officials acting on the authority of the commune.[63] This followed the pattern used by Martin, who had made it quite clear that anything magistrates might do would be done for him. In 1425 he had appointed two magistrates, stating that the office had lapsed and he wished to revive it. Lacking is any indication that they might bring honor to the commune or dignity to the Holy See; instead, he took the action as a corollary to his political interest in the city:

> Although we are delighted by the grace and flourishing of all the provinces of the world, according to the office entrusted to us from above, nevertheless not undeservedly we think it fitting and appropriate that we must have a greater care of our city of Rome, which was dampened by the spilling of the blood of the Prince of the Apostles, Peter, and of Paul, who was called to a similar lot, who are the central point of orthodox faith as well as of innumerable victorious martyrs, so that this city, which once flourished under divine and human laws, and it and its district now in our times, by the favor of divine clemency, should rise with good and should win approval with good success in the future.[64]

Three months later Martin empowered two agents to plunder ruined churches inside and outside the city of their colored marbles and fine stones to restore the pavement of San Giovanni in Laterano.[65] And when the magistrates' six-month term had expired, it seems that Martin had forgotten about them, because there is no evidence that the office was filled again until 1430.[66] Eugenius, perhaps on the basis of the 1430

[61]The office is known through Eugenius's reappointment of Martin's official; Theiner, *Cod. Dip.,* III, no. 254, p. 338. The man died in 1441, and Eugenius's appointment of his successor expanded his powers; ASV, Reg. Vat. 382, fols. cxliiij^v–cxlv^r.

[62]In 1431, a conservator of the banks of the river of Rome (ASV, Reg. Vat. 381, fols. xii^v–xiii^r) and a conservator of the waters of Marana, an appointment of Cardinal Condulmero (ASV, Reg. Vat. 384, fol. 128^v). The duties of each of these officials were given explicitly to the magistrates by the 1410 code.

[63]See the report published in Cugnoni, 1885, pp. 582–583, from the time of Calixtus III, which refers to an action from after 1440 during Eugenius's pontificate. Compare this with the troubles of Stefano Caffari beginning in January, 1449, reported in Coletti, 1885–86, 1886, pp. 592–593 and 601.

[64]Theiner, *Cod. Dip.,* III, no. 231, pp. 290–291; published in Müntz, *ACP,* I, pp. 335–337; *Etsi in cunctarum orbis,* 31 March 1425. The office was now for a six-month term; when it was extended from two months is not known.

[65]1 July 1425; see Müntz, *ACP,* I, p. 4 and p. 4, n. 1; also Tomei, 1942, pp. 7, 34. In 1431 Eugenius gave similar authority to the builders of the mint at the Vatican; Müntz, *ACP,* I, p. 35 and p. 35, n. 2. Such licences were frequent, although forbidden by the 1410 code, the 1452 code, and preservation bulls, for which see below, note 77.

[66]They are not mentioned in the March 1424 list of officers, nor in those of the next years, in ASV, Fondo Borghese, Serie IV, vol. 60, fols. 2^r ff., except for the list of January, 1430. The names given there are known from another source published by Re, 1920, appendix II, whose list is also void for the intervening years. The Fondo Borghese manuscript lists officials Martin appointed to the communal government between 1424 and 1430; see Partner, 1958, p. 164, n. 2.

appointment, tended from time to time to see to it that there were magistrates of streets and buildings, although surviving documents do not indicate that the office was always staffed or how its occupants were selected.[67]

There were magistrates active from time to time in Eugenius's Rome, however; as political order was established during the 1440s, there came an increasing awareness among both the Romans and the curia that orderly political procedures could produce a more orderly physical environment. Provisions included in the 1446 concordat derived from that awareness. One of the rubrics, which simply confirmed the recognition of the extant article in the 1363 statutes, stated that 100 florins of the senator's salary was to be retained for repairs to the Capitol and that the work was to be surpervised by the *conservatori*.[68] Payments of this sort, or for something similar, had been made in 1439, 1442, and 1443.[69] Other rubrics were meant to assure that the walls were kept in repair, that butchers, who tended to foul open spaces with the remains of their operations, be better controlled, and that carts, which impede pedestrians, not be allowed in the *viae rectae* (apparently the three major streets), with a one-ducat fine for offenders. The concordat did not mention the magistrates or specify a procedure for enforcing its provisions, but implicit in it is the idea that maintaining the city through political cooperation between the papacy and the commune was a concomitant to a tranquil political state.

In this context Nicholas promulgated a revised code for the street magistrates. Issued in 1452, it was not drafted for the narrow purpose of assisting him in his building program; instead, it was an integral part of his program for governing, a program that included the rebuilding of the city as well as the clarifying of its legal structure. A process of revision that had formerly been haphazard and sporadic now became integrated with a broader policy; an implicit relationship between political and physical order was now made explicit.

The new codification mixes together old and new elements, as is common in this sort of code; reading it only in the context of the 1410 edition lulls one into overlooking its place in Nicholas's program and obscures its innovative character.[70] The preamble simply makes the point that Nicholas issues this code "for the honor and state and exaltation of the most holy father in Christ and our Lord, Nicholas, . . . and for the holy Roman Church, and for the sacred college of the lord cardinals, and for the holy city of Rome." As had been the case in 1447, what is done for the good of Rome is done for the good of the Church of which Nicholas is head. But what is done in Rome for the Church is done by the Romans, and that is the point of these statutes, just as it had been of the bull of 1447.

The duties and procedures outlined in the magistrates' code of 1452 are based on the precedents of the 1410 edition of the magistrates' code and are coordinated with the 1363 communal statues. But there are important differences. The new code contains a greater emphasis on the public nature of the magistrates' office, and it makes the magistrates more responsible to the citizens they are to serve. Their duties and rights are defined as follows:

[They are to hold] counsel in the morning on the Capitol about all the

---

[67]See the lists in Re, 1920, appendix II. The office is not mentioned in Eugenius's appointment books, ASV, Reg. Vat. 381–383, nor in that of his *camerarius*, Reg. Vat. 384, although neither of these sets is complete.

[68]Archivio Storico Capitolino, Cred. IV, tom. 88, rubric xviii. The 1363 statute was book III, ch. i.

[69]Salimei, 1935, p. 184, n. 12; p. 187, nn. 18 and 19; p. 189, n. 22.

[70]The text is published by Re, 1920, appendix III, pp. 86–102; the reference to Nicholas's sixth year and the date 1452 places it between 6 March and 25 December 1452. The references below are to Re's edition.

public things and, as required, about private things written below, and they [the magistrates] are able and required to have the authorization of power to break down, cut off, tear out, and destroy everything that occupies streets, piazzas, alleyways, rivers, riverbanks, and other public places both inside and outside Rome, without any exception or condemnation to them; and similarly, of their making preparations for streets, they have the right to be able to build without any exception (article 1).

To their responsibility to make themselves available to the public is added their ability to undertake amelioration; these are two duties, and they are closely connected with one another.

Their counsel concerns adjudication in property disputes between private parties, as it had in 1410, but outside their jurisdiction are "differences...in public things, which...are and remain in the will of Our Father or, indeed, of him who has the orders of His Holiness."[71] But public improvements are within their jurisdiction; they may order the paving of streets and charge the cost to the benefiting property owners, and they may clear away impediments to open spaces and charge those who were responsible for them, even hiring the workmen and calling on the marshal to protect them. In both operations they are to be assisted by the counsel of an assessor and a submagistrate from a building trade, but in neither are they subject to the review of syndics after their tenure in office.

In all other operations they are both to be assisted by their assessors and submagistrates and to subject themselves to syndical review. These other operations are quite extensive. In addition to acting as judges in property disputes, they are to police the physical facilities of the city, tending to the maintenance of drains, fountains, riverbanks, walls, streets, piazzas, bridges, and ancient monuments. These duties are extensions of those found in the 1363 statutes and the 1410 code, although they now are more specific. An earlier duty the magistrates were given, that of cleaning the city, is now organized for the first time. The purpose for their attention to this, as is stated repeatedly in the code, is that precautions must be taken to promote good air in the city, especially during the summer months.[72] The magistrates are to make certain that no one randomly disposes of trash, building materials, and dead animals, and they are also to organize a refuse removal service. Every Saturday during May, June, July, and August they are to pick up the rubbish collected by householders and carry it to the Tiber at the property owners' expense; they are to be especially diligent along the three (unnamed) major streets, and they may levy a fine for noncompliance. At Easter and in July they are to use fees collected from carters and householders to have the banks of the Tiber cleared by throwing the accumulation of the year into the center of the stream. They are also to clear the city's open spaces after floods.

The magistrates received no salary,[73] although they did receive a portion of the

---

[71] Article 5; that would be the *camerarius* or *vicecamerarius*.

[72] See articles 32, 33, and 38. Better air had been mentioned in trecento documents quoted in Shiaparelli, 1902, but the *salubriter* of the 1410 code had moral overtones, rather than airy ones, an emphasis completely lacking in the 1452 code.

[73] Magnuson, 1958, p. 38, states that they were paid 100 florins but does not say by whom; his reference there to Re, 1920, in his note 131 is incorrect; Re, 1920, pp. 14, nn. 1 and 2, and p. 15, n. 1, shows that the payment of a fixed salary of 100 florins a year from the communal treasury was the practice after Sixtus IV's reforms of 1480. Martin V in 1425 had explicitly forbidden a salary. Tomassetti, 1897, pp. 357–359, listing officials normally paid by the papal camera and dating from about 1449, does not list the magistrates (for the date, see ibid., pp. 337 ff.). In the 1452 code, the magistrates' assessors and notaries were to be paid fixed rates, but there are lacunae in the manuscript where the amounts were to be specified.

fines they levied, fees for issuing licenses that attested that construction undertaken by private individuals would not "prejudice public things,"[74] and fees for adjudicating property disputes.[75] And they could perhaps turn a profit on their trash-removal operations. Abuse could be made difficult through the review of the syndics, who would use books that were kept by notaries and that were public records. The two magistrates, along with other officers, were selected by the *imbossulatura* procedure that Nicholas revived, and the offices were always filled.[76] Since at least 1446 the term of their office had been a year, the term specified in the 1452 code (article 1).

The magistrates were not agents of the pope; instead, they were officials of the commune. They were selected by the commune, responsible to their fellow citizens, and available to them at the Capitol. Procedures for reviewing their activities fitted within the structure established by the 1363 statutes. The magistrates were given the right to call on the communal marshals, and they were responsible to the judicial structure of the Capitoline courts. Nicholas's purpose in endowing them with a new code was not to extend his sway over Rome or even to invest one particular office with comprehensive responsibility for physical conditions in Rome. The magistrates were not given jurisdiction in public places that belonged to the pope, and they were not charged with responsibility for preserving ancient buildings.[77] Nicholas simply wished to introduce order into the procedures the commune used in governing its own affairs. This worked to the advantage of the commune because now, according to law, communal magistrates rather than papal officials bridged the gap between the several classes of property—that of private citizens, corporations, clerics and others who were immune from Capitoline jurisdiction, and that which was sacred or public (i.e., papal) property. Furthermore, the communal officials could now police and ameliorate the physical elements of the city as a comprehensive whole. Finally, the new legal arrangements meant that the papacy rather than the commune was responsible for financing public improvements. The pope could initiate whatever he wished, but he had to pay when a project was undertaken at the expense of a Roman's property. A system of expropriation hinted at in the 1410 code had been developed into a legal procedure entirely within the competence of the Capitol in the 1452 code.[78]

Documentary evidence is too fragmentary to give anything more than a hint of how these procedures worked in practice. It does show that the magistrates could function as papal agents, as when they were reimbursed in 1448 for expenses they had incurred in paving "the street from St. Peter's," presumably in the Borgo; the apos-

[74]See Re, 1922, for an example from 6 June 1452.

[75]See Caffari's case in Coletti, 1885–86, cited above, note 63.

[76]Tommasini, 1887, lists them; Re, 1920, appendix II, does not use Tommasini's publication, but through independent evidence confirms his list. Magnuson, 1958, p. 41, apparently overlooking Tommasini's article, incorrectly states that the pope selected them from a list provided by the *caporioni*, but cites no evidence.

[77]Preservation bulls continued to follow the pattern established in *Quia mundo posito*, 14 June 1423, of Martin V, cited above, note 60. These were Eugenius IV: *Quamquam in omnibus orbis*, 30 March 1436, in Theiner, *Cod. Dip.*, III, no. 271, p. 338, published in part in Müntz, *ACP*, I, p. 39, no. 3; an alternative version is *Quoniam in omnibus terrarum*, 28 March 1436, in *Coll Bull. Vat.*, II, pp. 89–90. Nicholas V: Only a reference to it is known. It appears in Raynaldus's digest of the bull of Calixtus III. Calixtus III: *Quoniam multiplicata est*, 25 March 1457, published in *Coll. Bull. Vat.*, II, pp. 156–157, a version that does not refer to Nicholas's bull but adds monetary fines to Eugenius's bull, which it does cite. See also Raynaldus, XVIII, ab anno 1457, no. 93. Pius II: *Cum albam nostram urbem*, May, 1462, the standard bull, often reissued and printed. It appears in Theiner, *Cod. Dip.*, III, no. 369, pp. 422–423; in Müntz, *ACP*, I, appendix; and Fenzonio, 1636, pp. 667–668.

[78]MacDougall, 1962, p. 68, recognized this in the 1452 code, but did not see its coordination with the judicial procedures of the 1363 statutes or its outgrowth from the 1410 code. Nevertheless, her hunch was correct.

tolic treasury paid, which was reasonable because the Borgo was not part of the commune of Rome, but that meant that the magistrates had no statutory jurisdiction there.[79] It also shows that the pope paid for improvements on the Capitol; payments from 1451, 1452, and 1453 were from the apostolic treasury, while some from 1447 and 1452 are from the communal treasury. The papacy paid considerably more than the commune, but no valid pattern can be derived from the random surviving documents.[80] And, finally, the pope—as was proper—paid for the improvements to the Ponte Sant'Angelo and for the street from the Vatican Palace to the bridge.[81] The bridge was narrow and encumbered at both approaches, a condition that allowed the disaster of December, 1450. Soon after, Nicholas repaired the bridge, opened the approaches on the Rome side by tearing down houses and shops, had the new piazza paved, had two commemorative chapels built, and opened new approaches into the piazza. Throughout 1452 and 1453 indemnity was paid to private citizens from the apostolic treasury through instruments handled by curial notaries.[82]

Each of these examples of Nicholas's administrative operations, especially his bull of 1447 and the code of 1452, shows that his operations were based on conceptions that held the communal government in respect; each also shows that he considered it desirable to coordinate its activities with those of the papacy so as to allow order to flourish in the political activities and building operations in the city. These operations would have been inconceivable earlier in the century when Rome was in constant agitation, but the greater stability of the city was only a precondition for Nicholas's operations. It is certain that neither Martin nor Eugenius, who believed it their right to enjoy temporal dominion in Rome, could have been guided by a conception that placed the trust in the Romans that Nicholas did. Nicholas imported to Rome an attitude about government that had long been prevalent in Florence, and once it had been implanted in Rome, it gradually took root. Each of Nicholas's successors little by little took away that which Nicholas had given, but each left intact the structure he had established. They, like Nicholas but unlike his predecessors, used the traditional legal structure of Rome to define how the citizens could act to produce a coordinated, visible political and physical order in the city. But only Nicholas allowed the Romans to act in those roles.

---

[79] Müntz, *ACP*, I, p. 157; 23 February 1448; see also Borgatti, 1931, pp. 157–158. Müntz, 1889, pp. 144–145, gives some additional documents for this work.

[80] Müntz, *ACP*, I, pp. 148–150.

[81] Müntz, *ACP*, I, pp. 152, 153; Borgatti, 1931, p. 169; these payments cover early 1450 through 1452.

[82] See Müntz, *ACP*, I, pp. 140–141, 154; Borgatti, 1931, p. 169; Rodocanachi, 1922, pp. 274, n. 1, 275, n. 2, and 304. Rodocanachi's comparative prices indicate that the pope was not generous, but it seems unlikely that the buildings were very substantial. The area was known as Piazza S. Celso.

5 The New Appearance of the City of Rome

What Rome appeared to be changed significantly during the quattrocento, because a new conception of the city was introduced there. This new conception affected the design of the new buildings, but more significant and fundamental was the effect of a new conceptual approach that was taken to the buildings in relationship to one another, in relationship to the city, and in relationship to their significance within the ordered political structure of the city. The new conception allowed people to see the city as a place within which individuals act and as a place that possesses a unique and visible relationship between political and physical structures.

The newly invented conception is conspicuous in views made of Rome after the middle of the century. Only after that time do they show Rome as a place where people lead their lives and as a place filled with significant buildings of every sort. Although the manufacture of those views cannot be attributed directly to Nicholas's influence, they do seem to have been a by-product of it; at least, they reveal a cognizance of his program, because the departure they represent from earlier views is in the direction of showing the city as he conceived of it, both politically and physically. To understand the importance of these views, it must be accepted that views of cities were never made without the intention of making some point; they were never mere illustration. By careful attention to a number of different views of Rome, a great deal can be learned about Nicholas's program.[1]

Fourteenth-century views convey the attitudes exemplified by Filarete's six major panels or Taddeo di Bartolo's Siena frescoes. They are primarily collections of images of buildings that are based on visual figures for buildings and are assembled according to traditional visual formats. The intention of their makers was usually to show that the city was politically orderly, and therefore they conveyed information about the political status of the city. There was little or no attempt to achieve visual verisimilitude or to represent the city in a spatial structure resembling that which fell under the eyes of the viewer.

A fine and representative example of this early type appears on the Golden Bull used by the imperial contender Louis of Bavaria from 1328 through 1340 (fig. 20).[2]

---

[1] For a categorization based purely on the visual appearance of the views of cities, which includes cities other than Rome and disregards an analysis of the kind of information views contain and purvey, see Krautheimer, 1970, p. 258, n. 11; and for a categorization that more closely resembles the one to be presented here, see Ettlinger, 1952, p. 164. For a discussion of the nature of the city that gave rise to the older category of views, see Braunfels, 1966, pp. 45–50, 131–139. For a brief review of maps of Rome, with bibliography, that supplements the material to be cited below, see Thelen, 1963.

[2] Frutaz, 1962, I, pp. 119–120, II, pl. 144; Erben, 1931, esp. ch. IV.

Its legend had appeared on imperial seals since the eleventh century—ROMA CAPVT MVNDI REGIT ORBIS FRENA ROTVNDI—but the form in which the city of Rome is shown was drastically altered. Other imperial seals showed a purely typological representation of a city that could be any city;[3] Louis's bull shows distinct buildings, but the only ones selected for representation are the ones that attest to the survival of Rome in the Holy Roman Empire that Louis claimed. In the center appear the two buildings that best represented ancient and modern Rome as the seat of imperial authority, the Colosseum and the Palazzo del Senatore.[4] The Palazzo is shown with two nearly equal towers rather than with clearly unequal ones, and there is no hill under the building. Other imperial buildings dominate the scene—the Mausoleum of Hadrian, the Pantheon, the Torre di Nerone (or dei Conti, or delle Milizie),[5] the Column of Antoninus (or, less likely, of Trajan), the Arch of Constantine (or, less likely, of Titus),[6] the Pyramid of Cestius, and the obelisk next to St. Peter's—all enclosed within the walls, gates, and towers of the city, including bridges across the Tiber. Because these buildings predominate, there is only room for three Christian basilicas, St. Peter's, the Lateran, and Santa Maria in Trastevere. These choices correspond to Louis's belief that his imperial dignity should overshadow that of the pope, whom he believed he should protect. Only those buildings that can reveal Louis's ideas are shown; topographic features are totally lacking, and no building is a ruin. This is a figure for Rome rather than a view of Rome; it was not meant to indicate anything that could not be learned from other sources, and its purpose was to fix one's focus on the visible evidence that Louis believed supported his anti-papal crusade.

Rome continued to be represented figuratively long into the quattrocento, in views that most likely derived directly from older archetypes or that may have been constructed from familiar figurative elements for a particular purpose. The purpose of such views was not to show something new about Rome, but to show something traditional—as traditional, for example, as Christian doctrine. Because Rome had long served as a literary figure for the Heavenly Jerusalem, it appears in two manuscript copies of Augustine's *City of God*, one made for Aeneas Sylvius (later Pius II) in 1456, and another dated 1459 and showing the image of Rome as Jerusalem appearing to Augustine as he sets out to write the book (figs. 21,22).[7] Views of Rome could also be used to associate an event with that city, but this was done by assembling typical buildings rather than by representing the city in a view that attempted to present it with topographic or spatial verisimilitude. In the various *cassoni* from the shop of Apollonio di Giovanni in Florence produced during the

---

[3]See, for example, the seal of Henry VII from 1312, which introduces an historiated column to designate Rome (Sella, 1934, no. 16), or the one of Charles IV from 1355, which shows a church with two towers rather than a city proper (ibid., no. 18).

[4]See Siebenhüner, 1954, pp. 17–36; these identifications are taken from Erben, 1931, pp. 61 ff. There is some dispute about some of them, for which compare Scaccia-Scarafoni, 1939, no. 107, and Frutaz, 1962, I, pp. 119–120. For the actual condition of the Palazzo del Senatore at this time, see below, pp. 92–94.

[5]Towers such as this one were believed to have been part of the palaces of ancient emperors; see Anonimo Magliabechiano, 1953, p. 126, and Perosa's note in Rucellai, 1960, p. 163, n. 21.

[6]The Arch of Constantine seems reasonable on an iconographic basis. See also Erben, 1931, p. 61. The forms of representation hardly allow a distinction to be made between the two.

[7]Aeneas Sylvius's manuscript is signed by Giacomo da Fabriano; it is Bib. Vat., Cod. Reg. Lat. 1882, fol. 2[r]; the other is signed Niccolò Polani; Paris, Bibliothèque Sainte-Geneviève, Cod. 218, fol. 2[r]. See Frutaz, 1962, I, pp. 134, 135; II, no. LXXXIV and LXXXV respectively, pl. 155.

decades following the middle of the quattrocento,[8] various Roman buildings appear in different relationships to one another (fig. 23). The views here are similar in their conception to those in the two manuscripts; that is, they are assembled with a similar disregard for topographic veracity.[9] The artists in the shop had easy access to a collection of figurative views of Roman buildings, and the *cassoni* indicate that the artists did not trouble to bring their images up to date. Many of the buildings in the *cassoni* appear in their fourteenth-century figurative form, even though they had been rebuilt during Nicholas's pontificate.

A different approach to the representation of cities began to develop during the same years in the quattrocento that a new conception of the city was being worked out. The new conception is hinted at first in views that belong primarily to the older tradition. One hint was given by Taddeo di Bartolo in the Palazzo Pubblico frescoes in Siena in 1413–14, where Rome appeared as the goal and recipient of the virtuous actions of the *exempla* assembled below it (fig. 25).[10] Taddeo produced the view by following the procedure of his predecessors,[11] but in response to the attitude that pervades the fresco cycle's program, he produced a view the character of which suggests something new. In addition to including the proper buildings in approximately their proper places by using inherited figures and a traditional format,[12] he has shown that Rome is a place that is inhabited and used. Boats now appear on the Tiber. Although there is no one in the city, there are at least a few tracks across the open spaces that must be roads. One of them follows (approximately) the via Papalis from the Ponte Sant'Angelo to the Capitol; another runs from near the Ponte Sant' Angelo toward the Piazza Navona, the approximate route of the via dei Coronari. In addition, Taddeo has introduced a few buildings that, in themselves, are completely unimportant. These are simply collections of humble structures where people live, one in the Borgo and another near the Pyramid of Cestius. He has introduced ele-

[8]Apollonio di Giovanni died in 1465, but his shop continued production. For examples, see Gombrich, "Apollonio di Giovanni," 1966, esp. figs. 20, 30, and 33; other *cassoni* are listed by Frutaz, 1962, I, p. 144; see also Huelsen, 1911.

[9]Gombrich, "Apollonio di Giovanni," 1966, p. 14, observes: "Quattrocento art offers no reportage of the places and personages of the time, for it operates with types and patterns, not with individualistic portrayals." Apollonio di Giovanni was assembling types to identify, not to report about, the place of the action. See also Krinsky, 1970, passim.

[10]For its location, see the diagram, fig. 1, and photograph, plate 17 (e), in Rubinstein, 1958.

[11]The process followed is similar to the one used by Fra Paolino, for which, see Gadol, 1969, pp. 162–164. The step-by-step procedure was something like this: first, the boundaries for the city were established, then some actual topographic features were added, and then the buildings were placed in the space more or less in the places they actually occupied relative to one another and probably as known through a standard archetype. An incomplete version of Fra Paolino's view of Rome (Paris, Bib. Nat., Cod. Parisiensis Lat. 1939, fol. 27ʳ), reported in Frutaz, 1962, I, p. 115, corroborates this description; it shows only the walls, and the interior area has been left blank. As Gadol points out, an important difference between Paolino and Taddeo is in their spatial conception of the city.

[12]This use of older prototypes and the failure of recently built buildings to appear in the view has led to the interpretation that the archetype for this view derives from before 1400; because the Aracoeli, or at least its set of steps, is lacking, it is assumed that the archetype even predates 1348. See Stevenson, 1881, passim. It seems unnecessary to go that far back for the archetype for the entire view, appropriate as it may be for some of the individual elements. It seems more reasonable to assume that Taddeo or someone else assembled the view from individual figurative elements, the same means of working as that apparently used by Apollonio di Giovanni, as Gnoli, 1941, pp. 4–5, has remarked.

ments that show an interest in the city as a place where people go about their business among the buildings of Rome.

Taddeo's additions reveal the frame of mind that would make an interpolation in a text rather than the one that would demand a completely new edition. Soon, however, Rome would be represented in a new form, as a place full of things (figs. 26, 27, 28). The city is seen as filled with buildings of every sort—the familiar figurative buildings and, in addition, humble houses, all shown from a single point of view and even merging in distant parts of the views to form a pattern made only of their roofs. The city is so packed that there are no piazzas or streets; the open areas in the views represent spots where no buildings existed, rather than active open areas surrounded by buildings. The city is conceived of as more than mere buildings; the hilly topography of Rome is handled with audacity, so that the Capitol dominates the upper center area by exaggerating the height of the hill, rather than by falsely distorting the grandeur of the buildings on it. And the city is surrounded by walls, including towers and gates, which merge into the many buildings and become part of the city, rather than merely satisfying the demand that the view of the city be enclosed.

Two examples of this form of representation are known. One was certainly executed by Masolino in 1435 at Castiglione Olona (Varese) for the collegiate church; the view appears between the annunciation of the birth of John the Baptist and the Visitation and is supposed to represent Jerusalem (fig. 26).[13] The other, which has the same character as the Castiglione Olona view, is known only from copies (figs. 27, 28). The original was probably in the hall of Cardinal Giordano Orsini at Monte Giordano in Rome, which was decorated with a cycle of famous men between 1430 and 1432, probably by Masolino.[14] The inventor of these views must have had a visual acquaintance with the city, and he must have responded to it as something other than a figure; the views seem to display a frame of mind that shunned views constructed only by assembling traditional figures within traditional formats. Masolino had visited Rome in the mid 1420s and again a few years later. These views perhaps show an attitude toward the city that he had acquired while working with Masaccio in producing the revolutionary frescoes in the Brancacci Chapel; there, one sees men acting in spaces resembling those inhabited by the viewer, just as in these views of Rome, one sees the city represented as a place in which men could act.

The supposition that originally the model of the view of Rome now known only through copies was on Giordano Orsini's palace walls is strengthened by the link that a view such as this one has with humanists' concerns. Its artist has tried to emphasize a credible topography and space in which a citizen could act. The humanists and others active during the first third of the quattrocento in Florence—Bruni, Dati, and, at the end of that period, Alberti, who was younger—were developing a new understanding about the role of the citizen in the city, and their attitude had had its impact not only on literary productions but on other areas as well. Taddeo di Bartolo, when representing Rome in a humanist program in Siena devoted to the role of citizens in governing the city, tried to represent the city as something more than a collection of typical buildings that identified a particular place. Orsini's artist may have attempted the same thing because he, too, was in close contact with humanist thought. Orsini was a learned bibliophile and patron of humanists. Those he favored

[13]In Frutaz, 1962, I, pp. 128–129; II, pl. 152.

[14]See Scheller, 1962, passim; Simpson, 1966, p. 137, n. 10, and passim; Mode, 1970, esp. pp. 70 ff. and 115. The copies are: 1) Milan, Crespi Collection; see Frutaz, 1962, I, pp. 131–132, II, no. LXXXII, pl. 154. For this group, see Toesca, 1952; Scheller, 1962. 2) Turin, Bib. Reale, MS. Varia 102, fol. 28ʳ; Frutaz, 1962, I, p. 133, II, no. LXXXIII, pl. 154. 3) ex-Cockerell and ex-Morris Chronicle, the relevant page of which is now in the Metropolitan Museum, 58.105.

were active in Rome and in touch with others in Florence during Martin V's pontificate and later, until the cardinal's death in 1438.[15] Furthermore, the next innovations in the representation of the city of Rome were made by a group that also included painters and humanists, among them Alberti. The revisions they made to the means of representing Rome, which will be discussed in a moment, were of the same character that this view represents relative to its predecessors. These revisions were made in the fourth decade of the quattrocento by a group familiar with Rome and active there, although its members were younger than Orsini's friends and lived long enough to profit from Nicholas's patronage. This group left Rome in 1434 with Eugenius and returned in 1443 with the curia; the participation of its members in events in Florence during the interval seems to have whetted their desire to use in Rome some of the skills and attitudes that they had developed while away.

After their return they quickly produced three new presentations of the city and its monuments. One was Alberti's *Descriptio urbis Romae*, which is probably to be dated just after 1444.[16] In these years, by developing his theories about art—and eventually about architecture—in directions suggested by his humanist culture, Alberti had begun to expand these theories into an understanding of the city as a place where men acted for the good. Another was Flavio Biondo's *Roma instaurata*, also written immediately after the curia's return to Rome, released in 1446.[17] The third was a view of the city that has been lost but the character of which may be known from various copies.[18] The view, which was probably produced either to assist Biondo in writing his *Roma instaurata* or as an illustration made soon after its composition and based on it,[19] survives most completely in a copy made by Alessandro Strozzi in Venice in 1474 (fig. 29).[20] It was also used selectively by Piero del Massaio in producing illustrations for Ptolemy's *Cosmologia* in Florence. One of these, probably from either 1453 or 1456, is now in Paris (fig. 30).[21] Another is dated 1469 and is now in the Vatican (fig. 31).[22] And a third, from 1472, was produced for Federigo da Montefeltro and is now also in the Vatican (fig. 32).[23]

Alberti's cartographic research, Biondo's archaeological investigations, and the view of Rome that was apparently produced between 1444 and 1447 have in common an interest in the city as it exists as a physical entity. Alberti sought to discover a means to represent where things were;[24] Biondo tried to uncover what purpose the ancient buildings had served and to introduce greater accuracy in the knowledge of ancient Roman topography;[25] and the draftsman of the view contributed his skill in making a visual representation of the city that emphasized visible spatial relationships between the buildings that defined the city. The artist's representation of the individual buildings was still for the most part based on figurative prototypes, but when

[15]Simpson, 1966, p. 140 and n. 22.

[16]See Lehmann-Brockhaus, 1960; Gadol, 1969, p. 71, n. 24. See also Orlandi, 1968; Vagnetti, 1968.

[17]See Weiss, 1969, pp. 66–70; Robathan, 1970, who has promised a critical edition.

[18]Scaglia, 1964, esp. pp. 137–138, 138 n. 4, 140, 153.

[19]The former position is taken by Scaglia, 1964; the latter, by Huskinson, 1969, p. 147, n. 81.

[20]Florence, Bib. Medicea-Laurenziana, Cod. Redi 77, fol. vii^v–viii^r; dated 1474.

[21]Paris, Bib. Nat., MS. Lat. 4802, fol. 133^r; Scaglia, 1964, pp. 139 n. 7, 140; Huskinson, 1969, p. 146, n. 79. For this and the next two Ptolemy manuscripts, see Fischer, 1932, I, pp. 365–375.

[22]Cod. Vat. Lat. 5699, fol. 127^r, a manuscript produced in the shop of Vespasiano da Bisticci; Frutaz, 1962, I, p. 137.

[23]Urb. Lat. 277, fol. 131^r, codex dated 5 January 1472; also probably from Vespasiano's shop. Frutaz, 1962, I, p. 139.

[24]See Gadol, 1969, pp. 157 ff., esp. 170.

[25]See Weiss, 1969, p. 70.

he placed them, he attempted to stress topographic relationships rather than purely conceptual ones. Rather than show only the buildings and their locations that would clarify or refer to nonvisual evidence about Rome, the artist attempted to reveal what can be seen, and the viewpoint from which he saw the city now approaches that of an observer near the city. The older category of views is still lurking within this one, however, because the artist showed only a select group of buildings. But these are buildings that illustrated a belief about the life of ancient Romans and the survival of ancient Rome in modern Rome; the artist based his selection on a conception of the city that considered it a place with buildings in which people did things in the past and continue to do them. Thus, in intention, his view is related to those of Taddeo and Masolino. In addition, he showed physical elements other than buildings; each of the copies includes a street passing through the Campo de' Fiori and the Piazza Giudea and arriving at the stairs before the Aracoeli, but the street and its piazzas are not shown as spaces defined by buildings. Some of the copies include other streets, indicating that the archetype may have been richer in them than any single copy suggests. And although the view is still clearly indebted to the method of construction used to make the traditional views rather than to the one explored by Masolino, it gives the impression that the city as a place seen and lived in is at least as important in its representation as is some external idea that the view is supposed to illustrate.

From then on views of Rome belonging to the new category would attempt to combine an emphasis on the city as a place full of things, as Masolino had demonstrated, with that on the city as a careful representation of actual spatial relationships within which people did things. In addition, there would be an increasing attention to what the buildings actually looked like, although their relationships to types familiar from figurative representations would remain prominent, as would the traditional political content. Two views of Rome from the second half of the century combine these many interests, but only one of them fully exploits the potential of the new category. The earlier view is still transitional in character; that is, while it appears to belong to the new category and to present the city as a site full of things in certain places, it really contains a collection of figurative types revised to represent the appearances of buildings, and it distributes the types according to vague spatial relationships rather than according to actual topographic locations. This view was painted in 1465 by Benozzo Gozzoli in the collegiate church of S. Agostino in San Gimignano, where Rome is shown in the background of the scene in which Augustine sets out for Milan (fig. 33). As a whole, Gozzoli's fresco is very similar to the one he had made six years earlier in the chapel in the Palazzo Medici in Florence, showing the arrival of the Magi. There the subjects are carefully dressed and posed in studied, decorous attitudes; they are stretched out across a shallow spatial shelf that is discontinuous with the background; the background forms a broad, deep backdrop for the thin shelf, and it includes hills, trees, flowers, people, *castelli,* and scenes from the hunt. The combination of these elements in a single painting is more conspicuous than an overpowering unity of space, light, and action that might hold them together. In San Gimignano Gozzoli handled the setting in much the same way, and his treatment of the physiognomy of Rome is quite similar to that given the portraits of the individual Medici included in the scene in Florence; while producing convincing representations, he altered what one would see in order to emphasize what one should see.[26] The view fits into a landscape setting based on the new form of

---

[26]See, for example, the comments accompanying plates VII (*Il più giovane dei Magi e i suoi paggi*), XIV (*Il Re "Moro"*), XX (*Paggio nel corteo del vecchio Re*), and XXI (*Il vecchio Re e il suo corteo:* details), in Toesca, 1958.

spatial construction exemplified by Castagno's works at Legnaia, but it is not a convincing demonstration of the principles that had guided Castagno. Similarly, the buildings in the view of Rome resemble more closely what the buildings actually looked like than they would if they were being shown as types, and their relationship to one another resembles that which appears from some particular viewpoint; but, again, the depiction of each particular building seems as indebted to some figurative source as it is to actual observation, and the spatial relationships crowd the topography rather than portray Rome. Gozzoli seems to have assembled the view to satisfy requirements dictated by the content of the painting—to make a convincing representation of Rome for Augustine to leave. His attitude toward the city resembles that of the *cassoni* masters and the illuminators of the *City of God*, rather than that of Taddeo, Masolino, or the artist associated with Biondo.[27]

Gozzoli constructed the view to represent Rome. Through numerous visits to the city he would have become as familiar with Rome's appearance as he was with that of the individual Medici. He had been there in 1447, in 1449, and again in 1458, and it seems clear that this view represents what he had learned of the city during each of his visits.[28] He learned not only what the buildings looked like, but what they were supposed to look like, and the view of Rome he constructed shows it as Nicholas had conceived it. In broad forms he has shown that St. Peter's and the Vatican dominate the city, that the Borgo is distinct from Rome, and that Rome is a mixture of ancient grandeur and contemporary activity taking place in the city under the supervision of the government on the Capitol.[29]

The last major quattrocento view of the city is clearly a new type. It was made in the last quarter, or even the last decade, of the century, but it survives only in copies. The example that seems closest to the archetype probably dates from the fourth decade of the sixteenth century; this example is preserved in ruinous condition in the Palazzo Ducale in Mantua (fig. 34).[30] The so-called "Mantua view of Rome" unifies into an easy harmony the most basic principles of the older and newer categories of views, making each distinct while clearly emphasizing the newer attitude toward the city. It profits from all the previous experiments; the city is full, the buildings are displayed relative to one another in something that resembles their actual physical and spatial disposition from a common and credible point of view, and each building

[27] Thus, the assertion of Magnuson, 1958, p. 10, that "this may be considered as the earliest *veduta* in the real sense of the word," cannot be sustained.

[28] Magnuson, 1958, pp. 108–109, who cites older literature (n. 58), argues that Gozzoli used sketches made in 1447 and 1449, because Nicholas's work on the Capitol is not shown, although he admits that the pope's work at the Castel Sant'Angelo is obvious, and he must discount the interpretation of others that the Tower of Nicholas V is shown. Its existence was perceived by Müntz, 1889, p. 139; Zippel, 1911, pp. 195–196; Ackerman, 1954, p. 4; Frutaz, 1956, pp. 24–25; idem, 1962, I, pp. 136–137; and Scaglia, 1964, p. 151, n. 84.

[29] Further comments in support of this interpretation will be given below, p. 101, in chapters 6 and 7, and in the Epilogue.

[30] See Frutaz, 1962, I, pp. 151–155; II, pls. 167–169. The best known derivatives from this type are in Jacobus Philippus Foresti (Bergomensis), *Supplementum chronicarum*, Venice, 1490, and Hartmann Schedel, *Liber chronicarum*, Nuremberg, 1493. Less well known uses occur in numerous northern paintings, as, for example, in the Musées Royaux des Beaux-Arts de Belgique, Brussels, from after 1527, showing the sack of Rome. See the list in Frutaz, 1962, I, p. 154; for the Brussels view, see Ehrle and Egger, 1956, pl. X, and p. 14. The prototype for this view was perhaps the map produced in Florence in Francesco Rosselli's shop; see Ettlinger, 1952. This shop has been connected with the views of Florence that show a similar attitude toward the city and that are represented by the *View of Florence with a Chain* (fig. 24) and its close mate, a panel in a private English collection, both from the late quattrocento. See Hind, 1938, I, no. B. III, 18 (pp. 145–146); Ettlinger, 1952, passim.

is represented more or less as it actually appeared to the viewer. And, although for the first time the city itself is the full subject of the view, it nonetheless has a rich political content, which is conveyed through the same means that had been used for the older category.

Like Gozzoli, the artist has represented each important building not only as it appeared to the viewer but also as a representative of its appropriate figurative type. This is especially conspicuous in his treatment of the Palazzo dei Conservatori and the Palazzo Venezia. He has shown some buildings in a size that is quite appropriate for their political importance but that is quite out of proportion to spatial verisimilitude—the Palazzo dei Conservatori, Palazzo Venezia, and Vatican Palace, for example—and he has emphasized those areas and spaces that were most important in the political conception of the city—the piazza and complex at St. Peter's, the via dei Coronari, the area around the Capitol and the Palazzo Venezia, the complex of the Ponte and Castel Sant'Angelo, and the gateway and section of walls at the very front of the view. Massive ancient monuments continue to attest to the valor of ancient Romans, but clearly Rome is now given order through the activities of Romans on the Capitol, in the palaces of important ecclesiastics, and, most importantly, in the Borgo. Interestingly, the Lateran is isolated from the fabric of the city and is more pertinent to antiquity than it is to modern Rome.[31] Although the visual information that the Mantua view reveals about precise topographic positions and the condition and appearance of individual buildings is inaccurate, this is the most faithful representation of the city of Rome as planned and visualized by Nicholas V.

Gozzoli and the artist of the Mantua view's prototype could represent Rome with clarity because Nicholas had conceived his project with clarity. The pope had understood the city as a whole that was to be rebuilt physically and politically (or institutionally) so that the citizens could act to make order in it. The physical rebuilding would allow the political organization to be clear to the perceptive visitor. None of the individual building projects the pope sponsored was designed as an isolated unit; each was designed and built as a part of a larger whole, although each was complete in itself.[32] And each of the building projects related directly to the larger program for government that Nicholas had conceived for the city of Rome and for the Church.

One group of buildings that the pope built, a group that is conspicuous both among the other buildings in Rome and in the views that show his conception of the city, was particularly important to the Romans. This group defined where justice was located in Rome. Nicholas rebuilt these areas. He made a clear demarcation between the area under the jurisdiction of the commune and the one that was under the direct sway of the pope. For the commune he supported a project for rehousing the government on the Capitol, which was its traditional and appropriate location. In antiquity the hill had been considered the *caput et umbilicus mundi*. From Ottonian times onward, it represented Rome. After 1144 it became the site of the renewed communal government of the city. Cola di Rienzo had used it as his base when he attempted to refound the Roman Republic, and Petrarch arranged to have himself made poet laureate there. In his *Trionfi*, the procession begins at the Capitol, and

[31]In front of the Lateran is the ancient equestrian monument with the legend, "Haec aenea equestris statua M. Aurelii Antonini Severi aut Septimii Severi nunc posita est Capitolia." It is, however, unclear whether or not the legend is a later addition to the Mantua example; therefore, the legend is not useful for dating it or the prototype. Frutaz, 1962, I, pp. 152–154, transcribes and locates the various inscriptions.

[32]The exception was the amelioration of the Ponte Sant'Angelo with the two commemorative chapels.

it was from the Capitol that the early humanists contemplated the evidence of fortune's operations in the affairs of men and of states attached to earthly fame.

Before 1447 the communal government had at its disposal a variety of buildings on the Capitol. Some apparently ramshackle ones were scattered around the hill within a legally prescribed sanctuary zone.[33] The Church of the Aracoeli was then, as it still is, the largest building on the Capitol. It seems to have had no special relationship to the communal government until after the quattrocento, except that its location made it convenient to the government. At times it was used as an assembly hall; justice was sometimes administered by the senator seated at the side entrance that looked toward the Palazzo del Senatore, and some of the guilds' tribunals were allowed to meet in the cloister.[34] The main seat of government was the Palazzo del Senatore. The building extant in 1447 had been built during the pontificate of Boniface VIII on the foundations of the Tabularium, the ancient Roman archives building, and on the remains of a twelfth-century structure (fig. 35).[35] It was well designed and equipped for the many functions that it had to serve. On its elevated ground floor was an open loggia where minor cases were adjudicated and where a prominent inscription explained that this was a place for executing sentences of justice.[36] The loggia was reached by a ramp, next to which was placed an ancient statue of a lion devouring a horse, a figure that visually corroborated the inscription's statement. The lion also identified this as a *ringhiera*, or place for announcing capital sentences, and as the rostrum for those in authority at public assemblies held in the area in front of the building.[37] The next floor was a council hall with an open arcade facing the open area; in the hall the senator presided over the meetings of the communal government. On the *piano superiore*, a minor floor above the *piano nobile*, were offices used by the organs of government that existed at one time or another—guilds, *banderesi*, *conservatori*, magistrates, etc. The bureaucratic staff and prisons were located behind the palace in older, makeshift structures built into the ruins of the ancient Tabularium. The palace turned its back to the ancient Forum and faced northwest toward inhabited Rome and in the direction of the Borgo. It was long, high, and shallow, and was given greater authority by towers of unequal size on the ends of the building. The larger one nearer the Aracoeli held the bell that the commune had captured in 1200 in a battle against Viterbo; it was rung to announce special occasions and to call the citizens to the Capitol for public assemblies.[38]

No substantial alterations were made to the fabric of the building during the fourteenth century, despite the battering it took whenever there was a violent change of government. Cola di Rienzo had filled in the loggia and the openings on the next two floors with temporary construction to protect the authority of his government. Earlier, he had had the building frescoed with scenes of the deprivations of the Romans and the warning that, if injustice continued, Rome would follow Babylon,

---

[33]For the sanctuary zone, see Re, 1882, pp. 25–34; Pietrangeli, 1948; Martini, 1965; and Siebenhüner, 1954, who gives a tentative reconstruction, fig. 6.

[34]Re, 1882, pp. 19–21; Colasanti, n.d., pp. 6, 12; and Cellini, 1955, p. 222.

[35]Pietrangeli, 1960, with its bibliography is basic; see also idem, 1964; Paul, 1963, pp. 253–260. Recent investigations have shown Siebenhüner's assertion (1954, p. 26) that the building of ca. 1300 had four wings around a court, with a tower at each corner, to be unfounded.

[36]For the inscription, see Pietrangeli, 1960, appendix.

[37]For the area, see Lavagnino, 1941, p. 106; corrected and largely superseded by Pietrangeli, 1960, p. 4. It was also known as the *parlatorio* and as the *luogo del leone*. See also Cecchelli, 1944, pp. 224–225; Marchini, 1962, pp. 53 f. The sculpture group is now in a garden within the Capitoline Museum.

[38]Pietrangeli, 1957, passim, for the bell.

Troy, Carthage, and Jerusalem into oblivion.[39]   The frescoes quickly disappeared, and during the next decades the enclosures and the fabric itself were damaged in the numerous political upheavals. Boniface IX (1389–1404) strengthened the flank on the right, away from the Aracoeli, by enlarging the tower and inserting a special window from which the senator could supervise executions at the Tarpian rocks nearby. Martin V—who, like both recent Bonifaces, considered the senator to be his special officer in Rome—enlarged and strengthened the other tower. Both towers now had crenellations. In addition, the bell had been removed to a new campanile that had been erected behind the council hall and slightly off-center by either Boniface IX or Martin.[40]

In this form the Palazzo del Senatore survived in 1447, when it was an unkempt building, the strongest visual forms of which were the towers, the ramp with the *ringhiera* and its lion, and a façade that was still apparently patchwork construction obscuring Boniface VIII's fabric. The form of the block between the towers had probably originally been built to evoke the *palazzo del comune* type in Lazio, or, more likely, that of the north Italian *palazzo della ragione*,[41] but by the mid quattrocento the building was in such a serious state of disrepair that its typology would not have been obvious. It seems instead to have been considered as little more than a building constantly in need of repair, as the Romans must have made clear to Eugenius's agents during the meetings in the 1440s. Its most recent additions seem to have been the painted arms of Cardinal Scarampo, *camerarius* from 1440 to 1465, and of Giovanni Filingeri, senator in 1446–47, perhaps joined by those of Eugenius, placed above those of the thirteen *rioni* and a number of others now unrecognizable. They decorated the area just to the right of the principal entrance.[42] Perhaps they were placed there to commemorate the concordat of August 30, 1446, but there was nothing else about the palazzo that would have indicated in visual form anything about the arrangements established then.

In the first year of his pontificate, Nicholas initiated an extensive rebuilding of the Capitol, through which he sought to make visible the relationship of the commune to the papacy that he had established by the bull of May 1, 1447.[43] In his new buildings he employed a set of architectural elements that he used elsewhere in his program to enclose spaces that served the same or related functions and that derived from standard and probably well-known sources. Through using elements consistently, he produced buildings that revealed the relationship between the physical facilities of Rome and his program for papal government. The way he used these elements parallels the purpose Alberti defined for ornament and the role artists gave figurative representation of buildings in the older category of views. It is clear here, as well as

[39]*Vita di Cola*, 1928, pp. 6–8 (book I, chapter 2). Paul, 1963, p. 258, suggests that the ramp dates from 1348.

[40]Paul, 1963, p. 259, suggests that the campanile is by Nicholas V. See, however, Pietrangeli, 1964, p. 197; Amadei, 1969, pp. 99–101.

[41]The former possibility is suggested by the similarity to the remains of the Palazzo del Comune in Corneto (Tarquinia) and the less similar but related palaces in Anagni, as well as in Fabriano, all from the mid thirteenth century. For these, see Paul, 1963, pp. 87, 193–194, 206–207. The latter was suggested by Siebenhüner, 1954, p. 26. It should be noted that the latter type, which may earlier have been related to the former type, was still being evoked in the quattrocento to house communal governments in the north, as in Vicenza's *palazzo* built between 1444 and 1460 by Domenico da Venezia, in imitation of that in Padua from the same period as Boniface VIII's Palazzo del Senatore. For Vicenza, see Barbieri, 1970, pp. 25–30.

[42]Pietrangeli, 1960, pp. 7 f.

[43]Payments in Müntz, *ACP*, I, pp. 146–150, while far from complete, show that work was underway by late 1447.

elsewhere among his buildings, that Nicholas was more concerned with emphasizing what Alberti called the quality of a building than he was with producing coherent architectural designs.

He brought about a major change in the quality and serviceability of the Palazzo del Senatore by extremely simple means (fig. 36). On the ground floor of the wall that faced the piazza on the Capitol he replaced Cola's temporary enclosures and later repairs with a blank wall. Above that, across the next floor, he walled up every other arched opening, and in the others he inserted large, square-crossed windows. This now became the indisputable *piano nobile*. Above it, he added a series of smaller windows opening into the upper hall and chambers, which were now made into the residence of the senator. The two rows of windows appear to have been in line with one another and in an even rhythm across the façade, as were the arched openings into which they had been inserted. He left the two towers and the ramp next to the lion untouched; one side of the ramp led directly to the ground floor, and the other went on to the main hall behind the new square-crossed windows. From the piazza the building now appeared to have an organized facade with regular windows on the *piano nobile*, with an easy entrance to the interior, and with a *ringhiera*, all enclosed within two towers. The effect of the design was totally to replace Boniface's building, with its emphasis on the two stories of loggias, by a building whose principal feature was a council hall on a dominant *piano nobile*.

Nicholas also began an important addition to the building (figs. 37,38). At the back, he walled up the portico in the Tabularium overlooking the Forum,[44] and at each end of the side facing the Forum he began a new tower. He completed one tower, which rose to the height of those in front, and terminated it in crenellations; at its base it stood away from the Tabularium. It was built of brown tufa blocks, was unbroken by mouldings, and had battered surfaces, and its corners were strengthened by grey peperino quoins. The other tower remained incomplete; it was begun with the same manner of construction, and its battered rise is visible up to the point at which it merges with the walls of the palace, which date from the sixteenth and seventeenth centuries and which begin from the top of the Tabularium's walls. Even without attaining its full height, Nicholas's tower would have projected above any contiguous walls in the quattrocento. On the flank of the building the tower projects out from the face of the wall, but at the back the surface of its foundations is flush with the face of the Tabularium. This seems not to be in accordance with Nicholas's desire: the foundations end on what would appear to be unstable material with even less promising ground beyond,[45] so apparently structural problems interfered with his plan. Even though it is flush and now rather inconspicuous, the truncated tower would have been highly visible in the quattrocento, and in later views of Rome it is shown as if it were completed (figs. 39,40).[46] These towers, both firmly identified with Nicholas by his coat of arms, converted the shallow, long palace of the four-

[44] Two of his *stemme* are still visible; three arches were reopened in 1939. See Colini, 1939, p. 201; Nash, 1961, II, p. 902.

[45] This side of the Tabularium is highly irregular; see Delbrück, 1907, pp. 23–46; Colini, 1942, pp. 5–6. The quattrocento ground level is difficult to ascertain; see *Roma cento anni fa*, 1970, pls. 21 and 24; also Egger, 1932, II, pls. 12, 13, 14, and 21.

[46] See the engraving dated 1577, by Antonio Lafreri after Etienne DuPérac, London, British Museum Map Room (Frutaz, 1962, no. CXXVII; here, fig. 39), and a panoramic view from about 1535, by Anonymous A copying Marten van Heemskerck (Egger, 1932, II, pl. 106; here, fig. 40). See also another view, by Hendrik von Cleve from 1550 (Egger, 1932, II, pl. 107). It should be remarked that only one tower at a time is mentioned by Müntz, *ACP*, I, p. 150, which does not preclude their having been undertaken sequentially rather than concurrently. The last payment is 9 March 1453, the general time when construction on most of the program seems to have terminated.

teenth century into a square building with an inner court, a tower at each corner, and a slim campanile rising somewhere near the center.

To the right of the Palazzo del Senatore, across the piazza from the Aracoeli, Nicholas built a new palace for the *conservatori* (figs. 36,41). There may have been a building there earlier, and its foundations—or some ancient remains—may have dictated or suggested the oblique angle it made to the Palazzo del Senatore, but there was most probably little or nothing above ground level to determine or influence the form given the Palazzo dei Conservatori.[47] Its form was extremely simple. A loggia composed of twelve arches stretched across the entire ground-floor length of the building. Above it was the *piano nobile;* a row of six square-crossed windows opened into two rooms,[48] one large and lit by four windows, the other small and lit by two windows. The *piano nobile* was extended to the full length of the ground-floor loggia by inserting a room at either end. These rooms opened onto the piazza on the Capitol through double-arched loggias. The one toward the Palazzo del Senatore came to be called the Sala del Cantone, and the one opposite was called the Loggia della Madonna. Across the full length of the building was a low *piano superiore,* which opened to the piazza through small windows; guilds and magistrates had offices here, as well as in wings that projected back from the front of the building on each end. The wing with its façade facing out toward Rome had a *piano nobile* loggia composed of three arches.[49] The other wing contained the staircase leading to the upper floors. These wings enclosed a *cortile* that had a cistern in the center; part of the side toward Rome opened into rooms through an arcade. From it survive three slightly pointed brick arches carried by stout columns with rugged Ionic capitals. The *cortile* was accessible from a portal apparently centered inside the loggia, in disregard of its placement opposite a column rather than an arch. The portal may have opened into a barrel-vaulted *androne.*[50]

The Palazzo del Senatore was the more imposing of the two buildings, as was appropriate, because the senator was the representative of the commune and because he was responsible for administering the highest level of communal justice. This he did with reason or intellect, and he executed it with the sword or arms. Older elements in the palace, retained in Nicholas's rebuilding, made this conception of his office clear. At the entrance stood the *ringhiera,* where the senator announced sentences and from which he presided over assemblies of the people. Michelangelo would replace it with the baldachino in the center of the new stairs.[51] Next to it was the ramp that gave access to the major hall on the *piano nobile* and to the smaller hall next to the senator's apartments on the top floor; here reason concerning justice transpired. The ramp's direct penetration of the building showed how easy was the citizen's access to the representative of his commune. The senator also wielded the sword of the commune to protect justice and to execute judgments established through reason; it was sheathed when not needed. This concept was shown to the senator in a visual figure during the ceremonies of his installation. On the landing of the ramp just outside the council hall was a painting showing a lion lying with one

[47]For the site's desolation see Re, 1882, p. 22, and Pietrangeli, 1964, p. 198, whose description of Nicholas's Palazzo dei Conservatori is most complete, correcting the earlier statements about an existing building made by, for example, Siebenhüner, 1954, pp. 34–35, and Paul, 1963, p. 259. For Giovanni Rucellai's statement about the Capitol, see below, Epilogue.

[48]Hermanin, 1948, p. 22, citing no evidence, states that the windows date from the time of Sixtus IV, which seems highly unlikely.

[49]These are visible, although walled up, in the present Sala dei Fasti. See also fig. 36.

[50]For this detail, see the analogy between this building and its copy mentioned below, p. 99.

[51]The new stairs are visible in fig. 36.

eye closed and the other trained on a puppy asleep between his paws. The senator was told that he must be like that lion when the people are as attentive to vice as the puppy is when asleep; he was then taken to the *ringhiera* and shown the lion devouring the unreined horse and told that when there was vice to be devoured by virtue, he must imitate this lion.[52]

The Romans could, through the architectural design of Nicholas's building, see the same two points made in architecture. Two familiar motifs constitute the building's design. One is the great council hall where reason prevailed. It lay behind the row of square-crossed windows on the *piano nobile* that dominates the façade. Wrapped around the hall, and protecting it as the sword protects reason, is another familiar motif, that of the *castello*, a square block with a crenellated tower rising at each corner. These two motifs, which determine the visual appearance of the building, would have been familiar to a quattrocento visitor and would have carried with them a clear meaning.

The visitor would have known the meaning through the use of these motifs in particular contexts. The source for the *castello* motif is difficult to locate with precision.[53] It may have been in the type of palace built in Lazio during the middle ages to house the militant arm of communal governments.[54] More likely, it derives from the type of fortress that dukes had been building for generations, most recently and most competently in north Italian cities since the fourteenth century (fig. 42). The *castelli* in Pavia (1360s), Milan (1360s), Ferrara (1385), and Mantua (1395)[55] each had a square plan and a stout, usually crenellated tower at each corner.[56] This would be an appropriate source for the Capitol, because the office of the senator of Rome had about the same relationship to the communal government as did that of a duke to the city in which he had his ducal seat. A duke was a legitimate representative of a city if he had a patent from the emperor or from his feudal superior, as well as the approbation of the people; the patent was given, in theory, only if he were distinguished in military valor. This was quite different from the situation in central Italian republican communes, where the construction of the *palazzo pubblico* or of the *palazzo del podestà* was often more sophisticated, but the functions of the officers housed in the buildings were much less analogous. In Rome the senator officially represented his city, as did a duke in a duchy; he was his city's ceremonial embodiment. The official duties handled by a duke or the senator were allocated in a different manner in a republican commune, where there was neither duke nor senator. The official representative of a republic was an elected *gonfaloniere della giustizia* (literally, the man who carries the flag of justice), but he had few real powers in executing justice. In a republic, a

[52]Pietrangeli, 1960, p. 13; Cecchelli, 1944, pp. 224–225. On p. 225 the epigram accompanying the lion and puppy is given: *Iratus recole quod nobilis ira leonis / In sibi prostratos se negat esse feram.* It appears, along with a variant form of the image, in the copy of the Marcanova manuscript in the Biblioteca Estense in Modena, reproduced in Huelsen, 1907, fig. 19, p. 20.

[53]A reference to the council-hall motif and its other appearances will be given below, chapter 7.

[54]See, for example, the collection of disparate elements including a tower at each corner, one of which still has crenellations, that constitutes the remains of the Palazzo dei Priori in Tarquinia (Corneto), which is a few blocks away from the Palazzo del Comune. For the variety of names given communal palaces, see Paul, 1963, pp. 41–42.

[55]It has recently been suggested that the Castel di San Giorgio in Mantua may date from the 1450s and be the work of Luciano Laurana (Saalman, 1971, p. 51, n. 15); if this is so, the point being developed here gains strength, because it would mean that the formal tradition was still very much alive then.

[56]Compare and contrast the remarks on a similar formal motif by Hersey, 1969, pp. 68 ff.; see also Zippel, 1907, fig. 3, for the papal *castello* of John XXII at Sargue from 1320, which he calls the earliest example. See also Hersey, 1969, fig. 94, for the thirteenth- and fourteenth-century Castello di Quattro Torri near Siena.

podestà executed justice as a duke usually did and as the Roman senator was charged to do. Like the senator in Rome, a *podestà* was a foreigner hired for a short term. Unlike a duke, the senator, or a republican *gonfaloniere della giustizia*, he was not the ceremonial representative of the commune that employed him. Thus, there was no talk of the *podestà*'s being the father or spouse of the republic, as was said of a duke and his duchy and of the senator and Rome.[57] Thus, the appropriate typological source for the Palazzo del Senatore was a ducal *castello*, not a republican *palazzo pubblico* or *palazzo del podestà*.

The senator was only one official in Rome, and he was a partner in government with the democratically selected Roman *conservatori*. The latter enjoyed a more intimate contact with their fellow citizens—who, like the *conservatori*, remained unarmed. This was revealed in the dominating and close relationship the Palazzo del Senatore had to the Palazzo dei Conservatori and by the design of the new palace. The elements from which the latter was composed were carefully selected to convey a particular meaning. The loggia was borrowed from the ground floor of Boniface's Palazzo del Senatore, where it had been the setting for minor adjudications. There, and in the chambers opening onto it in Nicholas's palace, one would have found representatives of the people, such as the street magistrates and members of the guilds' tribunals, arbitrating disputes among the citizens.[58] The two sets of square-crossed windows opening into the large and small council halls on the *piano nobile* exposed the role of the *conservatori* in acting as the *giunta* of the government. The *conservatori*, like the senator, had a responsibility to deliberate with reason, but their deliberations were conducted at a less austere level than that which prevailed in the Palazzo del Senatore. Nevertheless, their deliberations were important for the order of the commune.

Nicholas's buildings made the Capitol a positive space in the city of Rome. By building conspicuous monuments that described the government of the commune as it had been established in 1363 and as Nicholas had renewed it, the pope allowed the Capitol to be a piazza as Petrus Berchorius had described piazzas: "Since piazzas are areas in villages or cities, empty of houses or other such things and of obstructions, arranged for the purpose of providing space or set up for meetings of men, it should be remarked that in general through piazzas the condition of man in this world can be discovered."[59] The condition in this world revealed by the Capitol was the political status of the citizens of Rome acting in the city to establish order.

The buildings were appropriate settings for the citizens' actions—or, at least, they had appropriate architectural motifs that conveyed meanings and that could be considered analogous to Alberti's ornaments. But they were not buildings that satisfied all of Alberti's criteria for beauty; they were hardly coherent, finished, sophisticated architectural designs. This is suggested by the meager visual evidence that survives to give some indication of their appearance; they leave much to be desired when compared to contemporaneous buildings in central Italy—for example, the Palazzo Medici or Palazzo Rucellai in Florence, or the Palazzo Comunale in Montepulciano. There are several possible reasons for the Capitol buildings' seemingly dishevelled

[57]Cardinals were also considered fathers and spouses of Rome. See Biondo, 1953, III, lxxxviii, p. 318, and Signorili, 1953, pp. 162–165.
[58]See Re, 1882; Pietrangeli, 1948, appendix I; idem, 1964, p. 198; Martini, 1965, pp. 89 f. For the loggia's similarity to what Alberti suggested on ancient precedent for just such a function, see *De re aed.*, VIII, viii; for other remarks concerning loggias, see below, chapter 7.
[59]Quoted in Heckscher, 1955, n. 67. Contrast the purely figurative interpretation given piazzas in *De claustro animae*, IV, xiv–xvi (cols. 1150–1153, for Jerusalem) and IV, xxvii (col. 1166, for Heavenly Jerusalem).

aspect. One is that their purely visual appearance is best known through sixteenth-century sources. By that time they were nearly a century old and had both been altered and added onto; moreover, they were depicted by men who had little respect for the formal intentions of mid-quattrocento builders. These buildings would have represented a rather low level of architectural achievement when compared with the level of three-dimensional structural integration and classical understanding that had been demonstrated by later architects, such as Francesco di Giorgio, Bramante, the Sangallos, and Michelangelo. They were recorded by draftsmen who saw their dilapidation rather than their original contributions to solving problems that at the time had been exciting but that by then were outmoded and alien. Another reason they appear in this form is that they apparently were haphazard compared to sixteenth-century standards of construction. This could have been because Nicholas was unwilling to commit sufficient resources to their construction, or because the level of the building trades in Rome at the time was rather low, or because they did not receive the continuous attention of a skilled architect.

But despite their failure from the point of view of later standards of architectural design, they were quite successful when considered from another viewpoint. Seemingly even less sophisticated than the patched-up Palazzo del Senatore, the Palazzo dei Conservatori served as the prototype for town halls built in the Patrimonium of Peter, where there were states that the pope governed and that Nicholas tried to govern with the same principles he implemented when he revised Rome's legal position (figs. 43,44). The rebuilding of the Palazzo Comunale in Viterbo (fig. 43), which began in 1448 and was still underway after 1503, drew on the major motifs of the palace in Rome: the loggia with offices opening onto it and the *piano nobile* council area with square-crossed windows.[60] The façade bears the arms of Sixtus IV, whose name appears in each of the windows. The only difference between this building and its prototype is its greater coherence as an architectural design, a difference that could have been introduced because it was built later and because its designer could copy and clarify a prototype, rather than having to undertake the more difficult task of inventing one.[61] A much simpler and cruder reference to the prototype in Rome was produced in the rebuilding of the Palazzo Comunale in Narni (fig. 44), probably in the years immediately after the Roman building was finished. The collection of older buildings out of which the palazzo had been made was given a formal unity by inserting a more or less regular row of six square-crossed windows across its front.[62] The most important use of both of the Capitoline buildings as prototypes, however, was on the Capitol itself; Michelangelo only altered and did not efface any of the major motifs of the two buildings. He simply revised the forms and subjected the entire arrangement to the demands of his incredibly sophisticated system of architec-

[60] For the older building and the date 1448, see Paul, 1963, pp. 275–276.

[61] The formal relationship between the two buildings was first pointed out by Zippel, 1907, pp. 135–136. The Viterbese palace also seems to be similar in the disposition of other elements. Along the right side of the *cortile* is a series of arches (since rebuilt), which may have opened into communal offices; the entrance to the halls on the *piano nobile* is gained by a staircase on the left, although the stairs first run parallel to the length of the building and then turn back to the front. (The lintel at the head of the stairs is inscribed by Julius II.) These similarities could be as much the result of the topography of the site as the product of conscious copying of the prototype, however. But this does not seem to be the case with the expected location of the chapel on the *piano nobile*, which may again reflect the prototype on the Capitol. In Viterbo, a barrel-vaulted *androne* leads from the portal (which bears Sixtus IV's arms) to the courtyard, which suggests a similar arrangement for the entrance to Nicholas's Roman building.

[62] For the earlier state of the building, see Paul, 1963, pp. 236–237. Paul's reference to Rossellino as the architect is based on the completely spurious reference in Vasari, drawn from Manetti, in the life of Rossellino (Vasari, III, p. 99).

tural design. Perhaps the sanction of tradition stretching back to Nicholas's build-ings helped assure the eventual faithful execution of Michelangelo's design.

The buildings on the Capitol were only part of Nicholas's project for Rome, and they were only two of the three buildings that defined the structure of justice in the city. Just as the Palazzo del Senatore dominates the Palazzo dei Conservatori because its level of justice is higher, so too does the Castel Sant'Angelo dominate the Palazzo del Senatore, a building to which it is both formally and programmatically related. During the same early years in which Nicholas sponsored the work on the Capitol, he had another project underway at the Castel Sant'Angelo. The building had a rich and important history that was well known during the quattrocento.   Early in the Christian empire, Hadrian's mausoleum had been converted to a defensive position. In 590 Gregory the Great and the people of Rome saw a vision of the Archangel Michael atop the structure; later, a stone effigy of the angel was placed there.   During a procession in 1348, pleading for the lifting of the plague, the people of Rome saw the angel sheath his sword as he had in 590 to indicate once again that the end of their tribulation was near. From this tradition the building gradually came to be called the Castel Sant'Angelo, and the single bridge connecting the Borgo to Rome that lay at its foot took on the name Ponte Sant'Angelo.[63] Although the figure of St. Michael had been destroyed in 1379, the tradition of the miracle was alive during the quattrocento. Several representations of the legend of St. Gregory show the pro-cession, bridge, *castello,*and angel.[64] Each shows the *castello* in a way that evokes its ancient form, as Filarete had on his doors, but Filarete had naturally not included the angel (fig. 3).

In rebuilding the Castel Sant'Angelo, Nicholas satisfied both practical and figura-tive ends in an economic manner. Originally the structure had a square base inside of which rose a circular core with a square tower projecting from its top (fig. 45). Nicholas simply built a low, round, defensive tower at each corner of the base and increased the height of the square top of the central tower, adding a new bronze and wood statue of St. Michael.[65]   Here Nicholas had reproduced the *castello* type of a square building with a tower at each corner, although it now protected not the senator but the papal castellan. Nearly a century of Roman history had shown the strategic importance of the Castel Sant'Angelo; each pope entrusted it to his most faithful officer, the cardinals considered it their last redoubt during a papal inter-regnum, and the people of Rome weighed its possible role in any turmoil they might plan or undertake.   The Borgo was historically, politically, physically, and now, through Nicholas's construction, visually independent from and distinct from the city of Rome, as it had been in the Sigismund panel in Filarete's doors (figs. 6, 7). By re-building the Castel Sant'Angelo as a *castello* related to the one on the Capitol, Nicholas made it clear that just as the *castello* on the Capitol protected the justice dis-

[63]Borgatti, 1931, p. 119; Weil, 1968, pp. 9 ff., 116.

[64]See, for example, a predella in the Louvre (RF 672) by Giovanni di Paolo and another from Tuscany (no. 147 in the Museo Nazionale, Villa Guigi, Lucca) by Priam della Quercia. There is also a represen-tation prominent in the center of the frieze of a sacrament ciborium from Andrea Bregno's shop now in the Salviati Chapel, S. Gregorio Magno, Rome, dated 1469. See also Borgatti, 1931, pp. 204 ff.

[65]Only three of the low towers were completed; work was never begun on the fourth, which was the least important of the four because it lay within the Borgo fortifications. Each of the four corners re-ceived enlarged and slightly lower corner towers during the pontificate of Alexander VI; see Müntz, *ACP,* I, pp. 151–154, which shows that the main activity was between 1447 and 1453; Borgatti, 1931, pp. 157–163. Manetti, *RIS,* edition in Magnuson, 1958, appendix, sentence 45, mentions four corner towers. Included in the rebuilding, but not visible from outside, was at least one square-crossed win-dow. This element appears in Polani's 1459 view of Rome, fig. 22.

pensed by the senator, so too did the Castel Sant'Angelo protect the justice dispensed by the pope.

That it was a different form of justice was indicated by the difference between the two structures' crowning elements. The bell in the campanile on the Capitol called citizens to capital executions of the body; the angel Nicholas replaced atop the Castel Sant'Angelo wielded a sword that would be used at the Last Judgment affecting the soul.

The views of Rome produced after Nicholas's death use these buildings to reveal his program for governing Rome. The Mantua view presented it in detail, as well as in its broader character (figs. 34,75). The Castel Sant'Angelo is a conspicuous *castello* protecting the Borgo, and the angel on top is shown quite out of scale, as is the campanile at the Palazzo del Senatore. The towers of the *castello* motif at the Capitol are not shown, however, although the Palazzo dei Conservatori is conspicuous. This could represent the late date of the copy or even of the prototype, because as the century progressed, the trappings of communal independence remained intact, but the reality of power on the Capitol gradually flowed elsewhere. If a motif were to be neglected, it would be that of the *castello* towers of the Palazzo del Senatore, which indicated power. Significantly, the palace of Cardinal Barbo, later Paul II, is more prominent than the Capitol, and it is shown as a representative of a distinctive palace type. It is not only to the Borgo that the power gradually flowed but also to the cardinals' seats throughout Rome. Biondo had put it well when he said that senators and cardinals are equal and next to the pope.

Gozzoli's view also represents Nicholas's conception; indeed, it is even clearer in its presentation of the political structure than is the visually more sophisticated view in Mantua (fig. 33). Six structures dominate the view: the Column of Antoninus, the Pantheon, the Aracoeli, the Palazzo del Senatore, the Castel Sant'Angelo, and the Vatican complex, made up of St. Peter's and the Vatican Palace. The first two represent ancient *virtù*. The Aracoeli stands as a conspicuous Christian basilica used by the modern Christian Romans, who no longer worship pagan gods. The other three, which dominate most of the view, represent the present means by which order is achieved in Rome. The pope resides in the Vatican, protected by the Castel Sant' Angelo, which sharply divides Rome from the head of the Church; the angel on top of the *castello* calls Christians to the Last Judgment. It is juxtaposed with the campanile on the Capitol, which rises out of a building in which the *castello* towers, entrance, and council-hall windows are conspicuous.[66] Gozzoli, a veteran of the Medici palace environment in Florence, did not show the Palazzo dei Conservatori; perhaps he did not have a sketch of it handy, or perhaps he let the Palazzo del Senatore stand for communal government and therefore terminated its campanile with a pyramid rather than with a square top, thus evoking the distinctive campanile rising from the Palazzo Pubblico in Florence.[67] In a quite abbreviated way Gozzoli convincingly represented a distinctive characteristic of the Rome of Nicholas V. His view shows that the government of the city of Rome had been given autonomy and that its officers had been housed in conspicuous buildings, which added dignity to the city and allowed the Romans to act for their own virtue. The pope, meanwhile, resided in the Borgo, where he was able to devote his full attention to governing the Church. The angel at his Borgo *castello* reminded all that his program emphasized protecting the sacraments, and that only through the sacraments would actions in the world result in the enjoyment of the full pleasures of paradise.

[66]The tower on the left of the Palazzo del Senatore could be a baron's tower in Rome, rather than the Tower of Martin V; if so, the argument is not substantially altered.

[67]Lazzaroni, 1883, p. 9, commented on the similarity of the campanili.

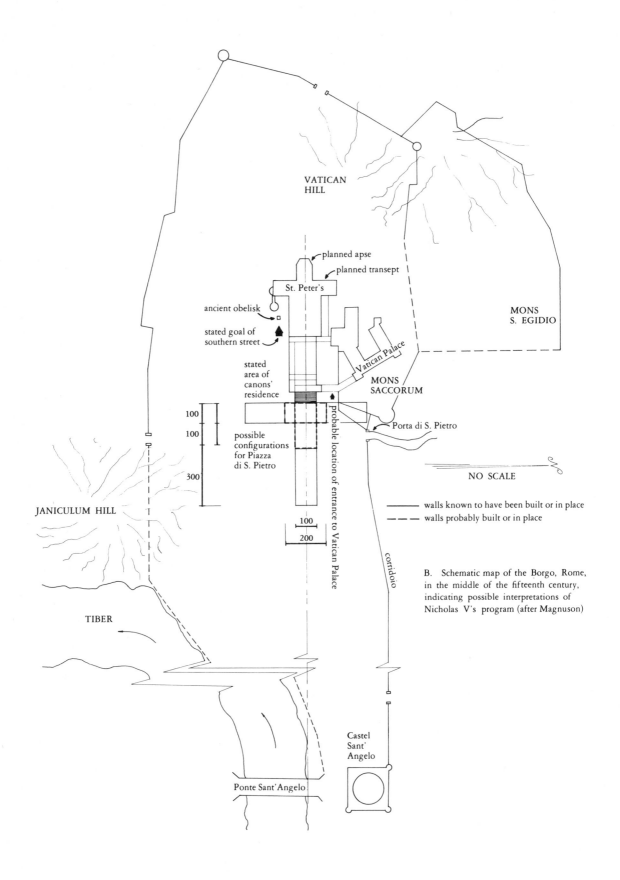

VATICAN
HILL

MONS
S. EGIDIO

planned apse

planned transept

St. Peter's

ancient obelisk

stated goal of
southern street

Vatican Palace

stated
area of
canons'
residence

MONS
SACCORUM

100

100

300

possible
configurations
for Piazza
di S. Pietro

probable location of entrance to Vatican Palace

Porta di S. Pietro

NO SCALE

JANICULUM HILL

100

200

walls known to have been built or in place

walls probably built or in place

corridoio

B. Schematic map of the Borgo, Rome,
in the middle of the fifteenth century,
indicating possible interpretations of
Nicholas V's program (after Magnuson)

TIBER

Castel
Sant'
Angelo

Ponte Sant'Angelo

6 Doctrine in the Borgo and at the Basilica

The public buildings on the Capitol were among those that demonstrated in actual architectural form the role of the pope in Rome and in the Church. The Capitol, which had long been the seat of the communal government, now had buildings coordinated with others that as a group visually defined the structure of government in Rome. This structure would remain intact for some time; although it was constantly subjected to minor revisions, what Nicholas first instituted in architecture survives even today. The Capitol still stands for Rome. The Ponte and Castel Sant'Angelo still define a separation between Rome and the Borgo. The Borgo is still more a suburb to the Vatican complex than it is a part of Rome. And St. Peter's and the Vatican Palace still dominate Rome and still constitute the seat of the head of the Church.

Nicholas's conception was the determining factor in all subsequent physical development in Rome. Despite minor tinkering with his proposals, the efforts at rebuilding Rome made by later popes followed Nicholas's sketch. The tinkering resulted both from an increased scale of building operations as time went on and from slight alterations in the conception of the papacy. Thus, under later popes and following the definitions of doctrine laid down at Trent, the divine clemency signified by St. Peter's was also made evident at the other major basilicas, and the major churches were tied together by a network of streets that spread throughout and beyond the city; but at the same time construction at St. Peter's was again taken up and the Vatican Palace was expanded. Similarly, under later popes the importance of Rome as the seat of the papacy was increased, at the expense of Rome considered as the home of its citizens; thus, the buildings at the Vatican became ever more important, while the Capitoline project of Michelangelo was brought to completion only very slowly. In the larger framework of the conception of the city of Rome, however, these alterations of Nicholas's project were inconsequential. Rome gradually did acquire a semblance of the physical structure he had envisaged for it.

The buildings Nicholas built would hardly have inspired his successors to implement his building program. Almost none of the most bulky and substantial physical fabric he hoped to raise ever got above ground level. The most complete element of his project was on the Capitol, and the two buildings there were rather ramshackle. They were also among the less important parts of his building program. They had apparently not been given the highest priority when funds, materials, energy, or talent were distributed. Nonetheless, perhaps because less was expected of them and because they were simpler and smaller, they were useful and serviceable in the form he gave them. They survived without major alteration until their reconstruction was begun more than a century later. Nicholas had made them conspicuous visual elements in the fabric of the city of Rome, and in that form they exerted their impact on other buildings, on the views made of the city, and on future projects on the Capitol.

The other and more important parts of the project were far less complete. They were more important because they represented higher levels in the hierarchy of the building program, and for that reason more would have been expected of them. They were to be bigger, they were to be built of more dignified materials, and they were to demonstrate a higher level of design competence. They required more time and money than the public, profane buildings on the Capitol, and they were in a less complete state at Nicholas's death in 1455. Still, even though less of each of them had actually been built, these buildings had a profound impact on future conceptions of the papacy and its buildings and on the many related ideas Nicholas's program had introduced.

The explanation of how a building project that was so incomplete could exert such a great influence on future practice must be that something other than the buildings conveyed the conceptual and practical intentions they had been planned to perpetuate. A person informed of the project as a part of Nicholas's comprehensive program for government could convey the idea for a time, but Petrarch's statement, "When the proof of our actions is gone, only the evidence of our speech will remain," is a good reminder that a written description could carry into posterity what unbuilt buildings and fond memories could not.

Giannozzo Manetti provided such a description. In the second book of his *Life of Nicholas* the secretary gave a lengthy and detailed report of the building program, and he claimed that he was reporting the pope's intentions.[1] Manetti's description has been handled with varying degrees of caution by art historians, for several reasons. His architectural terminology is vague; his seemingly precise information turns out to be inaccurate when compared to what is known from other sources, and it often cannot be coordinated with what was possible; and he fails to distinguish between what was completed, what was begun, and what was apparently only intended.[2]

These reasons point to serious problems in handling the text, but they do not require censure for Manetti's efforts. He was a rhetorician, not a chronicler.[3] His terminology is vague, but his treatment of buildings as places designed to promote the program of government Nicholas undertook is quite clear, and this was what he was attempting to convey. His precision is often faulty, but some of these faults can be forgiven because he was operating with quattrocento criteria of accuracy and importance, and he was citing information for quattrocento purposes rather than for modern purposes; his text must be carefully interpreted to yield proper results. And in treating the extent of the project's execution with optimism, he was attempting to produce clear rhetoric. He was also indicating that what Nicholas planned would be built, because what Nicholas planned should be built; therefore, so far as Manetti was concerned, it had been built. Furthermore, at the moment he was writing, it would

---

[1] Manetti, *RIS*, cols. 929–940. An edition based on several additional texts appears in the appendix to Magnuson, 1958; each sentence there is numbered, and future citations to the description will be to its numbered sentences either in the text or in the notes. For a translation of part of the description, see Magnuson, 1954.

[2] Magnuson, 1958, pp. 59, 98–99, discusses the problem; see also pp. 66–67, and 163 ff. Also Urban, 1963, and Westfall, 1971, for additional observations on the interpretation of the text.

[3] For the remarks which follow concerning Manetti's way of operating, see Baxandall, 1971, which appeared too late to be incorporated into the present text. This study does not discuss Manetti or deal with architectural description, but it does provide an insight into the context in which Manetti operated.

not have been clear whether or not Nicholas's successor would continue the project.[4] Manetti's attitude here is similar to his failing elsewhere in the *Life* to attribute any of Nicholas's ideas to anyone other than the pope. Nicholas was head of a hierarchical structure, and what was done under him and for him was done by him. Manetti's description, when used with caution and when assessed and interpreted in the context of external material that allows some control to be brought to bear on it, is an invaluable source for understanding Nicholas's building project.

This is true for another reason as well. Manetti framed his description within the same context in which Nicholas had conceived it. It is a part of Manetti's *Life of Nicholas,* and it was a part of the program Nicholas had developed for governing the Church. This gives it a special significance, because through Manetti's report it is possible to approach the building program from Nicholas's point of view. An attiude similar to Manetti's had informed the observations of others who mentioned the project when reporting about Nicholas's pontificate. They, too, distorted their reports of actual events for purposes similar to Manetti's, and they will be discussed later.

The pope's secretary and others writing at the time fail to make specific reference to some of the building activity that Nicholas did undertake, activity that is documented and that is mentioned later by others. For example, payment records exist for Nicholas's work at Santa Maria Maggiore, S. Stefano Rotondo, and other churches,[5] and he promulgated some bulls from the former church, but only after his death did this work become prominent in his biography.[6] Important as both projects were for the development of construction in Rome, they were relatively unimportant from the point of view that is reported through the sources that give the best insight into Nicholas's conception of the city. That conception, and not all of the building activity or even the contribution of that activity to Renaissance architecture, is the concern here. Therefore, Manetti's report must occupy a central, but not exclusive, position in recovering Nicholas's project for rebuilding the city of Rome, and some of Nicholas's other undertakings may be ignored.

Manetti stated that the pope undertook the building program to make the city memorable and commendable; he attended, Manetti said, to the city's ornament, to the salubrity of its air, and to its ability to instill a sense of devotion (s. 13). The program included five elements that, Manetti makes clear, were considered to progress in a hierarchical order. They move from concern for the practical facilities of the city to a concerted effort at the Basilica of St. Peter, and they stress strength at one end of the scale and devotion at the other. In filling out his description with details, Manetti followed the pope's priorities. He mentioned only enough of the first few elements of the program to convey to the reader some sense of what they included, and he went into elaborate, seemingly hyperbolic detail when he reached the more important elements.

The first part of the project Manetti listed was the repair to public works and buildings throughout Rome that had collapsed and become disused through neglect (s. 14). This could refer to what the commune itself undertook with the administra-

[4]See the exhortation by Giuseppe Brippi to Calixtus III (Brippi, Ricc. Cod. 361, fols. 3ᵛ–4ʳ, 12ʳ⁻ᵛ), in which the old scribe tells Calixtus that to continue Nicholas's program of government and of building would serve his own purpose of waging war against the Turks. It is undated, but must be from the first months of Calixtus's pontificate. Brippi died in 1457 at age seventy-nine; Forcella, VII, p. 361, n. 734. See also Valla, *Oratio,* which Professor Charles Trinkaus kindly brought to my attention.

[5]Müntz, *ACP,* I, pp. 139 ff.; Magnuson, 1958, pp. 58, 224; Urban, 1961–62.

[6]See Platina, p. 424 (Life of Nicholas V).

tive latitude Nicholas had given it, which Manetti did not mention (except perhaps obliquely in his reference to healthy air). It could also refer to the fortifications around the city, which were the pope's responsibility and which Manetti does mention (s. 21). Manetti also stated that the pope had attempted to rebuild and to ameliorate a major portion of the city, apparently referring to the built-up area between the Ponte Sant'Angelo and the Colosseum and extending on into the empty stretches beyond.[7] Indeed, in 1447 and again in 1448, the pope granted building and legal privileges to those who would build in the depopulated area between the Colosseum and the Lateran, probably along the via Papalis, in the rione Monte.[8]

Manetti did not mention Nicholas's repairs to bridges and aqueducts,[9] or his construction of fountains in the city.[10] He was more concerned with those parts of the project that related directly and conspicuously to the major program, and therefore he moved on to the repairs Nicholas had made at the Ponte Sant'Angelo. One landing of the bridge was in Rome, the other in the Borgo, but at this point Manetti mentioned only the work Nicholas had undertaken on the Borgo side of the bridge, even though his subject was the Roman side of the Tiber. His purpose was to show that Nicholas's project included an element that affected both the Borgo and Rome; in another context he returned to this element.[11] It would have been more appropriate at this point to have mentioned the two commemorative chapels and the piazza S. Celso formed in coincidence with them, but because they were incidental to the pope's carefully planned project, Manetti passed over them in silence here; his only reference to them had been in the context of the Jubilee elsewhere in the *Life*.

The second element in Nicholas's project was to rebuild the forty station churches, which, according to Manetti, had been set aside as a special group by Gregory the Great.[12] Nicholas did actually undertake a great deal of work at these churches, as well as at the next group Manetti mentioned, the old and revered seven major and minor basilicas. Nicholas devoted special attention to these, Manetti explained; some were to be strengthened, some repaired, some ornamented, and some renovated in a marvelous way (ss. 27–29). These basilicas were the greatest and the most celebrated, he continued, but among them the principal, most marvelous, and most revered one was St. Peter's, the only one of the group Manetti named. This the pope would rebuild from the ground up, along with the palace that was contiguous to it (s. 30).

Manetti has now reached the upper level of the hierarchy, and he slows the pace of his description to reveal a greater breadth in the pope's plans. He carefully progresses through the Borgo, the third element and one filled with figurative significance, then to the Vatican Palace, the fourth element, and finally reaches the last point of the program in the Basilica of St. Peter (fig. 46).

---

[7] Manetti's topographical references are quite vague; s. 22.

[8] Pastor, 1949, p. 171. The precedents for this had been established in the Borgo by Martin V and Eugenius IV; see above, chapter 1, esp. note 47.

[9] See Müntz, *ACP*, I, pp. 156–159.

[10] In August, 1447, he paid for a new fountain at the Maddalena (Müntz, *ACP*, I, pp. 156–157). In 1453 he opened a new Fontana di Trevi at the outlet of the Aqua Vergine; it carried the inscription: NICOLAVS V PON MAX POST ILLVSTRATAM INSIGNIBVS MONVM VRBEM DVCTVM AQUAE VIRGINIS VET COL REST 1453. Tomei, 1942, p. 108, points out that this is the first new fountain and first repair to an aqueduct since antiquity.

[11] This reference is in ss. 23–26; see also below.

[12] Manetti, s. 15; see Magnuson, 1958, p. 58. Nicholas mentioned them himself in his testament; Manetti, *RIS*, col. 950.

It is extremely difficult to know what the actual condition of the Borgo was during the first half of the quattrocento, and therefore it is difficult to know what actual, physical effect Nicholas's program had on it. Both Martin V, in 1421, and Eugenius IV, in 1437, had attempted to stimulate its development,[13] but so long as the Vatican was not the permanent seat of the pope, the blandishments—such as relief from taxes and immunity from prosecution for past crimes—that these popes offered had little important effect. The Borgo remained nearly unpopulated until there was a reason for establishing a residence there. When Nicholas began to rebuild the basilica and the palace at the Vatican, others apparently became willing to build at its foot in the Borgo. Perhaps to encourage settlement in the Borgo, perhaps to satisfy the demands of new residents, or perhaps simply to make access to the Vatican easier for visitors and pilgrims, a street across the Borgo was paved in 1448.[14] It may or may not have been one of the three streets Manetti mentioned in his description, which will be discussed below. Eventually the population of the Borgo did grow; after he was created cardinal in 1478, Domenico della Rovere built in its center a large palace with a large piazza, and Alexander VI built a major street down its central axis, cutting away a major part of the Meta Romuli, which stood near the Castel Sant' Angelo. The cardinal's palace and the pope's street, along with two other streets, are conspicuous in the earliest clear map of the Borgo, made by Leonardo Bufalini in 1551 (fig. 46), but it is impossible to know to what extent the arrangement of streets that appears there corresponds to what Nicholas intended.

Manetti's treatment of the Borgo is not very helpful for learning what was built there between 1447 and 1455. It implies more than it reveals, but within the context of his entire description and of statements made by others—as well as through careful attention to the way in which Manetti composed his description—the significance of the pope's project for the Borgo can be recovered with some clarity (plan B).[15]

The Borgo had long been considered a special place. Leo IV (847–55) had fortified it as an enclave distinct from Rome in order to protect the tomb of Peter, which had been sacked by the Saracens in 846. In fortifying the Borgo, Leo had founded a city; in the quattrocento it was commonly referred to as the Borgo Leonino. The area at the Vatican was also commonly believed to have been sacred to the divine office. Biondo, writing at the time of Eugenius and constantly stressing the survival of ancient Rome in modern Rome, saw a direct continuity of interest in the area from Nero through Constantine, Symmachus I, Honorius I, Donatus, I, and Nicholas III to Eugenius IV; each of the Christians had devoted attention to the basilica or the palace, or to both, and Biondo gave a special place in the sequence to Leo IV, because he had built the walls, thus founding the Borgo Leonino.[16]

In the middle of the quattrocento the Borgo was considered more important as a fortified papal enclave than it was as the possible site for Peter's martyrdom, or even as the original site of Peter's tomb. Peter's crucifixion was important as an event of significance within the history of salvation, and, like other similar events, it could be understood without critical inquiry into particularities concerning time or place. From Petrarch's understanding of history the idea began to circulate that knowing and representing time and place was an important complement to understanding

---

[13] See above, chapter 1, note 47.

[14] See above, chapter 4, nn. 79, 81.

[15] Thus, plan B shows the elements mentioned by Manetti that can be located with certainty and leaves out some things that cannot be precisely located.

[16] Biondo, 1953, III, xlvi–lvi, pp. 272–274; see also Vegio, 1953, p. 381; and the Anonimo Magliabechiano, p. 134. See also Ehrle and Egger, 1935, pp. 11 ff., esp. p. 17.

significance, as Masaccio and Castagno showed, but this conception did not yet prevail in Rome. It soon would, however. While there was not yet any unanimity in opinion about where Peter had been crucified, new thought was beginning to be given to the matter. Biondo proposed that the event had occurred within the Borgo, while Filarete and Vegio believed in the opinion that would eventually prevail, that while it had not taken place within the Borgo, it had occurred on the Borgo side of the Tiber.[17] Where agreement existed was in beliefs about the construction of St. Peter's Basilica; it had not necessarily been built above the original tomb of the Apostle, but had been raised as an appropriate shrine for his body after it was moved from its hiding place and installed there by Constantine and Sylvester. Manetti did not disturb the Constantinian emphasis on the basilica, but neither did he linger on any of these details. Instead, he emphasized the attention Nicholas gave to the Borgo as a fortified and ordered place, thus coordinating his remarks with traditions attached to the Leonine foundation of the Borgo rather than with traditions associated with the tomb.

Manetti's emphasis on the distinctness of the Borgo from Rome corresponds with the way it appeared to visitors after Nicholas's project was well under way. Views of the area show that there was no question about the distinction made between Rome and the Borgo through fortifications actually built at the junction of the two. One view, made between 1453 and 1465, is a careful assemblage of figurative elements that have been altered to include new construction (fig. 47). It shows an elaborate system of gates, towers, and walls on both the Borgo side and the Campo Marzio side of the Ponte Sant'Angelo.[18] Views that more closely approach *vedute* and are less indebted to a figurative tradition, and that were produced independently, make the same point. The Bergomensis, Schedel, and Mantua views of Rome, which all derive from the same lost archetype, correspond to what appears in a *veduta* attributed to the school of Domenico Ghirlandaio and dating from just before the alterations executed by Alexander VI (figs. 34,45,75).[19] Two square, crenellated towers, one on either side of the bridge and nearer it than the Castello, flanked a gate structure; walls ran back to the Castello to form a keep. This construction is a natural extension of the *castello* that Nicholas had made from the Castel Sant'Angelo. It is also what Manetti had described earlier when he had said that Nicholas had added towers and fortifications and had built facilities for warders on the Borgo side of the bridge (ss. 23–26).

This construction was to be considered a small part of the extensive fortification system that protected the entire Borgo; the system would render the Borgo so secure that only birds flying over the walls would be able to enter without the pope's permission (s. 45). In describing the system, Manetti worked figuratively. What he

[17]Huskinson, 1969, passim; see above, chapter 2.

[18]It is in the Marcanova manuscript in Modena. It shows the angel atop the Castel Sant'Angelo, which suggests but does not confirm the date 1453 as the *terminus post quem;* the manuscript is dated 1465. The corner towers on the *castello* are not shown; its base follows an older archetype, but its upper, circular part, with Nicholas's coat of arms, is an alteration of the archetype. A model of the *castello* has been placed on the roof of the gateway on the Rome side of the bridge, emphasizing with a figurative reference the defensive purpose of the complex; this supplements the battlemented top of the entrance structure on the Borgo side. For the possible artist of the Marcanova drawings see Huelsen, 1907, pp. 6 ff., where Ciriaco d'Ancona is suggested, and Lawrence, 1927, passim, whose suggestion is more reasonable. Huelsen's criteria (1907, p. 6) would apply well to the characteristics of a figurative archetype that may have been used in Padua by an artist unfamiliar with Rome. For the Marcanova manuscript's history, see Dennis, 1927; for a close copy of the Modena manuscript in Princeton, see Lawrence, 1927.

[19]For the first three views, see chapter 5, note 30; For the Ghirlandaio school view, see Codex Escurialensis, Egger, 1905–06, fol. 26[v], p. 90. See also fol. 30[v] for a view of the structure from the Borgo.

said about it does little to allow one to reconstruct an actual building project. He said that the plan of the walls would have four sides, that the walls would be crowded with towers, and that they would enclose the Borgo, the Vatican Palace, and St. Peter's (ss. 44–45). He gave no hint that the topography and extant walls made it impossible to enclose either the Borgo or the palace with walls of which the plan was a clearly four-sided shape. He also found it unnecessary to mention that Nicholas made extensive use of extant construction; by rebuilding walls that dated back as far as the ninth century, the pope had to build only a few stretches *ex novo* (plan B).[20]

Manetti said that the walls were built to satisfy three purposes. One was to make it possible to form a level platform. This was necessary, Manetti explained, because the new palace structures within the walls were to be important and great and therefore required a level site, as ancient architects had demonstrated.[21] The second purpose was to enclose the palace within walls and to have those walls reproduce the four-sided arrangement of the Borgo enclosures. To make clear their unifying and separating function, Manetti discussed this arrangement at the same time that he described the means of entrance from the Borgo to the palace (ss. 54–57, esp. s. 57). The third purpose was to fortify the palace as a part of the fortification system of the Borgo as a whole (ss. 50–53, and esp. s. 57). To stress the idea that the Borgo fortifications were tied in firmly to the entrance at the Castel Sant'Angelo, Manetti waited until he was describing the walls before he mentioned the four corner towers that Nicholas built at the Castello (s. 45).

To build these fortifications, and to build them with careful design, was to refound the Leonine city, and that was the point Manetti was making. Walls were an important figure for indicating the existence of a place and for demonstrating that, through their construction, a place had been founded and protected.[22] Nicholas had designed and built the walls, and Nicholas's palace, according to Manetti, would protect and perfect the Borgo (ss. 76–77). This would occur in two ways. First, the geometric configuration of the walls around the palace and around the Borgo would be analogous, linking the two indissolubly through design. And second, they would be closely integrated with one another physically, actually sharing some elements in common. Manetti's rhetorical structure makes these same points. His Borgo description had begun at the Ponte Sant'Angelo, and it had concluded with a description of the walls that terminated at the Castel Sant'Angelo, thus enframing within the description of the fortifications the description of that which the fortifications enclosed. And that description mingles with the description of the Vatican Palace; after he introduced his description of the palace, he took the occasion to describe the Borgo walls before he continued with the palace description.

His treatment of the walls, therefore, reveals that Manetti was less interested in being a reliable reporter of physical facts and achievements than he was in stressing something else. He wished to convey the figurative significance of his subject, and he wished to use the rhetorical structure of his description as an additional vehicle for conveying the significant content of the pope's building program. Like Vitruvius and like Taddeo di Bartolo and Biondo's map-making friend, Manetti did not see the walls as an architectural fabric that was part of a particular topographic situation

---

[20]The new stretches were begun in 1451 at the latest, according to the accounts in Müntz, *ACP*, I, p. 159. For more information about these walls, see below, chapter 7, and plan C, on p. 128.

[21]Manetti, ss. 46–48; compare Alberti, *De re aed.*, I, vii–viii.

[22]Braunfels, 1966, chapter II; Białostocki, 1964; Hale, 1965, pp. 470–471; see also Vitruvius, I, iv–v, who begins his discussion of the building of the city by explaining how the walls are to be laid out and then hardly refers to the walls again, an approach followed by Filarete, 1965, I, IV, and V.

in the Borgo; they were things or signs signifying that the pope's plans for the Borgo included its enclosure. This is particularly clear in the way Manetti handles the description of the inhabited area to be rebuilt within the walls.

The inhabited area, he explained, would extend from the entrance area at the Castel Sant'Angelo at one end and be bounded along one side by the Tiber and along the other by a wall running to the Castello; part of this wall would include a new extension to the great palace tower he describes elsewhere (s. 31). These were extant topographic features; in his description they are unrelated to the system of fortifications he describes at the conclusion of his treatment of the Borgo's interior arrangement, even though the topographic features include elements that would be found in the fortification system. Additionally, the pattern traced by these elements corresponds only in a very vague way to the more precise geometric pattern Manetti had said the fortification system would follow. They also serve poorly in the task he attributed to them, which was that of enclosing the interior, built-up area, because they leave one end of the area, that of the basilica, open. Manetti's point is that the Borgo has an interior arrangement and that it is circumscribed both by extant elements and by a new system of enclosures, but he did not reveal what relationship there might be between the interior arrangement and the exterior enclosures.

Manetti's emphasis in describing the interior of the Borgo is the same as the one that is found in his description of the system of fortifications. Once again, he stressed the order imposed through design in the city that he credited the pope with building at the base of the basilica and palace. The Borgo is to be inhabited by the curia, by which Manetti meant all those connected with the papacy and all those who lived in the area to serve it and their neighbors. In his testament, Nicholas had considered its residents to be the extensions of the members of which he was the head, and he stated that he desired to protect them and to give them their proper dignity.[23] Their dignity would be conspicuous in their ordered placement, and Manetti described three streets Nicholas planned for the Borgo that would contribute to the order of the Borgo through the care of their design. The first street is straight; it runs from a piazza at the Castel Sant'Angelo to the piazza at St. Peter's, and it is directed toward the central door of the basilica's five great entrances.[24] The second street, also straight and also departing from the same area at the Castel Sant'Angelo, runs along the right (north) side of the Borgo to the entrance of the Vatican Palace.[25] Across the Borgo along its left side is another street, and Manetti's description of it is impossibly vague. He said that it tended toward the Tiber and was directed toward an ancient obelisk that stood at that time on the left of the basilica. The street possibly curved, but it certainly terminated before the obelisk, at the new canons' lodgings contemplated for that area (ss. 34–35).

This section of Manetti's description is typical of his operations as a figurative reporter, in that it seems to be clear until one attempts to relate one element to another and to coordinate the combination of elements with the extant topography and buildings. Manetti is never precise enough to allow one to obtain clear urbanistic or topographic information, but he does explain how the design satisfied the demands made on it by the program. Manetti says that in the Borgo there would be an open area at the Castel Sant'Angelo. It would be open at the Castello and joined to the buildings in the Borgo, it would run on one side from the walls directed from the

[23] Manetti, *RIS,* col. 950.

[24] Manetti, ss. 32–33. This street might be related to the one mentioned above, chapter 4. See chapter 4, note 79.

[25] This street might be related to the one mentioned above, chapter 4. See chapter 4, note 81.

Castello to the palace and on the other side to the Tiber, and it would be produced by clearing the area near the bridge. He adds that from that piazza would run the three streets; these would divide the Borgo into three (*sic*) areas and have colonnades on each side. But he says nothing about the shape or decoration of the piazza at the Castello, nothing about where the three streets depart from it, and nothing about a regular or irregular pattern of the plan of the streets as they cross the Borgo. He sees these elements not as physical design elements placed in a considered relationship to one another—to expect him to do that would be to expect more of him than the mapmakers were capable of—but as things without which a city was incomplete. He treated them as separate things, introducing them in a sequence that hardly related them to one another, but after they had all been introduced into the Borgo the latter was complete, and he could claim that it had been designed. The streets are the most obvious example of his having thought in this way. They define the areas of habitation on either side and are not seen as defining blocks between their courses; thus, the three streets divide the Borgo into three areas, not into four blocks. These three areas contain three types of residents; that is, the streets order the inhabitants according to their classes and nations. The first, central street has the greater craftsmen—moneychangers, drapers, and bakers—the northern street the less important craftsmen, and the one farthest from the palace and nearest Rome and the Tiber has the lowest classes.[26] Political, not spatial, divisions still give order, but political divisions are beginning to be established consciously through conscious physical design.

The physical facilities Nicholas intended for the Borgo are very inadequately explained, as is clear in Manetti's description of the colonnades and buildings along the three streets. The colonnades are, he states, both beautiful and useful. Their beauty is obvious to those inside them in all the seasons of the year, and their usefulness resides in their protecting people from the inclemencies of the weather. Furthermore, the residences that accompany the shops within the colonnades are to be placed above the colonnades, in order to provide sufficient light (ss. 40–43). But what does this mean? That is to say, what architectural form would this combination of colonnades, shops, and residences have?

Manetti is apparently unaware that he is describing a design that is different from traditional shop design in Rome, and that its differences reside in the resolution of several different kinds of problems at once. Traditionally, shops were spread along Roman streets, each separate from the next, with the shop on the ground floor and the residence often crammed into a mezzanine level within the shop. Above the shops would be residences, and they would not necessarily be for the shopkeepers. The shops and their cramped quarters had little or no light, and the occupants practiced their crafts as much in the street as they did indoors. This clogged the streets with benches and other things that the magistrates of streets were empowered to cut down, tear out, and destroy. The activity of the craftsmen was probably as responsible as the carters who figured in the 1446 concordat were for impeding pedestrians.

When these buildings were faced with colonnades, as was not uncommon in parts of Italy, including Rome, they were often colonnades of short run and irregular face. They doubtless created as many problems as they provided amenities, and such problems were in the hands of the street magistrates, who could again cut down and cart off offending projections. It would appear that Manetti missed the point of

---

[26]Manetti, ss. 37–39. He does not elaborate on their national segregation.

Nicholas's design, which, as has been argued, is based on traditional practice[27] but which has transformed it from a nuisance into an amenity.[28] The design separates cart from pedestrian traffic, allows pedestrians, if they wish, to mix together with the craftsmen, provides a protected place for that conjunction, and puts the residences above in line with either the front of the colonnade or the shop within the colonnade. The latter seems more probable, because that arrangement would widen the opening to the sky and allow in the greater quantity of light Manetti mentioned.[29] Manetti catalogues the benefits the design would provide—beauty, usefulness, protection from the weather, and good illumination—but he does not indicate that the benefits were integrated into a single solution that resolved the problems inherent in similar, undesigned structures—disorder, encumbered circulation, exposure to the weather, and darkness. That solution accounted at the same time for visual pleasantness, usefulness, solidity, and proper ornamentation, each of which responded to problems of the public and private uses of physical facilities, and some of which also confronted the blasts of fortune. It was, in addition, a solution that was coherently inserted into a larger urban and political structure.[30]

The major elements in Manetti's Borgo were the entrance, the fortifications, the piazza at the entrance, the three streets with their colonnades, and the entrance areas into the basilica and the palace. In keeping with the unity he saw between the Borgo and the palace, a unity shared by the intimate conjunction of the Borgo and the basilica, Manetti did not draw a sharp distinction between his description of the third, fourth, and fifth parts of the project, which he had named when introducing his description. Without a break he goes on to discuss the palace and then returns to the Borgo to outline Nicholas's plans for the basilica. He begins his description of the basilica at the piazza in front of it. In following his report it becomes clear that the open space there is not to be considered as distinct from the Borgo, the basilica, or the palace. Instead, it is to be thought of as an urbanistic element that unifies the three and stands at the very center of Nicholas's scheme for the Borgo.

There is little or no evidence to show what the area was like in 1447 or in 1455. It is also difficult to discover what Nicholas planned there. Manetti's description is the only surviving direct evidence of Nicholas's intention, and a deficiency that prevents the text from yielding accurate figures for its dimensions is of little help.[31] This lapse may make little difference, however. Manetti may not have had accurate figures available to him, and even if he had them, he may have used rounded figures or other figures for some purpose now beyond our understanding. It is clear that when he used figures, he used them for a purpose that was more profound than mere description, as will be seen when he gives the dimensions of the basilica. And Manetti

[27]Magnuson, 1958, pp. 77–80.

[28]See MacDougall, 1962, p. 74.

[29]Magnuson, 1958, p. 78, interprets s. 43 to mean that the openings in the colonnades would be wide enough to allow light into the shops and the residences.

[30]Contrast the interpretation of this description with that of MacDougall, 1962, who objects to Magnuson's interpretations by stressing the visual unity that uniform colonnades would lend the area. See also Magnuson, 1958, p. 79, n. 28, who mentions what Manetti does not mention, the tradition that there was a roofed-over, colonnaded street running through the Vatican across the Ponte Sant'Angelo to an area just across the river, where it terminated in a triumphal arch. For it, see Thoenes, 1963, part I.

[31]Manetti, ss. 84, 85, and 121 in Muratori's text, gives the dimensions of the piazza as 200 by 100 cubits (*braccia*), but as Pagnotti, 1891, has pointed out, some texts give the dimensions as 500 by 100. The manuscript that Muratori used has not been traced; see Magnuson, 1958, p. 356, n. 23. Magnuson rejects both 500 and 200 cubits and offers no alternative; 1958, pp. 72–77. MacDougall, 1962, pp. 73–74, offers a reconstruction that is not preferable; it is that the 5 × 1 proportion is probably correct, but that the dimension 100 *braccia* excludes the depth of the portico on each side; for these, see below.

would probably have considered dimensionally accurate figures quite superfluous. His description is figurative, not concrete, and his emphasis is on the program, not on the architectural elements as architectural structures. The result may be, then, that there is no way to recover Nicholas's figures from anything Manetti has to say, and, furthermore, it might be that Nicholas himself never had specific figures available to him for this area.[32]

It seems highly unlikely that there is any way one can gain a concrete architectonic or urbanistic sense of the piazza from what does survive of Manetti's description. When interpreting his text, one must recall the limitations on Manetti's abilities to describe physical elements and his tendency to use his rhetorical structure for some larger purpose than mere description. When one reads Manetti's description closely, one finds little or no spatial unity. The piazza is little more than the space left over after the elements assembled around and in it have been put in place. Only his references elsewhere to the two streets at the extreme sides of the Borgo allow one to infer that these enter the piazza at opposite ends and define two of its sides. One of the sides would have the canons' residence near it, and the other would be terminated by the papal palace; each of these is related to the piazza, but neither would give definition to it. The canons' residence is not described at all, and the palace is described as a building with a series of elements the visitor encounters as he enters and visits, rather than as a block or a combination of elements integrated into a coherent design that presents a face to the piazza and that forms a backdrop for an open space.[33]

Manetti describes the piazza by mentioning elements that are found in it. At the upper end there would be a set of steps and a platform. Manetti gives the platform's dimensions as 75 by 120 cubits,[34] which is only a little smaller than the piazza if the text which gives the dimensions as 100 by 200 is considered correct; this is still not a small platform related to a piazza if the texts with the 100 by 500 dimensions are accepted.[35] On the opposite side of the piazza, apparently 200 or 500 *braccia* (or cubits) away in the direction of the built-up part of the Borgo, was to be a façade of the piazza with colonnades that recall those of the three streets leading through the Borgo (s. 85). Manetti states that this "most ample and ornate area," which the Greeks called a *platea,* was valued because it affords the most beautiful and rich spectacle of all sorts of beautiful things (ss. 85–86). One of these things is the obelisk, moved from its position at the side of the basilica and placed in the center of the lower, larger piazza, presumably in line with the central door of the basilica and the street of the Borgo, although Manetti simply says "in the middle." It was to be reestablished on its base, with its four bronze lions replaced by four bronze statues of the Evangelists.[36] Above them would be bronze statues of persons arranged each according to his dignity, topped by a great bronze figure of Christ the Savior holding a gold cross in his right hand (ss. 86–88). The other of these beautiful things would be the entrance to the basilica.

[32] Some ramifications of this argument will be discussed again below, Epilogue.

[33] Ss. 31–36, 44–45, 52–57, 101. Manetti gives no indication that the north and south sides of the piazza had colonnades.

[34] S. 90. It was, however, only about 30 *braccia* deep; Thoenes, 1963, p. 137, n. 40. Manetti must have included the steps in his platform dimensions, as it is shown in plan B on p. 102.

[35] Concerning the dimensions, see note 31 above.

[36] The lions were probably no longer under the obelisk in the mid quattrocento. Their earlier presence would have been known from older sources, however. See Squarciapino, 1962. That Manetti mentioned them again shows the extent to which he depended on material other than what was visible to him when he made his description.

Manetti describes the wall in front of the viewer approaching the basilica in figurative as much as in architectural terms. The steps are of marble, of porphyry, and of emerald colors,[37] a scheme Manetti will repeat later. Beyond them is the small platform discussed above, and beyond that rises a wall punctured by five noble bronze portals and terminated at each end by a tower. The latter are 100 cubits high and built of beautiful marbles; they strengthen the basilica and contain bells that ring out the canonic hours (ss. 90–91). It would seem that Manetti considers these towers as strengthening the basilica in much the same way Torquemada had when he referred to "campanile, sive turrim" as a figure for the defense of the Church rather than as a defensive installation,[38] an idea which would find its way also into Filarete's ideas about churches.[39]

Conspicuously lacking in this description is any sense of space and any sense of the buildings around the piazza as contributing to the piazza. The basilica is seen as a natural extension of the Borgo, and at the same time the Borgo is a mere forecourt for the basilica; intruding between them is a *platea* with objects in and around it. Manetti moves consistently toward the basilica; beyond the ample built-up area of the Borgo there would be a broad piazza, then a set of steps, then a platform smaller than the piazza and more broad than deep, and then the five great portals.

A sophisticated sense of space may be lacking in Manetti's description because the precise details for that area had not been settled by the time Nicholas died. Alternatively, it may be lacking because a sophisticated handling of open spaces treated as things designed had not yet become part of the rhetorical, conceptual, and visual vocabulary of those who were already adept in ancient forms of literary expression, as Manetti was, and in design with ancient architectural elements, as Brunelleschi and Alberti were.

Parts of cities had been designed since the late thirteenth century in Tuscany.[40] Spaces that fronted on important buildings had been manipulated to achieve a preconceived visual result. For example, the piazza around the baptistry and the space in front of the Palazzo Vecchio in Florence had been cleared during various campaigns in the fourteenth century. Buildings had also been manipulated in order to give a particular character to the space in front of them. For instance, ordinances were passed in the late fourteenth century that regulated the form of facades up to a height of more than thirty feet along a portion of the street connecting the piazzas at the cathedral and the Palazzo Vecchio in Florence; they were to be remodeled to imitate the form of the (old) Palazzo di Parte Guelfa, which stood in the same street. But these examples cannot be considered to be piazza designs of the same type as that which has been sought by recent interpreters of Manetti's description, and more importantly, they were not designed in the rigorous style congruent with what Manetti leads us to expect Nicholas wanted. Nicholas was clearly attempting to use an architecture based on the emulation of antique methods of design, and to design with the coherence and integration of elements that Brunelleschi had introduced in his buildings, that Castagno had used in the fictive architecture at Legnaia, and that

---

[37] Manetti, s. 85; compare the steps at the gate of purgatory in Dante, *Divina Commedia, Purg.* IX, lines 76 ff., and the steps to thrones for saints in contemporary paintings.

[38] Torquemada, *Consecratione*, fol. 5ᵛ.

[39] Similarly the next sentences, which refer to walls running back from these towers to the crossing of the basilica, should be thought of as structural rather than as military constructions. Alberti, *De re aed.*, I, viii, refers to the wall between the basilica and the palace, with its chapels, as useful for keeping the hill from sliding down into the basilica. MacDougall's defortification of Magnuson's basilica (1962, p. 74) is eminently reasonable.

[40] Braunfels, 1966, esp. pp. 116–122.

Brunelleschi's successors would show was possible in piazza design—for example, at Pienza (1458–62) and Vigevano (1492–94).[41] Thus, these late medieval piazzas hardly qualify as designed piazzas according to Nicholas's standards or according to those standards that would gradually be introduced during the quattrocento.

There are only three open spaces in Italy earlier in date than Nicholas's piazzas on the Capitol and at the basilica that could claim to have been designed according to the new criteria, and the claims of each are open to question. Brunelleschi probably did design the space in front of the Ospedale degli Innocenti in this way, but execution dragged on for a century. His piazza for the space between Santo Spirito and the Arno survives only in a meager statement of his intention, and our possible knowledge of a piazza intended for the area between San Lorenzo and his proposed but rejected Palazzo Medici depends upon even more tenuous evidence.[42] To wrest from Manetti's description a piazza with buildings, colonnades, arched entrances, portals, an obelisk, and other elements consciously designed and placed relative to one another with the intention of making a noble space with value in its openness is to draw more from Manetti than is there, and to miss his point as well.[43]

Manetti was unclear in his description, but he was probably intentionally deceptive as well in order to be clear rhetorically. To clarify his report, he indulged in simplification. His account of Nicholas's project is predicated upon stressing the dominance of St. Peter's over the Borgo, the independence of the Borgo from Rome, and the dominance of the Borgo over Rome. As he described the project, therefore, he had the visitor move from Rome through the Borgo and into the basilica. This was to ignore another means of access that was possibly more important and would hardly have been ignored by Nicholas. Pilgrims from the north avoided Rome, as Frederick III had when entering in 1452, by skirting Monte Mario and coming into the Borgo through the Porta di S. Pietro. This gate penetrated the *corridoio* that formed the wall running from the Castel Sant'Angelo to the Vatican Palace. It is conspicuous in all the versions of Biondo's friend's view of Rome (figs. 29–32, 71–74). Alexander VI rebuilt it and had Bramante install a fountain in the open piazza between the axis of the basilica and the gateway.[44] The pilgrim would enter an area that had been cleared and defined by the construction projects of Boniface IX (1389–1404) and John XXIII (1410–15), with the Borgo on one side and the Vatican Palace on the other.[45] The pilgrim's route and the area immediately within the Porta di S. Pietro remained unaltered until Pius IV (1559–65) rebuilt it. He laid a new street

[41] Lotz, 1968, passim.

[42] For the Santo Spirito piazza, see Manetti, 1970, lines 1512 ff.; for the San Lorenzo work, see Hyman, 1969. See also the illustration from the early sixteenth century in Krinsky, 1969.

[43] Especially important is the movement across the space in ss. 84–85. In contrast to the interpretation suggested here, see Magnuson, 1958, pp. 72–77, and pl. IA, and MacDougall, 1962, pp. 73–74. Both accept a reading of s. 85 to indicate that the axis of the piazza is parallel to that of the basilica. This may or may not be the case; an alternative reading, albeit based on a less usual interpretation of the Latin syntax, which places the long axis across the front of the basilica, would better fit the topography and Manetti's vision of the piazza elsewhere as an element tying together the basilica and the palace (see plan B on page 102). Manetti, for purposes of his rhetoric, had a clear interest in having the long axis parallel; his description proceeds across the Borgo into the basilica, and, as will be seen below, he uses the piazza's proportions in conjunction with those of the basilica. These two uses of the piazza would be better served by having the axis parallel than perpendicular, and there was no reason for him to report accurately on the matter. See also Magnuson, 1958, pp. 77–78, who introduces conjectures about the design of the points at which the streets enter the piazza, and MacDougall, 1962, pp. 73–74, who offers an alternative solution on equally conjectural grounds.

[44] Redig de Campos, 1967, pp. 80–81.

[45] Ehrle and Egger, 1935, pp. 87–89.

across the Borgo Pio, which he built as an extension to the Borgo Leonino, and he opened the Arco di Sant'Anna at the head of the street. He also enlarged and re-arranged the barracks' area of the Swiss Guards just inside the Borgo Leonino. These were the first extensive alterations to be undertaken in the area since the time of Nicholas V, and Pius's Borgo Pio project was linked by contemporaries with the original project of Nicholas, apparently through the agency of Vasari's discussion of it in the life of Bernardo Rossellino.[46] It seems unlikely that Nicholas would have ignored this entrance, or that he would have sponsored a project that diminished its importance as a means of access to the basilica, but because Manetti was describing the area within a context that stressed the movement through the Borgo to the basilica and to its contiguous and closely related palace, there was good reason for him to distort his description of this part and in the process to obscure Nicholas's complete intentions for the area of the piazza.

One final consideration suggests that Manetti's description has allowed rhetoric and figurative language to obscure the architectonic character of the piazza. The area in front of the basilica and the palace that included all these entrances and exits was highly irregular and probably in excess of 400 *braccia* square. If there were to be a colonnade around it, and if the colonnade were to describe a rectangle either 100 by 500 or 100 by 200, where would it have been placed, how would the streets and portals have been accommodated, and what would have filled up the space outside its limits (see plan B)? To answer these questions requires a great deal of conjecture; more sensible is the assumption that Manetti was writing figuratively. He simply used dimensions for a piazza that related to those he gave for the basilica in order to indicate that, figuratively, the piazza was an ordered forecourt to the great basilica and therefore an appropriate space in front of it, and that, in addition, the piazza tied together the entrances to the basilica and the palace when approached through the Borgo from Rome.

The pilgrim, no matter how he got into the area in front of it, is now ready to enter the basilica, the most important single element in Nicholas's building project. The pope spent much more here than anywhere else in Rome, which indicates the importance the building occupied in his program. He restored parts of the atrium and completed the restorations of the mosaics on the façade facing the atrium; he shored up and repaired the tilting nave and aisle walls; he destroyed and rearranged some chapels along the church's sides and at its east end; and he undertook the construction of a vast new transept and choir.[47] His intent was to restore and augment, not to replace the entire building. He laid a great deal of masonry beyond the eastern (i.e., west by the compass) parts of the Early Christian bema and apse; although these foundations reached a height of no more than thirteen *braccia,* and perhaps not even that much, and therefore remained rather inconspicuous, the sheer mass of the material there could not be ignored by any subsequent builder. Paul II added a little to what Nicholas had laid, but the energetic Julius II would profit most from what Nicholas had begun. The outline of the eastern apse and of the related sides of the arms of the great Greek cross church that Bramante began in 1506 was determined by Nicholas's foundations, as is clearest in one of the drawings (Uffizi

[46]For Pius's project, see Lewine, 1965, appendix (with n. 129 for reference to MacDougall's suggestion), and idem, 1969, who indicates that little had changed in a century.

[47]See Magnuson, 1958, pp. 163–214, and Urban, 1963, passim, for the most recent studies of Nicholas's actual construction.

20A) related to Julius's undertaking, which shows the Early Christian construction, Nicholas's foundations, and some of the sixteenth-century work.[48]

But once again, Manetti did not direct his attention to archaeology and construction activity. His description of the basilica is almost purely rhetorical. In it, he mixes together ornamentation and repairs undertaken by Nicholas and his predecessors and treats the extant Constantinian fabric as if it were all to be built by the pope. He continues to emphasize figurative rather than architectonic elements, and he constantly stresses the place the building occupies in Nicholas's comprehensive program for the papacy.

Manetti moves the visitor rather quickly through the areas in front of the great Constantinian nave. The platform at the head of the piazza, he reported, was sufficiently ample to hold many people; beyond it stood the five great portals, opening to a vestibule flanked by towers, and beyond it, entered through another five portals, was a second vestibule (ss. 89–91, 94). Following the vestibules would be the atrium. Transit from the second vestibule to the atrium would be made through five portals, with those on each end opening into the useful and beautiful porticoes on the sides of the atrium (ss. 94, 96). The atrium portico on the left would give access to the canons' residence, and that on the right would stand before the wall that separated the palace from the area of the basilica (s. 97). In the center of the atrium would be the *pigna*, restored to its former dignity as a fountain supplied with living water brought down from the hills behind.[49] In describing the area Manetti does not use the traditional terminology that called it a paradise.[50] At the base of the atrium would be an arcade opening directly into the vaulted narthex of the basilica, and, beyond that, the five decorated and ornamented portals of the basilica, including the one by Filarete, would greet the visitor.[51]

The description culminates inside the basilica. Manetti mentions the nave and east end in the same tone, without differentiating between Nicholas's intentions to repair and shore up the ancient nave and to replace great portions of the Constantinian fabric with new work. Here, as elsewhere, he treats intention as accomplishment, and he constantly describes the basilica as it would function and as it would be seen, not as it would be thought of by a builder or architect. Manetti reported that the nave with its four side aisles allowed an unencumbered view throughout the church, which pleased him.[52] Beyond the nave, a vaulted apse and vaulted transepts would project out from the crossing; had these been built, they would have vastly increased the space of the east end. The crossing would have a dome with a lantern allowing light to be diffused throughout the space.[53] The climax of the basilica—and, indeed, of the entire sequence of places from the Castel Sant'Angelo on—would be in the new projecting apse, which Manetti called the "head" and which, he states, is commonly called a tribune.

Having finished the general description, rudimentary as it is, Manetti concentrates

[48] For studies of the relationship between Nicholas's project, the extant building, and later construction, see, in addition to the material in note 47 above, Wolff Metternich, 1967, passim. For old St. Peter's, see Jongkees, 1966.

[49] Manetti, s. 95. Eugenius had already restored the fountain; see Müntz, *ACP*, I, p. 40, for the dates, 1437 and 1438.

[50] See Ehrle and Egger, 1935, p. 58, for a document from 1332; Ehrle and Stevenson, 1897, p. 11, n. 9, for 1488 and 1503. The documents referred to in Müntz, note 49 above, also call it a paradise.

[51] Manetti, s. 98; also ss. 99–102 for the entrance. The arcade with ten columns between the atrium and the vaulted narthex already existed, as did much else here. See Magnuson, 1958, pp. 180–185.

[52] Manetti, s. 103; there is no evidence in Manetti's text that Nicholas intended to vault the side aisles.

[53] Manetti, ss. 106–109. For a different statement about this light, see below, pp. 118,124.

on a few specific elements in the basilica. The tribune would be fitted out with seats for all the important persons, and it would be lit by great round windows that would serve also as ornaments (s. 112). The altar, ingenious, beautiful, and loaded with every sort of proper ornament—the only altar he mentions in the basilica—stands at the extremity of the crossing (s. 113), that is, beyond the actual location of the tomb of Peter, which Manetti does not mention, and within the circle of the dome. Beyond that, at the extremity of the tribune, in a position that would be clearly visible to all, would be the throne of the pope (s. 114). Manetti has described the kernel of the *concetto* that would guide later popes, especially those who patronized Bernini during the seventeenth century.

These elements relate directly to the functioning of Nicholas's basilica. The other elements Manetti places in the rebuilt east end are subordinate to those he has mentioned. They are included to allow the important elements to function more effectively. He describes this second group as supporting elements rather than as ornament or as parts of the architectural fabric. Windows in the nave would illuminate the individual parts, while those in the crossing would reveal the splendor of the area around the altar (s. 115). The dome's great, round windows would appear as a "glorious crown"; the dome would allow the rays of the sun to enter and "not only light up individual parts of the dome but also display an example of divine glory to all the devout onlookers."[54] The windows in the dome would, continues Manetti, resemble those throughout the basilica. The similarity would indicate that the entire structure is a unified whole. The materials of the pavement would be marble, porphyry, and emerald-colored, like those of the steps outside (ss. 117–18). In referring to the colored materials in the pavement, a Cosmati pavement that actually existed, and in reminding the reader that the visitor would have encountered them just before entering the basilica, Manetti is able to call attention to the unity that pervades the basilica from the entrance to the altar and pontifical throne.

Next, in a separate statement, Manetti turns to another important element in the complex:

> And lest so great, so fair, so holy, so admirable, and so divine rather than mortal a temple be defiled at all by any burials of deceased popes, he wished that sepulchres of this kind be established and constructed on the left hand outside the chapel. . . .

This area was toward the front of the basilica relative to the apse (s. 119). Manetti is referring here to an extant building, the circular mausoleum known by the names Santa Maria della Febbre and Sant'Andrea.[55] It was used for services by the canons of St. Peter's,[56] and in 1452 renovations were underway there in conjunction with its

[54]Manetti, s. 116. The image is hardly unusual; see Dante, *Divina Commedia, Paradiso,* X, XI, XII, XIII. It is found in the quattrocento in literature (see Manetti's "De pompis," to be cited below, note 64) and in architecture (Brunelleschi's Medici sacristy and Pazzi Chapel, both in Florence).

[55]For these names, and for another circular mausoleum next to this one, see Armellini, 1942, pp. 927–928, 913–915, 933–937, and the note added by Cecchelli to Armellini, 1942, p. 915. See also Krautheimer, 1965, p. 320, n. 47 to ch. 2. This was the mausoleum that was detached from the transept of the basilica.

[56]On 23 December 1449 Nicholas transferred the priests attached to S. Vincenzo to the chapter of the canons of St. Peter's and stated that they were to assist in the services at Santa Maria della Febbre; *Coll. Bull. Vat.,* II, pp. 130–131.

function as a sepulchre.⁵⁷ Elsewhere in the description Manetti had mentioned a sacristy in this area (s. 101). He placed it beyond the proposed canons' residence, but his description seems to suggest that he was referring not to Santa Maria della Febbre but to S. Petronilla, another circular mausoleum also thought to be ancient and attached to the transept of the basilica.⁵⁸

Manetti's explanation for the pope's desire to be interred outside the basilica recalls Alberti's counsel against placing the dead within churches, as has often been mentioned.⁵⁹ But Alberti at this time was involved in at least two designs that contradicted the position he had announced in his treatise. At SS. Annunziata in Florence and San Francesco in Rimini, tribunes were being fitted out to receive the mortal remains of the patrons of the buildings. Manetti's explanation, while vague, suggests that the mausoleum and the sacristy would occupy two separate buildings, but recent Florentine practice shows that the two functions would not have been incompatible in a single centralized building. At San Lorenzo the sacristy served as the sepulchral chapel for the parents of Cosimo de'Medici, and it, like the tribunes at SS. Annunziata and in Rimini, had a centralized plan covered with a dome. The crypt below the crossing at San Lorenzo also became a sepulchre.

Domed, centralized burial spaces recalled not only ancient and early Christian practice but also a conspicuous pontifical tomb in the church itself. The tomb of Boniface VIII, which stood inside the Basilica of St. Peter against the center of the entrance façade, was also centralized in that its altar was covered by a canopy.⁶⁰ The brief remark in Manetti's text is too vague to suggest which, if any, of these precedents Nicholas was evoking, and the practice of four of his successors, who placed their tombs in centralized spaces, does not clarify the issue. Calixtus III was buried in Sant'Andrea (Santa Maria della Febbre). Pius II and Sixtus IV established their tombs in centralized chapels conjoined to St. Peter's.⁶¹ And Julius II would later have Bramante and Michelangelo begin to convert the entire Basilica of St. Peter into a colossal centralized mausoleum for himself and St. Peter. But no matter what Nicholas may have intended, after his death his body was placed in a small tomb in the left side of St. Peter's. Its principal ornament was a glowing epitaph composed by Aeneas Sylvius Piccolomini, the future Pius II.

Having finished enumerating the various elements that comprise the basilica, Manetti turns to several characteristics of the entire complex. First, he introduces the dimensional relationships that pervade the basilica as a whole. He had given some of the dimensions earlier, but here he repeats the major ones to stress the unity throughout the building—the dimensions for the piazza, for the length of the basil-

---

⁵⁷See *Coll. Bull. Vat.*, II, pp. 140–141, a document dated 12 July 1453, addressed to Francesco Orsini, prefect of the city of Rome. The pope states that because the Chapel of St. John the Baptist is being removed "pro fundatione et constructione quas circa ampliationem Tribunae Basilicae Principis Apostolorum de Urbe sumptuoso et mirifico opere fieri facere fecimus," the Orsini Chapel is being removed to Santa Maria delle Febbre. For related payments from 1452, see Müntz, *ACP*, I, pp. 123–124, and for payments for other works there, see ibid., pp. 121–124. For the Chapel of St. John, Armellini, 1942, pp. 937–938. For later reports about Nicholas's work at Santa Maria delle Febbre, see Müntz, *ACP*, I, p. 121, n. 2 (citing Platina) and n. 3 (citing Panvinio).

⁵⁸For it, see notes above to Santa Maria delle Febbre. Magnuson, 1958, pp. 190, 206, considers Manetti's reference to both the sepulchre and the sacristy to be too vague to be useful. He does not refer to the documents concerning the Orsini tombs.

⁵⁹Alberti, *De re aed.*, VIII, i.

⁶⁰Gardner, 1969, pp. 109 f.

⁶¹For Pius, see Rubinstein, 1967, pp. 31–32; for Sixtus, see Ettlinger, 1953, pp. 268–271. Ettlinger suggests a relationship between Sixtus's chapel and the Medici sacristy.

ica, for the breadth of the transepts, and for the height of the vaults and dome. They seldom correspond to the ones he had already given;[62] his purpose is not to render possible a reconstruction but to demonstrate the unity of the fabric. The larger dimension of the piazza, for example, is equal to the distance through the forecourts and nave to the pontifical throne. In citing dimensions he can also make it clear that proportions have been used in designing; they will be repeated once more in a later passage to show the relationship between the basilica and its prototype.

Next Manetti stresses the unity between the basilica and the contiguous papal palace. He first mentions the portal that allows the pope and the prelates to enter from the palace, with proper dignity, directly through a special side entrance (s. 126). The next three sentences are also meant to relate the basilica to the palace and both of these to their prototypes, which will be introduced later in the description, by naming three elements that were common to the buildings and their prototypes—a special staircase, a particular type of roof, and special materials used in their construction. At this point in the description Manetti states that the pope and prelates reach the side entrance of the basilica by means of a marvelous spiral staircase (s. 127), and we are told that the basilica has a lead roof and that it is built of stones brought specially along the river from the small town of Tivoli near Rome to the building site in the Vatican.[63]

In a certain sense everything that Manetti has mentioned up to this point has been an elaborate stage setting for his final remarks, which concern the content of the basilica. Extensive as his comments had been, up to this point he had acted as a reporter rather than as an interpreter; now he becomes not only an interpreter but also a visitor. He now explains what figurative content and doctrine the design held, and he then concludes with observations about the place of Nicholas's undertaking in the history of architecture.

Manetti explained the content and doctrine in a special section, which he carefully set aside from his description. He wished to present these comments as the result of his own reflection. Here, and only here in the *Life of Nicholas,* he claims to have speculated on his own. He states that the similarity between the basilica and the body of man is clearly visible. The vestibules and the tribune correspond to the location of the feet and the head, and the transepts correspond to outstretched arms (ss. 130–34).

This anthropomorphic analogy was not new in either descriptive and interpretative literature or in Manetti's works. When describing the cathedral in Florence in 1436 he had made a similar comparison and had done so with careful technical language. He had explained that the shape (*figura*) of the Duomo resembled the form (*forma*) of man and that the form (*forma*) of man surpassed the shapes (*figurae*) of the most perfect things.[64] But Manetti carefully revised his earlier version of this traditional anthropomorphic analogy and added a great deal of other material in order to adapt it to his new purpose. In Florence he had said that such an analogy has often been noted; now he points out in general language that these visible similarities are his own conclusions, although others would be able to see them as well. His lan-

[62] Compare: Manetti, ss. 121 with 84 and 85; 122 with 90, 99, and 110; 123 with 99 (see also 160); 124 with 107; and 125 with 108 (see also 161).

[63] Manetti, ss. 128–129. Manetti's purpose for these remarks will be treated below, p. 150.

[64] Manetti, "De pompis," fols. 261ᵛ–262ʳ; Manetti: Battisti, pp. 311–312. Urb. Lat. 387 originated in the library of Federigo da Montefeltro. Manetti: Battisti is a publication of the copy in Vat. Lat. 2919. Contrast Magnuson, 1958, pp. 185–200, who refers to this work.

guage then becomes technical. He adds that the form (*forma*) of man is the most noble among all the shapes (*figurae*) of all animate and inanimate things, that it is similar to the entire created world, and that it "indeed was held by some of the most learned men to have been made in the likeness of the entire world," for which reasons the Greeks call it "microcosm" (ss. 135–136). He then adds, again as he had not in Florence, that Noah had built the Ark to save mankind, that he had built it after the most perfect construction (*fabrica*) of the human body, and that Nicholas had wanted to imitate that construction in his own divine temple. "The proportion of these dimensions [of the Ark] could not be kept in the form (*forma*) of our temple; nonetheless, he kept the likeness of the design (*lineamentorum*) in the shape (*in figuris*)" (s. 138).

Manetti then concludes his own comments by saying that in his construction Noah had had divine inspiration directly from God. The Ark was the proper model to imitate and copy when constructing a building meant to save mankind, and Nicholas, through reading and study of proper authors, had desired and wanted to imitate that construction in undertaking his own divine temple (ss. 139–140).

Manetti's comments show that he had used the building as a figure for study. He followed the traditional pattern of letting it serve as a point of departure for speculation about doctrine, and he did not examine it as an architectonic structure. But he did frame his comments as part of his description of the building as a piece of architecture, and he did make some fundamental changes that show that he had an awareness of its architectonic character.

The first indication that he was adapting an older convention rather than inventing something new occurs in his reference to the Ark. It was one of the most common figures for the Church, and it allowed him to prepare for the reference a few lines later to the Temple of Solomon, which was often analogous to the Ark when either was used figuratively. He was also following the traditional interpretation that had long referred to the Ark or the Temple when he found the basilica to be similar in one way or another to man and to all created things.[65] Augustine had explained that the Ark, whose three dimensions signify the human body (*significant corpus humanum*), had many other significations as well, and he indicated that few of them depended upon precise knowledge of the Ark as a physical structure.[66] In this way Augustine had authorized a purely non-architectonic use of the Ark as a figure. An example of such a use is Hugh of St. Victor's explanation that the three elements of the Ark, which is the Temple of God in man, are *locus, materia,* and *artifex;* defining who would be the builder of the home of God, he said, "Ipse artifex eris, cor tuum locus, cogitationes tuae materia" ("You are its builder, you build it in your heart, your thoughts are its material").[67] This recalls Augustine's reason for condemning those who misunderstood the prophecy to David that Solomon would build the Temple of God. They had failed to recognize that the Temple would be Christ and even man. As he quotes Paul, "'For the temple of God is holy, which temple you are.'"[68]

The elaborations and commentaries of medieval authors wander constantly farther from the architectural figure that had served as their point of departure; similarly, the more the figure was embroidered, the more feeble its impact became. In patristic writings the analogy between the various things referred to by the figure had been

---

[65] See Cornelius, 1930, pp. 3 ff.

[66] *City of God*, XV, xxvi, xxvii.

[67] Hugh of St. Victor, *De Arca Noe Morali*, IV, i, col. 664.

[68] "Templum enim Dei sanctum est, quod estis vos"; Augustine, *City of God*, XVII, viii; I Corinthians 3:17.

clear, because the terminology was simple and the argument was pointed. Ambrose had said simply that the Ark was built in the shape (*figura*) of the human body and had demonstrated that the human body and created things that were made by God were similar because they were both carefully constructed according to their *congrua mensura ratioque*.[69] Similarly, Augustine had depended only upon the terms *figura*, *mensura*, *constructio*, and *signum*.[70] Hugh's analogies between the Ark, the Temple, the Church, the body of man, and created things is lost in his welter of other analogies and figurative meanings. He used the term *forma* to refer to form, but the term *figura* referred to a non-architectonic and non-formal sign for contemplation as a figure within an allegory to be interpreted literally, allegorically, tropologically, and anagogically.[71] Manetti used *forma* as Hugh had, but with the term *figura* he referred to shape, thus making the thing itself more substantial and concrete as an object of study.

Manetti's cogitations within the basilica belong to the figurative tradition that includes Ambrose, Augustine, and Hugh of St. Victor, but his means of expressing the results of his reflections give them the impact of the Fathers rather than the complexity of their successors. There are, however, differences even between Manetti's report about the Duomo in Florence and the basilica in Rome; they are major conceptual differences and may not be adequately explained by an additional two decades of exposure to patristic sources and rhetorical experience. It seems highly possible that they may be attributed to his contact with his friend Alberti. Alberti was equally literate in ancient and patristic writings and had recently completed *De re aedificatoria;* the new comprehension of architecture that is found there seems to lie behind the sounder understanding of architecture that is found in Manetti's later description.

Alberti had explained that architecture is design (*lineamenta*) and construction (*structura*), and that the operations of the architect must be an imitation of the operations of God as he creates in nature. The stress was on the thing in process of creation, not on the finished, immutable form to be subjected to cogitation. Alberti was writing about how the architect designs and builds. He had considered man only one of the many things that God made and whose construction the architect should imitate in his own operations. This attitude is clear in a passage in which he referred to older sources. The ancients, he said, invented three orders of columns, taking their separate form (*modus*) and measure (*dimensio*) from the variety in the bodies of men. From this correspondence, he continued, the commentators of our sacred books have

---

[69]"Itaque et Deus auctor nostri corporis, naturaeque fabricator astruitur, et opus ipsum perfectum esse iis sermonibus significatur . . . ut in iis quoque congrua mensura ratioque concurrat: . . . ." *De Noe et Arca*, vi, cols. 387–388.

[70]". . . Procul dubio figura est peregrinantis in hoc saeculo Civitatis Dei. . . . Nam et mensurae ipsae longitudinis . . . significant corpus humanum. . . ." "Et cetera quae in eiusdem arcae constructione dicuntur ecclesiasticarum signa sunt rerum." *City of God*, XV, xxvi.

[71]In *De Arca Noe Morali*, Hugh of St. Victor stressed *forma*, while in *De Arca Noe Mystica* he stresses *figura*. In the former work he defines *figura:* "Figura, res, veritas, ut idem intelligas esse umbram et figuram, idem corpus et rem, idem spiritum et veritatem. Unde umbra dicuntur illa, quae ante adventum Christi sub lege naturali, et sub scripta lege corporaliter et visibiliter gesta sunt ad praefiguranda ea, quae nunc post adventum Christi in tempore gratiae corporaliter et visibiliter geruntur, quae ideo umbra dicuntur, quia corporalia erant et figura corporalium" (IV, ix, col. 679). In the latter work he uses it in that manner, as, for example: "Si enim arca Ecclesiam significat, restat ut longitudo arcae longitudinem figuret Ecclesiae" (iii, col. 685). And: "In ipsa fronte arcae facio parvam quadraturam ad figurandas quatuor partes mundi. . ." (iv, col. 686).

come to the opinion that the Ark of Noah was patterned on the shape of man.[72] In this passage Alberti refers to columns, the noblest ornaments of a building but still mere elements in it, and does not refer to the entire building. He also refers to commentators on scripture, not to scripture itself. Ancient practice and Vitruvius's theory were valuable to Alberti, but the commentators, who wrote of an entire structure based on man's body, were of little use to him. Similarly, an entire building that was made out of elements would serve Alberti as a figure for contemplation, but its individual elements would not. A building would reveal the order that derives from God and that is immanent in the world he creates. This, however, is a slightly different doctrine from the one Manetti coaxes out of the basilica.

Although his approach was different, Manetti was on the track Alberti had set for him, as is evident in his revisions of the original description. In the earlier work on the Duomo in Florence, Manetti had made no pretense of presenting his own ideas or discoveries. Instead, he explained in the preface that it was his intention to describe the ceremonies presided over by Eugenius IV when he had consecrated the building, and that he would do so in as brief a form as possible. In his brevity, he continued, he would imitate the technique of ancient painters who, *pro artis lineamenta*, were able to concentrate on the essential elements of an action without diluting the representation with unnecessary detail.[73] In what follows, although he describes the cathedral, there is little in his wording that makes the cathedral a concrete, substantial architectonic structure, and, although he describes the ceremony, there is little sense of the activity as an event held within the architectural setting of the great church. Together, these deficiencies vitiate the reader's response to the event as an action that occurred in a setting. In contrast, although in his description from twenty years later he describes no specific event, he has treated the architecture as a part of a larger program of building that the pope undertook as a part of his program for government, and he has placed the pope in the tribune of the basilica, lit by the light from the dome, presiding over the hierarchy of the Church.

A more significant revision also suggests familiarity with Alberti's ideas. In the earlier work, similarities between the body of man, the Duomo, and all created things were to be noted in the relationships of the forms (*formae*) and shapes (*figurae*). These were finished objects that could be examined in sequence as their similarities and correspondences were noted. In the later work, forms and shapes are supplemented by construction (*fabrica*), in the case of the human body, and by design (*lineamenta*), in the case of the likeness of the shape of the basilica to the Ark. The term *lineamenta*, which had been used in the earlier work as a vague term referring to general characteristics of the painter's operations and does not appear elsewhere,[74] is now used in the sense Alberti had given it in *De re aedificatoria*. Similarly, the human body is now a construction, a thing made rather than a thing finished, a thing that might be studied in its process of fabrication rather than a thing finished and ac-

---

[72]"Quod ipsum nostri sacrorum interpretes advertentes, arcam per diluvium factam ad hominis figurationem autumant." *De re aed.*, IX, vii, p. 835; Alberti: Leoni, p. 200. Zoubov, 1958, p. 257, cites Augustine, *City of God*, XV, xxvi, as the source, but this would be a source in only a vague way, consonant with Alberti's vague "sacrorum interpretes," a phrase Zoubov mentions. See also Vitruvius, III, i, 1–2, who speaks of symmetry "ad hominis bene figurati membrorum," and of the "Corpus enim hominis. . . natura composuit."

[73]Manetti, "De pompis," fol. 261ʳ; Manetti: Battisti, p. 310, reads "per artis liniamenta."

[74]Compare Facius in Baxandall, 1964, p. 99, and Ghiberti in Krautheimer, 1970, pp. 230 f., and revision, p. xx. The term does not occur in this context in Augustine, Ambrose, or Hugh of St. Victor; for them, it would refer to insignificant aspects of their figures.

cessible through analysis of its extant and unchanging shape or form alone. Manetti's new sense of the body of man as a construction and of the shape deriving from design seems to be an important indication of his familiarity with Alberti's theory of architecture. It corresponds to his careful stress in his treatment of the basilica on proportions, on the building materials, and on the response of the building to the specific requirements of those who would use it, indications that recur throughout the description. All this seems to show that Manetti was familiar with his friend's new ideas about architecture or that he had profited from the same sources and outlook that Alberti had. This familiarity comes to a climax in the section that Manetti attributes to his own discoveries inside the basilica, for here he is able to treat the building as a design, as an architectonic structure that serves as a figure for his own contemplation.

The conclusions he draws from his contemplation, however, could hardly show a more distinct difference of interpretation of legitimate sources for design from those Alberti had laboriously explained. Manetti, not Alberti, believed—and Manetti himself claims uniquely to have discovered—that the design of the basilica is related to the body of man, to all animate and inanimate things, to what the Greeks call a microcosm, and to the Ark of Noah. Manetti makes a case for the appropriateness of these models for the basilica's design, notes that he had seen them in the design, states that Nicholas desired and wanted to imitate the Ark, and then concludes his thoughts. Significantly, he does not say that, like Noah, Nicholas had had direct inspiration from God in designing the basilica. Nicholas had had to study the proper authors.

After finishing his contemplation, Manetti again becomes a reporter. He now moves on to discuss the place of Nicholas's building project in the history of architecture. He reports that Nicholas's works are greater than those of Philo as described by the Greeks (s. 144), and that it ought to be conspicuous to all that they far surpass those of Solomon. Nicholas's excellence in design is easily seen by comparing his great buildings with the seven wonders of the world, which include the city of Babylon and the Capitol of ancient Rome.[75] Manetti reports that Nicholas, shunning the oracles of Apollo and the writings of Socrates, imitated Solomon, "the wisest of men through the power of God," and studied what had been written of Solomon's buildings in sacred literature, which gave him access to the sentences (*sententia*) of omnipotent God (ss. 155–156).

Nicholas could have found any number of doctrines in Solomon's writings and in commentaries on them, including beliefs about the figurative correspondence of a basilical church to the Ark, to man, and to the universe. Manetti and Nicholas may have been particularly aware of another of the sentiments of Solomon, who had said that God had "ordered all things by measure and number and weight."[76] This had become an accepted statement about the structure of the universe, and Augustine had related it to Platonic teaching to show certain similarities between Christian and pagan doctrine.[77] Alberti's ideas about architecture may have made the pope and the secretary sensitive to the statement. In the terminology Alberti taught, measure and number would stand for *lineamenta* or design, and weight would refer to *structura* or construction, which included the moving, lifting, and placing of great weights in the

---

[75] Manetti, ss. 144–145. Compare Manetti's earlier compressed reference to the seven wonders and to the works of Philo, which the Florentine cathedral surpasses; "De pompis," fol. 262ᵛ; Manetti: Battisti, p. 313. Frezzi, in the *Quadriregio*, compared the church in the domain of Faith (discussed above, chapter 3), to the Capitol, to Ilion, and to the Temple of Zion (1914, IV, xv, lines 7–9).

[76] Wisdom 11:12.

[77] Augustine, *City of God*, XII, 19.

fabric.[78] That Manetti was referring to Solomon as glossed by Augustine and developed by Alberti is suggested by the way he had carefully incorporated into his own description clear references to the dimensions, proportions, and materials Nicholas had used when building the basilica. Even though Manetti did not reach the level of sophistication in handling them that Alberti did, Alberti had perhaps introduced them to him as important considerations in architecture.

Manetti went on to quite specific references to Solomon's writings. He quoted the scriptural descriptions of Solomon's constructions and then pointed out the differences between the basilica and the Temple and between the palace at the Vatican and the one Solomon had built. Nicholas's basilica was superior in its dimensions; it was longer, wider, and higher. It was also superior in other ways; it had three vestibules rather than one, round windows rather than long ones, and vaults and a dome rather than three flat roofs (ss. 160–165). Manetti concluded his description of the basilica and of Nicholas's building program by stating that although Solomon's buildings were great, Nicholas's were greater, just as the religion of Christ is to be preferred and is known to have replaced the divine Law of the Old Testament.[79]

Manetti's description—carefully constructed to reveal the basilica as the dominant element in the entire fabric of Rome, included as a coordinate part of the *Life of Nicholas,* and imbued with the new attitude toward architecture that he shared with Alberti—corresponds to Nicholas's program for papal government as it may be known from other sources. It therefore gives an insight into that program that is not available elsewhere. It reveals how the buildings built by the pope would have provided moving settings for his actions, and it adds detail to the justification of the building program that Nicholas had himself made to the cardinals on his deathbed.

Laetentur Coeli had defined the pope as successor to Peter, Vicar of Christ, and "head of the universal Church and father and teacher of all Christians." Nicholas made this doctrine conspicuous through building. He ensconced himself in the Vatican at Peter's shrine, where he could concentrate on the sacred affairs of the Church. The Jubilee bull had explained, on the basis of traditional doctrine, that the Jubilee is a special time when God's mercy is specially shown. The Flood, circumcision, the Law, and, finally, grace have been the agencies for saving mankind, and now the pope, celebrated throughout Christendom as the head of the Church, Vicar of Christ, and successor to Peter, is making available God's gift of grace to the faithful. The Jubilee is a special sign of God's mercy; the sacraments are signs of God's gift of grace, which is always available to the faithful. The pope's administering of the Jubilee and of the sacraments are signs of, or figures for, his concern for those of whom he is head, father, and teacher, and the basilica allows him to be seen in this role at all times. No gaudy spectacle would goad the pilgrim into the basilica, but once inside he would be moved by the dignity and the splendor of the place. There he would see the pope, a conspicuous *exemplum* of the administrator of God's apparatus of salvation, the Vicar of Christ, a man whose love for God allows him to act with charity. As Manetti's description explains, Nicholas is to be visible beyond the altar on his raised throne illuminated by the light flowing down from the dome.

This was the most obvious representation of Nicholas's program for papal government in the design of the basilica; coordinated with it were many subtleties. One of these is the triumph of the Christian religion over pagan religions, which could be shown through the use of classical elements. This was the principal way in which Nicholas's program was a conscious revival of classical, pagan antiquity. Nicholas

[78] See *De re aed.,* preface.
[79] Manetti, ss. 170–171. See also below, chapter 7.

did not revive antique architecture; he used it. Antiquity was present in the design, but not as a standard of achievement that haunted the pope or as an object of jealous rivalry. The Church and its pope had long since triumphed. It was legitimate, therefore, to incorporate pagan materials into Christian buildings. Some of the columns Nicholas intended to use in the crossing of the basilica had been hauled over from the ruins behind the Pantheon.[80] The Castel Sant'Angelo, known to have been the Mausoleum of Hadrian, was refitted and reequipped with the angel of the Last Judgment. The obelisk that had stood beside the basilica would have had the urn on top that was believed to contain the ashes of Caesar, topped with Christ the Savior.[81]

Manetti said almost nothing about this spoilage of antiquity, and when he did mention the obelisk, he did not refer to its ancient function but only to its intended Christian use. Antiquity could be plundered and put to better use in a Christian context, and nothing need be said about it. Augustine had sanctioned the operation: the pagans "gave their gold, silver, and clothing to the people of God fleeing from Egypt, not knowing that they yielded those things which they gave 'unto the obedience of Christ' (2 Cor. 10:5). That which was done in Exodus was undoubtedly a figure that it might typify these things."[82]

Nicholas was not the first pope to consider antiquity a legitimate stockpile of material for the use of Christians. From the earliest phase of monumental Christian architecture in Rome, pagan buildings had been plundered by Christian builders. What was new in Nicholas's construction was the self-conscious attempt to evoke antique forms, even if this meant using antique architectural elements in an architectonic syntax different from the one they had had before or different from the one then prevalent in construction. And the period of antiquity to which Nicholas chose to refer was also self-conscious. His forms were meant to evoke Christian antiquity, that is, the period when the early Church first became established in Rome.[83] This accounts for the simplicity and the monumentality of the basilica's tribune as Manetti described it. The Early Christian character of the old and revered building Nicholas was rebuilding would not have been violated; instead, it would have been emphasized.

Christian antiquity is also present in another passage in Manetti's text, although only implicitly. In the works of Ambrose there is a short account of the Ark of Noah that included a statement Manetti might have picked up, although Ambrose had attributed it to Solomon and Manetti might have considered the earlier source to be the proper one when he used it himself. Ambrose had said that Solomon had said, "The wise man has eyes in his head" (Eccles. 2:14); therefore, Ambrose continued, it is proper that he who presides in an imperial council hall should be where he can see all, and, being seen, he sits in greater splendor.[84] Nicholas, according to Manetti, presided over the hierarchy in the part of the basilica that Manetti called the "head" and the "tribune." The only other worthy sight in the building would have been the single altar between the tomb of Peter and the throne of the pope. Alberti had pointed out that to have but a single altar in a church would be a welcome and beneficial return to the practice of the early Church.[85] The altar had been built by Constantine,

---

[80] See Muffel, 1953, pp. 360–362; for this, and other plunder destined for St. Peter's that might not have retained its ancient form, see Müntz, *ACP*, I, pp. 83, 108 ff., 118–119.

[81] For the ashes of Caesar, see Rucellai, 1960, p. 72.

[82] *On Christian Doctrine*, 1958, II, xl, 61; see also II, xl, 60. Augustine uses this figure to summarize book II, which deals with the Christian's exegesis of signs.

[83] Wittkower, 1962, I, 1, pp. 5–6.

[84] *De Noe et Arca*, vii, cols. 389–390.

[85] *De re aed.*, VII, xiii. See Wittkower, 1962, I, 1, p. 5.

whom the pope replaced as the head of the empire after it had become Christian, and it was placed there to mark the tomb of Peter, the rock on whom Christ had founded the Church and whose successor Nicholas was.

Nicholas would be visibly dominant over the hierarchy of the Church, which would find its properly ordered place in the tribune around him. He would clearly be the head of the Church; the Church's members would clearly be there at his disposal. Manetti's description stresses this arrangement, and therefore it must be seen as another point of doctrine that Nicholas intended to make clear through his building project. It corresponds directly to Nicholas's choice of Peter's arms as his own; those arms, Nicholas made clear, had been given by Christ to Peter and the popes for the Church and not by Christ to Peter and the Church for the popes. The pope, not a council, handled them.

The keys were called knowledge and the power to judge matters of the soul, and they were therefore superior to arms and corporal judgment executed against the body, the instruments of earthly states. The keys ruled the sword; the head governed the body; the pope as priest presided over the hierarchy, which there in the tribune would include the temporal officers of states under his jurisdiction. Nicholas's transportation and renovation of the Vatican obelisk would have been a clear visual figure for this point of doctrine, which corresponds to Biondo's statement: "The princes of the world revere and honor the supreme pontiff, the perpetual dictator, successor not of Gaius Caesar, but of the fisherman Peter, and vicar of the aforementioned emperor."[86]

Knowledge was the greatest attribute of the pope; it was essential that the successor to the Fisherman, who administered the sacraments through which God gave the gift of paradise, demonstrate his knowledge. It therefore followed that he would design the project. Nicholas used his intelligence as sharpened in his investigations of the most holy authors and sacred books of omnipotent God to conceive and design in mind and spirit both the basilica and the project of which it was a part. When built, it would accomplish Nicholas's purpose; it would continually confirm and daily corroborate by great buildings, which are perpetual monuments and eternal testimonies seemingly made by God, vulgar beliefs founded on doctrines of learned men. "In this way," Nicholas had continued in his testament, "belief is preserved and augmented, and in this way it is laid down and held fast by a certain admirable devotion."

Manetti explained some, but not all, of this in his description. His description of the pope's comprehensive program is a rounded but not a complete one, but when supplemented with other elements that correspond to its major points, it becomes clear that Nicholas's program was an extensive and unified whole. It was the first to allow a program for government based upon theological and political conceptions to be consciously, intelligently, and carefully rendered in the architectural design of an entire city. The Borgo dominates Rome; the palace dominates the Borgo; the basilica dominates the palace and the Borgo. The climax of the project is inside the basilica, where, beyond the altar in the well-lit and undecorated tribune beyond the dome, sits the pope, surrounded by the hierarchy, clearly visible to the faithful. In Nicholas's project, an intelligent theory and method of architectural design has been expanded to embrace an entire city that has been conceived of as a place where men, through their activities, establish order.

[86]Biondo, 1953, III, lxxxvii, p. 318.

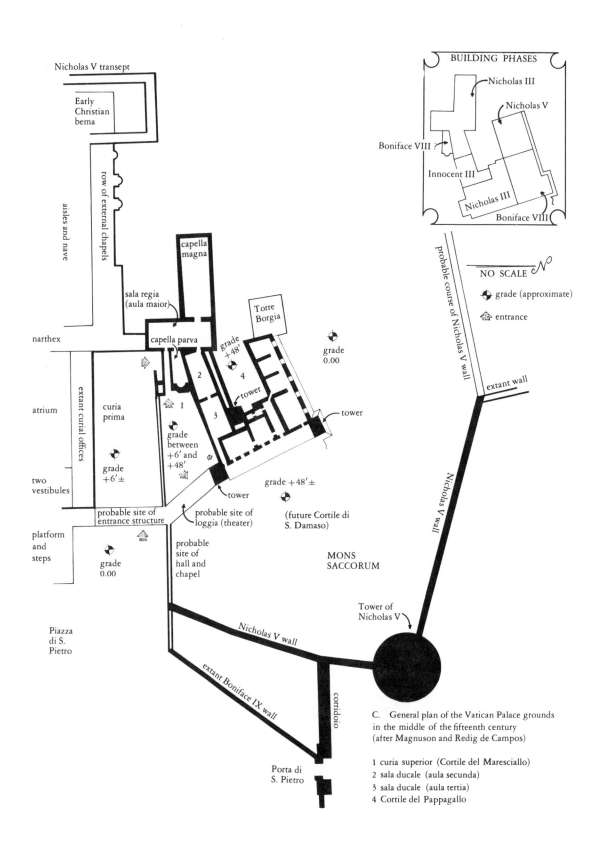

Nicholas V transept

Early
Christian
bema

row of external chapels

aisles and nave

capella
magna

sala regia
(aula maior)

Torre
Borgia

narthex

capella parva

grade
+48'

grade
0.00

atrium

extant curial offices

curia
prima

1

2

4

grade
+48'

tower

3

tower

narthex

grade
between
+6' and
+48'

two
vestibules

grade
+6'±

grade +48'±

(future Cortile di
S. Damaso)

platform
and
steps

grade
0.00

probable site of
entrance structure

probable site of
loggia (theater)

MONS
SACCORUM

probable
site of
hall and
chapel

Piazza
di S.
Pietro

Nicholas V wall

Tower of
Nicholas V

extant Boniface IX wall

corridoio

Porta di
S. Pietro

C. General plan of the Vatican Palace grounds
in the middle of the fifteenth century
(after Magnuson and Redig de Campos)

1 curia superior (Cortile del Maresciallo)
2 sala ducale (aula secunda)
3 sala ducale (aula tertia)
4 Cortile del Pappagallo

BUILDING PHASES

Nicholas III

Nicholas V

Boniface VIII ?

Innocent III

Nicholas III

Boniface VIII

probable course of Nicholas V wall

NO SCALE

N

grade (approximate)

entrance

extant wall

Nicholas V wall

7   The Papal Palace
in the Vatican

Nicholas had given the cardinals two justifications for his building project, one particularly relevant to the basilica, the other to the Vatican Palace. Each justification was related to the other, just as each building was also. Through his ecclesiastical building program, "belief is preserved and augmented, and in this way it is laid down and held fast by a certain admirable devotion." The pope then continued directly:

> With a view to this devotion of the Christian peoples toward the Roman Church and the Apostolic Seat, certain fortifications of towns and cities are added, [places made] safe for the inhabitants themselves and a source of fear to enemies. These are made more secure through the rearing of great buildings against foreign enemies and internal ones who are eager for revolution, conspiring daily to plunder and revolting to the terrible harm of their churchly governors.

He listed these places—Gualdo, Fabriano, Assisi, Castellana, Narni, Città Vecchia, Spoleto, Viterbo, "and in many other places of our Church"—and then went on: "We built several distinguished things for the sure and expressed effect, both of devotion and fortification." He was especially zealous, he continued, in his attention to the ornamentation and fortification of Rome, the most celebrated city among all Christian peoples, and to St. Peter's, to the palace next to it, and to the great and new city adjacent to it. These he made secure and dignified for the head, the members, and the curia.[1]

Nicholas's project for the palace was as laden with significant content as was his scheme for the basilica, but a different approach must be taken in its interpretation. Manetti's description is useful, if not essential, but the secretary was less complete in his report about the content of the palace than he was about the more important basilica. Nicholas's project for the palace was closely tied to quickly changing notions concerning the proper setting for a secular governor, while his scheme for the basilica was immersed within a much longer and more slowly evolving ecclesiastical and sacred tradition. The sacred tradition has been the subject of more study than its concomitant secular elements, and so Nicholas's basilica project is more easily comprehended than is his project for the palace. And, although Manetti's report was important for transmitting the pope's intentions for the palace to a later period, the actual construction Nicholas raised within the palace precinct was not insignificant,

---

[1] Manetti, *RIS*, cols. 949–950.

and the impact of what he built was in some cases immediate. Some of his work is only now being brought to light and identified, much has been lost, and much was never executed. Nevertheless, the role of the palace in the pope's program for governing the Church and for rebuilding the city of Rome may be grasped with some clarity, but only if the whole is understood in each of its parts.

The parts are the extant construction and Nicholas's additions to it, the decorations within the palace, and the surrounding areas as they were planned but only partially completed. After these parts have been surveyed, the meaning or content of the project can be grasped.

Both tradition and extant construction at the Vatican were important in the project Nicholas formulated for the palace. Innocent III was the first pope to reside at the Vatican for any length of time, and he began what survives as the nucleus of the present building. Nicholas III was the next pope to devote any extensive attention to it; Boniface VIII also resided there on occasion and added to the palace. During the Babylonian Captivity, when what was said about Rome was more important than what the popes in Avignon were doing about Rome, the Lateran loomed ever larger in rhetoric and conception, and by 1420, when the basilica at the Lateran was the principal church of the city and of the world, the residential facilities there doubtless shared its august position. But when Martin V returned, the Lateran Palace was less habitable than the Vatican Palace, which had been kept in some sort of repair by popes resident in Rome. The Lateran had been damaged by fires in 1308 and 1361, as well as by earthquakes and riots. Repairs had been undertaken there by Urban V (1362–70) and by Gregory XI (1370–78), who considered the Lateran basilica to be "greater than all the other churches and basilicas... in the honor of priority, dignity, and preeminence." Because the Vatican complex was more immediately serviceable, the curia was installed there, and both Martin V and Eugenius IV devoted attention to its repair, although neither considered it his expected residence when in Rome. After 1447 the Vatican Palace, linked to the status Nicholas had given the basilica of the Prince of the Apostles, became the expected—if not official—residence of the popes. With brief and insignificant exceptions, the popes have remained where Nicholas put them (see plan C, on p. 128).

Before the Babylonian Captivity, Innocent III and his successors had built most of what survived at the Vatican Palace in 1447, although Biondo said that the palace was that of Pope Symmachus (498–514).[2] The most imposing parts were the public, ceremonial facilities required at the residence of any important governor of the period. These were a large chapel (*capella magna*), later replaced by the Sistine Chapel, and a large council hall lying next to it and called the Sala Regia (also *aula maior*), which was refitted in the sixteenth century as the present Sala Ducale. Opening off the Sala Regia was the first of two smaller council halls, lined up with one another, each called the Sala Ducale and differentiated from each other by the additional terms *aula secunda* and *aula tertia*. Next to the *aula secunda*, and likewise opening into the Sala Regia, was the *capella parva*, or Chapel of St. Nicholas. Next to this chapel was a corridor leading to the Sala Regia from the *curia superior*, also known as the Cortile del Maresciallo. This enclosed space extended from the end of the chapel and the entrance to the corridor next to it to a point a little beyond the *aula tertia*, where it gave access to the *mons saccorum*, a garden area for the palace; along the

---

[2] Biondo, 1953, I, liii, p. 273. Shortly after, Platina would point out that Nicholas V had added to the palace of Nicholas III; Platina, p. 324 (Life of Nicholas III). He does not say that the palace was among Symmachus's many works.

fourth side it was separated from the lower-lying *curia prima*, which was the first of the spaces within the palace precinct to be entered from the area in front of the basilica and palace. This entrance court abutted the vestibules that formed the entrances into the basilica; it opened at the back, and perhaps along the side toward the atrium, into curial facilities between the palace and the basilica's atrium and northern flank.[3]

The more intimate facilities and the private apartments of the pope were in a wing set at right angles to that composed of the two *sale ducali*; it projected north, away from the basilica, and it was accessible directly from the Cortile del Maresciallo in its corner at the *mons saccorum*. There was a tower on the inner corner where this wing joined the *aula tertia*, and a tower on each end of the wing's exterior (eastern) façade. This façade—now higher, masked by the loggia Bramante began, and one of the three sides that encloses the Cortile di San Damaso—faces in the direction of the Castel Sant'Angelo. Originally it offered an extensive view over the Borgo and Rome. Below it stretched the *mons saccorum*, where there was a palace garden. The garden's boundaries were ill-defined to the north, but walls built in the early quattrocento clearly separated the garden on the *mons saccorum* from the Borgo. The garden area itself was further divided by walls with smaller towers.[4]

The topography of the site, the relationship of the palace's site to that of the basilica and to the Borgo, and the failure to have had a comprehensive scheme for construction, but instead to have built piecemeal, had produced a palace precinct that fell into roughly three areas. At the far west were facilities for the curia and the functionaries of the papal household; next, down the hill to the east, were the entrances and the ceremonial halls; and farthest to the east and nearest Rome were the papal apartments and gardens. Nicholas had to work with the same topographic considerations as had his predecessors; but, in addition, he accepted the distinction between the three areas that had been bequeathed him by the extant construction and the traditional uses of the buildings. Manetti's description makes it clear that Nicholas meant to leave the western, uphill area largely intact; it explains briefly that the pope would add stables, kitchens, and workhouses with their necessary gardens, orchards, and courtyards to the extant structures in the western area. Next, farther down the hill, he said there would be a chapel, the library, facilities for the most important officials of the curia, and the papal apartments.[5]

Manetti, and Nicholas, concentrated their attentions on the last two areas, the public, ceremonial facilities and the private apartments of the pope with the rooms for the curia's activities. The greatest uncertainty surrounds Nicholas's intentions for the part of the palace that dated back to Innocent III and Nicholas III. Neither Manetti nor surviving documents or buildings indicate that the pope had any extensive plans for renovating this part, but the area did not remain untouched. Fra Angelico worked in the *capella parva*, most probably for Nicholas. Vasari reported that his work included "some stories from the life of Jesus Christ" and portraits of Nicholas V, Frederick III, the archbishop of Florence St. Antoninus, Flavio Biondo, and Ferrante

[3] For a more detailed analysis of these areas, including the facilities for the curia and treasury, see Ehrle and Egger, 1935, pp. 61 ff.; Egger, 1951, esp. pp. 497 ff.; and the literature to be cited in the next note.

[4] See Ehrle and Stevenson, 1897, pp. 14, 19; Ehrle and Egger, 1935, p. 68, esp. n. 5, and pp. 69, 98; Magnuson, 1958, pp. 103–104, 107–110, 118–126; Redig de Campos, 1941–42, passim; idem, 1959, passim; idem, 1960, passim; idem, 1967, pp. 25–41, 48; idem, 1971, passim.

[5] Manetti, ss. 67–73. For the area, see Ehrle and Egger, 1935, pp. 62 ff.; Magnuson, 1958, pp. 98 ff.; and Redig de Campos, 1967, pp. 19–52. For more precise designations for these last three facilities, see below.

of Aragon,[6] while the Anonimo Gaddiano said that the chapel "was truly a paradise."[7] Such a cycle seems inappropriate for a chapel; its location next to the entrances to various council halls, as well as the failure of its usual ecclesiastical designation to appear in documents during Nicholas's pontificate, suggests that perhaps Angelico was given the task of fitting it out as a reception hall.[8]

That is the single hint available about Nicholas's intentions for the older, ceremonial nucleus of the Vatican Palace. It seems more than likely that the pope intended to replace its facilities with a new complex elsewhere in the precinct; this complex will be discussed below. Meanwhile, the pope devoted a great deal of energy to renovating the wing with the private reception halls and apartments farthest down the hill toward the Borgo. His intended program included all the facilities one would expect in a papal *casa regia* at this moment. By understanding what Nicholas inherited, what he added, and how he decorated it, the Vatican Palace can be understood within the context of other quattrocento palaces—both ones built and ones described in treatises—but to interpret it in that context is beyond the scope of this study. Here, attention will be directed at the role of the palace in Nicholas's comprehensive scheme for governing (plan D).

On the top floor, the second above the basement level, in what had been the inner corner tower between the private wing and the *sala tertia*, Nicholas made a small private chapel that was decorated between 1447 and 1450 by Angelico, with Benozzo Gozzoli as an assistant.[9] Its decoration stressed the transmission of doctrine from the Evangelists in the vaults through the eight doctors in the corners of the vaults and the examples of the protomartyrs of the early Church, Stephen and Lawrence. On the same floor was a small *studiolo*, richly decorated with intarsia walls and gilded frieze, cornice, and capitals; its decorative program is unknown.[10] On the floor below, Nicholas decorated two small rooms (the Stanza della Falda and a smaller room), the smaller of which he used as his bedroom; in the center of its ceiling he placed a painted half-bust of Peter holding the keys and a book.[11]

[6] Vasari, II, pp. 516–517. Ehrle and Egger, 1935, pp. 133–135, place the work in 1453–55 and point out that Calixtus III was most likely the sponsor of Ferrante's portrait, which would have been executed by a pupil of Angelico (Angelico died in Rome about three weeks before Calixtus became pope). See also Pope-Hennessy, 1952, p. 207. Orlandi, 1964, pp. 88–95, 128–143, places the decoration in the last year of Eugenius's pontificate and the first years of that of Nicholas, even though there would have been little reason at that time to include Frederick III and Antoninus. He proposes that in 1453–55 Angelico was working for Cardinal Torquemada at Santa Maria sopra Minerva.

[7] Anonimo Gaddiano: Fabriczy, 1893, p. 277, in his remarks about St. Peter's, which he visited in 1544–46 when the chapel was being torn down by Paul III. Earlier, in the section devoted to Angelico, pp. 76–77, he had said simply, and apparently inaccurately, "Im [*sic*] Roma dipinse a papa Eugenio una capella," a statement he had taken from the Libro di Antonio Billi: Fabriczy, 1891, p. 361.

[8] Ehrle and Egger, 1935, pp. 108–109, list the references. If it were a reception hall, its history scenes and portraits of famous men may have fitted the type that Taddeo di Bartolo and Castagno had painted.

[9] This was the "capella parva superior," and should not be confused with the "capella parva sive capella parva Sancti Nicolai"; see Ehrle and Egger, 1935, pp. 103 ff., who addressed this problem. For the tower, see Redig de Campos, 1947–49, p. 385; idem, 1967, pp. 22–24. For the dates of Angelico's work, see Pope-Hennessy, 1952, pp. 187–188; Orlandi, 1964, pp. 85–87, with numerous documents.

[10] Müntz, *ACP*, I, p. 76; Pastor, 1949, p. 187, where the common confusion between the *studiolo* and the chapel appears; Biagetti, 1932–33, passim, reassessed the evidence and showed that they were in separate parts of the palace but on the same floor. See also Ehrle and Egger, 1935, p. 94; Redig de Campos, 1967, p. 51.

[11] Redig de Campos, 1967, p. 25, and p. 49, where he points out that, in addition to Nicholas's coat of arms in the ornamentation, one finds those of Boniface IX in the remains of the frieze in the attic of the bedroom, and that above that level are the remains of a frieze from the thirteenth century. See also Redig de Campos, 1960, pp. 242–243. The work is perhaps to be connected with the payments of 1450

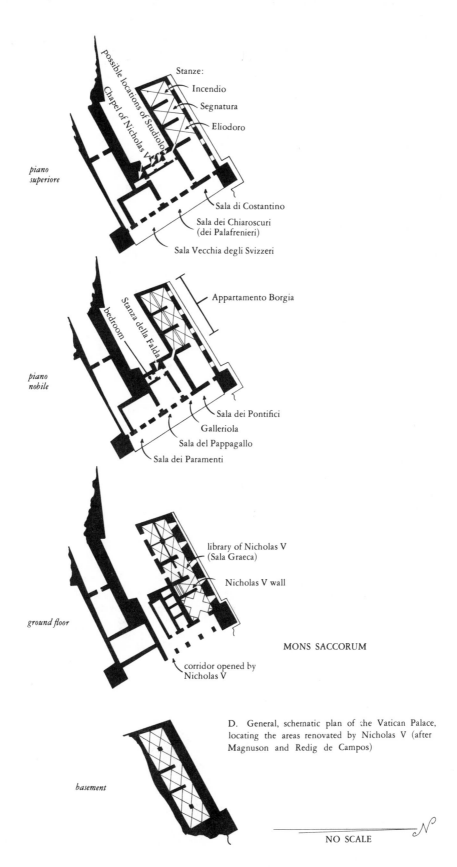

*piano
superiore*

Stanze:

possible locations of Studiolo
Chapel of Nicholas V

Incendio

Segnatura

Eliodoro

Sala di Costantino

Sala dei Chiaroscuri
(dei Palafrenieri)

Sala Vecchia degli Svizzeri

*piano
nobile*

bedroom

Stanza della Falda

Appartamento Borgia

Sala dei Pontifici

Galleriola

Sala del Pappagallo

Sala dei Paramenti

ground floor

library of Nicholas V
(Sala Graeca)

Nicholas V wall

MONS SACCORUM

corridor opened by
Nicholas V

D. General, schematic plan of the Vatican Palace,
locating the areas renovated by Nicholas V (after
Magnuson and Redig de Campos)

basement

NO SCALE

These rooms were on the interior side of the wing toward what in the next century would become the Cortile del Pappagallo. On the opposite side, overlooking the garden, the Borgo, and Rome, the pope had at his disposal a series of large rooms. These were more public; here he presided over small ceremonies and interviews and conducted similar official business. On the same floor level as the bedroom were four rooms. The two nearer the entrance were called the Sala dei Paramenti and the Sala del Pappagallo, names that are often encountered in palaces of popes and princes.[12] The first perhaps took its name from the activity done there (preparation) or, more likely, from its decoration (tapestries, i.e., "Paramento, vale anche Ornamento, Drappo, col quale s'adornano le pareti de'templi, e delle case..."[13]), while the second was named after the live parrots that popes had around them in receptions or in their residences from at least the early fourteenth century.[14] Parrots were among the rare and delightful birds and animals that carried rich connotations and were a necessary element to include in the settings where princes pursued chivalric goals.[15] The third room, the Galleriola, was deep and narrow; the fourth, the Sala dei Pontifici, was used by Nicholas and his predecessors as a small consistory room.[16] Only the Sala del Pappagallo has revealed quattrocento decoration, the fragments of a painted frieze.[17]

Above these rooms, on the level of the chapel and *studiolo*, was a series of rooms that formed a *piano superiore*. They were apparently used for activities more closely associated with the internal papal household. Nearest the Cortile del Maresciallo was the Sala Vecchia degli Svizzeri, next was the Sala dei Chiaroscuri (also known as the Sala dei Palafrenieri), and, finally, there was the larger Sala di Costantino. There are

---

and 1451 in Müntz, *ACP*, I, p. 129. The painted fragments from the walls of these rooms are now in deposit in the Pinacoteca Vaticana.

[12]The earlier remarks by Magnuson, 1958, p. 284, n. 112, may now be supplemented by Diener, 1967, pp. 45 ff., who gives references to older literature and valuable additions to it. For designations of the "Camera del Papagallo" from the Vatican Palace, the "palatio tunc apostolico iuxta sanctum Laurentium in Damaso," the papal residence at Santa Maria Novella in Florence, the Palazzo Venezia, and the papal palace at Bologna, dating from March, 1431, through January, 1503—including six from the period of Nicholas—drawn from the Vatican archives, see Diener, 1967, pp. 51–54, and discussion, pp. 56 f. To his list may be added a notice that the Florentine ambassador had an interview with Nicholas in the "Camera del Papaghallo" on 9 July 1451; ASF, Dieci di Balia: Carteggio responsivo, 22, fol. 30ʳ. There are also references to the "aula palatii sui, quae paramenti camera appellatur" in the palace of Cardinal Giordano Orsini, in which Poggio mentions a series of sibyls (cited in Simpson, 1966, p. 138, n. 13); the "antecamera quae est paramentorum" where Cardinal d'Estouteville made his will (quoted in Mancini, 1967, p. 55); the "camera paramenti" between the dining room and garden in the papal palace at Avignon, mentioned from 1342 (Ehrle, 1890, pp. 692 n. 641, 694–695); and a "camera paramenti palatii apostolici" at the Vatican mentioned in Müntz, *ACP*, I, p. 13, from 1420. These two are the only names for rooms in the Vatican Palace for which records contemporaneous to Nicholas exist; the names of all other rooms are later.

[13]Crusca, s.v., no. 1. For tapestries, see below, p. 138.

[14]Diener, 1967, pp. 64–67.

[15]See the information given in Diener, 1967, pp. 98 ff.; and the analysis of the broader motif in Schlosser (1895) 1965, pp. 30 ff.; and below, pp. 155–161.

[16]For the consistory room, see Ehrle and Egger, 1935, p. 70. This room terminated the palace to the north; its west wall was also an outside wall before Nicholas V added his wing to it. See Ehrle and Stevenson, 1897, p. 33, and Redig de Campos, 1967, pp. 35–36, 44–45, who analyzes the condition of the wall under the *Expulsion of Heliodorus* in the Stanza d'Eliodoro on the level above. For a plan, see Redig de Campos, 1971, fig. 1.

[17]Biagetti, 1924–25, p. 492; published in Biagetti, 1926–27, pp. 244–245, figs. 5 and 6. The room is also known as the Camera dello Spogliatoio and is directly below the Sala dei Chiaroscuri. Calixtus III had a crucifixion painted in 1456 in the Camera del Papagallo; Diener, 1967, p. 50, with references to other, later work.

intriguing, extensive remains of decorative painting from the first two rooms, of which the technique, form, and means of integration with older work are similar to the remains from the Sala del Pappagallo and the two small rooms on that lower floor. Such similarities suggest that these fragments represent a meager survival of a much more extensive decorative program, which covered the entire palace (figs. 48–62). The surviving decorations are described here, so that later in this chapter their significance within Nicholas's comprehensive program for the palace can be understood.

The fragments are of decorative painted friezes in the first two rooms of the suite.[18] In the Sala dei Chiaroscuri a fictive architectural frieze executed for Nicholas III, which contains lively, wing-flapping doves between large fictive consoles, runs around the top of the wall (figs. 48,49; the uppermost parts have been lost). Below this frieze is a new one that may be securely dated to Nicholas V's pontificate (figs. 50–52).[19] Nicholas's addition complemented the doves; from the top, it begins with a rich spiral moulding that is met by a Cosmati pattern below it and is terminated by mouldings. It then turns into a series of thin, interlocking, circular frames enclosing luxuriant acanthus leaves and flowers against a blue ground, with long-beaked birds perched among the foliage against a bright red ground. The plants and birds surround smaller circles, which have three decorative motifs against red grounds that alternate around the remaining three sides of the room—a tiara, a simple boss, crossed keys, a boss, a tiara, etc.[20]

In the Sala Vecchia degli Svizzeri the program is more complex (figs. 53–62). Here it seems that Nicholas built a new ceiling lower than the older one; it totally cut off from view the thirteenth-century frieze above it.[21] Immediately below the new ceiling, which has now disappeared, was added a frieze that survives in part along each of the four walls.[22] It began immediately below the plane of the ceiling with a thin Cosmati-pattern strip that rested on a moulding, which was in turn supported by a row of trellislike dentils and by fluted pilasters, all rendered fictively. The surviving pilasters suggest that there was a more or less regular pattern that determined their placement, but there is no way to tell how far down the wall this may have continued.

The pilasters articulated a continuous frieze composed of rich and fantastic foliage, mostly acanthus, set in long rectangular bands framed by a decorative strip (fig. 53).[23] These bands alternated with quadrilobes set within square fields, which were also

---

[18] The friezes are between the false, flat, coffered ceilings from the sixteenth century and the floor of the Segretario di Stato above, also originally a sixteenth-century addition. In the 1960s the ceiling was reinforced and the floor above completely rebuilt.

[19] In this room it seems likely that Nicholas did not lower the ceiling and that the entire range of thirteenth-century work remained visible after he had made his additions. The two levels of fresco are carefully joined to one another, the pattern is continuous, and the thirteenth-century level seems to show no damage by the work that would have been necessary to have lowered the ceiling in conjunction with the new frieze. There is damage to the level of Nicholas's work and to the thirteenth-century level, which does not correspond to the work of the sixteenth-century ceiling, and which does not seem to form any coherent pattern of its own. The south wall has fragments on its entire length; the west and east walls have fragments over to the present north wall; the present north wall is part twentieth-century and part older, but it has no trace of thirteenth- or fifteenth-century frescoes.

[20] See Redig de Campos, 1941–42, pp. 71–76.

[21] The thirteenth-century work appears in the upper portion of fig. 53, where the zone of damage between the two levels, one with birds, the other with the Cosmati-like pattern, is quite distinct. This zone is continuous. See also Redig de Campos, 1967, fig. 12, where a thin band of the quattrocento work is visible.

[22] Reported and illustrated in Redig de Campos, 1967, p. 49, and idem, 1969, passim.

[23] One such strip is barely visible, returning along the left side of the pilaster in fig. 53.

trimmed with the decorative strip.[24]   Within the quadrilobes were three different motifs. The full program contained within the quadrilobes is impossible to recover, but some of its features are visible.   On the south wall (toward the Cortile del Maresciallo) were keys and a tiara, apparently in alternating quadrilobes.   On the opposite, north wall (toward the Sala dei Chiaroscuri) only one quadrilobe survives; it has two putti, one catching richly colored butterflies, the other bending down and doing something that is now impossible to decipher, but doing it with great care (figs. 54,55).   More putti appear in the quadrilobes along the east wall, which opened into the loggia overlooking the *mons saccorum*. First, from the north, is a putto riding a white bird with a long neck and beak (fig. 56).   Next is a putto pulling energetically on a bow (fig. 57).   Next, and centered in the wall, are crossed keys topped by a tiara against a red ground (fig. 58).   Next is a putto who puts his full effort, with bulging cheeks and eyes, into blowing a bagpipe (fig. 59).   Finally, in the last quadrilobe at the south is luxuriant foliage with blooming flowers.

On the opposite wall, which is also divided into five fields with the crossed keys and tiara in the central quadrilobe, were the four cardinal virtues.   From the south end, opposite the foliage-filled quadrilobe, is Fortitude, twice-labeled and further clarified, like the other virtues, by attributes (fig. 60).   He is a broad-shouldered warrior in full armor engaged in some strenuous activity lost beyond recall by the damage to the wall.   Behind him, rising from a fortress that is topped by a strong cornice and square crenellations, is a tower with full battlements.   On it are written the attributes of Fortitude: *magnanimitas, magnificentia, p(er)severantia, co(n)stantia, fidutia, paciencia, securitas, tollerantia, et firmitas*.[25]

Next is an unlabeled virtue—the area where the label and attribute would occur is damaged—who is a tousle-haired girl fixing her eyes on an object lost in the distance (fig. 61).[26]   She holds a book in her left hand, the inscriptions of which identify her as Justice: *religio, pietas, gratia, obse(r)vantia, veritas, obedientia, in(n)ocentia*, and *co(n)co(r)dia*.[27]

The next passage of wall is so badly damaged that no trace of the motif survives, but surely Temperance was here.   The last space, at the north end of the wall, is

[24]The strip is visible along the top of fig. 57.

[25]This and the following expansions are from Redig de Campos, 1969.   The chart in the appendix of Tuve, 1966, p. 442, suggests possible sources for the elements and will be used here and below.   Macrobius and Cicero are sufficient and seem likely; all of Macrobius's elements appear here, and *tolerantia* is unique to him, but from Cicero have come the additions of *perseverantia* (also in Frezzi) and *pacientia* (also in Frezzi), both lacking in Macrobius.   Tuve's other two sources either lack some of these elements or contain some that do not appear.   Frezzi is insufficient; he has only two more, *magnaminitas* (shared between Macrobius, Guillaume de Conches, and Alanus; lacking in Cicero) and *fidutia*, common to all.   Frezzi's elements of Fortitude appear in 1914, IV, vi, lines 103 ff.

[26]Redig de Campos, 1969, p. 127, identifies the figure as male and believes that the representation refers to "le virtù religiose."   The sex is indeterminate on visual evidence, but Justice, like the other virtues, including Fortitude, is usually a female.

[27]Again, Macrobius and Cicero are sufficient, and neither in itself is complete, but there is one element not found in any of those cited by Tuve—*obedientia*. *Religio* is common to Cicero and Macrobius; *pietas* to Cicero, Macrobius, and Frezzi; *gratia* only in Cicero (but also Alanus, an unlikely source); *observantia* and *veritas* are in Cicero and Frezzi only; and *innocentia* and *concordia* in Macrobius, who lent them to Guillaume and Alanus. Frezzi (1914, IV, xii, lines 124 ff.) has *pietas, observantia*, and *veritas* and adds *latria* (which he plays off against *lodi* and *godi*), *gratitudin delli doni*, and *vendetta*, which really does mean giving due to "chiunque vuol che colpa sia punita,/se non ha emenda" (lines 139–140). Contrast Burckhardt, 1958, pp. 430 ff., and compare Dante, *Divina Commedia, Purg.* XXI, lines 1–6; *Par.* VI, lines 88–93, and VII, lines 20 ff.

filled with Prudence, who is identified by a label (fig. 62). She holds a lighted candle in her right hand and gazes at it with her head cocked intently in its direction. Resting on her lap and held by her left hand is a shield, the inscription on which reminds one that he must never flag in this virtue; thus, at its top appears *nox*, and at the bottom, *dies*, and around its edge, *infantia, t(em)pus, p(raese)ns, pueritia, adolesce(n)tia, preteriu(m), iuve(n)to,* and *sen(e)ct(us),* followed by a cross indicating death. On the body of the shield are listed the attributes of Prudence: *memoria, intelligentia, prudentia, circu(m)spectio, docilitas, caucio, e(t)ratio.*[28]

The cardinal virtues were a common decoration in a place of government. They are found, for example, in the Palazzo Pubblico in Siena in conjunction with Roman heroes, and in the tiny antechamber to the chapel in the Palazzo Vitelleschi in Corneto (Tarquinia), executed in about 1438 (fig. 63). Here, personifications of the virtues appear enthroned and in color between scenes of the chivalric romance of Lucretia and the Tarquins. Lucretia is deceived, and the Tarquin heroes vindicate her honor after she had killed herself so that "'not in time to come shall ever unchaste woman live through the example of Lucretia'" (Livy, I, lviii, 10; B. O. Foster, trans.). The six history scenes are *en grisailles;* in the lunette of the entrance wall is Vitelleschi's cardinalate coat of arms in color, and opposite it, also in color and covering the entire end wall, is Christ among the doctors.[29] Elsewhere in Vitelleschi's palace, both in the large council rooms and in smaller rooms, were friezes that included coats of arms, Evangelists, and mythological scenes apparently related to Vitelleschi, although they are now in a quite fragmentary condition (figs. 64,65).[30]

One remarkable characteristic of the decoration in the Vatican Palace is the similarity in the motifs and the formal execution of the work carried out for Nicholas III, Boniface IX, and Nicholas V, a similarity shared with Vitelleschi's work (figs. 48,53,57,63–65). The original decoration belongs to a pattern related to ancient Roman and Early Christian forms that is found in a number of ecclesiastical cycles done in Rome through the agency of vigorous papal and curial patronage in the last quarter of the thirteenth century.[31] One important change is a continuing deterioration in the quality of execution as time passed, although Nicholas V's work is still of high quality and, although later, is much better than the decoration in Corneto. Another change is that the foliage in Nicholas V's friezes is more luxuriant, as if it were cut from healthier plants. But the virtues and putti are executed in an entirely different style from the purely decorative portions.

There is no clear evidence concerning when or by whom any of these decorations were executed, although it is clear that they were done neither by Angelico nor Gozzoli, nor by any of the other Tuscans Nicholas had working for him elsewhere in

---

[28] Again, the sources are not unexpected. Six are shared with Macrobius and with Alanus de Insulis, who have only those six, and four with Guillaume de Conches (he deletes *ratio* and *intelligentia*). Cicero includes only *intelligentia* and *providentia* (Nicholas's *prudentia*) from the six and adds *memoria*, which is found only in Frezzi and in Nicholas's room. Frezzi includes the six, but his addition, *solerzia*, referring to ability in the arts, is not found in these examples or in Nicholas's room. Thus Cicero, not Frezzi, seems to be the source for the single addition to the Macrobian schema. For Frezzi's elements of Prudence, see Frezzi, 1914, IV, x, lines 94 ff.

[29] Published by Bertini Calosso, 1920, pp. 197–199. He makes no attribution for this cycle.

[30] In one room (TCI, *Lazio*, p. 119, room V) appear the arms of Eugenius IV and of the archbishop of Florence; this was Vitelleschi's office from October, 1435, through August, 1437.

[31] Gardner, 1969, pp. 207 ff., 239 ff., 254 ff. Contrast two other cycles, each different, one in the palace decorated for Innocent III at Anagni (Marchetti-Longhi, 1920, pp. 399–410), and the late thirteenth-century work at the Aracoeli (Cellini, 1955, pp. 224–228).

the palace.[32] The purely decorative passages could have been done by any competent artist or shop based in Rome and working in its territory, but the figures show a freshness of observation combined with an interest in representing an outer character appropriate to each virtue or putto. In addition, there is an ease and fluidity that seems most allied to the art of north Italian princely courts as represented by the works of Pisanello. Like so much else in Nicholas's project, as will be seen again, these friezes are a happy mixture of tradition, innovation, and collaboration. Lazian artists provided the setting, someone perhaps specially imported from a north Italian court rendered the putti and figures, and the program for the cycle was perhaps provided by someone in Nicholas's circle, who had invented it for this particular setting. Collaboration of this sort could turn out badly, but here it resulted in a great deal of good quality work, accomplished under difficult conditions in a short length of time.

The purpose of such decorations, especially those with the virtues, was to remind the governor what virtues he should attempt to exercise. At the Vatican they were probably complemented by tapestries hung below them and showing heroes in action. Rather than the chivalric heroes and battles that were common in the palaces of princes, the pope's tapestries showed heroes of the Church, although there is a reference in a 1518 inventory of Nicholas's tapestries to one large one that showed "men fighting between themselves, divided into two parts."[33] In addition to scenes of the life of Christ, Nicholas's tapestries included scenes of the creation of the world, David crowning Solomon, David slaying Goliath, another subject involving David, the story of Moses, the story of Peter, the passion of Peter, and "virtues and certain prophets." Nicholas spent a great deal of money and attention on tapestries, importing French artisans and establishing a factory in Rome that must have been a part of his general program related to the rebuilding of the Vatican Palace.[34]

This part of the palace seems to be part of the area Manetti was referring to when he said that farther down the hill from the utilitarian facilities the pope intended to build a chapel, a library, and facilities for the officials of the curia. The private chapel in the apartment wing is probably that chapel, and the public and private rooms in the renovated section would have accommodated curial activities, but the library and additional facilities were installed in a new wing that Nicholas added to the palace (fig 66, and plan D, on p. 133).

The new wing was built at nearly a right angle to the older one and ran in a direction away from Rome toward the west. This location corresponds to Manetti's description, which stated that additions were built up the hill from the apartment wing but down the hill from the western portion of the palace precinct. It seems certain that there was no older construction on the site; it had formerly been part of the orchards and gardens extending to the north.[35] Nicholas welded his new wing onto a

[32]See Redig de Campos, 1969, pp. 127–128, for speculation that the artists were a certain Bartolomeo di Tommaso da Foligno and/or Antonio da Orte, for whom there are payments. The payments, in Müntz, *ACP*, I, p. 132, are for work "del fregio che fa al presente nela sichonda sala" in 1453, a rather imprecise designation.

[33]The inventory was done for Leo X and carefully lists the tapestries that had Nicholas's arms on them; it was published by Müntz, *ACP*, I, pp. 179–180.

[34]Müntz, *ACP*, I, p. 179.

[35]The area had been called the *pomerium* or *viridarium* before Nicholas's period, for which see Magnuson, 1958, p. 105, and Redig de Campos, 1959, pp. 374 f.; during his and successive pontificates it was commonly referred to as the *vigna*, the term—or a variant of it (*vinia*)—that had been used for the *mons saccorum* in the thirteenth century. See the accounts in Müntz, *ACP*, I, relating to the palace, and Ehrle and Stevenson, 1897, p. 33, and, for a later period, pp. 19–20; also Ehrle and Egger, 1935, pp. 40–47 for the thirteenth century, and pp. 95–96 for the fifteenth century. Julius II would eventually build the Belvedere here.

short projection to the palace that Boniface VIII had built. This had contained a room on each of four levels, the Sala del Costantino, the Sala dei Pontifici, a room at the level of the *mons saccorum,* and one below that level that nestled into the slope that dropped off from the *mons saccorum* level. Boniface also built a tower at the northern extremity, which terminated the eastern façade of the palace. The tower had a battered basement, it rose above the roof level of the apartment wing, and its eastern face projected beyond the eastern face of the façade looking toward the *mons saccorum.*[36]

Boniface's rooms were approximately twice as deep as they were wide, and Nicholas's wing projected westward along their long axis. On each of the four levels Nicholas added a suite of rooms. On the lowest level were two great vaulted areas used for storage.[37] A door was cut in the northern end of what had been the western wall of Boniface's basement room to give access to Nicholas's basement, where a door on the northern end of the transverse wall gave access from the first room, which was square, into the second, which was rectangular.

The structure of the floor above was similar, but the rectangular space at the western end was divided into four smaller rooms. How one entered the northeast room remains obscure, but the two on the southern side were entered directly from the area later called the Cortile del Pappagallo. Nicholas had connected that area with the *mons saccorum* by opening a corridor through the ground floor level of the old apartment wing.[38] The square room on this level that abutted Boniface's room was very probably Nicholas's library.

The location of Nicholas's library has often been the subject of dispute.[39] Although there is no definite evidence, this room seems the most likely to have been it. Its vaulting system sets it off from the other spaces in the two basement levels. Of the six square spaces in the two basement levels, this is the only one to have a transverse arch between its two rectangular groin vaults, a characteristic it shares with the three square rooms on the *piano nobile.* It was entered directly from the future Cortile del Pappagallo, making it easily accessible from the palace. The room is in the part of the palace in which Manetti, insofar as he wrote with precision, had located it. Sufficient light entered through the tall, narrow window in the north wall to satisfy its function, which was to accommodate the eight chests with the more than 1,100 books that Nicholas left at his death. There they were safe from the penetration of damp and from constant contact with busy officials, who did not read them

[36] Redig de Campos, 1967, pp. 35–36; p. 48 for the basement level. It is uncertain how high the tower's battering went; Redig de Campos, 1967, isometric drawings 5 and 10 shows it only to the level of the *mons saccorum,* although the section now exposed in the northwest corner of the Cortile di S. Damaso seems to show the battering continuing on up at least to the level of the present post-Bramante *cortile*-level loggia vaults. See also Redig de Campos, 1971.

[37] For the floor level, see Redig de Campos, 1967, p. 44. For the structural fabric of the basement levels, see Redig de Campos, Bibliotheca Graeca, 1967. The floor level of the lower basement was approximately that of the present Belvedere. To remove earth from around the Torre Borgia was one of the first tasks paid for by Julius II when he began the Belvedere; for that and the subsequent history of this area, see Ackerman, 1954, p. 48 and doc. 2(d), pp. 87–88, 117.

[38] See Redig de Campos, 1967, pp. 30–32.

[39] For a belief that the Sala Graeca did house Nicholas's library, see Zippel, 1919, pp. 83–85. For the opposing view, see, among others, Fabre, 1895, p. 455, who cites little substantial evidence, and Magnuson, 1958, p. 119, who ignores the character of quattrocento libraries that were for storage. Similar in placement to Nicholas's library was that in the palace in Urbino, for which see Rotondi, 1969, fig. 49, no. 93. Yuen, 1970, pp. 730 f., who supports the idea that this was Nicholas's library, errs in designating it a *studiolo.* Magnuson errs in his analysis of the frescoes in the room, for which frescoes see below, pp. 140–141.

there but checked them out to their own quarters. And the location was pleasant. Later, when there were more books and when readers used them in their places of storage rather than elsewhere, Sixtus IV would make minor alterations in this room when he converted the entire floor into the Vatican library.[40] At that time this room would be given the name Bibliotheca (or Sala) Graeca.

The room was beautifully decorated, and this decoration gives additional and independent evidence that the room was important (figs. 67–70). Interpreting the decoration, however, raises problems. Nothing about it indicates that the room was a library, but neither does it contradict that supposition. The decoration is difficult to date with precision, but when the renovations and restorations are accounted for and the original form of the room is examined, it seems clear that the room was decorated for Nicholas.

Here, as is characteristic in Nicholas's project, several individuals appear to have been at work, but none can be identified with certainty.[41] What is clear is that in no case was the executor up to the standard set by the designer. Someone with an advanced knowledge of perspective and architecture designed a fictive architectural scheme that shows a robust colonnade and entablature around the four extant sides of the square space (see figs. 67,68). Originally there was a wall that divided the space into two chambers corresponding to the two rectangular groin vaults; the fictive architecture may have appeared on this wall as well. The window on the north wall was given fictive surrounds, which are well integrated with the fictive architecture. That decoration, along with the *stemme* of Nicholas V in the vault bosses (see fig. 69), the ribbons streaming out from them, and the delicate stripping along the intersections of the vault fields, was surely done for Nicholas. Even in its presently mutilated and restored condition the design—when considered as the decoration of two rooms within the present Bibliotheca Graeca, one entered from the south, the other lit from the north—is coherent. But the execution is faulty. Whoever rendered it on the wall did not understand the principles of perspective that lay behind the design.

Above the fictive entablature is an addition to the scheme that demanded some skill to execute but less to design (fig. 70). A colorful marble parapet resting on the entablature supports pots with plants and streamers. The character of the parapet's architecture is both simpler and entirely different from that of the lower part. But because the design of this addition is integrated with that of the lower part, because both its design and execution do not fit the character of the restorations executed later for Sixtus IV, and because the Sistine additions are rather crudely placed on top of this decoration, it seems clear that the additions to the lower decoration date from the same period as the lower part, and that they too were done for Nicholas. The design

[40]See Müntz and Fabre, 1887, pp. 141–142; Clark, 1899, esp. pp. 20–29; Zippel, 1919, pp. 81–85, for a correction of the documents in Müntz, *ACP*, III; Redig de Campos, 1967, pp. 57 ff.; and Ruysschaert, 1969, who stresses the role of Nicholas as collector of books in contrast to Sixtus, the library's founder. Julius II, the next to expand the Vatican Library, arranged for more space in the floor above the level of the Stanze, on the south side of the Cortile del Pappagallo; see Einem, 1971, part iii.

[41]For an attribution of the entire scheme to Piero della Francesca, see Zippel, 1919, pp. 81–86; for an attribution of the spirit of the scheme to Alberti, see Lanckorońska, 1935, p. 115, followed by Börsch-Supan, 1967, p. 242, who places them during Nicholas's pontificate. For a reexamination of the scheme, with an attribution to Castagno working with Alberti, and of Alberti's attempt here to bring a classical villa to life, see Yuen, 1970, who does not refer to Lanckorońska or to Börsch-Supan. (For a suggestion of Castagno's own direct contact with now-lost Roman wall painting as shown by his Legnaia frescoes, see Kennedy, 1963, p. 39.)

of the additional decoration does not reveal a firm basis in perspective, and, even at that, the execution of the perspective parts of the design is faulty. There is no reason to suppose that the designer or executor was the same person as the decorator below. In the north lunette are two busts. These reveal strong suggestions of Castagno's forms, but they fit only poorly into the general scheme. They were perhaps done by yet another person adding richness to the room, again for Nicholas. The decoration concentrated on the upper parts of the wall is rich, while the *quadratura* system below the vaults and lunettes is kept simple. It would have established an architectural framework for the chests in which Nicholas's books were stored. The character of the entire decoration is, therefore, appropriate for the use of the room as a place for storing books, and it was, as Manetti said, an ornament of the palace.[42]

Above this level were two more floors of different and unequal character. The more important, *piano nobile* level was tied into the private apartments and public reception rooms through Boniface's Sala dei Pontifici. This level had the rectangular groin vaults of the stories below and was apparently built for important curial activities. Nicholas's decorative scheme for it, if any, is unknown. Alexander VI had Pinturicchio decorate this level, and through that pope's continued residence there it acquired the name "Appartamento Borgia."

The next, final floor was originally subordinate to the one below it and had wooden ceilings in its three square rooms. Julius II and Leo X used these rooms for their official business and kept Raphael and his studio active there producing the Stanze. Like Sixtus and Alexander, they also found that the rooms Nicholas had built for curial business could continue to serve that purpose.

Both the program and the design of the palace were based on a carefully conceived model. It contained suites of rooms on three floors, one a basement with each room entered from outside, and two above with rooms connected directly with one another by doors near an outside wall. Peculiarities of the site caused this model to be altered. The basement floor here turned out to be two stories high and to be nearly equal in height to that of the two floors above. But that was rendered less conspicuous by showing the basement to be a robust foundation for what it supported. Its battering, determined by the battering on Boniface's addition to the palace, was continuous through both basement floors and was terminated by a strong, half-round moulding at the point where the wall turned to a vertical face.[43] The moulding and the basement were of peperino, and the materials above were stucco over brick.

The junction between Boniface's and Nicholas's construction was made as inconspicuous as possible.[44] The same battering, mouldings, and stucco surface placed over Nicholas's wing was spread across Boniface's, and the same type of windows used in Nicholas's palace were opened in Boniface's.[45] In the basement they were thin slit windows. On the *piano nobile* they were large, square-crossed windows, one placed in each of Nicholas's three rooms and two inserted at nearly the same spacing

---

[42]Manetti, *RIS*, col. 926; see above, chapter 2, p. 31.

[43]Ehrle and Stevenson, 1897, pp. 31–32, mention traces of the moulding behind the lower balcony. For these balconies, which were added by Julius II (top), Leo X (at the level of Raphael's Stanze), and Pius IV (at the level of the Appartamento Borgia), see Redig de Campos, 1971, p. 288.

[44]The junction is clearly visible as a crack in the prerestoration photograph in Ehrle and Stevenson, 1897, p. 9 (discussed p. 33).

[45]There were already two windows in the north wall of Boniface's room; Redig de Campos, 1967, pp. 35–36. There may have been slits or other openings in the lower story; the present *bocche di lupa* are later additions; ibid., p. 47.

into Boniface's large wooden-ceilinged room.[46]   None of the windows on the north façade of this or the next floor carries either an inscription or an emblem to identify its builder, a possible indication of an early date for their installation.[47]   The original windows of the floor above were apparently smaller than the *piano nobile*'s square-crosses.   After the façade was finished, the brick fabric of the walls and the stucco surface was disturbed around the windows of this floor and of the *piano nobile*, and the top floor seems to have remained without windows for some years.[48]   Between 1454 and 1455 the wooden ceilings in Nicholas's three top-floor rooms were replaced with the present square cross-vaults, which still carry the coat of arms of Nicholas V.[49]   Perhaps at that time work was begun on the marble window sills and Cosmati-like floor in the Stanza della Segnatura, which Julius II and Leo X would finish.[50]

This façade, then, would have originally had a dominant *piano nobile* and a subordinate upper floor, but during Nicholas's last year it may have been intended to give equal stress to each story by changing the windows to conform to the new vaults that had just been installed.   Above the entire top floor the building terminated with full battlements, including machicolations and crenellations.[51]   The entire façade above the moulding of the battered basement was covered with stucco.   At the top a zone of white stucco ran immediately below the machicolations.[52]   It would have served as a fictive frieze for an entablature whose cornice was the battlemented top, a common element in quattrocento representations of ancient Roman architecture.   A natural corresponding element to such a strip and to the large moulding at the top of the battered basement would have been a string course between the *piano nobile* and

[46]It is possible that at least some of the windows were installed by 1450.   See the payments in Müntz, *ACP*, I, pp. 116, 122, and 137 (all for 1450); pp. 138 and 138–139 (for 1451, 1452, and 1453).   Ehrle and Egger, 1935, pp. 98–99, point out that Müntz's documents do not allow the windows to be accurately identified.

[47]Compare the Palazzo Capranica, completed about the middle of the century.   Its older windows bear the coats of arms of a cardinal (the central crest is effaced, but the hat and tassels are legible); its new square-crosses have no inscription or emblem.   Perhaps it had not yet been decided how an emblem was to be worked into the form.   The square-crosses at the Palazzo Venezia (begun 1455) apparently provided the answer that was then followed.

[48]There is no explanation for the disturbances on the *piano nobile* and no certain evidence for the date of the replacement of the windows above.   Ehrle and Stevenson, 1897, pp. 32–34, suggest Calixtus III or Pius II and indicate that the window seats of the top floor could be "from the time of Nicholas V."   Magnuson, 1958, pp. 120 ff., agrees about the windows; Redig de Campos, 1967, p. 46, suggests Alexander VI.   Pius seems the most reasonable person, because Piero della Francesca was painting on that floor in 1458–59; for which, see note 49 below.   The windows on the opposite side of the Stanze bear the arms of Julius II; originally, these walls were probably without fenestration.

[49]Ehrle and Stevenson, 1897, p. 33, mention the change from the wooden ceilings to the present vaults; additional investigations reported by Redig de Campos (1967, p. 48), placed the work indubitably in the period 1454–55, although he claims, without evidence, that Nicholas planned to add an additional story.   In 1458–59 Piero della Francesca executed frescoes in the Stanza d'Eliodoro; see Zippel, 1919, pp. 91–92; Gilbert, 1968, pp. 12–15, 48–51.   Redig de Campos, 1967, p. 48, reports the discovery of fragments of older frescoes under Raphael's work in the Stanza della Segnatura, but he does not speculate about their authorship.

[50]Ehrle and Stevenson, 1897, p. 34, who suggest that the material came from the basilica.   But from what part?   Does this suggest that Nicholas's work involved extensive construction inside as well as outside the choir where the foundations were built?   See also Einem, 1971, p. 10.

[51]The crenellations were removed by Julius II, who replaced them with a balustrade; the present superstructure is even more recent.   The modillions of the balcony were originally the corbels sustaining Nicholas's crenellations.   Ehrle and Stevenson, 1897, pp. 31 ff. and 36 f.; Ackerman, 1954, p. 50, n. 1; Redig de Campos, 1967, p. 35.

[52]Ehrle and Stevenson, 1897, p. 33; in their discussion on pp. 36–37 they do not indicate that they sought to discover a string course behind the present balcony at the floor level of the Stanze.

the original *piano superiore*. The string course would have demarcated the two distinct floor levels of the palace. The palace would have appeared to have been built of large, squared stones because, in the grey-brown stucco, fictive mortar beds were drafted in white. The date on the stucco covering is 1454.[53]

It would seem that Nicholas intended the wing to terminate at the west with a tower; it might have been meant either to dominate or to complement Boniface's tower. A tower was built later in the century, and Nicholas's construction seems to have made allowance for it, although the evidence is far from definitive.[54] The Torre Borgia closely resembles the form one might expect a Nicholine tower to have had. It projects above the palace wing; it had an arcuated loggia at the top, which has been walled up, and it was surrounded by machicolations and crenellations (now obscured by the addition of another story).[55]

The wing of Nicholas V was a conspicuous addition to the Vatican Palace. The library on the lower floor was both an ornament to the palace and accessible to the prelates, as Manetti had said. In the rooms on the *piano nobile* and *piano superiore*, seen rising above the strongly battered basement walls and protected by the towers of the palace, the pope and his intimates conducted the business necessary for governing the Church. The sequence of square-crossed windows on the dominant *piano nobile* is probably the source for the use of the motif at the Palazzo del Senatore and the Palazzo dei Conservatori, where related activities took place, while the pattern of the new wing is probably to be connected with subsequent palace construction in Rome and in its territories, where the precedents for the wing's formal motifs are to be found.

The old nucleus, the renovated apartments, and the new wing were not the most important parts of Nicholas's palace project. Nor were they the parts he himself had referred to in his testament. They were mere housing and were unfortified in themselves. More important than the housing was the landscaping, or, less prosaically put, more important than the palace was the garden and its enclosures. These together satisfied the two purposes both Nicholas and Manetti attributed to the palace.

Nicholas had explained to the cardinals that he had undertaken the project for both devotion and strength. Manetti had explained through his rhetoric that the fortifications around the palace had both figurative and functional purposes. The conspicuous additions to the fortifications Nicholas actually did build in the Borgo and at the palace demonstrate their functional role in protecting the papacy, while their form and reports about them attest to their figurative meaning. They enclosed the palace.

Because the walls protected it, the pope's palace had a different character from that of the other two palaces Nicholas built as seats of governors. In Rome, the senator in the Palazzo del Senatore was protected, perhaps only conceptually, by towers. In the Borgo, the papal castellan was physically protected by the towers added to the Castel Sant'Angelo. Nicholas's Vatican Palace was unlike either of these, and also unlike the traditional Roman residences of Roman barons. It was conceptually and

[53]See Ehrle and Stevenson, 1897, p. 33, who state that the stucco application was begun in 1450.

[54]Ibid., pp. 29–30, 36–37. The Torre Borgia was built by Alexander VI. Julius II had Bramante add a wooden and lead cupola to its top; the cupola burnt in 1523. See Ackerman, 1954, pp. 47–48, who supposes it replaced a pointed roof of the original tower.

[55]For a reconstruction of the façade as it appeared in about 1500, see Ehrle and Stevenson, 1897, p. 31; published also in Tomei, 1942, fig. 25. Certain details need to be changed to reproduce the scheme from before 1454; Boniface's tower should be added, the windows on the *piano superiore* should be smaller, there should be no miniature square-crosses in the windows of the library level, and the tower should perhaps not be quite so large as the Torre Borgia turned out to be.

actually protected only by the addition of walls, which had both the potential and the appearance of strength. Thus, the palace of the pope within those walls did not need to have the appearance of a fortress.[56]

Manetti was more generous in his description than the walls warranted. Nicholas had placed new walls in conjunction with those already on the site, stretches of which he restored, but the pattern of the plan of his walls was not so regular as Manetti claimed it to be. However, the walls were regular in another way; all of them, particularly those nearest the palace and therefore most important for advertising the strength of its fortification, seem to have been built to the same design. They were not very high, they had a battered lower level that ended at a large, half-round moulding, and they had full battlements.[57] Their form resembled that of the lower level of the wing of Nicholas V, and a visitor would have seen a considerable portion of the Vatican Palace from outside them.

The portion of the walls nearest the palace was planned with a pattern that had a central nodal point. The walls were not built quite where Manetti described them, but the resemblance between what was built and what he described is close enough to be recognizable. He said that the three walls came together at the great, round tower now called the Tower of Nicholas V (figs. 71–75).[58] The Borgo and palace fortifications were welded together at the tower. One wall from the tower was splayed to the north of the basilica's axis and ran back up the hill, probably in a straight line, before it eventually turned and joined the Leonine walls that Nicholas restored.[59] A pilgrim on the road leading to the Porta di S. Pietro would have been able to see the wing of Nicholas V beyond this wall.[60] Another stretch of wall ran from the tower along the division between the palace precinct and the Borgo and terminated at or near the point where one entered the palace from the piazza at the basilica.[61] The third stretch was the Borgo *corridoio*, which did not join the tower but intersected the wall from the tower to the piazza. It already existed, and Manetti included it among the Nicholine

[56] Redig de Campos (1967, p. 46, and 1971), has proposed that Nicholas continued a scheme launched by Nicholas III or Innocent III to build a square *castello* with an inner *cortile* and with a tower at each corner, and that the wing of Nicholas V should be read in this context. It seems unlikely, however, that Nicholas's palace design continues this tradition, the very existence of which seems unlikely. More likely, it seems that he looked upon the palace as unfortified and separated from the walls that surrounded it; also, it seems to have belonged to a tradition existing in Rome and its territories rather than to one narrowly confined to the Vatican.

[57] See Magnuson, 1958, pp. 69–70, and the illustrations from the period in Hale, 1965.

[58] For Manetti's description, ss. 46–53; for the tower, see also Frutaz, 1956; Hale, 1965, pp. 474–476; and below, p. 145.

[59] Magnuson, 1958, pp. 117–118, 123, 129, 136, does not believe that the stretch from the east side of the Belvedere across the *vigna* (now the Belvedere) to the Leonine walls farther up the hill was built, but that it was only planned and reported in Manetti. For this area see above, note 35. Magnuson does not analyze the views of the area, for which, see below, p. 145.

[60] This stretch from the tower to the Belvedere, as well as the Nicholas V wall to be mentioned in the next sentence, has been altered; if the northern stretch of wall did cross the *vigna*, it was removed to make way for the Belvedere. The remaining segment was refaced under Pius X; neither of Nicholas V's remaining walls now has battlements, and other alterations are possible, but the shape—battered rise and vertical top—seems to have come from traditional practice and would have provided the core for the present form. For the alterations, see Magnuson, 1958, pp. 116–118.

[61] Slightly to the east of Nicholas's new wall was a wall built by Boniface IX that ran from the Porta di S. Pietro in the direction of the basilica (see Plan B). Nicholas's new wall was a redundancy, and he apparently intended to remove the older wall. It remained, however, and eventually was used to form one side of the enclosure for the Swiss guards. The Boniface IX wall was torn down to make way for Bernini's colonnade. See the details from Roman views and maps, and discussion, in Lewine, 1969, esp. pp. 28, 33–34, 37–38. For the original construction of the wall, see above, chapter 6, n. 45.

walls joining the tower, in order to indicate that it, too, formed part of the carefully designed system of walls Nicholas had planned.

Manetti was not the only one to indicate that the tower was an important and conspicuous element that tied together the fortifications of the Borgo and of the palace. The same emphasis appears in views of Rome that derive from the view made by Biondo's friend in the 1440s. In the Paris version, produced in Florence probably either during or just after Nicholas's pontificate and sold to Alfonso of Aragon,[62] the tower and several walls running out from it are prominent and obviously represent a revision to that element in the view (figs. 30,71). Departing from the base of the tower is a low wall, probably the one running around—not across—the *vigna*.[63] Next to it is the Porta di S. Pietro, with the Borgo wall nearly tangent to the tower. Against it is a massive, high, buttressed wall, which is linked to another beyond it, enclosing the palace. The tower itself is four stories high, not the squat tower now on the site. In the example from Urbino—also produced in Florence, but not until 1472—the tower is lower and the forms are reduced nearly to a figurative representation of walls in general (figs. 32,72). The Vatican (1469) and Strozzi (1474) views are identical to one another; they no longer reveal an attempt to revise the 1440s archetype in the palace area (figs. 29,31,73,74).[64]

The peculiar tall tower in the earliest of these views, the one in Paris, may be explained by Manetti's text (fig. 71). Nicholas, he reported, had intended to carry the tower up to a hundred *braccia*, but had limited it instead to thirty.[65] In the 1450s Massaio had tried to show the tower as Nicholas had intended it, but later he did not. The other curious and unique element in this view, the square, battlemented walls next to the palace and enclosing part of it, may also be explained by Manetti's text. This would seem to be the level site appropriate for building as ancient architects taught was proper, which was formed by the walls.[66]

Gozzoli's view and the view in Mantua resemble the earlier rather than the later versions of the 1440s prototype (figs. 33,34,75). In Gozzoli's view, the tower is shown low and with crenellations. In the Mantua view it more closely resembles its actual appearance and that of the Castel Sant'Angelo. The tower in Gozzoli's view receives on one side the wall that encloses the Borgo, and on the other it is joined by the wall that comes from around the *vigna*. In the distance the latter joins the Leonine wall, which is shown running from the top of the hill past the *vigna* junction and into the palace complex. In the Mantua view the tower and the Castel Sant'-Angelo are the dominant elements. They are clearly united by the *corridoio*, while the tower is also joined by the wall around the *vigna* and the one between the palace and the Borgo. These are the parts of the Nicholine work that are most conspicuous in the Mantua view. It makes clear that the fortifications around the Borgo are no less important than those around the Vatican Palace.

Manetti had considered not only the walls but also the portal from the piazza into

[62] Scaglia, 1964, p. 140; it was sold in either 1453 or 1456.

[63] The wall surrounding the *vigna* and enclosing the top of the *mons sancti Aegedii*, where Innocent VIII built his Belvedere villa, was restored by Nicholas. Manetti, s. 76; Magnuson, 1958, pp. 70–71.

[64] That the tower is lacking altogether in the Strozzi version suggests that this one is most closely related to the common archetype, as has been suggested by Scaglia, 1964; see above, chapter 5.

[65] Manetti, s. 46. Magnuson, 1958, pp. 63–64, 127, interprets the next sentence as giving the reason for the limitation—unstable foundations—in conjunction with a vague document which refers to the collapse of "la torre nova." The sentence, however, seems to state that the purpose of the tower and, by inference, of the walls joining it, was to provide a level place for building, as stated above, chapter 6.

[66] Some sort of leveling would be called for; it should be recalled that the level of the *mons saccorum* was at least a full story above that of the *vigna* north of the wing of Nicholas V.

the palace as an element that fortified, separated, and linked the Borgo and the palace. The portal was to be at the end of the northern street across the Borgo, and it was to open into the palace from the piazza in front of the basilica. Manetti's description suggests an important analogy between the basilica and the palace; at each, there was to be a formal reception area beyond a formal entrance structure that faced the piazza. Manetti indicates that the palace's *curia prima* and *curia superior* would have been rebuilt and probably unified with colonnades and porticoes, apparently with the intention of forming a *cortile d'onore* with an appropriate solemnity, formality, and dignity (s. 55). The entrance structure would have stood in the wall running from the great tower over toward the entrance to the basilica. Manetti said that it was to have two great towers enclosing an arch to form a triumphal arch (s. 54).

This arrangement for an entrance was not uncommon. Manetti's few words bring to mind the form of the entrance to the Borgo at the Ponte Sant'Angelo and the design for entrances to numerous other important places. The arch of Alfonso I at the Castel Nuovo in Naples is one example (fig. 76). Its decorative elements, which celebrated one of the rare triumphs actually held by a Renaissance prince, rendered in permanent form the chivalric trappings of the temporary equipment and ceremony of the actual event of 1443. Nicholas probably knew something about it. In 1447 a permanent arch was to have been set up within the city, and the pope cooperated in this phase of the design by sending some statues to Naples, but in 1451 it was decided to transfer the scheme to the Castel Nuovo and insert it within the *castello* towers, the renovations of which at that moment were nearing completion.[67] Both portals belonged to a common type—two towers flanking an arched opening—that was used repeatedly as a gateway to Rome in figuratively constructed views,[68] and the nearly constant use of this type in scenes set in Jerusalem during the period hardly needs to be mentioned. But the Neapolitan arch was an actual piece of architecture, not a figurative one, and in another example, in which the type is used to refer exclusively to Rome, the figurative type has taken on a similar architectonic substance that had been lacking earlier, perhaps under the impact of some known scheme for Nicholas's portal. This is the gateway to Rome at the very front of the Mantua view, which perhaps renders some actual Roman gateway that had been Nicholas's architectural model (fig. 34). Like Alfonso's arch, the design of which may postdate Nicholas's and may also reflect a Nicholine design,[69] the round turrets here are squat, and the towers and connecting wall are crenellated; but unlike it, the distance between the towers is broad and the arched opening is generous. This form is nearest the design of the entrances to the *castelli* at Capua and Castel del Monte, designed, according to contemporary belief, by the emperor Frederick II himself; that at Capua contained elements which consciously attempted to evoke ancient triumphal arches.[70] This is the form used for the Porta di S. Pietro when it was rebuilt under Alexander

[67]Seymour, 1966, pp. 134–138. See also Hersey, 1969, pp. 7–8, 11; Magnuson, 1958, pp. 144–145, 157–159.

[68]See the views of Taddeo di Bartolo, the Paris and Strozzi examples from Biondo's friend's archetype (but not the Urbino and Vatican examples), and the type available in Apollonio di Giovanni's workshop (figs. 23, 25, 29, 30).

[69]Hersey, "Arch," 1969, p. 22, has suggested that the arch represented in the Museum Boymans-van Beuningen in Rotterdam is from 1446 and that it represents "not a preliminary design [of Alfonso I's Arch], but rather a design for a preliminary version, a rehearsal, as it were, for the unfinished marble monument." This would move the design date for Alfonso's arch closer to 1451, within the range of the possible date for Nicholas's portal's design. For dates, see below, Epilogue.

[70]Magnuson, 1958, p. 158, mentions the similarity and the belief; Weiss, 1969, pp. 12–13, for the revival; Battisti, "Simbolo e classicismo," 1960, pp. 16 ff., who developed each of these themes.

He placed a portal opening

VI.[71] It seems that there had been a close interplay between an old figure and actual construction, and that revisions to the figure, even in visual representations, had been made to give these entrances a greater architectural substance. Nicholas's entrance to the Vatican Palace must have been intended to fit within this figurative tradition.

But Nicholas did not build the portal, and when the Florentine Gozzoli was representing the area, he apparently knew that there was to have been a portal but did not know its intended location or form. He placed a portal opening between the Borgo and the Vatican Palace immediately to the left of the tower and gave it the same form Florentines usually used for gateways—for example, the form Massaio used, and the one which appears in the *View of Florence with a Chain* (figs. 24,33). It is placed among a cluster of buildings that include three elements that must be meant to represent the basilica—a large, navelike structure, a campanile, and a low entrance structure. The basilica and the palace are related to one another, each is distinct from the Borgo, the palace has an imposing entrance structure, and it is firmly enclosed.

The enclosures around the palace that these many visual sources stress were among the most common epitomies used to refer to it in other sources as well. They serve that purpose in two apologies written immediately after Porcari's execution in January, 1453. The authors agree that the pope was building in order to govern and that most people in Rome knew that and were pleased with it. Only Porcari and his band were not, they explain, and the pope's swift justice was appropriate for men held totally in sway by *superbia*. Giuseppe Brippi, a minor functionary in Nicholas's curia, cited Nicholas's repair of churches, his amplification of St. Peter's, and then his founding of a "marvelous palace." This was a fortress protected by a stupendous tower and walls built with high spirit and prudence (*alto animo prudenteque*).[72] Petrus de Godis, another minor official who defended the pope's judgment, recited a long list of buildings as evidence of Nicholas's care in his office and included among them the palace next to St. Peter's. It was largely rebuilt, he explained, in a magnificent form, with towers and walls enclosing the palace, which was one of the largest and most marvelous of foundations.[73] Later in the list he returned to St. Peter's alone, indicating that in the earlier passage he was referring to the palace and not to the basilica. The adjectives he lavished on the basilica are different from those he had used for the palace.[74]

In another reference to the palace it is again the enclosures that are specially emphasized, although in a purely figurative way, which is at the same time very revealing. In 1450 Giovanni Rucellai visited the papal palace and described it, quite simply, as the "palazzo of the pope, a most beautiful abode, and attached to the Church of St. Peter with great and small gardens, and with a fish pond and fountain of water and with a *conigliera*."[75] "*Conigliera*" now designates a rabbit hutch, but in the quattrocento it referred to grounds that could contain the furry little animals that figured in chivalric lore.[76] Of all that he saw, Rucellai preferred to stress the gardens and to indicate their character by citing the *conigliera*, which was probably on the site enclosed by the system of walls spreading out from the tower of Nicholas V.

Rucellai's enclosures were not fortifications against rabbits. In each of the other descriptions it could be argued that the fortifying rather than the figurative function

---

[71]Illustrated in Redig de Campos, 1967, fig. 37, discussed pp. 80–81. See also above, chapter 6.

[72]Brippi, Vat. Lat. 3618, lines 107–112.

[73]De Godis, Vat. Lat. 3619, fol. 7ᵛ.

[74]Ibid., fol. 8ʳ. See also Platina, p. 424 (Life of Nicholas V).

[75]Rucellai, 1960, p. 72.

[76]Crusca, s.v.

of the walls is being stressed, but not in Rucellai's. The walls were doubtless strong, but in this as well as in other representations, they were also something more—they enclosed a garden, and in order to have a significant garden, it was necessary to have strong enclosures. One thing contained within significant rather than merely fortifying enclosures was a garden, and this area had traditionally been a special private garden for the popes.

It was apparently the hope of enjoying the gardens that had persuaded Nicholas III to undertake his works there and to make the Vatican a residence for popes; at least, the single reference to his construction in his *Life* in the *Liber Pontificalis* indicates this.[77] Other sources, including a marble inscription, make the same point: Nicholas III enclosed the gardens, planted many trees, and supplied water to the walled space.[78] Maintaining the gardens from then on posed a problem, but the problem was faced from early in the Babylonian Captivity. To maintain the gardens was as important as maintaining the palace and basilica.[79] In a touching letter from Avignon, filled with figurative language that carried specific instructions, Urban V (1362–70) charged his spiritual vicar in the city of Rome to remove the tares from the garden, repair the walls, and cause the trees to flower and produce fruit.[80] Maintenance of the garden continued; in 1433 Eugenius paid a "keeper of the garden of the holy palace," and in 1447 at least two gardeners were included in the list of members of the pope's "family" who received black crepe for the pope's obsequies.[81]

When Nicholas became pope the garden was probably more enclosed than flower-filled. On the *mons saccorum* there was a *hortus secretus* defined by low, crenellated walls in an irregular rectangle with a small crenellated tower at each corner.[82] The new enclosures Nicholas built rendered the old ones unnecessary, and he must have intended to rebuild the garden from the palace out to the new walls. Gozzoli's view, which when properly interpreted has been seen to reflect Nicholas's intentions quite well, stresses the garden in this area. In it the artist shows a tree, shrubs, and a fountain, and on the Tower of Nicholas he shows a curious open structure or pergola.[83] The garden was accessible from the area west of the palace across the intended *cortile d'onore*, and through the corridor Nicholas drove through the ground floor of the apartment wing.

[77]The only reference to the palace reads in full: "Hic palatium sancti Petri multum augmentavit, et quamplurima edificia fieri faciens, iuxta illud pratellum inclusit, et fontem ibidem fieri paravit, meniis et turribus iardinum magnum diversis arboribus decoratum includendo." *Liber Pontificalis*, II, p. 458; also quoted in Ehrle and Egger, 1935, p. 39, where other places of publication are given.

[78]See citations in Ehrle and Egger, 1935, pp. 38 ff.; and Redig de Campos, 1960, pp. 240 ff.

[79]See Ehrle and Egger, 1935, p. 55, nn. 2,3, and p. 56, n. 1.

[80]Theiner, *Cod. Dip.* II, no. 408, p. 430; dated 13 November 1365.

[81]Beltramo Lombardo, "gubernator ortus sacri palacii," received twenty-five florins with which he paid others; the crepe was given to Iaquemino *ortulano* and two other gardeners. Bourgin, 1904, pp. 213, and list, pp. 214–224.

[82]For its location, see Magnuson, 1958, pp. 107 ff. and 132 ff.; it appears on his plate II as the area enclosed by LW, T5, T6, and MW. For access to it see Ehrle and Stevenson, 1897, pp. 13–14. They appear in the Heemskerck view of the palace.

[83]Müntz, 1889, p. 139, was the first to note both the tower's function and the structure on its top: "Cette tour—crénelée—semble avoir été convertie en jardin, en 'orto pensile'; elle contient au centre une sorte de pyramide, peut-être une volière." Zippel, 1911, pp. 195–196, states that the structure is the "pergola di Nostro Signore" built by Paul II, and adds (p. 196, n. 3) that the fountain or fish pond is also visible. Ackerman, 1954, p. 4, accepts Müntz's interpretation and calls the structure on top of the tower "the small conical turret of a pergola"; Frutaz, 1956, pp. 24–25, also accepts Müntz's interpretation. Gozzoli also shows another garden on the site of the *vigna* north of the new wing. This is clearly meant as a kitchen garden and orchard.

The façade of the apartment wing that overlooks the garden would have been renovated in conjunction with Nicholas's garden-building. At that time the façade was composed of three stories of arcades terminated at each end by towers. Gozzoli shows the towers and a two-story loggia, the ground floor with a pier arcade and the upper floor with a columnar arcade. This probably gave the façade a more dignified appearance than it actually had, unless Nicholas did rebuild it, which is possible. The Mantua view—which, along with others of that type, shows the *hortus secretus* still on the site—is probably a truer representation of the area as it actually existed, but Gozzoli has shown it as it was intended to be. Gozzoli's view corresponds to Manetti's brief reference to a loggia, which he mentioned when he described the private apartments of the pope.[84]

But all this is minor material compared to Manetti's description of the area between the loggia and the enclosures connected with the Tower of Nicholas. His description goes far beyond what anyone else mentioned or showed. In this fortified area on the *mons saccorum* was to be the most important part of the Vatican Palace Nicholas had planned. The order in which Manetti presented the elements in the palace precinct conveys the sense of the important ceremonial function this area was to serve. After having described the triumphal gateway and the related walls, and after having briefly mentioned Nicholas's plans for the entrance space behind the gateway, Manetti stated that there was to be a most beautiful and large garden filled with all the herbs and fruits that grow, watered by a fountain supplied from the hills behind (ss. 54–59). He continued:

> In this most perfect space of paradise there stood three most beautiful and excellent buildings. First among them, from the lower part, is a sort of theater, noble and extraordinary, raised on marble columns raised up into a high vault. To the right of this theater there was built a sort of atrium for assemblies, conclaves, and pontifical coronations, in a vaulted room with two additional spaces facing one another above and below, in the side of which an apostolic treasury is designed, where the treasures of the Church are stored. Above this atrium a great banquet room was fitted out, designed for anniversaries and the regular blessings of the highest pontiff, which banqueting hall looks toward the eastern bridge of the Castel Sant'Angelo. From the left there is a sort of large chapel with a great vestibule from the upper part, likewise founded in the manner of a vault (ss. 60–64).

His next sentences discuss the utilitarian structures of the curia, and do so with reference to the walls around the palace precinct, thus stressing once again the enclosed nature of the palace. Then, before turning to the pope's private apartments, which overlook this paradise and with which he concludes the description of the palace, he returns to paradise imagery. In this way he forcefully links the apartments to the paradise and its buildings, and he sets them off as a unit from the other buildings within the precinct:

---

[84]For this façade, see Redig de Campos, 1971, pp. 6–17. His evidence confirms the existence of the porticoes forming the loggia. That the extant portico was also a loggia giving access from room to room is clear by a number of other references. Diener, 1967, p. 51, cites a document from 28 January 1432, which refers to the "lodia prefati palatii [palatii apostolici] iuxta cameram papagalli," and others of the same tenor (30 March 1432; 23 April 1432; 24 April 1432). A document from 1374 refers to this area as the "deambulatorio, quod est supra viridarium seu supra vineam dicti palatii" (quoted in Ehrle and Egger, 1935, p. 68, n. 5; see also 31 March 1479, on p. 54). Manetti, s. 79, used the word *ambulatoria*.

> But why do we inquire further about the individual buildings of this sacred palace, although so many, so great, and so diverse were the dwellings designed by that divine ability (*ingenium*) founded upon an especially great magnitude of spirit, with the result that they might seem an incredibly beautiful and distinctive labyrinth, as it were, yet not an intricate and convoluted one as was depicted by the poets, but rather a kind of dazzlingly beautiful paradise (s. 74).

Here is the part of the palace that is worthy of complementing the great basilica, which he will describe next;[85] here is the most important part of the new papal palace. Here the pope would govern.

Manetti stressed the importance not only through his rhetorical structure and through his listing of buildings that, as will be seen, were essential for governing, but also through his use of these elements from the palace for his comparison of Nicholas's and Solomon's works. After he had finished the description of the basilica, he quoted the description of Solomon's palace as given in the Bible, then said that the four major elements of the building in Jerusalem could be discerned in the palace in the Vatican and added that he had carefully selected only some parts from the complex for the comparison (ss. 166–167, 170). His selection was based on the same criteria he had used for the basilica—those that stressed appearance and the use of design on the one hand, and those that made clear the function of the palace on the other.

When Solomon's palace was being built, Manetti reported, the sound of the hammer, the ax, and metal instruments was not heard, such was the perfection of the stones that went into it. Manetti did not claim the same. He hoped that the reader would recall that the stones for the basilica had come from Tivoli, but he was also to recall that, while Solomon had been working with abundant divine assistance, Nicholas had been using his God-given intellect and *virtù*. Manetti therefore said only that in Nicholas's palace new, squared stones were conspicuous (s. 168). Design had been used, but the design had produced two categories of squared stones, a real one in the enclosing walls and in the basement of the new wing, and a fictive one in the new wing's two upper floors. The difference between real and fictive stone was probably insignificant; what was important was that they were squared. They had been cut to a pure geometric shape—or had been made to appear as if they had been—and therefore were as well worked as Solomon's had been. In this form they also satisfied the requirements established by the representation of Roman ashlar construction in figurative representations of ancient Rome and its buildings.[86]

The second and third elements that show the similarities between the palaces were functional. The entrance to Solomon's palace stood in the middle of a wall; in the midst of the defenses of the palace stood Nicholas's great triumphal arch, which gives access to the palace precinct (s. 169). Here Manetti stressed once again the distinctness of the Borgo from the palace and the special character of the palace as a place set aside and protected. The next element also stressed the distinctness, but in addition

---

[85]See also Vasari, who took Manetti literally about the authorship of the project but read the description figuratively, as Manetti intended; Vasari, III, pp. 100 ff.

[86]See, for example, the ground-floor level of the Castel Sant'Angelo in Peter's martyrdom on Filarete's doors, in Masolino's views, in the Polani view, and in Gozzoli's view; see also the Palazzo del Senatore in the Golden Bull and the buildings labeled ROMA in the fourth narrative panel in Filarete's doors. For this traditional figure, see Battisti, "Simbolo e classicismo," 1960, pp. 26 ff. The same form of masonry appears in ancient Roman buildings and in actual *vedute;* see, for example, the Ghirlandaio school view in Codex Escurialensis, Egger, 1905–06, fol. 26ᵛ, and also 25ʳ.

showed how the pope became accessible to the people in the Borgo. Manetti referred to the spiral stair that ascended to the loggia (*coenaculum*) above the palace of Solomon, and drew an analogy to the loggia in the palace which, he said, had three orders of vaults, one above the other (s. 169). This would be the place atop the hall in the paradise, from which the pope would give blessings on special occasions. Only from this point within the palace precinct would the pope be visible to the people in the Borgo. For them, this was a vantage point equivalent to the throne in the basilica; from either place, the pope would be seen officiating over the hierarchy.

The final element refers to the design used in the building and links the palace to the basilica. In the Biblical palace there had been cedar paneling, floors, and works; Manetti proudly states that, instead, sheets of lead were used to cover all of Nicholas's buildings.[87] Throughout these comparisons Manetti had stressed the unity of the two buildings by treating them in a reverse order from the one he had used when first describing them. The two were a single unit; together they bore comparison to Solomon's two buildings, temple and palace, and together they showed the congruence of Solomon's and Nicholas's intentions.

But Nicholas was not another Solomon; Nicholas was a *new* Solomon, as Manetti said in his concluding sentence. Together, the basilica and palace showed this:

> And if veneration for sacred scripture, and due respect for King Solomon as well, had not checked me in my brief comparison of such elements [i.e., those which clarified the comparison, s. 170], I would certainly have added many other details which have been passed over in silence. Those would have shown that Solomon's structures are surpassed by our own to the same degree that the new religion of Christ, as we all know, is to be preferred and set above the old divine Law (s. 171).

Solomon had governed; now Nicholas governs. The area Manetti described as a paradise contained the accommodations necessary for the governor of the Church. The pope governed through ceremony, and the paradise would have accommodated those ceremonies. Ceremonial activities deserve more important settings than bureaucratic activities, but, as is usually the case, the necessities of bureaucracy were satisfied before the needs of government. Although Nicholas built the new wing, he only planned the paradise that would have replaced the old, inadequate halls of Innocent III and Nicholas III. The buildings in the paradise—a chapel, a conclave hall, and a theater—would certainly not have been unexpected in the palace of the pope.[88]

A chapel and assembly and ceremonial halls are found both at the Lateran and in the papal palace in Avignon. A chapel calls for no explanation; if Nicholas were converting the old *capella parva* into a reception hall and transferring the functions that formerly had taken place in the halls near it to the new buildings he intended for the *mons saccorum*, a chapel would certainly be included among them. Even if he were not, Manetti, on the basis of similar chapels in both papal and princely palaces, would include a chapel among any new ceremonial facilities the pope might have had in mind.

Manetti's statement that the new hall was to be suitable for "assemblies, conclaves, and pontifical coronations" suggests that he was referring not only to cere-

---

[87]Manetti, s. 169. See also s. 128 for the lead roof of the basilica.

[88]The following observations, which compare Nicholas's Vatican project to other papal residences, are sketchy in the extreme. It is hoped that enough is included to give a sense of the place of the palace within the urban project; no attempt has been made to be thorough from the point of view of the history of architecture.

monies in which the pope installed an officer, but also to the selection and installation of the pope himself. Apparently Nicholas intended to transfer the installation ceremony from the steps of St. Peter's to the Vatican Palace. Consonant with this, but less striking and unexpected, was Manetti's reference to the benediction loggia proposed for the top of the hall. On the end of the great consistory hall at the Lateran, Boniface VIII had built a loggia that overlooked the piazza.[89] At Avignon there was a window attached to the entrance hall to the great chapel, above the stairs from the consistory hall below the chapel. From the window the pope gave his blessings to the faithful assembled below in the larger courtyard.[90] At Constance Martin V gave blessings and promulgated bulls from a loggia—or, more properly, a bay window—at the palace in which he resided.[91] In the time of Urban V there was a wooden benediction loggia near the site of Nicholas's Vatican garden, if it was not within it. Martin V repaired it, and it was still functioning after Nicholas's death.[92] Nicholas simply wished to render in monumental form within an integrated design the kind of facility that was traditional in papal ceremonial. Such a loggia was, furthermore, expected at a time when rulers, princes, and others of importance appeared to people in settings that placed them apart and made them more dignified by their conspicuous setting.[93] Pius II did eventually begin such a loggia, but not where Nicholas had planned it, although it was in nearly the same context as his predecessor had thought proper for it.

The third building, the theater, has provoked unnecessary misinterpretations. As Jacob Burckhardt indicated, this is to be understood as a loggia,[94] although of a different type from the one just discussed. In referring to it as being in the lower part of the paradise, Manetti meant that it was the nearest of the three buildings to the *curia prima* and *curia superior*, which were to be replaced by a *cortile d'onore*. A loggia, perhaps next to the conclave hall, would fit nicely in the area defined by the south tower of the private apartment wing and the wall Nicholas built running from the great tower to the atrium of the basilica, nestled into the space between the *mons saccorum* and the new *cortile* (see plan C). One would pass from the piazza through the triumphal portal into the *cortile*, and then through the loggia into the new garden, with its new ceremonial facilities opening onto it. By calling the entrance structure

---

[89]Mitchell, 1951, passim; Battisti, "Simbolo e classicismo," 1960, pp. 31 ff.

[90]Mollat, 1963, p. 312; Gagnière, 1965, pp. 86 ff.

[91]Richental, 1961, pp. 173, 177, 180–181.

[92]Ehrle and Egger, 1935, p. 64; Müntz, *ACP*, I, pp. 12, 14. Scaglia, 1964, p. 150, claims—probably justly—that the Strozzi view of Rome shows this loggia. It also seems to show the old steps leading up to the entrance to the Paradisus (atrium). The revisions to this area in the other three views support the position that the Strozzi map is closest to the prototype that originated in Biondo's circle (figs. 71–74). In the Paris version (1453 or 1456), in which the Tower of Nicholas appears as three stories above its battered basement, the loggia has disappeared and the steps lead directly to the basilica, obliterating the Paradisus. In the Urbino example (1472) a loggia reappears, and it seems to be a different loggia from the Strozzi one; this one resembles the Florentine Loggia Rucellai type, while the Strozzi view resembled the public loggia in front of the Palazzo Pubblico in Siena—square rather than three bays by one bay, with a low hip roof rather than a parapet on top. This type, not the type in the Strozzi version, is what appears in the Nuremberg Chronicle, contrary to Scaglia's opinion (ibid., n. 78) that "the original loggia of benediction still appears" in the Chronicle. In the Vatican version (Vat. Lat. 5699) the loggia has again disappeared, and the steps are more regular than ever but lead directly to the basilica, which has a portico but no Paradisus in front of it. As was the case with the revisions made to the Tower of Nicholas, then, the Paris and Urbino versions show more careful revisions to this area than do the Strozzi and Vatican versions.

[93]For the pervasiveness of this motif and its impact on quattrocento art, see Ringbom, 1965, pp. 42–46.

[94]Burckhardt, 1955, p. 174. See also Zippel, 1911, p. 183. It should not be confused with the loggia that Gozzoli showed fronting on the papal apartments or the one atop the new hall Manetti described.

a theater rather than a loggia or portico, Manetti was able to emphasize its ceremonial function and to relate it programmatically to the garden and its other facilities.

The use of the word "theater" in other contexts shows what Nicholas had in mind here. It had been used throughout the middle ages, but not to designate a particular building type; instead, it referred to whatever could accommodate certain activities. These were formal ceremonies that were called *ystoriones* and that should not be confused with the presentation of dramatic narratives in mimic form.[95] The term *ystoriones* also referred to scenes showing chivalric heroes in tapestries and frescoes in princely castles, and the word as a verb could be used, for example, to indicate that a room was "historiated with the most beautiful figures, which represented hunts and fishing and jousts, with other various representations of the dukes and duchesses of this state."[96] Thus, a chivalric act, whether committed in a battle of the past or a ceremony of the present, was an *istoria*, and *istorie* were presented or held in theaters.

Visual evidence, which will be discussed below, corresponds with verbal evidence and suggests that *istorie*—that is, chivalric acts such as battles or ceremonies—in the past or in the present, were represented or held in theaters. In quattrocento Rome the term "theater" had been used to designate the hall in the palace of Cardinal Orsini on Monte Giordano, in a list prepared in 1432 of the dozens of famous men who had recently been painted on his walls, probably by Masolino.[97] In 1450 Giovanni Rucellai said that the palace was "historiated with good figures."[98] These heroes from all ages were there as *exempla* for the Cardinal, who conducted acts of government in the hall. This was a private setting; in locations where acts took place for public consumption, the setting was called a *pulpitum*, or theater. The term *pulpitum* is more common; it referred to a simple platform overlooking an area where the people could see the action.[99] In Rome in the middle of the quattrocento, *pulpitum* was the term used to designate the benediction loggia begun by Pius II in front of the entrance to the Basilica of St. Peter.[100] The activity conducted in such structures was ceremonial —the swearing of oaths, the receiving of ambassadors and important, visitors, and other such activities of governors.[101] A loggia, a theater, and frescoed *exempla* went together in Pistoia. The city officials took their oaths of office in what was called the "loggia del giuramento, o del theatro" as early as 1409, and in 1475 this loggia was frescoed with famous men: Scipio Africanus, Gaius Fabricius, Cato, and Marcus Curtius.[102]

As Alberti made clear in *De re aedificatoria*, a patrician's acts in a republic were often public acts that produced order in the city. There are numerous references to

---

[95] Bigongiari, 1964, pp. 167 f.

[96] See the inventories and descriptions in Schlosser (1895) 1965, docs. A–N; quoted here, doc. L, from 1570, referring to works in the Castello in Pavia.

[97] Simpson, 1966, p. 150, where the term "sala theatri" appears in the title of the list published there. For the view of Rome that is included, see above, chapter 5.

[98] Rucellai, 1960, p. 76.

[99] See Bigongiari, 1964, p. 179; both Vitruvius (V, vi, 1) and Alberti (*De re aed.*, VIII, vii, p. 731), used this term for the stage of a theater.

[100] Müntz, *ACP*, I, pp. 280–283.

[101] For the important place of oaths in the papal administration of the Patrimonium, see Jones, 1952, pp. 341–342; for the oath sworn to the pope by the senator of Rome, see Anonimo, 1881. Among the first uses of the benediction loggia begun by Pius II was the installation of Borso d'Este in his dignity as duke of Ferrara (1471; Paul II); Zippel, 1911, p. 188 (for the ceremony, Celani, 1890, pp. 435–436). A temporary wooden loggia apparently served Paul on Christmas Day, 1468, when he received Frederick III; Zippel, 1911, pp. 187 ff., esp. p. 188, n. 1. See also Vasari, III, p. 101.

[102] Mode, 1970, p. 235. For other Italian examples, see Bigongiari, 1964, p. 178; Buchthal, 1971, p. 60.

loggias as the setting for such acts, among which would be Rucellai's relation of the marriage celebration held in his loggia (fig. 77).[103] Acts were no less important in principalities, and they, too, were held in spaces called theaters or loggias. Public activities occurring in the piazza in front of the cathedral in Ferrara conferred on it the designation "theater" in a manuscript produced for Ercole d'Este.[104] In 1487, Ercole was greeted in a loggia and garden at the Vatican by Innocent VIII.[105] One of the more elaborate descriptions of an act of government concerned a meeting in a loggia in the ducal *castello* in Ferrara; it was narrated by Pierantonio Paltroni, the secretary of Federigo da Montefeltro. Borso d'Este, the duke of Modena, had carefully arranged a meeting in 1457 between Federigo, then count of Urbino, and Sigismondo Malatesta. After extensive and difficult negotiations, the two men met in "a loggia that was there, and there he [Sigismondo] met the lord duke of Modena and Count Federigo and, both extending their hands, they touched hands making the sign of reverence, and both turned quickly to the lord duke of Modena, showing again that act of touching the hands was made only for satisfaction and compliance of the lord duke, because no words had gone between them concerning how they might act when they met." The duke spoke to them there in the loggia and then had them return to their individual rooms. More negotiations were required before an actual interview took place.[106]

Just such a ceremony would be an act of government for the duke of Modena; any of these acts would have been the sort of activity Nicholas would have conducted in his theater or loggia. Manetti wanted to show that it was an impressive building and described it as raised up on marble columns into vaults. The description could be a precise reference to what was intended. For example, a vaulted loggia or vestibule is found directly behind the Arch of Alfonso I in Naples, which was built at the same time as the chivalric central portion of the entrance to the *castello*.[107] Nicholas's acts were to be conspicuous, and the term Manetti used and the form and site he described indicate that they would have been visible from within the enclosed paradise, the ceremonial center of government for the Church. Here Nicholas would govern in his loggia, hall, chapel, and garden.

When Manetti used the word "paradise" to refer to this area, he was not using hyperbole. It was a word rich with connotations, and the connotations were the ones sought by governors. In descriptions that are less rhetorical and more literal, the connotations are glossed to make the point explicit. In a description of a reception held at the Vatican to celebrate the elevation to the papacy of Alfonso Borgia (Calixtus III), Nicholas's successor, the gloss is literally paradisiacal. The festivities included hymns, orations, and feasting. The event demonstrated that concord existed between the clerics and the people, and between the men, the women, and the magis-

---

[103]See above, chapter 3. See also Alberti, *Della famiglia*, p. 210; Pitti, 1967, p. 32; Vespasiano, 1963, p. 159; and the "Libro di matematica di Giuliano de' Medici," Bibl. Riccardiana, Florence, Ricc. 2669, fol. 110ᵛ, which shows a ceremonial act in a setting resembling Rucellai's loggia (fig. 77). For the Rucellai loggia, see Kent, 1972.

[104]Battisti, "Scena classica," 1960, p. 98.

[105]Ehrle and Stevenson, 1897, p. 13, n. 9, citing a passage from Burchardi's diary (Thuasne ed., I, p. 262).

[106]Paltroni, 1966, pp. 114–115.

[107]Hersey, 1969, p. 11. That these vaults were "Catalan Gothic" can be attributed to local tradition. See also the arch in the drawing in the Museum Boymans-van Beuningen in Rotterdam (Hersey, "Arch," 1969) and the arch at Capua (discussed by Battisti, "Simbolo e classicismo," 1960, pp. 20 n. 1, 21 ff., 22 n. 3), where features that made explicit reference to the entrance to paradise are discussed.

trates who were in attendance; that is, it continued, there was concord between "the senate and the people." The description explained that those who had participated had known that they were in a "paradise fertile with fruit trees." Here they were at the gate of heaven, with the dove of the Spirit and the single beautiful Bride without blemish or wrinkle, within the enclosed garden with the fountain of living and purifying water, with fruits of the flowering trees. Here indeed, it concluded, the Church was governed through divine clemency.[108]

Calixtus died only three years after this celebration of his having become pope. His successor, Pius II, spent little more time than that in Rome, but when there he made full use of the area. He greeted ambassadors, gave counsel, and enjoyed his meals in a setting at the Vatican that he described as lush with plants and stocked with domestic and exotic animals.[109]

Descriptions, and glosses on descriptions, of activities that indicated that they took place in a paradise are not an innovation. Indeed, the *topos* that related acts of government to paradisiacal settings had a long tradition. The settings in which acts of government occurred were named paradises, and in descriptions they were equipped with what were considered the appropriate elements to make the identification of the place clear. The paradise *topos* indicated that certain things would be found in a paradisiacal setting, and therefore the entire list of things would not need to be named, and, conversely, when enough of the prescribed elements were named, the term "paradise" did not need to be used. Italians were more prone than other Europeans were to make their paradisiacal points with imagery that was actually decorative or architectural.[110]

In Milan there had long been a tradition of making explicit the paradisiacal connotations of the places in which government was conducted. Azzo Visconte's *castello* there had a courtyard and some rooms with paradise decorations as early as 1340.[111] Filarete's constant repetition of the figure in his architectural treatise, written for the Sforza duke in 1461–64, wove together Visconte and Sforza history and imagery; it was an attempt to provide the trappings of legitimacy for the new ducal family by showing the Sforza's participation in traditional chivalric, Milanese, and Viscontean concerns.

In Florence the imagery was less often or less blatantly and explicitly employed, but when a Milanese delegation was there in 1459, its members found a paradise. In a report to Galeazzo Maria Sforza about an official reception for them, held at the palace of the principal patrician of the republic to which the duke of Milan was allied in the Lega Italica, they stressed the paradise elements at the Palazzo Medici. One of the councilors described the palace with careful precision and proper awe, and then broke out, "*In somma*, it is believed by all that in the world there is not another earthly paradise like this."[112] In a more finished dispatch, this time a poem, produced later to report on the palace and the ceremonies, the crucial term is reserved for the moment when "the sun of paradise" is representative of the marvel produced by the

[108]Quoted in Raynaldus, ad anno 1455, no. 21. The term "the senate and the people" ("Senatus populusque") is used as a figure, not as a reference to the government of Rome.

[109]Zippel, 1911, pp. 195–196, relates Pius's description to what Manetti described as Nicholas's invention.

[110]For an early study, which only introduces the richness of the *topos*, see Schlosser (1895) 1965. For an encyclopedic review of visual material, see Börsch-Supan, 1967, esp. pp. 219–224. For a recent study, which works only from obvious, known sources but which demonstrates the breadth and importance of the *topos*, see Comito, 1971.

[111]See the description in Schlosser (1895) 1965, doc. K, pp. 109 f.

[112]Hatfield, 1970, appendix, p. 246.

torches that illuminated the evening festivities.[113] Elsewhere in the poem the equipment of an earthly paradise is listed, but the term is not used.[114] The equipment was
there to be seen, however, and it appears in one of the earliest representations of the
palace (fig. 78). In a Virgil manuscript illustrated in Apollonio di Giovanni's workshop (ca. 1460–65), Dido receives the emissaries of the Trojans, who are led by a
smartly dressed, youthful Cupid. Behind them is the Palazzo Medici; conspicuous
are the open arches on the corner of the palace, which were called the loggia, and in
this view it is clear that the loggia was considered a means of access into the *cortile*
and the enclosed, tree-filled garden beyond. This was a setting appropriate for such a
ceremonious activity.[115] Generally, the Florentines were less likely to use the term,
although they knew what its constituent elements were.[116] It was a more conscious
and familiar element in princely states than it was in republics.

In principalities, paradisiacal settings are used to show the acts of government that
establish order and peace through the two principal means, letters and arms. The
example of three scenes that show the use of reason or intellect within a paradise
might indicate the motif's flexibility. In each, the most common collection of the
fewest elements used to render the *topos* as a visual figure—a loggia fronting on an
enclosed greensward—provides the setting for the act being performed. One is in a
miniature that shows the presentation of a learned treatise to a patron (fig. 79). Origi-
nating in Lombardy (1431–47), it has Eugenius IV surrounded by cardinals; he is
wearing his tiara and is seated on a throne in an enclosed, flowery, and grassy garden,
where he receives the book from its kneeling and tonsured author.[117] Another is in a
Life of St. Benedict produced in Padua in the middle of the quattrocento (fig. 80).
Here, the protagonists of a miracle act in a paradise setting with a fountain, tree,
flowers, enclosure, and loggia.[118] The last is in Borso d'Este's Bible (1455–61), where
Solomon, the *exemplum* of kingly or princely wisdom, is seen in an elaborate setting
(fig. 81). He sits on a dais in a loggia, looking at the rising sun across a rich landscape. On the right side, the landscape is enclosed by a woven wicket fence, and on
the other it is bathed by the light of the newborn sun. With the king in the loggia
are ladies and gentlemen of the court, who dance to the music of musicians. The
illustration combines many paradisiacal delights with connotations of wisdom conveyed by the figures of Solomon and the sun.[119]

The imagery of paradise was as important in the representation of heroes of arms

[113]Ibid., appendix, p. 248; lines 16–18 of fol. 41ᵛ. The sun is a figure for paradisiacal illumination; thus,
by analogy, the torches had lit an "ordered" realm.

[114]Ibid., appendix, p. 247, lines 9–26.

[115]The arches were filled by Michelangelo in 1517; for the manuscript, see Gombrich, "Apollonio di
Giovanni," 1966. It is the Riccardiana Virgil, Bibl. Riccardiana, Florence, Ricc. 492, fol. 74ᵛ.

[116]See, for example, Rucellai's description of his villa at Quaracchi, 1960, pp. 20–25. For the villa
owner and its governor, see Alberti, *Villa*, passim. The setting for book III of Alberti's *Della famiglia*
is "vostri bellissimi orti"; p. 153.

[117]Antonio da Rho, "Tre dialoghi sugli errori di Lattanzio Firmiano," Vat. Lat. 227, fol. 4ᵛ; reproduced
in *Miniature del Rinascimento*, 1950, cat. 99, pl. XVII.

[118]Gregorius I, "Dialogorium Liber II Vita S. Benedicti," The Pierpont Morgan Library, New York,
M. 184, fol. 14ᵛ; the location of the miracle of the poisoned bread is the courtyard of the Abbey of
Monte Cassino; see Harrsen and Boyce, 1953, cat. 62, pl. 53.

[119]Modena, Este Library, Ms. V.G. 12, vol. I, fol. 280ᵛ; attributed to Taddeo Crivelli (Salmi, 1954, pp.
58 ff., pl. LIII). See also *Sarah and the Pharaoh*, vol. I, fol. 9ᵛ (Salmi, 1954, pl. L). See also a manuscript
from the same time, derived from styles used in Milan slightly earlier, showing Anthony's death in a
loggia fronting on a greensward, within an enclosure that forms part of Cleopatra's city; British Museum, Add. Ms. 22318, fol. 44ᵛ (Mitchell, 1961, pl. 2, pp. 8–17; also pp. 5–10, for its use for princely
edification).

as it was when showing *exempla* of intellect. The occupations of knights in Naples reported by Pierantonio Paltroni—triumphs, jousts, and hunts—were commonly shown in paradise settings.[120] A triumph was simply a display, in one form or another, of heroes. Dante encountered Hector, Aeneas, and Caesar, and Socrates, Plato, and Cicero, as well as other ancient heroes in limbo after having reached

> al piè d'un nobile castello,
> Sette volte cerchiato d'alte mura,
> difeso intorno d'un bel fiumecello.
>
> Questo passammo come terra dura;
> per sette porte intrai con questi savi;
> giugnemmo in prato di fresca verdura.
> (*Inf.* IV, lines 106–111)

These unbaptized heroes were shielded by their *castello* and had not been consigned to the place Dante next encountered, the "parte over non è che luca" (*Inf.* IV, line 151). In paradise he encountered the warrior-heroes of God in the realm of Mars, and again he described their setting as a similar *prato di fresca verdura;* now of heavenly quality, it was at the

> quinta soglia
> del'albero che vive della cima,
> e frutta sempre e mai non perde foglia.
> (*Par.* XVIII, lines 28–30)

Frezzi traversed a succession of *prati di fresca verdura* peopled with examples of the virtues, some resident in *castelli,* and all installed in paradise settings. In limbo he found a paradise containing the First Parents and their successors from the periods *ante legum* and *sub legum,* including Moses "and King David and all the prophets/ lacking in heaven, where the First Monarch is."[121] He asked Minerva, his guide there, where he could find the learned, the poets, and the ancient Romans. Minerva responded:

> In these wide meadows
> there are none of those with their vaunted abilities;
> as has been said, they have a higher place.
>
> Their *virtù* and fame have made them worthy
> to stay with Mars and to stay with the Muses
> and with Apollo in a more splendid realm.[122]

These later heroes had "that dear Baptism" that those in limbo had lacked.[123] Farther on, in the realm of the virtues, Frezzi would find the heroes of arms and the learned in knowledge who had ministered to the Church in the period *sub gratiam,* and who

---

[120]See below, pp. 159–160.

[121]Frezzi, 1914, II, iv, lines 137–138; his description of the garden is in lines 28 ff.

[122]Ibid., II, iv, lines 142–147. Compare this with the cycle in the Palazzo Pubblico in Siena, discussed above, chapter 3. Immediately after leaving this area the topography changes; it turns tortured and spiney, a "loco incolto/tra rovi e spin, che mai producon rose"; II, v, lines 1–6.

[123]See Frezzi, 1914, II, iv, line 42.

would therefore find their reward near the vision of God that Frezzi himself enjoys at the end.

Visual sources are more scrupulous in segregating the strong men from the intellectuals and even more elaborate in their paradise imagery. These sources include cycles that are meant to present groups of heroes standing in triumph as *exempla* for a prince to emulate. They almost always show the heroes in an enclosed, grassy meadow or *castello* and often in a loggia. The popular *neuf preux* cycle, established by the early fourteenth century, was composed of three groups of three men, each of whom had fought for his religion. Hector, Alexander the Great, and Julius Caesar were the pagans, Joshua, David, and Judas Maccabeus the Jews, and King Arthur, Charlemagne, and Godfrey de Bouillon the Christians.[124] In their representation in a manuscript of *Le Chevalier Errant*, written in 1394 by Tommaso III, Marquis of Saluzzo, and illustrated for him, they are shown with their paramours (figs. 82, 83). The men are spread out in a line within a *castello* that appears in the guise of a loggia, with a crenellated cornice and fortified towers at each end, while the ladies are in a more delicate loggia.[125] At La Manta, the seat of the marquisate of Saluzzo, the figures reappear without the loggia, but as one element within a complex setting in a hall decorated at some point well into the first half of the quattrocento (figs. 84, 85). The heroes and their paramours stand on a grassy, flowered vale between trees and against an arboreal backdrop, which acts as an enclosure.[126]

To earn their places in these cycles, the heroes had exercised arms for their states and for religion; this could be done equally well in actual battle or in a joust. Representations of either an actual heroic act, such as St. George's slaying of the dragon, or of a joust almost invariably show the *castello*, loggia, and enclosed, flower-speckled greensward of the paradise motif. From the late middle ages, chivalric acts were particularly popular subjects for mirror cases and marriage chests and for manuscript illuminations and tapestries.[127] A hunt was simply another form of joust; it

---

[124]Schlosser (1895) 1965, p. 36; Huizinga, 1956, pp. 72 ff.; Ross, 1963, p. 105; Loomis, 1967.

[125]Bib. Nat., Paris, Fr. 12559, fols. 125^{r-v}; repr. in d'Ancona, 1905, pp. 190 and 191, and Wyss, 1957, figs. 17 and 18. Contrast a similar setting, without the paradise overtones, from mid-trecento Naples (London, British Museum, Royal 20D.I, fols. 49^v, 53^r, and 110^v; repr. in Buchthal, 1971, pls. 13 and 30a, discussed pp. 16 ff.).

[126]For the dating of 1420, see d'Ancona, 1905, and Wyss, 1957; for that of 1437–40, see Mallè, 1956, p. 149, n. 13, which is generally accepted, along with the attribution to Giacomo Jaquerio. See also Griseri, 1960. For easily accessible, related examples, see the *cassone* "delle virtù" in the Bagatti-Valsecchi collection, Milan, from the second half of the quattrocento, repr. in *Arte Lombarda*, 1958, cat. 438, pl. CLXX,a. Also, six heroes from antiquity in a Plutarch manuscript from the same period (Bologna, Bibl. Univ., Ms 2325, fol. 1^r; repr. in Salmi, 1954, p. 61, pl. LVI). Also, the heroes that appear in the elaborate setting in the Palazzo Trenci in Foligno, from 1421–24, which includes references to Frezzi's *Quadriregio* (Frezzi enjoyed Trenci patronage) and which deserves extended study; see Salmi, 1919, pp. 153–159, 159–164, and Weiss, 1969, p. 57. And, the old throne room in the Palazzo Ducale in Urbino from just after the mid century; Rotondi, 1950, pp. 155 ff. (his reconstruction is unreliable). The loggia setting was one of two types; the Siena and Castagno examples are related to it. An alternative was to show the heroes against a plain background, as in the Orsini palace on Monte Giordano (see Toesca, 1952, and other literature cited above, chapter 5), and earlier, in the famous Greeks and Trojans in the Guido manuscript in Geneva (Bibliotheca Bodmeriana, fols. 25^v–27^v; repr. in Buchthal, 1971, pls. 46 and 47) produced in Venice around 1370 (see ibid., ch. V and pp. 44–45).

[127]See the illustrations in Loomis, 1919; Kurth, 1942; and Ross, 1948. See also Donatello's St. George relief, Or San Michele, Florence, and a painting of the subject from the second half of the quattrocento (Brescian?), with two figures watching from a loggia above *castello* walls (repr. in *Arte Lombarda*, 1958, cat. 292, pl. C). Also, several figures watch the scene of St. George slaying the dragon from a castle and its mountain, in a miniature in the copy of the miracles and martyrdom of St. George, made for the author of the book, Cardinal Jacopo Stepheneschi (Vatican, Archives of the Chapter of St. Peter, Ms C. 129, fol. 85^r), produced in Avignon before 1343 by the Maestro del Codice di S. Giorgio, under the influence of Simone Martini; Salmi, 1954, p. 28, pl. XX.

was a figure for heroic activity that demonstrated proficiency at arms and well-directed love. In a flowered *prato di fresca verdura* the knight would pursue furry little animals, capture stags, or slay boars as signs for his vigorous pursuit of the love of God, his eagerness to attend to the human soul, or his anxiety to put down concupiscent desires.[128]

Julius von Schlosser long ago observed that the figure of St. George and the dragon was the "origin and model of all chivalric events."[129] The militant and heroic knight slays the monster to save the virgin; the Christian exercising his *virtù* slays the adversary to protect the Church. The concept was chivalric, and so was Nicholas.

The major states and statesmen in Italy were directly linked to the papacy through a variety of chivalric ties, formal and informal. The kingdom of Naples was a papal fief. The counties of Ferrara and Urbino (later duchies under Paul II and Sixtus IV, respectively) were papal vicarates. The duchy of Milan was an imperial territory, the emperor was a sworn officer of the papacy, and Francesco Sforza could not have become duke of Milan in 1450 without the pope's approval. Florence, through its Guelf tradition and other ties, was woven into this fabric of political relationships, which included the pope.

In governing the Church Nicholas called upon knights of the Church militant. One of the most successful projects he undertook followed the loss of Constantinople. In late 1453 and early 1454, he called ambassadors to a congress at the Vatican, where he attempted to forge the Italian states, united in peace, into a weapon that he could turn against the Turks. His efforts were frustrated by the continued abrasions afflicting the fringes of states, by jealousies, and by his own gouty and failing health, but he continued to sponsor negotiations among the chivalric princes and republican patricians.[130]

Eventually, as Paltroni put it, the major powers realized that by building on a series of little pacts among themselves, they could establish a general peace that would satisfy the best interests of all.[131] The early participants worked diligently to incorporate the king of Naples into the league, which was a precondition for bringing in the pope, who had initiated the project. Without the pope's participation the league lacked a crusading ideal and a context of universality that would allow it to transcend particularism.[132] Finally, Nicholas's project bore fruit when the Lega Italica was established. Ratification followed difficult negotiations in Naples where the expenses, Paltroni said, were generously supported by the king of Naples, by other princes, and of course by his own patron—and therefore paragon of princely generosity—Federigo da Montefeltro. The negotiations had been long, and Paltroni reported that the participants "occupied themselves during that time with many most solemn and grand triumphs, with jousts, with hunts, and with most dignified banquets."[133] The conclusion of the negotiations in Naples was celebrated by a mass and a joust.[134]

The entire affair was a display of chivalry. Knights with their love set on God were conquering lusts; order was being established; charity was vanquishing *superbia*. The

[128]See Robertson, 1962, pp. 263–264.

[129]Schlosser (1895) 1965, p. 44.

[130]For Nicholas's support of Fra Simone Camerino, who prodded the various early signatories, and their interest in a crusade, see Soranzo, 1924, pp. 12 ff., 51, 125 f., 138 ff.

[131]Paltroni, 1966, pp. 107–109.

[132]See Cessi, 1942–43, pp. 116–117, 121–123, and earlier, for emphasis on the necessity that the pope preside, see Soranzo, 1924, pp. 146 ff. For modern assessments of the Lega Italica, see Soranzo, 1924, passim; Ilardi, 1960, esp. pp. 141, 143 ff.

[133]Paltroni, 1966, p. 109.

[134]Soranzo, 1924, pp. 116 ff.

intellect guiding the arms of the knights was that of the pope. Nicholas was governing with charity and overcoming the *superbia* of the world.

Gratian's *Decretals* and the canon law that stemmed from them had supported the medieval monarchical constitution of the Church on this New Testament and Augustinian doctrine.[135] Torquemada, Nicholas's stout defender of papal primacy, included the doctrine naturally and easily within the commentary on penance he had composed for Nicholas.[136] In another treatise he had given seven reasons why the *paradiso terrestri* could be compared to the Church. His gloss on the figurative meaning of the parts of paradise that allowed sin to be cleansed and health to be restored to the soul included elements from Nicholas's program for government, and elements that were to be found on the *mons saccorum*.[137] Christ is at the head of the Church and directs the Church militant, he said, and the Church is the seat of judgment and has divine knowledge; furthermore, paradise was the home of the First Parents, it was placed in the east, it had trees and flowers, it had fruit trees and cedars, and pure water ran there. Elsewhere he had said that the *fons vitae* is a figure for charity and that charity overcomes *superbia*.[138] Nicholas had concluded his testament with similar figurative language. He explained to the cardinals that the Church is the Bride of Christ, the Seamless Tunic that the soldiers could not rend, the Ship of Peter that rides over the storms of the world. It deserves all your body and spirit, he continued to the cardinals; it will be invincible through your service of charity.[139] As the apostle Paul had explained, "There are three things that last forever: faith, hope, and charity; but the greatest of these is charity."[140] Frezzi had explained that charity was the greatest virtue and that *superbia* is the principal vice:

> *Superbia* is grand, it is the first presumption
> against the rational [mental] law and divine [law],
> and it was the first [vice] that man gave way to.[141]

Superbia caused the expulsion from the garden; charity made it possible for mankind to return to paradise.

Acts of charity rendered in a garden were figures for this doctrine. As the Augustinian doctrine, which was prominent throughout the middle ages in literature, has been summarized, "When Christ is the gardener, the garden is ruled by wisdom and suffused with the warmth of charity. Otherwise, it is ruled by worldly wisdom or *scientia* and suffused with cupidity."[142] As Dante had said, a living consciousness of charity

> tratto m'hanno del mar dell'amor torto,
> e del diritto m'han posto alla riva.
>
> Le fronde onde s'infronda tutto l'orto
> dell'ortolano eterno, am'io contanto
> quanto da lui a lor di bene è porto.
> (*Par.* XXVI, lines 62–66)

[135]Buisson, 1958, ch. I.

[136]See for example *Poenitentia*, fols. 49ᵛ ff.

[137]See *Consecratione*, fol. 126ʳ.

[138]*Poenitentia*, fol. 54ᵛ.

[139]Manetti, *RIS*, col. 956.

[140]I Corin. 13:13.

[141]Frezzi, 1914, III, ii, lines 79–81.

[142]Robertson, 1951, p. 32.

Love, whether rightly or wrongly directed, stood at the center of this doctrine. Love of the world was wrongly directed and equal to *superbia,* and love for God and one's neighbor was rightly directed, or charity.

Nicholas's projected paradise was a carefully designed architectural project, which would have shown that the pope governed with charity. Within an enclosed place, a papal *castello*—made strong through carefully designed walls and towers that protected fresh, watered gardens abundant with all the herbs and fruits that grow—the pope governed the Church. Here he had all the facilities needed for the elaborate chivalric ceremony of government. He received ambassadors in the theater. He dined in the triclinium, presided in the hall, and officiated in the chapel. He blessed the people from his benediction loggia. And he gave counsel in the apartments that looked eastward over the garden, the Borgo, and Rome. Here he used his intellect to direct the arms of his members to bring to the affairs of the world a semblance of the order of the first paradise.

But Nicholas's paradise was left incomplete, and because what was completed was later effaced, the palace's role in giving architectural form to a common *topos* has been ignored. In the middle of the century, when it was a new undertaking, it would have stimulated a great deal of excitement. Some of that excitement seems to have led to the programs that Pius II used at Pienza, that Paul II drew on at the Palazzo Venezia, that Federigo da Montefeltro built in Urbino, and that Filarete incorporated into his architectural treatise. Those interested in knowing more about what Nicholas had projected had available to them Manetti's description, reports of others who were privy to the pope's project, and other material such as Gozzoli's visual representation, as well as the actual buildings and decorations and their own acquaintances with the project. They would have examined this material with an understanding of what went into the project and would have recognized that the figures taken from Biblical, ancient, and romance literature and from the decorative material that accompanied it had been rendered in architectural form to give a proper setting for the pope, the Vicar of Christ, the gardener of the garden of wisdom.

But the parts of the project mentioned so far would have left one element in the *topos* ambiguous. How was the visitor to know whether Nicholas considered the paradise to be a place protected from the temptations and disorders of the world outside the walls, or an ordered territory that could serve as an example of what the governor within sought to impose on the world outside through his actions? The question was a quattrocento one, and Nicholas was the first to give an answer in visual form.

The question had come up during the trecento, and it turned on the belief that chivalric acts could be *exempla* for a proper or for an improper love. Two different systems had been sketched out to show which love directed one's actions. Each had been extensively developed and had come into wide use by the middle of the quattrocento. One was more common in north Europe. It used references to concupiscent love as warnings to those who were reflecting about an action they might take. It stressed the idea that just as knowledge controlled arms, so too the intellect, through reason, controlled the passions and directed the love to God. Knowledge and government were best pursued in an earthly paradise protected from the world through arms and intellect. There the love could seek God in isolation *from* the outside world.[143]

[143]The literary material has been most actively studied, and the related art historical material has only recently begun to receive attention, both for its own content and for the uncovering of chivalric themes related to the literary *topoi*. For literary studies, see Patch, 1950, esp. chs. IV, V, and VI; Robertson, 1962, pp. 386–389; Curtius, 1963, pp. 194–202; Giamatti, 1966, pp. 3–129. For specialized studies connected with the Castle of Love, see Loomis, 1919; Cornelius, 1930, ch. VI; Saxl, 1942, "Pictures without

The other system was more common in Italy. Petrarch had given it body by declaring that love was the strongest passion of the soul. It used references to divinely directed love as admonitory *exempla* to those who would undertake an action. It demanded active engagement *in* the world. Among those who adhered to this new position were Nicholas and his associates in Rome in the middle of the century. The paradise on the *mons saccorum* represents its implementation in architecture and in decoration.[144]

From this dignified seat at the head of the Church the pope was an active participant in the affairs of the world. He was an *exemplum* of charity. As his humanist friends explained, the results of his actions would reveal his intentions and show whether he was driven by a love for God or by the Satanic lusts of pride of life or of knowledge, love of the world for its own sake, or desire for the dignity, pomp, and power the world offered. His achievements in governing and in building would reveal that he had clearly desired to use his knowledge, the riches of the Church, and the office he held to protect and amplify the sacraments and to protect and to dignify the papacy. The evidence would surround them in the rebuilt Rome, reconstructed basilica, and enlarged palace. These would outlast their builder. The voice of Petrarch the poet can be heard in the background: "Our life will be judged by our conversation; when the proof of our actions is gone, only the evidence of our speech will remain."[145]

And it would be clear in the figures used in the decorative program within the palace. Although only a fragment survives of what was probably a much larger program, that fragment is revealing. In the Sala Vecchia degli Svizzeri, one saw the four cardinal virtues (only three survive), which represent the means the pope used to exercise his secular office as princely pope (figs. 60–62). The cardinal virtues, however, represent only one part of the decorative program; the playful putti (figs. 54–57, 59), who are rendered in the same size and appear in decorative frames of the same design as those which hold the cardinal virtues, supplement the meaning conveyed by the cardinal virtues. The putti indicate that Nicholas used the cardinal virtues to govern in order to exercise his love for God in this world in the hope of enjoying paradise in the next world. Like any putto, these represent a form of love, in this case, a love for God that can overcome *superbia* through governing.

The putti in this room are able to signify love for God because they present a visual figure for the doctrine of charity that had been slowly developed since the late thirteenth century. In the last decades of the thirteenth century, a new interpretation of the theological virtue of Charity began to circulate in literature, probably first in the context of secular love themes.[146] Giotto's visual representation of Charity in the Arena Chapel in Padua (1303) shows the newly developed interpretation (fig. 86). She stands with the goods of the world beneath her feet, holding fruits and flowers

Commentary"; Kurth, 1942; Fleming, 1969, ch. 2. Further material in Patch, 1927, ch. IV; idem, 1950, pp. 179–180, 222–224; Robertson, 1951. Important precedents for Torquemada's ideas are in Hugh of St. Victor, *De Arca Noe Morali*, II and III. Frezzi himself seems to refer to the difference between French and Italian attitudes towards the role of love and the passions; in the Realm of Venus, where the blond ladies are dancing and enjoying themselves in a way that the good bishop comes to dislike, he is told "Né Fiandra, né Roma, ovver Fiorenza,/ né leggiadria giammai che di Francia esca,/ mostraro ninfe di tant'apparenza." 1914, I, xvi, lines 55–57.

[144]The context within which Nicholas's program is to be interpreted has been lamentably neglected; for the little that has been done on chivalric themes before Politian and Lorenzo and Giuliano de'Medici, see Schlosser (1895) 1965; Vallone, 1955; Mitchell, 1961; and Ruggieri, 1962.

[145]Quoted above, chapter 2. See also above, p. 53.

[146]For that background, see Freyhan, 1948, part II.

that overflow from a basket to show the abundance of earthly goods. She holds her heart aloft to God to represent her drive for the love of God that guides her actions. And a flame is included behind her head to depict the *armor Dei* that burns for union with God.[147] Charity, for Nicholas, was a more highly developed version of the same concept. The putti show that his love was directed toward God and resulted in action in the world.

Probably no more than three putti are lost from the scheme, and more likely five of the probable total of six survive.[148] As a group, they have two characteristics in common that set them apart from other representations of paradisiacal sprites in other contexts. They are not blindfolded; they are, therefore, shown as clear-sighted, which indicates that they see with the illumination that comes from knowledge of God.[149] And they enjoy themselves with things of the world. Prodded by their "most violent passion," which is directed toward God, they may play safely in the rooms overlooking the paradise in Nicholas's palace. Two play at traditional antique games; one pulls a bow, and another rides a bird (figs. 56, 57). Two others have a richer meaning.

One blows the bagpipe (fig. 59). In Italian art bagpipe-blowing angels had appeared, making celestial music, in the presence of an angelic orchestra in paradise around an enthroned saint, at the coronation of the Virgin, at the birth of Christ, or at some other event connected with Christ and the history of salvation.[150] And there is a bagpipe-blower in the paradisiacal foliate border of the Porta della Mandorla in Florence, which includes the cardinal virtues.[151] But Nicholas's energetic musician meant something quite different from the bagpipers in angelic choruses. Nicholas took him from the decorative borders of manuscripts, where he had served along with grotesques, various animals, and other figures as a gloss that added another level of allegorical meaning to the text. The texts where such borders appeared were usually

[147]Ibid. Earlier, Wind, 1937–38, part 2; both cite variations, for which see also Panofsky, 1970, pp. 148 ff. For Dante, who conceived of charity in a similar way, see Freyhan, 1948, p. 79. These were Petrarch's sources for his more systematic development of the idea.

[148]Three exist in the three quadrilobes of the east wall (figs. 56, 57, and 59); two (in one quadrilobe) are on the north wall (figs. 54, 55). It is likely that none was on the south wall, and that only one, from the west end of the north wall, is lost. It is possible, however, that there were two on the south wall, although they would not have been directly opposite those on the north.

[149]For clear-sighted putti, see Panofsky, 1962, ch. IV, esp. p. 126; Gilbert, 1968, pp. 82–84; idem, 1970, p. 305. Frezzi, 1914, III, xiv, explains the three kinds of love one may have on earth and states that the love of Venus, "cioè concupiscenza,/ nasce Amor cieco, fanciullesco e vano"; lines 71–72. See also III, xv, lines 52–54.

[150]See Hammerstein, 1962, who cites four interesting examples: in the scene of St. Francis enthroned attributed to Puccio Capanna, ca. 1350, in the chapter room of the monastery of San Francesco, Pistoia (pl. 68, p. 226); on the doors to a tabernacle in the Oratorio della Madonna, San Giovanni Valdarno, weakly attributed to Masaccio (pl. 102, p. 241); among those attending the angelic companions for the enthroned Madonna and Child by Giovanni Boccati, Pinacoteca, Perugia, 1447 (pl. 115, p. 244); and in Filippino Lippi's *Assumption of the Virgin*, Caraffa Chapel, Santa Maria sopra Minerva, Rome, ca. 1490 (pl. 98, p. 240). His remarks concerning their having joined the angelic chorus occur on pp. 218 ff., 236–238, and 239. Two others may be mentioned. One is an early quattrocento statue, part of a series, from the Duomo in Milan; see *Arte Lombarda*, 1958, cat. 150, pl. XXXVI,d. The other appearance is two bagpipers among the fourteen musicians on the Lateran Cope, Pinacoteca Vaticana, of English manufacture from the late thirteenth century. This list is far from exhaustive, but it does demonstrate their appearance in angelic choruses from time to time.

[151]See Seymour, 1966, pp. 31 ff.; Panofsky, 1970, pp. 149 f., n. 4; and Krautheimer, 1970, pp. 279 ff. Bagpipers also exist in the borders of the doors to the baptistry. None is found in Filarete's doors. One is found in the border decoration of Cardinal Aeneas Sylvius's *City of God* (Biblioteca Vaticana, Cod. Reg. Lat. 1882, fol. 2ʳ) on the page with the view of Rome (here, fig. 21), where he is one of the numerous, happy, terrestrial putti-musicians (fig. 87). The manuscript is dated 1456; perhaps this putto comes from Nicholas's decoration.

those of vernacular romance literature. In northern European manuscripts, a bagpipe player represented an antitype of charity; he showed that an individual had opted for the rasping sounds of earthly, concupiscent love rather than for the sweet tones of godly love.[152] His appearance here indicates that Nicholas has chosen active participation in the world. As Alberti had written in support of the active life in the city, "He who has not heard the sound of the bagpipe cannot judge whether the instrument is good or not good."[153] Only through the exercise of his *virtù* in the world can the pope bring order to the Church.

The last putto carries a similar meaning (fig. 55). He, too, enjoys himself as he catches butterflies. Dante had learned their significance upon entering Purgatory:

> O superbi cristian, miseri lassi
> che, della vista della mente infermi,
> fidanza avate ne'retrosi passi;
>
> non v'accorgete voi che noi siam vermi
> nati a formar l'angelica farfalla,
> che vola alla giustizia sanza schermi?
> (*Purg.*, X, lines 121–126)

But Nicholas's little friend represents a completely revised means by which the *vista della mente* is made healthy, and it presents a different idea about the purpose a healthy intellect is to serve. Not intellect, but love, gives clear sight, and man is not a worm but a butterfly engaged in enjoyable play with a clear-sighted child of love while still on earth, within a surrogate for paradise.[154] The world had been made by God and contained God's justice in it. Driven by love for God, Nicholas could render proper judgments about the unprotected soul and give just counsel with his clear sight, here in this setting.[155]

Nicholas's paradise therefore is a counterpart to the basilica next to it. There, the pilgrim finds an eloquent figure for God in the design of the building and a moving example of charity in the figure of the pope presiding over the hierarchy and protecting the sacraments of the Church. Here, the visitor would be a member of the chivalric orders. He would find just government and a pope actively governing the world as the Vicar of Christ and successor to Peter, Prince of the Apostles. In both places, the architectural setting and the acts of the pope—acts made conspicuous through their architectural settings—would provide figures which revealed that the doctrine of charity directed the governor of the Church. As Nicholas explained in his testament, he built these fortifications "for the sure and expressed effect both of devotion and fortification";[156] as he summarized it for the cardinals, he built in order to put

---

[152]See Robertson, 1962, pp. 128, 130, 132, 482; Randall, 1966, figs. 307 (antitype of constructive harmony, and support for the cowardly knight who drops his sword and flees at the sight of a snail) and 595 (antitype for celestial music at the top of the margin).

[153]*Della famiglia*, p. 201; quoted above, chapter 3, p. 57.

[154]For Frezzi's home of the First Parents with butterflies, see 1914, II, iv, lines 28 ff. Ladner, 1961, esp. pp. 318–322, establishes a context that might allow an interpretation of the enigmatic foliage-filled quadrilobe. It perhaps refers to the new life brought through reform, as well as to the lushness that is paradise.

[155]The fragmentary scheme here presages the more elaborate but quite similar program on the south wall of the Stanza della Segnatura, which Einem, 1971, has demonstrated was decorated for Julius II's tribunal; for a review of the interpretation and literature concerning the putti there as theological virtues in conjunction with the cardinal virtues, see Dussler, 1971, p. 76.

[156]Manetti, *RIS*, col. 950.

down blind *superbia* and so that the papacy might enjoy its proper authority, power, and dignity.[157] These attributes would be visible from the Borgo, which was directly under the jurisdiction of the pope and was protected and perfected by the palace, and it would be visible from Rome across the Tiber. The ancient empire had made possible the dissemination of the doctrine of charity throughout the world.

The cross atop Caesar's ashes on the obelisk in front of the basilica had now, finally, superseded the imperial sword as the sign of universal jurisdiction, and the pope himself now sat enthroned beyond the tomb of Peter and the altar in the church that stood next to the palace of the Fisherman's successor.

[157]Manetti, *RIS*, col. 952.

Epilogue   The Designer and the Date

When did Nicholas conceive and begin his comprehensive building project, and who was responsible for its invention? These questions are important because the project had an immediate and significant impact on the conceptual and physical development of Rome, on the ultimate shape given the buildings at the Vatican, and on subsequent architectural practice in Italy.

The two questions are intimately bound together. The tendency among historians has always been to examine the available material to discover if Alberti, the obvious candidate, can be connected with it; and he usually can be. This examination in turn has yielded a date that is generally taken to represent a moment when Alberti made a decisive intervention in Nicholas's construction. The approach has depended primarily upon interpreting what Nicholas's project was and what Alberti's ideas about architecture were at certain dates and then rendering a judgment about the possible congruence of the two. It was first mapped out in 1880 by Georg Dehio, whose brief and penetrating analysis suggested to all later historians the form and much of the substance of their interpretations. Dehio's immediate primary material was little more than Manetti's and Alberti's texts, which he interpreted in the context of his broad understanding of the period. He concluded that Alberti had given the pope the essential advice and that the spirit of the project is Alberti's, even though, as Manetti had said, the architect was Bernardo Rossellino. He proposed that Alberti had intervened in a project Nicholas had already undertaken, and that the date for that intervention was 1452.

Three questions contained in Dehio's interpretation continued to haunt historians —how much did Nicholas do before Alberti intervened, what did Rossellino do, and when did Alberti intervene? Historians somehow misinterpreted each of these questions by failing to consider them in the larger context within which each belonged, but they nevertheless were able to bring more evidence to the interpretation and to support what they understood to be Dehio's answer. Thus, his original case was made more conclusive than it had been, and no one questioned its elements. But in light of more recent information and interpretation, several elements in Dehio's analysis have been shown to be glaringly inadequate. They should not have taken on the importance given them by later historians, but it was natural that they would because they touched on what historians have most wanted, that is, a decisive date and firm evidence of the intervention of the great Renaissance architect.

Ludwig von Pastor, who followed Dehio closely, presented the issues in full grandeur. His argument is worth recounting at length, not least of all because it shows the disproportionate weight given to the statement in the chronicle of Mattia Palmieri, a Pisan familiar with Rome. The pope, Pastor claimed, conceived the project, and Alberti intervened after it was well advanced, giving it shape and form, even, rather grandly, advocating the complete destruction of the basilica, which the pope had begun only to repair. The seminal moment was Alberti's presentation of *De re aedificatoria* to the pope in 1452:

> The impression produced was instantaneous, profound, and convincing. A comparison between Palmieri's statement [in the chronicle], the testimony of the earlier account books, and Manetti's description places the matter beyond doubt. Clearly the perusal of this book, further supported by the eloquence of its gifted author, was the turning point with Nicholas in his building plans. The earlier conservative designs were discarded "by Leon Battista's advice," and the new colossal scheme adopted.[1]

Neither Eugène Müntz nor Pastor had been able to find a reference to Alberti in the account books that covered the project, but Girolamo Mancini, Alberti's great biographer, had discovered that Nicholas had given Alberti a priory. This, said Pastor, confirmed an earlier hypothesis that the pope had remunerated the eloquent author and architect in a more worthy way than with a bag of coins.[2] Pastor did not mention the fragmentary condition of the accounts Müntz had published and did not say that the date Alberti received the priory was December 7, 1448, more than three years before the "instantaneous, profound, and convincing" impression made by the architectural treatise.

Pastor also failed to note that Müntz had discussed Rossellino's place within the organizational structure of Nicholas's building projects and had shown that he occupied a relatively unimportant position.[3] Later historians have continued to attempt to construct an oeuvre for him, but it seems most reasonable to adopt a current view that sees him in a subordinate position in Rome and to accept that position as appropriate for him. In architecture, he represents a shop of executors associated with Alberti, and in Rome his name is connected only with the supervision of a few elements in the vast project.[4]

Finally, it now seems certain that *De re aedificatoria* could not have made the "instantaneous, profound, and convincing" impression Pastor believed it did. To believe so demands that one believe the book and the thoughts it contained were unknown to Nicholas before 1452, and that before that year there may even have been no book. Until recently, it was often argued that before 1452 Alberti had not really put his thoughts about architecture in order and that what Mattia Palmieri reported was the presentation of a kernel, or perhaps only notes for the book, which was slowly completed in the following years. This interpretation tended to shake the belief that Alberti's intervention was decisive in any way.[5] In 1956, however, Richard Krautheimer argued that internal and external evidence, as well as the spirit of the

[1] Pastor, 1949, p. 178; see pp. 169 ff. for the project. The quotation is from Palmieri; the "new colossal scheme" was for St. Peter's. The documents he mentions are the ones Müntz had published. At the conclusion of the passage here he cites Dehio, 1880, p. 253.

[2] Pastor, 1949, p. 177, n. 1; referring to Mancini's first edition (1882). See Mancini, 1911, p. 277 n. 1, and p. 93 n. 4.

[3] Müntz, *ACP*, I, pp. 79–87.

[4] See Magnuson, 1958, pp. 91 f., and notes there and pp. 213 f. See also Müntz, *ACP*, I, pp. 79–87; and Frutaz, 1956, pp. 15–16, for other personnel. Rossellino will be discussed again below.

[5] See in particular Magnuson's study of the Borgo, 1954, which discounts Alberti as much as possible and which provided the framework for his larger study, 1958. There (p. 90, n. 56), he revised his opinion about the date of *De re aedificatoria* but did not alter his assessment of Alberti's possible involvement in the project and the date of his nonintervention.

work, suggests a date for the beginning of the treatise in 1447 at the latest, more likely in 1444, and possibly in the 1430s; indeed, "the further the date of the preparatory phase can be pushed back into the forties and thirties, the more plausible it becomes."[6] Further investigations by Cecil Grayson have added depth to this argument.[7] The work was not composed in a day; on the other hand, it was perhaps not completely finished in 1452, the date Palmieri gave for Alberti's presentation of it to the pope.

What, then, is the value of Palmieri's statement? Paul Hoffmann in 1883 was the last to give serious thought to it. He showed that the chronicle in which Palmieri's statement occurred was probably composed after 1475. Its early entries occupy the space between 1449, when the previous compiler, the Florentine Matteo Palmieri (d. 1475), ceased making entries, and the period that was closer to the interest of the Pisan continuer, Mattia Palmieri (d. 1483).[8] There is a marked difference in the length and character of the first new entries up until 1475 and those between 1475 and 1482, when it ends. It is highly probable that Mattia Palmieri made no entries until 1475, and that he then filled in the years since 1449 from memory. The entries concerning Nicholas's pontificate begin in 1450 with a reference to the Jubilee, to the catastrophe on the Ponte Sant'Angelo, and to the building of the memorial chapels—events that are easily memorable, clearly related to one another, and tied to an unforgettable date. There is no reference to Nicholas under 1451. In 1452 there is a series of them. It begins with Frederick III's coronation, then mentions three events unconnected with Nicholas, and then returns to Nicholas's Rome:

> The pope, having undertaken to surround first the Vatican Hill and then the papal palace with a strong wall all the way to the Tiber and the Mole of Hadrian, wherefore he might safely place his people therein, completed this work in large part.
>
> The pope, wanting to make the Basilica of the Blessed Peter a greater adornment (*ornatio*), laid deep foundations and erected a wall of thirteen *braccia*, but he stopped this great work, which could be compared to that of any of the ancients, by the distinguished advice of Leon Battista, and then an untimely death cut short this enterprise.
>
> Leon Battista Alberti, a scholar endowed with sharp and penetrating intelligence and an excellent education, and well versed in doctrine, presented these learned books on architecture, which he had written, to the pope.[9]

This is the last entry for 1452. The first for 1453 concerns Alfonso of Aragon; no more is heard of the building project, and Porcari's uprising is ignored.[10]

Mattia Palmieri knew Rome well. He had been in the curia under Pius II and perhaps earlier under Nicholas.[11] But more than twenty years had elapsed between Nicholas's death and the moment Palmieri began to set down the events of his pontificate. He would naturally collect the important events into bundles and hang

---

[6]Krautheimer, 1970, n. 28 (p. 270) and p. 268; see also pp. 268–276. The 1970 edition is a reprint of the 1956 edition with a new preface.

[7]Grayson, 1960, esp. pp. 155–156.

[8]Hoffmann, 1883, pp. 10 f.

[9]Palmieri, 1748, col. 241, entry dated 1452.

[10]Palmieri, 1748, col. 241; for Palmieri, working with a Florentine dating system (Nicholas's death is listed under 1454), Porcari's uprising occurred in 1452.

[11]Hoffmann, 1883, p. 10. His epitaph in Santa Maria Maggiore names him as an "abbreviator, et secretario ap[ostolic]o"; in Cosenza, s.v., p. 2564.

them on convenient pegs. The thing to look for in his chronicle is the reason for the bundles and their pegs, not the precise information in each entry. It is significant, for example, that Palmieri has separated the project that Manetti described from the sad events at the Ponte Sant'Angelo and its rebuilding, just as Manetti had. It is noteworthy that he formed a group of the construction of the Borgo and palace walls, the amplification of the basilica, and Alberti's presentation of the treatise to the pope. But why did he group his information in this way, and why did he choose 1452 as the peg for it?

A reasonable guess is that this group was formed around the visit of the emperor Frederick III in 1452. It was an important event that made that date memorable, and it was an event that was related to Nicholas's building project programmatically. The project had presented the emperor with irrefutable visual evidence that Nicholas was his superior. Pius II and Infessura each reported, in his own way, how thoroughly that point had been made to Frederick.[12] Alternatively, it may have been the 1453 (1452 for Palmieri) uprising of Porcari's crowd, who, according to apologists, should have seen in the buildings of the pope that papal government was benevolent.[13] But if the conspiracy were the unifying point, it would seem that Palmieri would have mentioned it. These observations are only speculation, however, and are meant to suggest that the important meaning of Palmieri's report is not the date—which must be suspect, because Palmieri bundled events together to fit convenient dates more than twenty years after the mid century—but the unity of the three things he mentions. He made it clear that Nicholas rebuilt the Borgo, that the tribune of St. Peter's would dominate it, and that Alberti and his treatise were somehow connected with the pope's project.

It is unfair to try to extract much more than a sense of a coherent bundle from the entries, and it is misleading to use Palmieri to supply a date for the project. There is, for example, no corroborative evidence in Müntz's admittedly fragmentary documents—nearly all the documents that we have—which date between January, 1450, and October, 1454, to suggest any significant change in the project in 1452.[14] Furthermore, Palmieri's middle entry itself is obscure; it is unclear whether the thirteen *braccia* is a vertical or a horizontal measurement.[15]

This analysis casts doubt on the importance of Palmieri's chronicle as evidence. It seems fair to conclude that an approach that stresses Alberti's late intervention is no longer useful. To believe it one must believe that Nicholas began building, that Alberti began writing, and that neither was in contact with the ideas and activities of the other until 1452, or 1450,[16] and that when they discovered they could make common cause together, Alberti made a radical intervention in the

---

[12] Aeneas Sylvius reported that cardinals, not the pope, met Frederick outside Rome, an indication for him that the pope was greater than the emperor; see Gregorovius, 1900, VII, i, p. 125, and Pastor, 1949, p. 150. Elsewhere, in his *Europa*, Aeneas Sylvius compared Nicholas's achievements in rebuilding Rome to the works of the ancient emperors and found that Nicholas had surpassed them; quoted in Tomei, 1942, pp. 8–9. Infessura, pp. 50–53, mentioned only the visit of the emperor under the year 1452; he reported that the emperor recognized the senator and shunned the cardinals, which would seem to indicate that the emperor interpreted the composition of the welcoming delegation in much the same way Aeneas Sylvius did. See, however, a different opinion posited by Pastor, 1949, p. 150, n. 1, who always distrusts Infessura's reporting.

[13] See below, pp. 179–180.

[14] Müntz, *ACP*, I, pp. 121–124, for the basilica.

[15] Urban, 1963, pp. 135, 164 n. 27, has suggested that Palmieri's dimensions may be read as breadth rather than as height.

[16] For this date, see below, p. 171.

project. Alternatively, one may propose that when Nicholas became pope he began building on his own and either waited some years or never got around to soliciting any substantial advice from Alberti. It also requires that one presume that Alberti was at first aloof and uninterested in an undertaking that moved others profoundly.

Much of this flies in the face of common sense, and some of it is confounded by evidence not available in the nineteenth century. The date 1452 seemed a reasonable one for Alberti's intervention, because it was presumed that after a five-year absence he had returned to Rome in that year from some unknown place. But we now know more. He was definitely in Rome not only in 1447 but also before 1450, in 1451, and in 1453. Mancini believed he was also there continuously between 1452 and 1455.[17]

Another reason for emphasizing the year 1452 has more substance, but only for the presentation of the treatise, not for an intervention. Mancini suggested that the treatise was undertaken at the instigation of either Leonello or Meladusio d'Este. The former died on October 1, 1450, and the latter on January 25, 1452,[18] when it may have been near a state of completion. It now lacked a recipient, and so Alberti presented it to another prince, a man whom he had known well and continuously since their student days together in Bologna and who was now pope in Rome.[19] A recollection of that event at that date may also have given Palmieri the peg for the bundle of buildings, but that explanation seems as unlikely as the one involving the Porcari uprising. Palmieri's statement is not the only one that shows that Nicholas was offered the book,[20] but it is the only one that gives the date, which accounts for its popularity.

The other date sometimes cited for the initiation of the project may also be dismissed. It is 1450, given by Manetti. He explained that while the pope had leisure in Fabriano, while escaping the plague brought to Rome by the Jubilee pilgrims, he occupied himself by rebuilding Fabriano. This spurred him into developing plans for Rome, which the pilgrims' alms now made financially possible on a grand scale.[21] This was probably simply Manetti's way, in retrospect, to link one great manifestation of Nicholas's program with another. The juxtaposition of the Jubilee and the building program with the plague also allowed him to link the building program to Nicholas's desire for a healthy city, a theme that recurs in reports of the project. Had Nicholas lived longer and brought the project to completion, Manetti would perhaps have said that from the first the pope sought to do what he had indeed done. Death, however, cut him short, so Manetti linked the project to the great success of his pontificate, the Jubilee.

When, then, did Nicholas begin to rebuild Rome following a comprehensive program? It seems clear that the entire program, including that for the rebuilding of Rome, should be placed in 1447, when Nicholas became pope. There are three areas of circumstantial evidence to support this supposition. The first is in the biographies of the pope. It was suggested above that Manetti's transcription of the testament accurately records the content of Nicholas's statements on his deathbed and that the testament is the pope's retrospective reflection on how well he had accomplished

[17]Hoffmann, 1883, p. 29 for 1451; otherwise, Mancini, 1911, pp. 278 ff., 297 ff.; Grayson, "Alberti," p. 706.

[18]Mancini, 1911, p. 281.

[19]Mancini, 1911, pp. 59–60, 276–277; Grayson, "Alberti," p. 706; and others, for the longstanding contact between Nicholas and Alberti.

[20]For Biondo and Aeneas Sylvius, see Hoffmann, 1883, pp. 10–15; Mancini, 1911, p. 352.

[21]See Magnuson, 1958, pp. 60–63, who takes this statement literally and interprets evidence to support it. He cites little of the material used in the present argument. See also Vasari, III, p. 98.

the program for government that he had pursued throughout his pontificate.[22]   The pope's testament contains the sketch of the building program that Manetti merely filled out in his lengthier description in Book II of his *Life of Nicholas*.   This suggests that the description is not Manetti's posthumous invention.   That both the original sketch of the building program and its place within the larger framework of the pope's original program for government are to be placed early in the pontificate is demonstrated by the close analogy of Manetti's biography to that of Michele Canensi's shorter and less polished one, which was written during the pope's lifetime, late in 1451 or early in 1452.

Like Manetti, when Canensi discussed the building program, he linked it to the governing of the Church, attention to ceremonies, the search for peace, and the liberal support of humanist enterprises.   After discussing the election of the pope, Canensi mentioned the immediate praise, peace, and unity his election provoked, the recognition that the Church was now unified and strong, and the role that Nicholas would play as *exemplum*.[23]   He then turned directly to the various building projects.   In the author's mind, these were not merely random undertakings; like Manetti, he described them as parts of a comprehensive program.   He listed the churches Nicholas rebuilt, beginning with St. Peter's and continuing with San Paolo fuori le mura, the Lateran, Santa Maria Maggiore, and others.   Next he referred to the rebuilding of Rome's walls, then to work in Bologna, Fabriano, and Assisi, and then to that at the Vatican Palace.   The new palace, Canensi stated, would show the pope's power and intelligence to all, and it would be directly connected to a new "magnificent and honorable community" (the Borgo) protected by walls and anchored at one end by the palace and at the other by the Castel Sant'Angelo.[24] Before citing specific works undertaken at the basilica, Canensi stated that the construction would strengthen the faith, and he again included references to Nicholas's attentions to ceremonies and to the pope's administration of the Jubilee, to his sponsorship of humanists, and to his avid search for peace.[25]   In his rhetorical structure, Canensi had used the building program and its most important element, the rebuilding of the basilica, to bracket his discussion of the pope's government.   Similarly, in the epitaph he composed for Nicholas, he included all the topics found in both his and in Manetti's biographies, along with four lines that referred to the residences, the temples of God, and walls of Rome and of the Borgo that the pope had restored.[26]   While it is important that both Manetti and Canensi considered the building program an integral part of the pope's comprehensive program for government, it is more significant that both stressed the pope's desire to reveal intelligence through designing and his wish to reveal doctrine through leaving permanent testimonies in the form of buildings.

Canensi's and Manetti's biographies reflect policies that had been shaping actions since the first years of Nicholas's pontificate, and those actions constitute the second area of circumstantial evidence for the early initiation of the building program. Immediately upon becoming pope, Nicholas set out to institute *Laetentur Coeli*. Peace had to be established in the Latin west and ratification for union had to be secured from the Greeks.   To accomplish these ends required the wisdom of Solomon.   Through the arts of the pope (*artes pontificalis*), Manetti reported, Nicholas

[22] See above, chapter 2.
[23] Miglio, 1971, pp. 513–516 (fols. 18ᵛ–22ᵛ).
[24] Ibid., pp. 516–517 (fols. 22ᵛ–24ʳ).
[25] Ibid., pp. 517–520 (fols. 24ʳ–28ᵛ).
[26] The epitaph is published in Miglio, 1971, p. 485.

had exercised his office. Both the Lega Italica, the great domestic success, and the fall of Constantinople, the great international catastrophe that marred his last days, were in the future. But Solomon may have been his *exemplum* from the beginning, and Manetti had known that Solomon had built as he governed.

Solomon served as a figure with many significations. Dante had placed the Jewish king in paradise with the first circle of lights, the only pre-Christian and the only man of activity admitted among the theologians, whose presence Aquinas explained: "entro v'è l'alta mente u' sì profondo/ saver fu messo," as the true words of the Bible explain.[27] When he was allowed by God to choose what he wanted, it was he "che chiese senno/ acciò che re sufficiente fosse," Aquinas continued.[28] Dante had placed him above the realm of Venus, in a realm where contemplative knowledge fulfilled love. Frezzi pointed out that Cupid had made sport of Solomon as he had of Aristotle,[29] and he related the story of Solomon and Sheba when he first introduced the pilgrim into the paradisiacal setting of the Realm of the Virtues.[30] Frezzi did not, however, find a place for Solomon among the theological virtues; instead, he allowed him to stand above Priam, Quirinus, and Alexander as the finest example of Justice, Frezzi's ultimate cardinal virtue.[31]

In Florence during the Council of Union and its preparation, Nicholas would have been exposed to another use of Solomon. As Professor Krautheimer has concluded, the union of the churches was understood under the figure of the meeting of Solomon and Sheba. The pope was both Solomon, "who had enjoyed greater glory than any other man," and Christ.[32] Nicholas would doubtless have been familiar with the meaning of the concluding panel on Ghiberti's second bapistry doors, which contained all the themes he stressed in his program for governing the Church. Through attention to the Church of which he was the Bridegroom, through attention to Christ's immaculate and whole Tunic, through attention to his priestly office as protector of the sacraments that were the new law, he might bring into the Church the souls who were apart from it.

To bring them into the Church meant to restore them to Rome. Rome was the place where the Church was healthy and unified. An essential part of Urban V's program to bring the Greeks back into the Church in 1365 was the return of the papacy from Avignon to Rome.[33] At Constance the cardinals had elected Cardinal Colonna to the papacy in part because he was Roman, and with his election came secure indications that the reunited Church would be returned to Rome. Filarete's doors had shown the happy result of Eugenius's management of the Council of Union in the figure of the oriental churches entering Rome to continue the council. Nicholas's attention to Rome was simply another form of the same idea that linked the dignity of the Holy See with the city of Rome, and this identification would have been as clear in the first moments of his pontificate as in the last, just as his belief that St. Peter's should dominate Rome was made clear immediately after his election to the Throne of Peter.

In the first moments of his pontificate he emphasized the Petrine basis of the papacy, taking the arms of Peter as his own and elevating St. Peter's above all

[27] *Par.* X, lines 112–113.

[28] *Par.* XIII, lines 95–96. See also Solomon's speech, *Par.* XIV, lines 37–60.

[29] Frezzi, 1914, III, xv, lines 55–57; for the *topos*, see Ross, 1948.

[30] Frezzi, 1914, IV, i, lines 154–166.

[31] Ibid., IV, xiii, lines 106–108.

[32] Krautheimer, 1970, p. 186.

[33] Mollat, 1963, pp. 156–157; see also pp. 161 ff. for the reasons for Gregory XI's return.

other churches in papal rhetoric and through his immediate and intense attention to it.[34] His building program was simply another clear sign of the same program predicated upon instituting *Laetentur Coeli* in Rome.

The major subordinate part of his program, his establishing the communal government in a semi-autonomous state on the Capitol, was also instituted in the first moments of his pontificate. The structure he established had been prepared by his predecessor, and he could have disbanded it. Instead, he amplified it, establishing thereby the preconditions for the revisions to the street code of 1452, which were perfectly consonant with the 1447 concordat and with the earlier negotiations between the Romans and Eugenius's agents, in which Parentucello had probably participated. The scanty records that survive indicate the likelihood that the building project that Nicholas sponsored on the Capitol, which meshed with his construction both at the Castel Sant'Angelo and in the new wing at the Vatican Palace, could have been undertaken in the earliest years of his pontificate. Those three parts of the more comprehensive project made explicit the political relationship that he supervised throughout his pontificate from the 1447 concordat, through the troublesome period with Porcari and with Spinelli, up to his last years.

To give the Romans as much political autonomy as possible was an integral part of Nicholas's program for papal government in Rome. While he concentrated on administering his office as pope, he attempted to encourage the Romans to see to their affairs as if they were Florentine republicans. From the point of view of his experience with Florentine humanism, his emphasis on the sacramental role of the pope was the proper complement to his granting appropriate autonomy to the Romans. As Alberti had explained in *De jure*, leave to God the care of divine things and leave to the laws of men the deposition of human affairs which, in the justice of judgment, should pay honor to God.[35] The two key elements in his program as it was rendered in architecture, the rebuilding of the Capitol and the rebuilding of the rest of the city in order to stress the Basilica of St. Peter above all else, were already implicit in his actions in 1447.

It would not have been immediately explicit; buildings take time to become conspicuous, but they seem to have been conspicuous between February 10 and March 8, 1450, when Giovanni Rucellai visited Rome. The description of his pilgrimage is the earliest extant record of Nicholas's comprehensive project and the third area of circumstantial evidence for the early initiation of the building program.

Rucellai and his family found themselves in Perugia escaping the plague in Florence, he reports, and because a Jubilee had been instituted, he set out for Rome with two relatives. In the morning he visited the four basilicas specified in the Jubilee indulgence, returned to his lodgings for lunch, remounted his horse and went "searching and investigating all those ancient walls and worthy things of Rome, returning in the evening to the house, making records of those things that one will see noted here."[36] What one sees are the results of his editing, most likely while in Rome or soon thereafter, as he transcribed his records in 1457 at his "castello di

[34] In addition to the documents cited above, chapter 2, see the transfer of canons attached to S. Vincenzo to the chapter of St. Peter's; they were located between the basilica and the Vatican Palace and had to be moved because Nicholas had meditated how "in Ecclesiis Urbis Divinus Cultus non solum celeberrimus servaretur, sed in illis multo amplior & perfectior augeretur"; dated 23 December 1449, in *Coll. Bull. Vat.*, II, pp. 130–131, and mentioned above, chapter 6, n. 56. Furthermore, Nicholas's repairs to the portals between the atrium and the basilica carried the inscription NICOLAVS PP. V MCCCXLIX; Müntz, *ACP*, I, p. 120, n. 3.

[35] See Mancini, 1911, p. 143; compare *De re aed.*, VII, i, and see Wittkower, 1962, I, 1, pp. 6–7.

[36] Rucellai, 1960, p. 68.

sancto Giminiano," where he again found himself with his family while once again avoiding plague in Florence.[37]   That they were edited is clear from the order in which he presents his observations; he could not have encountered the objects he lists in the order in which he lists them.   That they were edited either in Rome or soon after he left is clear from the structure he gave them; it corresponds nearly perfectly to the purpose for which he undertook his pilgrimage and to the conception of the city that Nicholas had set about to impose on Rome, about which he would have learned at that time.   The record of his visit not only shows him to have been religious, to have had an eye for beautiful things, and to have wanted to note antiquities as well as objects related directly to his pilgrimage;[38] it also represents one of the earliest coherent presentations of the city as a combination of political and physical forms, an idea that had been developed in Florence and that was to find its first mature representation in the written works of Alberti and in Nicholas's project.   It was not for nothing that Rucellai was one of Alberti's patrons, and it does not seem unlikely that in Rome the merchant would have had the services of his architect as cicerone.

His purpose in going to Rome was to participate in the Jubilee, with full contrition for the sins he had committed.   His pilgrimage was an act of penance through which he would gain the release from purgatory of ten years for each mortal sin.[39] In listing the prescribed basilicas he followed Nicholas's order, not that of Nicholas's predecessors, and he saw the pope as protector and governor of the Church as Nicholas had established himself.   He also saw the city of Rome as subservient to the papal priest ensconced in the Vatican.

Rucellai's record is divided into three sections.   The first lists the four major Jubilee basilicas with the usual information about their relics, indulgences, and historical importance, and then turns to Trastevere, by which he means only the Borgo. This section begins: "First and before all, the church of St. Peter...."[40]   The next three, in order, are San Paolo fuori le mura, Santa Maria Maggiore, and San Giovanni in Laterano.   His remarks concerning the first two are traditional, but what he says about the Lateran is not traditional, as may be seen through what he does not say rather than through what he does say.   He notes that, "It is said that the palace of the emperor Constantine was in the same place where the above-mentioned church is," and, "This church of San Giovanni is the vescovate of Rome and in the past the pope often lived here as bishop of Rome."[41]   Biondo, the most recent author to touch on the Lateran, had said that in the past it had been the residence of the popes, and he had explained that it was now nearly in ruins.[42]   Rucellai explained that the pope had taken up residence elsewhere by pointing out that this was the seat of the pope when the pope was stressing his office as bishop of Rome. By using the past tense, the Florentine could indicate that the pope no longer considered himself to be primarily that.   Rucellai's remarks seem to be predicated on

---

[37] Ibid., p. 2; see Perosa's preface, p. xiii.

[38] This is the characterization of the most recent author to deal with Rucellai's record, a characteristic that follows the context established by earlier scholars; see Weiss, 1969, p. 73, and Perosa's n. 1, pp. 159–160, in Rucellai, 1960.

[39] See above, chapter 2; also Rucellai, 1960, p. 67, for ten years. Elsewhere, when listing the Jubilee among the great events of 1450, Rucellai had said "si dicie che per ongni pecchato mortale vi s'à a stare dentro sette anni" (p. 52).

[40] Ibid., p. 68.

[41] Ibid., pp. 70–71.

[42] Biondo, 1953, I, lxxxiiii, p. 279; see above, chapter 1.

the position the Vatican occupied in Nicholas's conception of the papacy, as well as on the importance of the basilica in the framework of the Jubilee.

"In Trastevere are the things that are noted below," he begins the last part of this first section.[43] "First, the Castel Sant'Angelo, which, it is said, was the sepulchre of Hadrian the Emperor"; then the obelisk that at that time stood to the south of St. Peter's, of which he noted the dimensions and material, concluding, "and in the top a round vase of bronze, in which, it is said, are the remains of the bones of Caesar." Next, "la meta di Romolo," with notes of its shape and dimensions and the remark that "it is said to hold the remains of the bones of the said Romulus." Next he concludes with the reference to the Vatican Palace that stresses its gardens and its close association with the basilica, with which he had begun this section.

His selection in this section of burial places that were worth noting is significant, because only when mentioning burial places within the Borgo did he mention that they contained the remains of Romans. He did not mention the obelisk on the Capitol or mention that it was said to contain the remains of Octavius. Nicholas Muffel pointed it out.[44] Muffel was a Nuremberg patrician with a famous collection of antiquities; he would be hanged in his home town in 1469 for embezzlement. In 1452 he had accompanied Frederick III to Rome, and in his travel notes he tended to mention antiquities with imperial associations whenever he encountered them. Muffel was closer to following standard practice than his Florentine peer was. Poggio mentioned the tombs of Augustus and Hadrian together, and noted the sepulchre of Remus; those of Augustus and Remus were not in the Borgo and did not appear in Rucellai's notes. Poggio's concern was the operation of Fortune in the affairs of men, and the tombs of great emperors made his point quite well.[45] Anonimo Magliabechiano said that the bodies of Trajan and of Antoninus Pius were under the great columns each had erected, but Rucellai mentioned only their "stories of victory" and said that they erected columns instead of triumphal arches.[46] Rucellai was concerned about the operations of the Church, which dispensed the gift of grace to the faithful, and therefore, in the section devoted to the Borgo wherein lived the pope, successor to pagan Rome and protector of the sacraments, he listed the tombs of the founder of Rome, of the founder of the empire, and of the emperor who had used the Borgo as a holy place in pagan Rome. The tomb of the founder of the Church in Rome, also in the Borgo, was a natural fourth element in that list, and therefore it would be recalled in the context of founders' burial places.[47] The garden-residence of the Fisherman's successor, the living pope, was an appropriate conclusion to the section devoted to the living Church.

The next section deals with ancient Rome; this Rucellai presented in three different ways: the item he listed was either an ancient building converted to some Christian use, a curiosity that caught his eye but in itself was without current significance, or an example of the collapse of an ancient institution from its former high standing and importance.[48] Once again, Christian Rome has superseded pagan Rome. The Pantheon, Santa Maria della Rotonda, appears first. It is a functioning church

[43] Rucellai, 1960, p. 72, for what follows.

[44] Muffel, 1953, p. 362.

[45] Poggio, "Var. fortu.," 1953, pp. 239–240, 245.

[46] Anonimo Magliabechiano, 1953, pp. 131–132.

[47] Rucellai claimed that the bodies of Peter, Paul, Simon, Taddeus, and Andrew were in St. Peter's; 1960, p. 69. He found only a little dust and some trinkets of St. Paul at San Paolo; ibid., p. 69.

[48] Ibid., pp. 72–76, to which the following remarks refer. From time to time Rucellai simply inserts brief notices of curiosities or of buildings without any particular importance.

with marvelous architectural elements, the dimensions of which Rucellai gives, and is worthy of note as the product of "a private citizen whom one called Marco Agrippa." The list includes the Aracoeli, Santa Maria sopra Minerva, SS. Apostoli, and others, each of which Rucellai connects with ancient and modern Rome. A list of churches that he did not believe deserved additional comment is followed by triumphal arches, which also require no explanation, and by baths and other structures that are noteworthy for their grandeur but are clearly only ruins. In this spirit he reaches the conclusion of this section:

> The prison where Cicero held the prisoners Catiline and Cethegus and Lentulus, where at present a church is today.
>
> The Capitol, where at present the senator lives, in great part collapsed; in ancient times it was the fortress of the world and also the senate and other offices assembled there.
>
> The ancient mint of Rome, which appears to have been built of beautiful walls.
>
> The Tarpea, where the Romans held their treasure, next to the Capitol.
>
> And conduits, or rather aqueducts, the greatest arches, where one conducted water, twenty or twenty-five miles in length.
>
> The Templum Pacis [Basilica of Constantine], which one says was a temple of idols and which, the Romans said, would last until a virgin gave birth, and it fell in and was ruined on the very night that our saviour Jesus Christ was born, and there is at the base of it a twisted marble column twelve *braccia* in diameter.

That his emphasis was on fallen, pagan Rome is clearly seen by comparing these remarks to what he had said elsewhere and with what he must certainly have seen. He had already mentioned the Catiline prison, stating that it was a little underground church where St. Peter and St. Paul had been held and that it had a miraculously born fountain of water inside.[49] The Capitol was certainly not in the condition he said it was; his use of the past tense indicates that he was presenting its present condition in contrast to its ancient grandeur. Not even Michelangelo's design would have stood up under scrutiny in that context.[50] Rome's subordinate position relative to the papacy, which Nicholas was making conspicuous through his designs for the Capitol and for Rome, were accurately reported by Rucellai. So, too, with the mint,[51] the Tarpea, and the aqueducts. Great in antiquity, they are now mere ruins. The Romans knew that their empire would give way to a new one based on a different understanding of God, and that is Rucellai's point in presenting the Templum Pacis, or Basilica of Diocletian and Constantine. He probably believed that it had been

---

[49] Ibid., p. 74.

[50] Rucellai's statement, therefore, should not be taken as evidence of the state of the Capitol in 1450, as is commonly done. He makes no reference to anything except the dilapidation of ancient buildings and says nothing about extant or new construction. There certainly was a senator during his stay; he was Andrea Donati, a Venetian (ASV, Reg. Vat. 435, fol. 169ᵛ) whose administration during the Jubilee was of such excellence that his abilities were referred to in specific terms, uniquely during this period, in his appointment for a term by Calixtus III (ASV, Reg. Vat. 465, fols. 165 f.).

[51] Compare an insertion made by a later hand in Dati's guide to Florence: "la Zecca dove si battono li Ducati grossi e altri più minute monete, tutta di pietra laborata con bellissime finestre ferrate che è una bellezza a vedere"; Dati: Gilbert, 1969, p. 45. The ancient mint would have been at least as grand as that in Florence.

built by Augustus to house a statue of Romulus;[52] its collapse, therefore, signified the end of the realm founded by Romulus and Remus and was a fitting conclusion to his section of the Christian uses of Rome and its pagan collapse. It was also a fitting introduction to the next and last section.

His last section deals with the facilities that figured in the daily life of modern Romans.[53] First he makes observations about the governors in the city. The Roman equivalents to Florentine patricians, such as himself, were the cardinals.[54] He first lists the palace of the powerful French cardinal d'Estouteville, a representative of the foreign nations present in the court in Rome, and then that of Cardinal Latino Orsini, a member of a Roman baronial house that had included Cardinal Giordano Orsini and that had traced its ancestry back to the ancient Romans.[55] Orsini lives on Monte Giordano, Rucellai reports, "where there is a beautiful hall decorated with histories of good men (*storiata con buone figure*) and with certain windows of alabaster in place of glass."[56] Next, he lists the piazza Navona, where "one jousts and they make other festivals, with steps where the people are allowed to stand in order to see," and then refers to its ancient prototype, the Circus Maximus, also equipped with seats and overlooked by the major palace (Palatine), where "also one was able to stand in order to see."[57] There follow then Testaccio, where there were popular games, a description of the carnival, some antiquities that caught his eye, towers—which were believed to have been palaces of ancient noble Romans—and walls, and then notations about the number of churches and inns, speculation about the income from the altar at San Paolo, and other miscellaneous mercantile musings. He concludes with the Bocca di Verità, which he seems to have believed worked only in antiquity: "A round stone in the manner of a millstone with a face in relief in it which one calls the *lapida della verità*, which in ancient time had the *virtù* of showing when a lady had *fatto fallo* to her husband."

Rucellai's editing was anything but random. He remained independent of the structures for editing such works that others were using at that time—for example, Poggio, in his lament about the operations of Fortune in the affairs of men and of states, and Biondo, in his hopeful assessments about the survival of ancient Rome in modern Rome. He also avoided using the long-standing format of pilgrims' guides, the nature of which made it difficult to reveal political ideals because they concentrated on objects of devotion rather than on the city. His selections were pointed and his remarks pithy. They made the point that the city had been restructured and that this new structure for the meaning of the city of Rome was evident in its buildings. All sorts of buildings showed this, and as a Florentine he would have been familiar with the ability of buildings of every type to reveal the order of a city. His own palace, to which he had begun to add a façade to Alberti's design in 1446, was clear evidence of that. But Rome was not a republic. Rucellai was so familiar with the conception that had allowed the order of the Florentine republic to be revealed in its buildings that he was able to ignore the republican institutions in Rome and see in its buildings its princely constitution. He saw it even though the buildings that revealed it were just then taking shape. Nicholas's project must have been formulated by the time he visited, and someone must have explained it to him. At any

[52] See Graf, 1915, pp. 252–254.

[53] Rucellai, 1960, pp. 76–78, from which the following citations are taken.

[54] See Biondo, cited above, chapter 5, n. 57.

[55] See the anonymous "Carmen Laudatiuum" from 1405–6; published by Simpson, 1966, pp. 141–149, esp. p. 148, lines 17 ff.

[56] Rucellai, 1960, p. 76; this section runs from p. 76 to the conclusion, p. 78.

[57] Compare Poggio, "Var. fortu.," 1953, p. 239.

rate, his short guide is more than a record of his pilgrimage. It is the earliest clear evidence that Nicholas had launched his program in Rome.

Who was responsible for the invention of this project? To answer this question, we must recall that Palmieri's information was blown out of proportion because it offered the material that the historians were primarily interested in finding: a date and the identity of an architect for a number of buildings. But neither Palmieri nor anyone else during the quattrocento looked at buildings the way post-Dehio historians have. These historians approached the question the way they did because they did not think that either Nicholas or Alberti cared much about the city, but each instead had lavished his attention on individual buildings considered in isolation from one another within the city. Quattrocento commentators looked at the entire project in a different way. Their statements make it clear that they considered the pope's project to be the pope's invention, and they were relatively unconcerned about who its architectural designer might have been. They considered the project to include buildings throughout Rome and not simply individual buildings related to other buildings within the formal evolution of a Renaissance architect's style. Therefore, the direct information they give to allow one to insert the project or its buildings into modern historical conceptions and stylistic categories is negligible. It would be different if more of the project had been built and had survived, because then the buildings could be examined. The surviving evidence is useful, but not for these questions. The material left by Brippi, de Godis, Palmieri, Canensi, Manetti, and Alberti, to move from the more obscure to the clearer thinkers on the subject, shows that they understood architecture to be something considerably different from what we do today. To understand the conception, the authorship, and the importance of the project, as well as to interpret the role of the surviving buildings in it, one must understand the conception of architecture and the city held by those in the quattrocento who were involved in the project.

At the beginning of the quattrocento in Rome, a building was mentioned only as the result of what happened when superintendents, workmen, and materials were collected on a building site under the sponsorship of someone whose career in office could be considered great through his support of building activity. The biography of Martin V by the continuer of Ptolemy of Lucca's biographies is typical. It considers the mere fact of construction as evidence of the pope's greatness in much the same way Petrarch, Poggio, and Giovanni Rucellai had used buildings as figures. The pope's construction at St. Peter's, the Lateran, SS. Apostoli, and elsewhere is lumped together with his pacification of the papal states, his returning of the papacy to Italy, and his other acts as pope that made it proper, according to the biographer, to call him not pope but father of his country.[58] His building activity is another activity, not an activity related to a unified program that could be interpreted in its totality as charitable activity, and it is not evidence of intellect but merely of governing. Those who reported about Nicholas's project thought differently about it, or at least they presented a different sort of interpretation. They spoke of Nicholas's buildings as a part of a unified program for governing based on a conscious approach to each of that program's parts. They were vague about the details of the building project because their abilities to recognize and to report about design were limited. They therefore saw the forest rather than the trees, but they did recognize that Nicholas's urban project was a unified one and that through it he had made his intelligence evident throughout the city.

Nicholas, said Brippi, gave to you Romans justice, honor, praise, and fame; he

[58] Ptolemy of Lucca, *Vita*, cols. 867, 864. The Life was written during Eugenius's pontificate.

governed you well. His laws, his care, his buildings are all evidence of his charity. "He magnifies you, exalts you, and reforms you; he restores your lovely churches; in addition, he augments the sacred Church of Peter and founds magnificent palaces. He strengthens the fortresses with walls and builds a tower to be marveled at, and he does this with high spirit and prudence (*alto animo prudenteque*), lest perchance a violent flank of foreign arms or a few of your faithless offspring, lest any tyrant from mother Rome, be strong enough to drive out any pope with arms." No pope for a thousand years has built so many temples, palaces, and walls, or has so repaired and cleansed the city, all for the glory of God and for the everlasting fame and guardianship of Rome, the Apostolic Seat.[59] De Godis's list is longer, but his point is the same; Porcari should have recognized the goodness of the pope by having understood his benevolent intentions in undertaking his buildings.[60] Neither attributes the design of the buildings to the pope, but neither names anyone else or denies Nicholas's responsibility for the project. Each stresses his having built for a purpose, and each used the undertaking as evidence of the pope's having accomplished that purpose.

Nicholas claimed that he had conceived the buildings himself, and Manetti stated that the pope had designed them. He designed them in his mind and spirit (*mente animoque*), and the products of his intelligence surpassed those of his *exemplum*, King Solomon. In building, neither the oracles of Apollo nor the writings of Socrates were as valuable as were the reports of Solomon's buildings in the scriptures of God. Manetti's point throughout the *Life* is that Nicholas's accomplishments were acts of government that merit his receiving earthly fame and eternal glory.

When Manetti speaks here he sounds like Alberti, who might have said that Nicholas demonstrated his *virtù* through designing. Manetti expressed the same concept in a Biblical *topos*. Solomon and Nicholas had designed, and Hiram of Tyre and Bernardo of Florence had executed the works. Manetti even said that Rossellino was as intelligent and as accomplished in diverse arts as Hiram was (s.145). Manetti probably named Rossellino, not because he was responsible for more than others were in the various parts of the project, but because he was a Florentine. He had been sought out in a distant realm to assist the great governor, a man who would show that the condition of trust and felicity between the pope and Florence resembled that which existed between Solomon and King Hiram of Lebanon. Furthermore, as a fellow citizen, Bernardo would bring honor to Florence. But Solomon and Nicholas designed. The Roman project had to be the pope's invention, because it was the work of a prince and a demonstration of Christian doctrine. Nicholas was the head of the hierarchy, and he took credit for his works. The project had to be his invention, because his governing of the Church was a demonstration of his *virtù* as pope, and the building project was a part of his personal program for governing. The main point of the *topos* is that what the pope built was designed and that the design was by the pope.

In architecture, Alberti at this time was identified with designing rather than with executing, that is, with the theory of architecture rather than with the building of buildings. Biondo had called him the "outstanding geometrician of our age";[61] Palmieri had called him a sharp scholar. Were Manetti to mention him, it would have to be on the level of theory, of design, and not on the level of practice and

[59] Brippi, Vat. Lat. 3618, lines 108–125. See also Brippi, Ricc. Cod. 361.

[60] De Godis, Vat. Lat. 3619, fols. 7ᵛ ff. For four other references—those of Poggio Bracciolini, Nicodemo da Pontremoli, Lampugnino Birago, and Orazio Romano—that juxtapose the building program and the conspiracy, see Miglio, 1971, p. 489, n. 55.

[61] Quoted in Krautheimer, 1970, n. 28 (p. 269) and p. 268.

execution. To mention Alberti in the context of execution would have been insulting; Alberti's point in *De re aedificatoria* is that intellect must guide execution. Manetti had no reason to mention excellence of execution. But he could not have made a reference to Alberti's involvement in the other part of the undertaking, that which required intellect, because Nicholas had to be the designer.

Manetti was constrained from naming Alberti in the description because he was writing a biography of the pope, but, beyond that, it is quite improbable that Manetti would make a point about an intelligent Alberti designing buildings in Rome in any context. Only Alberti at that time explained that an architect should gain fame and glory through the exercise of his intelligence in architecture.[62] He apparently made little effort to publish his theories broadly,[63] and much of what he said could only be practiced by a republican or a prince. A republic was guided by the intelligence of all its citizens; a principality was guided by the intelligence of its prince. Perhaps this difference between a republic and a principality explains why the treatise, written by a republican, has a strong republican bias, even though it was apparently instigated by the d'Este and presented to Nicholas, all princes. Alberti had shown in the treatise how the intelligent, gifted, and energetic architect might assist in bringing order to the republic. Some in a state are suited to be learned and to direct affairs through counsel, some to be skilled in the arts that assist the state, and some to be blessed with the goods of fortune and to provide the state with an abundance of goods.[64] An architect in a republic belongs primarily to the second class; his fame will be assured through his exercise of his *virtù* for the state.[65] But even in republican Florence this idea is precocious, as Professor Gombrich's investigation of Medici patronage has demonstrated. Cosimo de' Medici paid for the works, and his is the fame for them. Architects are seldom mentioned, and when they are, they are placed in much the same relationship to Cosimo that Hiram was to Solomon.[66] The exceptions are Brunelleschi and Alberti. Brunelleschi's *Life* by Antonio Manetti, written between 1482 and 1489 with knowledge of Alberti's treatise, reiterates the point that Brunelleschi was naturally equipped, worked indefatigably, brought praise to his city, merited the honor which he sought, and was politically active, able, and conscious,[67] while Alberti is praised for his theoretical work on architecture.[68] These were the most conspicuous examples of the new breed of architect, and even when praising Brunelleschi, Antonio Manetti discusses the role of those who hired his hero and their intelligence in doing so as much as he does the personal fame his subject received for his labors.

In a principality, in which one man represented one class and the people constituted the other, there would have been even less chance for Alberti's theory about the famous architect to receive a hearing; the princes claimed the glory and the fame. A prince who was later to patronize Alberti, Sigismondo Malatesta, built a *castello* in Rimini (1437–46), and it was apostrophied by Maffeo Vegio: "Sismundo nomen

---

[62] See Westfall, *SR*, 1969, esp. pp. 69–70; also Boskovits, 1962–63, 1962, p. 250, and 1963, pp. 152–155. Boskovits fails to draw the conclusion that the architect or painter would receive credit for establishing the order he so well describes.

[63] See Grayson, 1960, p. 155, for the manuscript and text tradition.

[64] *De re aed.*, IV, i.

[65] See also Westfall, *SR*, 1969, esp. pp. 69–70.

[66] Gombrich, "Medici as Patrons," esp. pp. 41 ff. See also Jenkins, 1970, passim, and, for Brunelleschi's troubles with authorities who did not respect his ideas, Manetti, 1970 (e.g., pp. 97–99 [see also p. 142, nn. 116, 117], 101, 125–127).

[67] Ibid., e.g., lines 18–25, p. 43, lines 385–387, lines 576–578, lines 973–976, pp. 95 and 121.

[68] Ibid., lines 383–384.

mihi, Sismundus et auctor" ("Sigismondo is my name, and Sigismondo made me").[69]
Pius II claimed credit for Pienza. He named Bernardo of Florence as his architect,
and he was forced to defend the Florentine—however, not for his design, but for
his execution.[70] Another of Alberti's friends knew that Tuscany was the "source
of architects," and when he found none there, he did manage to find one elsewhere
who was "learned and instructed in this art" of architecture. This was Federigo da
Montefeltro, who found his architect in Mantua. In his patent to Luciano Laurana he
stated that his architect was to be followed "not otherwise than our own person
himself" would be.[71]

Alberti's attitude about famous architects was both out of place in a princely
situation like Nicholas's and incongruous with the authorities appropriate for guiding
a pope's activities. It was based on a society defined by Socrates,[72] and Manetti had
explained that Nicholas had followed the precedent of Solomon, not the teachings of
Socrates. Nicholas was a prince, and Solomon was an *exemplum* for holy princes.
Alberti was the architect for republics, but Vitruvius had explained the relationship
between architects and princes, and Alberti's authority could hardly hold its own
against that of the great Roman.

Vitruvius explained in the preface to the third book of his architectural treatise
that among the Greeks, some painters and sculptors received fame through their
works, but they "had got it by working for great states or kings or famous citizens."
For those who desire fame and are neither highborn nor likely to work for a great
patron, it is better to trust in the cultivation of knowledge than in the practice of
craftsmanship, he concluded.[73] He had already explained in the preface to the first
book that he dared to present his treatise to Augustus because "I observed that you
cared not only about the common life of all men, and the constitution of the
state, but also about the provision of suitable public buildings; so that the state
was ... made greater through you by ... the majesty of the empire [which was] also
expressed through the eminent dignity of its public buildings."[74] The treatise
Vitruvius presented was to be of service to Augustus when the emperor made public
and private [i.e., for the imperial household] buildings that "will correspond to the
grandeur of our history, and will be a memorial to future ages."[75] Vitruvius would
gain only so much fame as he earned through his making the empire and its emperor
famous.

This was the position taken by Filarete when he explained the arcana of architecture to Francesco Sforza, duke of Milan, between 1461 and 1464. He modeled his
preface on that of Vitruvius and sought not to intrude on the duke's attention to
war and peace. Here are things, he said, that will be "useful for your glory."[76]
To build for both utility and fame and without regard to expense reveals that a

[69]Quoted in Mancini, 1911, p. 304, n. 3. See Arduini, 1970, pp. 177–209.

[70]Pius II, 1959, pp. 288–289.

[71]The patent is given most recently in Heydenreich, 1967, p. 3, n. 8; it is dated 1468. Heydenreich
attributes a decisive influence on the design to Federigo. For Alberti's longstanding intimacy with
Federigo, see the letter to the duke from Cristoforo Landino, ca. 1475; Alatri, 1949, no. 87, pp. 102–
103. For material more closely related to Federigo's building activity, see Saalman, 1971, p. 51, and
for the literature, passim. The patent is given in translation in Chambers, 1971, pp. 165–166.

[72]See *De re aed.*, IV, i, where Socrates is cited as the best authority for the state Alberti is outlining.

[73]Vitruvius, III, pre., 3.

[74]Vitruvius, I, pre., 2.

[75]Vitruvius, I, pre., 3.

[76]Filarete, 1965, I, p. 4, n. 5, where there is a transcription of the preface from Bib. Naz., Florence,
Pal. 1411.

man is truly worthy of being a prince, he adds. Throughout his treatise he competed with Vitruvius in humbling himself before his patron, extracting the best designs for the most important buildings from that patron, and claiming only a supervisory capacity for himself.[77]

Although Alberti's idea that an architect might receive recognition for his work did not catch hold immediately, his idea that someone would receive such recognition when construction was based on intelligent design did. Before Alberti's theory was expounded, only Vitruvius conveyed an idea of what an architect might receive for his labors. Manetti's attribution of *virtù* to Nicholas because the pope had conceived of the buildings in his mind and spirit is the earliest recognition of Alberti's concept of design and of the role of the architect in formulating it. One might go further; it might be that the *topos* that links the pope with Rossellino as Solomon had been related to Hiram is Manetti's way of attributing the design to Alberti, whom he cannot, or would not, name. A reader familiar with the threads Alberti was collecting to weave into *De re aedificatoria*, threads taken from ancient authors, from discussions with his friends, and from the perusal of their works, might have seen that Manetti owed a debt to Alberti for instruction in architecture and that within the *topos* Manetti was amortizing it. At any rate, the reader would have been struck by the similar approach the two took to the central issue involved—that the buildings in the treatise and in Nicholas's Rome had been carefully conceived, that is, designed.

Was Alberti the inventor of the building project? As Dehio answered, could anyone else have been? The question finally and once again becomes the same, and the answer still depends upon one's interpretation of Alberti's thought and of Nicholas's project. Are they congruent? When the project is understood in its quattrocento context, there seems little room for doubt that Alberti was its inventor. The city at that time was considered as a whole composed of coordinated parts. Alberti's treatise on architecture is the first articulation of a substantial understanding of how buildings could be designed and woven into the fabric of a whole city that was considered as a combination of both buildings and institutions that made some point about order and design. Alberti had most probably developed this understanding by 1447, and Nicholas's long association with Alberti would suggest that if the theorist had conceived of a way to make the pope's program explicit in architecture, that way would have been available to the pope.

But Alberti's involvement in what resulted from the design should not be exaggerated. To explain the procedure as he himself did, he probably worked up in his mind ideas of buildings that he greatly approved, and, as circumstances arose, he modified those ideas to produce actual designs.[78] He would have based his ideas and designs on a comprehensive understanding of the pope's governing program and of Rome, both ancient and modern. He would then have provided instructions for the builders, who would have executed the parts. Some of these parts, such as the new wing at the Vatican Palace, the Palazzo del Senatore, the Palazzo dei Conservatori, the Castel Sant'Angelo, and the first phase of the new east end of St. Peter's, were given early and vigorous attention, and therefore may show Alberti's direct involvement in the designs. But the designs were then executed by others, who were limited in their abilities, in the assistance Alberti gave, and in means, and therefore the buildings may only imperfectly reflect Alberti's intentions. The project as a whole doubtless never existed in the form of models, drawings, diagrams, explanations, statistics, and analy-

---

[77]The contrast to the dedication to Piero de'Medici is informative; the Florentine was praised for his wealth, liberality, and *virtù*. Filarete, 1965, II, fol. 1ʳ, p. 3.

[78]Alberti, *De re aed.*, IX, x, pp. 861–863; Alberti: Leoni, p. 207.

ses, which precede modern undertakings and which often serve as a surrogate for the projects they represent. Instead, it existed in the form of a concept that embraced the entire city and that was worked out in detail as time and circumstances demanded. Something simple, like the rebuilding of the Palazzo del Senatore, or something urgent, like the new wing at the Vatican, were both designed and built; more extensive elements, like the piazza in front of St. Peter's, and elements that were more desired than essential, like the three buildings in the paradise, were perhaps only conceived and never worked out in detail. But the urban project, completed in some details but truncated in others due to the pope's death, must have existed, and Alberti's must have been the intellect hidden behind the Solomonic Nicholas in Manetti's description.

A new attitude about the city had been instituted through conscious and comprehensive urban design. "The violence, the tumult, the storm of the city, of the piazza, of the town hall," which old Giannozzo Alberti would reject for the peace of his villa, would continually be less meaningful to princes and patricians who built cities. Although the city may not have become the place where "one learns to be a citizen, acquires *buone arti*, sees many *exempla* to teach him to flee vices," and discovers that fame is comely and glory divine, it had become what it had not been before the pontificate of Nicholas V, the place where one finds "the workshops of the greatest dreams, governments, constitutions, and fame."

Bibliography

Abbreviations:

ASRSP   *Archivio della Società Romana di Storia Patria*
JSAH   *Journal of the Society of Architectural Historians*
JWC   *Journal of the Warburg and Courtauld Institutes*
PL   *Patrologia Latina.* Edited by J.-P. Migne. Paris, 1842 ff.
RIS   Muratori, Lodovico Antonio. *Rerum Italicarum Scriptores.* 25 vols. Milan,
          1723–51

Ackerman, 1949
Ackerman, James S. "'Ars sine scientia nihil est': Gothic Theory of Architecture at
the Cathedral of Milan." *The Art Bulletin* 31 (1949), pp. 84–111.

Ackerman, 1954
Ackerman, James S. *The Cortile del Belvedere.* Vatican City, 1954.

Alatri, 1949
Alatri, Paolo, ed. *Federigo da Montefeltro: Lettere di stato e d'arte, 1470–1480.* Rome,
1949.

Alberti, *Della famiglia*
Alberti, Leon Battista. *I Libri della famiglia.* Edited by Cecil Grayson. In Leon Battista Alberti, *Opere volgari,* 1, pp. 3–341. Scrittori d'Italia, no. 218. Bari, 1960.

Alberti: Leoni
Alberti, Leon Battista. *Ten Books on Architecture.* Translated by James Leoni, from the
Italian translation of Cosimo Bartoli. 1st ed. 1726; this ed. London, 1755, reprinted
with notes by Joseph Rykwert, London, 1955. Reprinted London, 1965.

Alberti, *To Matteo de' Pasti*
Alberti, Leon Battista. *An Autograph Letter from Leon Battista Alberti to Matteo de'Pasti,
November 18, 1454.* Edited, with an introduction, by Cecil Grayson. New York,
1957.

Alberti, *De pictura*
Alberti, Leon Battista. *On Painting and on Sculpture.* Latin texts edited by Cecil Grayson, with translations. London, 1972.

Alberti, *Della pittura*
Alberti, Leon Battista. *Della pittura.* Edited by Luigi Mallè. Raccolta di Fonti per la Storia dell'Arte, no. 7. Florence, 1950.

Alberti, "Porcari"
Alberti, Leon Battista. "Commentarius de porcaria conjuratione." In *Opera inedita et pauca separatim impressa,* edited by G. Mancini, pp. 257–266. Florence, 1890.

Alberti, *Profugiorum ab aerumna*
Alberti, Leon Battista. *Profugiorum ab aerumna (Della Tranquillità dell'animo).* Edited by Cecil Grayson. In Leon Battista Alberti, *Opere volgari,* 2, pp. 107–183. Scrittori d'Italia, no. 234. Bari, 1966.

Alberti, *De re aed.*
Alberti, Leon Battista. *De re aedificatoria.* Edited, with an Italian translation, by G. Orlandi. Introduction by P. Portoghesi. 2 vols. Milan, 1966.

Alberti: Spencer
Alberti, Leon Battista. *On Painting.* Translated by J. R. Spencer. Rev. ed. New Haven and London, 1966.

Alberti, *Theogenius*
Alberti, Leon Battista. *Theogenius.* Edited by Cecil Grayson. In Leon Battista Alberti, *Opere volgari,* 2, pp. 55–104. Scrittori d'Italia, no. 234. Bari, 1966.

Alberti, *Villa*
Alberti, Leon Battista. *Villa.* Edited by Cecil Grayson. In Leon Battista Alberti, *Opere volgari,* 1, pp. 359–363. Scrittori d'Italia, no. 218. Bari, 1960.

Alberti: Watkins
Alberti, Leon Battista. *The Family in Renaissance Florence.* Translation of *Della famiglia,* by R. N. Watkins. Columbia, S.C., 1969.

Allen, 1971
Allen, Judson B. *The Friar as Critic.* Nashville, 1971.

Amadei, 1969
Amadei, Emma. *Le Torri di Roma.* 3rd ed. Rome, 1969.

Ambrose, *De Noe et Arca*
Ambrose, St. *De Noe et Arca. PL* 14, cols. 381–438.

d'Ancona, Paolo. "Gli Affreschi del castello di Manta nel saluzzese." *L'Arte* 8 (1905), pp. 94–106; 183–198.

Anonimo, 1881
"Formule dei giuramenti del Senato Romano nel pontificato di Paolo II." *ASRSP* 4 (1881), pp. 268–278.

Anonimo gaddiano: Fabriczy, 1893
"Il Codice dell'anonimo gaddiano (cod. magliabechiano XVII, 17) nella Biblioteca Nazionale di Firenze." Edited by Cornelius von Fabriczy. *Archivio Storico Italiano,* s. 5, 12 (1893), pp. 15–94; 275–334. Reprinted London, 1969.

Anonimo magliabechiano, 1953
"Tractatus de rebus antiquis et situ urbis Romae." In *Codice topografico della città di Roma,* edited by R. Valentini and G. Zucchetti, 4, pp. 101–150. Rome, 1953.

Apollonj, 1937
Apollonj, Bruno Maria. "Fabbriche civili nel quartiere del Rinascimento in Roma."
I Monumenti italiani, rilievi raccolti, edited by the Reale Accademia d'Italia, fasc. 12.
Rome, 1937 (actually 1939).

Arduini, 1970
Arduini, F., et al., eds. *Sigismondo Pandolfo Malatesta e il suo tempo: Mostra storica,
città di Rimini.* Vicenza, 1970.

Argan, 1969
Argan, Giulio Carlo. *The Renaissance City.* Translated by S. E. Bassnett. New York,
1969.

Armellini, 1942
Armellini, Mariano. *Le Chiese di Roma dal secolo IV al XIX.* Edited by Carlo Cecchelli.
2 vols. Rome, 1942.

Arte lombarda, 1958
Arte lombarda dai Visconti agli Sforza. (Exhibition catalogue, Palazzo Reale, Milan,
1958). Milan, 1958.

Augustine, *City of God*
Augustine, St. *The City of God.* Translated and edited by G. E. McCracken, et al.
5 vols. to date. Loeb Classical Library. Cambridge, Mass., and London, 1957—.

Augustine, *City of God*, 1958
Augustine, St. *The City of God.* Translated by G. Walsh, D. Zema, G. Monahan,
and D. Honan. Edited by V. Bourke. Garden City, New York, 1958.

Augustine, *On Christian Doctrine*, 1958
Augustine, St. *On Christian Doctrine.* Translated by D. W. Robertson, Jr. Indianap-
olis, 1958.

Bandini, et al., 1934
Bandini, Carlo, et al. *Gli Anni Santi.* Edited by the Istituto di Studi Romani. Turin,
1934.

Barbieri, 1970
Barbieri, Franco. *The Basilica of Andrea Palladio.* Corpus Palladianum, vol. 2. University Park and London, 1970.

Bardus, 1565
Bardus, M. Antonius. *Facultates magistratus curatorum viarum, aedificiorumque pub-
licorum & privatorum Almae Urbis.* Rome, 1565. (Sometimes cited as ASV, Arm. IV,
vol. 74, fols. 1–36; ASV, Arm. IV, vol. 88, where the book has been disassembled
and is the first title in a collection of miscellaneous printed documents. A complete
copy is available in the Biblioteca Casanatense, Rome, I, xiii, 1.)

Baron, 1938
Baron, Hans. "Cicero and the Roman Civic Spirit in the Middle Ages and the Early
Renaissance." *Bulletin of the John Rylands Library* 22 (1938), pp. 72–97.

Baron, 1966
Baron, Hans. *The Crisis of the Early Italian Renaissance.* Rev. ed. Princeton, 1966.

Barraclough, 1968
Barraclough, Geoffrey. *The Medieval Papacy.* London, 1968.

Battisti, 1958
Battisti, Eugenio. "L'antichità in Nicolò V e l'iconografia della Cappella Sistina."
In *Il Mondo antico nel Rinascimento: Atti del V convengo internazionale di studi sul Rinascimento* (1956), pp. 207–216. Florence, 1958.

Battisti, "Scena classica," 1960
Battisti, Eugenio. "La Visualizzazione della scena classica nella commedia umanistica." In *Rinascimento e Barocco*, pp. 96–111. Turin, 1960.

Battisti, "Simbolo e classicismo," 1960
Battisti, Eugenio. "Simbolo e classicismo." In *Rinascimento e Barocco*, pp. 3–49. Turin, 1960.

Battisti, "Roma," 1960
Battisti, Eugenio. "Roma apocalittica e Re Salomone." In *Rinascimento e Barocco*, pp. 72–95. Turin, 1960.

Bauer, 1965
Bauer, Hermann. *Kunst und Utopie: Studien über das Kunst- und Staatsdenken in der Renaissance.* Berlin, 1965.

Baxandall, 1964
Baxandall, Michael. "Bartholomaeus Facius on Painting." *JWC* 27 (1964), pp. 90–107.

Baxandall, 1971
Baxandall, Michael. *Giotto and the Orators: Humanist Observers of Painting in Italy and the Discovery of Pictorial Composition, 1350–1450.* Oxford, 1971.

Bernardino, 1936
Bernardino da Siena, St. *Le Prediche volgari.* Edited by Piero Bargellini. Milan and Rome, 1936.

Bernardo, 1962
Bernardo, Aldo S. *Petrarch, Scipio and the "Africa."* Baltimore, 1962.

Bertini Calosso, 1920
Bertini Calosso, Achille. "Le Origini della pittura del quattrocento attorno a Roma." *Bollettino d'arte* 14 (1920), pp. 97–114; 185–232.

Biagetti, 1924–25
Biagetti, Biagio. "Relazione: Sala dei Chiaroscuri." *Pontificia Accademia Romana di Archeologia: Rendiconti* 3 (1924–25), p. 492.

Biagetti, 1926–27
Biagetti, Biagio. "Relazione: Soffitto della Sala dei Chiaroscuri o dei Palafrenieri." *Pontificia Accademia Romana di Archeologia: Rendiconti* 5 (1926–27), pp. 243–245.

Biagetti, 1932–33
Biagetti, Biagio. "Una nuova ipotesi intorno allo studio e alla cappella di Niccolò V nel palazzo Vaticano." *Pontificia Accademia Romana di Archeologia: Memorie* 3 (1932–33), pp. 205–214.

Białostocki, 1964
Białostocki, J. "The Power of Beauty: A Utopian Idea of Leon Battista Alberti."
In *Studien zur toskanischen Kunst, Festschrift Ludwig Heydenreich*, edited by W. Lotz and
L. L. Möller, pp. 13–19. Munich, 1964.

Bigongiari, 1964
Bigongiari, Dino. "Were there Theaters in the Twelfth and Thirteenth Centuries?"
In *Essays on Dante and Medieval Culture*, pp. 155–181. Florence, 1964. Reprinted
from *The Romanic Review* 37 (1946), pp. 201–224.

Biolchi, 1954
Biolchi, Dante. "La Casina del Cardinale Bessarione, Roma." Riparto Antichità e
Belle Arti del Comune di Roma. Rome, 1954.

Biondo, 1953
Biondo, Flavio. *Roma instaurata*. In *Codice topografico della città di Roma*, edited by
R. Valentini and G. Zucchetti, 4, pp. 256–323. Rome, 1953.

Blunt, 1940
Blunt, Anthony. *Artistic Theory in Italy, 1450–1600*. 2nd ed. Oxford, 1962.

Boase, 1933
Boase, T. S. R. *Boniface VIII*. London, 1933.

Boccaccio, *Concerning Famous Women*
Boccaccio, Giovanni. *Concerning Famous Women (De claris mulieribus)*. Translated by
G. A. Guarino. New Brunswick, N.J., 1963.

Börsch-Supan, 1967
Börsch-Supan, Eva. *Garten-, Landschafts- und Paradiesmotive im Innenraum*. Berlin,
n.d. (1967?).

Boethius, 1960
Boethius, Axel. *The Golden House of Nero*. Ann Arbor, Mich., 1960.

Bonvicinus de Rippa, 1898
Bonvicinus de Rippa. *De magnalibus urbis Mediolani*. Edited by Francesco Novati.
Bollettino dell'Istituto Storico, no. 20, 1898.

Borgatti, 1931
Borgatti, Mariano. *Castel Sant'Angelo in Roma*. Rome, 1931.

Boskovits, 1962–63
Boskovits, M. "'Quello ch'e dipintori oggi dicono prospettiva', Contributions to
Fifteenth-century Italian Art Theory." *Acta Historiae Artium: Academiae Scientiarum
Hungaricae* 8 (1962), pp. 241–260; 9 (1963), pp. 139–162.

Bourgin, 1904
Bourgin, Georges. "La *familia* pontificia sotto Eugenio IV." *ASRSP* 27 (1904), pp.
203–224.

Bouwsma, 1968
Bouwsma, William J. *Venice and the Defense of Republican Liberty*. Berkeley and Los
Angeles, 1968.

Braunfels, 1966
Braunfels, Wolfgang. *Mittelalterliche Stadtbaukunst in der Toskana*. 3rd ed. Berlin, 1966. 1st ed., 1952.

Brippi, Ricc. Cod. 361
Brippi, Giuseppe. "Exhortation to Calixtus III." Florence, Biblioteca Riccardiana, Riccardiana codex 361.

Brippi, Vat. Lat. 3618
Brippi, Giuseppe. "Lament Concerning Porcari." Vat. Lat. 3618. Published by O. Tommasini, "Documenti relativi a Stefano Porcari," *ASRSP* 3 (1880), pp. 63–133; 111–123.

Bruni, "Laudatio," 1968
Bruni, Leonardo. "Laudatio Florentinae Urbis." Edited by Hans Baron. In *From Petrarch to Leonardo Bruni: Studies in Humanistic and Political Literature*, pp. 232–263. Chicago and London, 1968.

Buchthal, 1971
Buchthal, Hugo. *Historia Troiana: Studies in the History of Mediaeval Secular Illustration*. Studies of the Warburg Institute, vol. 32. London, 1971.

Bueno de Mesquita, 1960
Bueno de Mesquita, D. M. "Ludovico Sforza and His Vassals." In *Italian Renaissance Studies*, edited by E. F. Jacob, pp. 184–216. London, 1960.

Bueno de Mesquita, 1965
Bueno de Mesquita, D. M. "The Place of Despotism in Italian Politics." In *Europe in the Late Middle Ages*, edited by J. R. Hale, J. R. L. Highfield, B. Smalley, pp. 301–331. London, 1965.

Buisson, 1958
Buisson, Ludwig. *Potestas und Caritas: Die päpstliche Gewalt im Spätmittelalter*. Graz, 1958.

Bull. Rom. noviss.
Bullarium Romanum novissimum, vol. 1. Edited by Laertij Cherubini; newly edited by D. Angelo Cherubino. Rome, 1638.

Burchardi: Thuasne
Burchardi, Johannis. *Diarium, sive rerum urbanarum commentarii (1483–1506)*. Edited by L. Thuasne. 3 vols. Paris, 1883–85.

Burckhardt, 1955
Burckhardt, Jacob. *Die Baukunst der Renaissance in Italien*. In *Gesammelte Werke*, 2. Basel, 1955. 1st ed., Stuttgart, 1868.

Burckhardt, 1958
Burckhardt, Jacob. *The Civilization of the Renaissance in Italy*. Translated by S. G. C. Middlemore. 2 vols. New York, 1958

Calisse, 1887
Calisse, C. "I Prefetti di Vico." *ASRSP* 10 (1887), pp. 1–136; 353–594.

Cecchelli, 1944
Cecchelli, Carlo. "Il Campidoglio nel medio evo e nel Rinascimento." *ASRSP* 67 (1944), pp. 209–232.

Celani, 1890
Celani, E. "La Venuta di Borso d'Este in Roma l'anno 1471." *ASRSP* 13 (1890), pp. 361–450.

Cellini, 1955
Cellini, Pico. "Di Fra' Guglielmo e di Arnolfo." *Bollettino d'arte*, s. 4, 40 (1955), pp. 215–229.

Cerulli, 1933
Cerulli, Enrico. "Eugenio IV e gli Etiopi al Concilio di Firenze nel 1441." *R. Accademia Nazionale dei Lincei: Rendiconti della Classe di Scienze morali, storiche e filologiche*, s. 6, 9 (1933), pp. 347–368.

Cessi, 1942–43
Cessi, R. "La 'lega italica' e la sua funzione storica nella seconda metà del sec. XV." *Atti del R. Istituto Veneto di Scienze, Lettere ed Arti:* Part 2, *Classe di Scienze morali e lettere* 102 (1942–43), pp. 99–176.

Chambers, 1971
Chambers, D. S. *Patrons and Artists in the Italian Renaissance*. Columbia, S. C., 1971.

Clark, 1899
Clark, J. W. "On the Vatican Library of Sixtus IV." *Proceedings of the Cambridge Antiquarian Society* 10 (1900), pp. 11–61.

Clark, 1944
Clark, Kenneth. "Leon Battista Alberti on Painting." *Proceedings of the British Academy* 30 (1944), pp. 283–302. Reprinted Oxford, 1946.

De claustro animae
Hugonis de St. Victore? Hugonis de Folieto?. *De claustro animae*. PL 176, cols. 1017–1183.

Colasanti, n.d.
Colasanti, Ardvino. *S. Maria in Aracoeli*. Rome, n.d.

Coletti, 1885–86
Coletti, Giuseppe. "Dai Diari di Stefano Caffari." *ASRSP* 8 (1885), pp. 555–575; 9 (1886), pp. 583–611.

Colini, 1939
Colini, A. M. "Notiziario: Campidoglio." *Bollettino della Commissione Archeologica del Governatorato di Roma (Boll. d. Comm. Arch. Comunale di Roma)* 67 (1939), pp. 200–201.

Colini, 1942
Colini, A. M. "Aedes Veiovis inter arcem et capitolium." *Bollettino della Commissione Archeologica del Governatorato di Roma (Boll. d. Comm. Arch. Comunale di Roma)* 70 (1942), pp. 5–55,

Coll. Bull. Vat.
Collectionis Bullarum Brevium aliorumque Diplomatum sacrosanctae Basilicae Vaticanae, vol. 2. Rome, 1750.

Comito, 1971
Comito, Terry. "Renaissance Gardens and the Discovery of Paradise." *Journal of the History of Ideas* 32 (1971), pp. 483–506.

Cornelius, 1930
Cornelius, Roberta D. *The Figurative Castle: A Study in the Mediaeval Allegory of the Edifice with Especial Reference to Religious Writings.* Bryn Mawr, 1930.

Cosenza
Cosenza, Mario Emilio. *Biographical and Bibliographical Dictionary of the Italian Humanists.* 5 vols. Boston, 1962.

Crusca
Vocabolario degli Accademici della Crusca. 6 vols. Florence, 1729–38.

Cugnoni, 1885
Cugnoni, C. "Diritti del Capitolo di S. Maria della Rotonda nell'età di mezzo." *ASRSP* 8 (1885), pp. 577–589.

Curtius, 1963
Curtius, Ernst Robert. *European Literature and the Latin Middle Ages.* Translated by W. R. Trask. New York and Evanston, 1963. 1st ed., 1948.

Cusin, 1936
Cusin, Fabio. "L'impero e la successione degli Sforza ai Visconti." *Archivio Storico Lombardo,* n.s. 1 (1936), pp. 1–116.

Dante, *Divina Commedia*
Dante. *Divina Commedia.* Edited by V. Rossi and S. Frascino (Società Editrice Dante Alighiere). *Inferno,* 6th ed., 1958; *Purgatorio,* 5th ed., 1963; *Paradiso,* 2d ed., 1956.

Dati: Gilbert, 1969
Gilbert, Creighton. "The Earliest Guide to Florentine Architecture, 1423." *Mitteilungen des kunsthistorischen Instituts in Florenz* 14 (1969), pp. 33–46.

Dehio, 1880
Dehio, Georg. "Die Bauprojecte Nicolaus des Fünften und L. B. Alberti." *Repertorium für Kunstwissenschaft* 3 (1880), pp. 241–257.

Delbrück, 1907
Delbrück, Richard. *Hellenistischen Bauten in Latium.* 2 vols. Strassburg, 1907–12.

Dengel, 1913
Dengel, Philipp. *Palast und Basilica San Marco in Rom.* Rome, 1913.

Dennis, 1927
Dennis, Holmes van Mater, 3d. "The Garrett Manuscript of Marcanova." *Memoirs of the American Academy in Rome* 6 (1927), pp. 113–126.

Dict. Théo. Cath.
Dictionnaire de Théologie Catholique. Paris, 1930–50.

Diener, 1967
Diener, Hermann. "Die 'Camera Papagalli' im Palast des Papstes." *Archiv für Kulturgeschichte* 49 (1967), pp. 43–97.

Doren, 1922–23
Doren, A. "Fortuna im Mittelalter und in der Renaissance." *Vorträge der kunstwissenschaftlichen Bibliothek Warburg* 2 (1922–23), pp. 71–144.

Dussler, 1971
Dussler, Luitpold. *Raphael.* Translated by S. Croft. Rev. ed. London and New York, 1971.

Eden, 1943
Eden, W. A. "Studies in Urban Theory: The *De re aedificatoria* of L. B. Alberti." *Town Planning Review* 19 (1943), pp. 10–28.

Egger, 1905–06
Egger, Hermann. *Codex Escurialensis: ein Skizzenbuch aus der Werkstatt Domenico Ghirlandaios.* 2 vols. Vienna, 1905–06.

Egger, 1932
Egger, Hermann. *Römische Veduten.* 2 vols. 2nd ed. Vienna, 1932.

Egger, 1951
Egger, Hermann. "Die päpstliche Kanzleigebäude im 15. Jahrhunderts." *Mitteilungen des österreichischen Staatsarchivs* (special issue) 1951, pp. 487–500.

Ehrle, 1890
Ehrle, Franz. *Historia bibliothecae romanorum pontificum tum Bonifatianae tum avenionensis.* Rome, 1890.

Ehrle and Egger, 1935
Ehrle, Franz, and Egger, Hermann. *Der vaticanische Palast in seiner Entwicklung bis zur Mitte des XV. Jahrhunderts.* Vatican City, 1935.

Ehrle and Egger, 1956
Ehrle, Franz, and Egger, Hermann, with A. Frutaz. *Piante e vedute di Roma e del Vaticano dal 1300 al 1676.* Vatican City, 1956.

Ehrle and Stevenson, 1897
Ehrle, Franz, and Stevenson, Henry. *Gli Affreschi del Pinturicchio nell'Appartamento Borgia.* Rome, 1897.

Eimer, 1961
Eimer, Gerhard. *Die Stadtplanung im schwedischen Ostseereich 1600–1715 (mit Beiträgen zur Geschichte der Idealstadt).* Stockholm, 1961.

Einem, 1971
Einem, Herbert von. "Das Programm der Stanza della Segnatura im Vatikan." *Rheinisch-Westfälische Akademie der Wissenschaften: Geisteswissenschaften: Vorträge G. 169.* Opladen, 1971.

Elling, 1950
Elling, Christian. *Function and Form of the Roman Belvedere.* Copenhagen, 1950.

Erben, 1931
Erben, Wilhelm. *Rombilder auf kaiserlichen und päpstlichen Siegeln des Mittelalters.* Graz, Vienna, and Leipzig, 1931.

Ercole, 1929
Ercole, Francesco. *Dal Comune al principato.* Florence, 1929.

Ettlinger, 1952
Ettlinger, L. D. "A Fifteenth-Century View of Florence." *The Burlington Magazine* 94 (1952), pp. 160–167.

Ettlinger, 1953
Ettlinger, L. D. "Pollaiuolo's Tomb of Sixtus IV." *JWC* 16 (1953), pp. 239–274.

Eubel
Eubel, Conradum. *Hierarchia catholica medii aevi.* 7 vols. Regensburg and Pavia, 1913–68.

Fabre, 1895
Fabre, Paul. "La Vaticane de Sixte IV." *Mélanges d'archéologie et d'histoire* 15 (1895), pp. 454–483.

Fenzonio, 1636
Fenzonio, Giovanni Battista. *Annotationes in statuta sive ius municipale Romae Urbis.* Rome, 1636.

Filarete, 1965
Filarete (Antonio Averlino, called Filarete). *Treatise on Architecture.* Facsimile of Florence, Bib. Naz., Magliabechianus II, IV, 140, with translation by J. Spencer. 2 vols. New Haven and London, 1965.

Filelfo, *De paupertate*
Filelfo, Francesco. *Commentationes florentinae de exilio,* book 3: *De paupertate.* In *Prosatori Latini del quattrocento,* edited by E. Garin, La letteratura italiana, storia e testi, pp. 494–517. Milan and Naples, 1952.

Fillastre, 1961
Fillastre, Guillaume. *Diary of the Council of Constance.* Translated by Louise Ropes Loomis. In *The Council of Constance,* edited by J. H. Mundy and K. M. Woody, Columbia University Records of Civilization series, no. 63, pp. 200–465. New York and London, 1961.

Firpo, 1954
Firpo, Luigi. "La Città ideale del Filarete." *Studi in memoria di Gioele Solari,* 1, pp. 11–59. Turin, 1954.

Fischer, 1932
Fischer, Josef. *Claudii Ptolemaei Geographiae, Codex Urbinas Graecus 82.* 2 vols. Liepzig, 1932.

Fleming, 1969
Fleming, John V. *The Roman de la Rose: A Study in Allegory and Iconography.* Princeton, 1969.

Fois, 1969
Fois, Mario. *Il Pensiero cristiano di Lorenzo Valla.* Analecta Gregoriana, vol. 174. Rome, 1969.

Forcella
Forcella, Vincenzo. *Iscrizioni delle chiese e d'altri edifici di Roma dal secolo XI fino ai giorni nostri.* 14 vols. Rome, 1869–84.

Fortuna, 1957
Fortuna, Alberto M. *Andrea del Castagno*. Florence, 1957.

Freyhan, 1948
Freyhan, R. "The Evolution of the Caritas Figure in the Thirteenth and Fourteenth Centuries." *JWC* 11 (1948), pp. 68–86.

Frezzi, 1914
Frezzi, Federico. *Il Quadriregio*. Edited by Enrico Filippini. Scrittori d'Italia, no. 65. Bari, 1914.

Frugoni, 1950
Frugoni, Arsenio. "Il Giubileo di Bonifacio VIII." *Bollettino dell'Istituto Storico Italiano per il Medio Evo e Archivio Muratoriano*, no. 62 (1950), pp. 1–121.

Frutaz, 1956
Frutaz, Amato Pietro. *Il Torrione di Niccolò V in Vaticano: Notizia storica nel V centenario della morta del pontifice umanista*. Vatican City, 1956.

Frutaz, 1962
Frutaz, Amato Pietro. *Le Piante di Roma*. 3 vols. Rome, 1962.

Fumi, 1910
Fumi, Luigi. "Nuove rivelazioni sulla congiura di Stefano Porcari." *ASRSP* 33 (1910), pp. 481–492.

Gadol, 1969
Gadol, Joan. *Leon Battista Alberti: Universal Man of the Early Renaissance*. Chicago and London, 1969.

Gagnière, 1965
Gagnière, Sylvain. *The Palace of the Popes at Avignon*. N.p., 1965.

Galbreath, 1930
Galbreath, Donald Lindsay. *A Treatise on Ecclesiastical Heraldry*. Part 1: *Papal Heraldry*. Cambridge, 1930.

Gardner, 1969
Gardner, Julian. "The Influence of Popes' and Cardinals' Patronage on the Introduction of the Gothic Style into Rome and its Surrounding Area, 1254–1305." Ph.D. dissertation, Courtauld Institute, University of London, 1969.

Garin, 1959
Garin, Eugenio. "I Cancellieri umanisti della repubblica fiorentina da Coluccio Salutati a Bartolomeo Scala." *Rivista Storica Italiana* 71 (1959), pp. 185–208. Reprinted in E. Garin, *La Cultura filosofica del Rinascimento italiano*, Florence, 1961, pp. 3 ff., and in idem, *Scienza e vita civile nel Rinascimento italiano*, Bari, 1965, pp. 1–32.

Garin, 1961
Garin, Eugenio. "La Cité idéale de la Renaissance Italienne." In *Les Utopies à la Renaissance* (colloque international, Brussels, 1961), pp. 13–37. Brussels and Paris, 1963.

Garin, 1964
Garin, Eugenio. *L'umanesimo italiano: filosofia e vita civile nel Rinascimento*. Bari, 1964. 1st ed., 1947. Translated by P. Munz as *Italian Humanism*, New York, 1965.

Giamatti, 1966
Giamatti, A. Bartlett. *The Earthly Paradise and the Renaissance Epic*. Princeton, 1966.

Gilbert, 1959
Gilbert, Creighton. "The Archbishop on the Painters of Florence, 1450." *The Art Bulletin* 41 (1959), pp. 75–87.

Gilbert, 1968
Gilbert, Creighton. *Change in Piero della Francesca*. Locust Valley, N.Y., 1968.

Gilbert, 1970
Gilbert, Creighton. "Blind Cupid." *JWC* 33 (1970), pp. 304–305.

Gill, 1959
Gill, Joseph, S. J. *The Council of Florence*. Cambridge, 1959.

Giovannoni, "Case," 1935
Giovannoni, Gustavo. "Case del quattrocento in Roma." In *Saggi sulla architettura del Rinascimento*, pp. 29–47. Milan, 1935.

G(iovannoni), 1937
G(iovannoni), G(ustavo). "Roma: villa del Cardinale Bessarione." *Palladio* 1 (1937), p. 34.

Giovannoni, 1946
Giovannoni, Gustavo. *I Quartieri romani del Rinascimento*. Rome, 1946.

Gnoli, 1938
Gnoli, Umberto. *Facciate graffite e dipinte in Roma*. Arezzo, 1938.

Gnoli, 1941
Gnoli, Umberto. *Piante di Roma inedite*. Quaderni del Centro Nazionale di Studi di Storia dell'Architettura, no. 1. Rome: Istituto di Studi Romani, 1941.

de Godis, Vat. Lat. 3619
Godis, Petrus de. "Dialogus de coniuratione Stephani de Porcariis." Vat. Lat. 3619. (Another ms, Vat. Lat. 4167, fols. 202–210. Defective publication by M. Perlbach, *Petri de Godis*, Griefswald, 1879.)

Golzio and Zander, 1968
Golzio, Vincenzo, and Zander, Giuseppe. *L'arte in Roma nel secolo XV*. Bologna, 1968.

Gombrich, "Apollonio di Giovanni," 1966
Gombrich, Ernst. "Apollonio di Giovanni: A Florentine cassone workshop seen through the eyes of a humanist poet." In *Norm and Form: Studies in the Art of the Renaissance*, pp. 11–28. London, 1966.

Gombrich, "Artistic Progress," 1966
Gombrich, Ernst. "The Renaissance Conception of Artistic Progress and its Consequences." In *Norm and Form*, pp. 1–10. London, 1966.

Gombrich, "Medici as Patrons," 1966
Gombrich, Ernst. "The Early Medici as Patrons of Art." In *Norm and Form*, pp. 35–57. London, 1966.

Graf, 1915
Graf, Arturo. *Roma nella memoria e nelle immaginazioni del medio evo*. Turin, 1915.

Grayson, "Alberti"
Grayson, Cecil. "Leon Battista Alberti." In *Dizionario biografico degli italiani,* 1, pp. 702–709. Rome, 1960.

Grayson, 1953
Grayson, Cecil. "Studi su Leon Battista Alberti." *Rinascimento* 4 (1955), pp. 45–62.

Grayson, 1960
Grayson, Cecil. "The Composition of L. B. Alberti's 'Decem libri de re aedificatoria'." *Münchner Jahrbuch der bildenden Kunst,* s. 3, 11 (1960), pp. 152–161. (See also the discussion in *Kunstchronik* 13 [1960], pp. 359–364.)

Gregorovius, 1900
Gregorovius, Ferdinand. *History of the City of Rome in the Middle Ages,* vol. 7, part 1. Translated by A. Hamilton. London, 1900.

Griseri, 1960
Griseri, Andreina. "Percorso di Giacomo Jaquerio." *Paragone* 11, no. 129 (1960), pp. 3–16.

Hale, 1960
Hale, J. R. "War and Public Opinion in Renaissance Italy." In *Italian Renaissance Studies,* edited by E. F. Jacob, pp. 94–122. London, 1960.

Hale, 1965
Hale, J. R. "The Early Development of the Bastion: An Italian Chronology, c. 1450–c. 1534." In *Europe in the Late Middle Ages,* edited by J. R. Hale, J. R. L. Highfield, B. Smalley, pp. 466–494. London, 1965.

Hammerstein, 1962
Hammerstein, Reinhold. *Die Musik der Engel.* Bern and Munich, 1962.

Harrsen and Boyce, 1953
Harrsen, Meta, and Boyce, George K. *Italian Manuscripts in the Pierpont Morgan Library.* New York, 1953.

Hartt and Corti, 1966
Hartt, Frederick, and Corti, Gino. "Andrea del Castagno: Three Disputed Dates." *The Art Bulletin* 48 (1966), pp. 228–234.

Hatfield, 1970
Hatfield, Rab. "Some Unknown Descriptions of the Medici Palace in 1459." *The Art Bulletin* 52 (1970), pp. 232–249.

Heckscher, 1955
Heckscher, William S. *Sixtus IIII Aeneas insignes statuas romano populo restitudendas censuit.* The Hague, 1955.

Hermanin, 1948
Hermanin, F. *Il Palazzo di Venezia.* Rome, 1948.

Hersey, "Arch," 1969
Hersey, George L. "The Arch of Alfonso in Naples and its Pisanellesque 'Design'." *Master Drawings* 7 (1969), pp. 16–24.

Hersey, 1969
Hersey, George L. *Alfonso II and the Artistic Renewal of Naples, 1485–1495.* New Haven and London, 1969.

Heydenreich, 1967
Heydenreich, Ludwig. "Federico da Montefeltro as a Building Patron." In *Studies in Renaissance and Baroque Art Presented to Anthony Blunt on his Sixtieth Birthday,* pp. 1–6. London, 1967.

Hind, 1938
Hind, Arthur M. *Early Italian Engraving.* 4 vols. London, 1938—.

Hoffmann, 1883
Hoffmann, Paul. "Studien zu Leon Battista Albertis zehn Büchern: *De re aedificatoria.*" Ph.D. dissertation, Leipzig University. Frankenberg i.S., 1883.

Hollander, 1969
Hollander, Robert. *Allegory in Dante's "Commedia."* Princeton, 1969.

Horster, 1955
Horster, Marita. "Castagnos florentiner Fresken 1450–1457." *Wallraf-Richartz Jahrbuch* 17 (1955), pp. 79–131.

Howard, 1966
Howard, Donald R. *The Three Temptations: Medieval Man in Search of the World.* Princeton, 1966.

Huelsen, 1907
Huelsen, Christian. *La Roma antica di Ciriaco d'Ancona.* Rome, 1907.

Huelsen, 1911
Huelsen, Christian. "Di alcune vedute prospettiche di Roma." *Bollettino della Commissione Archeologica Comunale di Roma* 39 (1911), pp. 3–22.

Hugh of St. Victor, *De Arca Noe Morali*
Hugh of St. Victor. *De Arca Noe Morali. PL* 176, cols. 617–680.

Hugh of St. Victor, *De Arca Noe Mystica*
Hugh of St. Victor. *De Arca Noe Mystica. PL* 176, cols. 681–740.

Huizinga, 1956
Huizinga, Johan. *The Waning of the Middle Ages.* Garden City, N.Y., 1956. 1st ed., 1924.

Huskinson, 1969
Huskinson, J. M. "The Crucifixion of St. Peter: a Fifteenth-Century Topographical Problem." *JWC* 32 (1969), pp. 135–161.

Hyman, 1969
Hyman, Isabelle. "New Light on Old Problems: Palazzo Medici, and the Church of San Lorenzo." Paper presented at Society of Architectural Historians Conference, January, 1969, Boston; abstract in *JSAH* 28 (1969), p. 216.

Ilardi, 1960
Ilardi, Vincent. "The Italian League, Francesco Sforza, and Charles VII (1454–1461)." *Studies in the Renaissance* 6 (1960), pp. 129–166.

Infessura
Infessura, Stefano. *Diario della città di Roma.*   Edited by O. Tommasini. Rome, 1890.

Jacob, "Conciliar Thought," 1963
Jacob, E. F. "Conciliar Thought." In *Essays in the Conciliar Epoch*, pp. 1–23. 3rd ed. Manchester, 1963.

Jacob, 1965
Jacob, E. F. "Christian Humanism." In *Europe in the Late Middle Ages*, edited by J. R. Hale, J. R. L. Highfield, B. Smalley, pp. 437–465. London, 1965.

Jaffé, 1885
Jaffé, Philippus, ed. *Regesta pontificum romanorum.* 2 vols. 2nd ed. Leipzig, 1885–88. Reprinted Graz, 1956.

Jedin, 1957
Jedin, Hubert. *A History of the Council of Trent.* Translated by E. Graf. 2 vols. London, 1957–61.

Jenkins, 1970
Jenkins, A. D. Fraser. "Cosimo de' Medici's Patronage of Architecture and the Theory of Magnificence." *JWC* 33 (1970), pp. 162–170.

Jones, 1952
Jones, P. J. "The Vicarate of the Malatesta of Rimini." *The English Historical Review* 264 (1952), pp. 321–351.

Jones, 1960
Jones, P. J. "The End of Malatesta Rule in Rimini." In *Italian Renaissance Studies*, edited by E. F. Jacob, pp. 217–255. London, 1960.

Jones, 1965
Jones P. J. "Communes and Despots: The City State in Late-Medieval Italy." *Transactions of the Royal Historical Society*, s. 5, 15 (1965), pp. 71–96.

Jongkees, 1966
Jongkees, J. H. *Studies on Old St. Peter's.* Archaeologica Traiectina, no. 8. Groningen, 1966.

Kaske, 1963
Kaske, R. E. "Chaucer and Medieval Allegory: Review Article." *ELH* 30 (1963), pp. 175–192.

Kennedy, 1963
Kennedy, Ruth W. "The Contribution of Martin V to the Rebuilding of Rome, 1420–1431." *The Renaissance Reconsidered: A Symposium, Smith College Studies in History*, 44 (1964), pp. 27–39.

Kent, 1972
Kent, F. W. "The Rucellai Family and its Loggia." *JWC* 35 (1972), pp. 397–401.

Klein, 1961
Klein, Robert. "L'urbanisme utopique de Filarete à Valentin Andreae." In *Les Utopies à la Renaissance* (colloque international, Brussels, 1961), pp. 211–230. Brussels and Paris, 1963.

Klotz, 1969

Klotz, Heinrich. "L. B. Albertis *De re aedificatoria* in Theorie und Praxis." *Zeitschrift für Kunstgeschichte* 32 (1969), pp. 93–103.

Krautheimer, 1942 (1969)

Krautheimer, Richard. "Introduction to an 'Iconography of Medieval Architecture'." *JWC* 5 (1942), pp. 1–33. Reprinted with postscript in *Studies in Early Christian, Medieval, and Renaissance Art,* New York and London, 1969, pp. 115–150.

Krautheimer, 1965

Krautheimer, Richard. *Early Christian and Byzantine Architecture.* Baltimore, 1965.

Krautheimer, 1970

Krautheimer, Richard, and Krautheimer-Hess, Trude. *Lorenzo Ghiberti.* 2nd rev. ed. Princeton, 1970.

Krinsky, 1969

Krinsky, Carol Herselle. "A View of the Palazzo Medici and the Church of San Lorenzo." *JSAH* 28 (1969), pp. 133–135.

Krinsky, 1970

Krinsky, Carol Herselle. "Representations of the Temple of Jerusalem before 1500." *JWC* 33 (1970), pp. 1–19.

Kristeller, 1964

Kristeller, Paul Oskar. *Eight Philosophers of the Italian Renaissance.* Stanford, 1964.

Kurth, 1942

Kurth, Betty. "Mediaeval Romances in Renaissance Tapestries." *JWC* 5 (1942), pp. 237–245.

Ladner, 1961

Ladner, Gerhart B. "Vegetation Symbolism and the Concept of Renaissance." In *De Artibus Opuscula XL: Essays in Honor of Erwin Panofsky,* edited by M. Meiss, pp. 303–322. New York, 1961.

Lanckorońska, 1935

Lanckorońska, Karoline. "Zu Raffaels Loggien." *Jahrbuch der kunsthistorischen Sammlungen in Wien,* n.s. 9 (1935), pp. 111–120.

Lang, 1952

Lang, Susan. "The Ideal City from Plato to Howard." *Architectural Review* 112 (1952), pp. 90–101.

Lavagnino, 1941

Lavagnino, Emilio. "Il Campidoglio al tempo del Petrarca." *Capitolium* 15 (1941), pp. 103–114.

Lavedan, 1941

Lavedan, Pierre. *Histoire de l'urbanisme.* Vol. 2: *Renaissance et Temps modernes.* Rev. ed. Paris 1959. 1st ed., 1941.

Lawrence, 1927

Lawrence, Elizabeth Baily. "The Illustrations of the Garrett and Modena Manuscripts of Marcanova." *Memoirs of the American Academy in Rome* 6 (1927), pp. 127–131.

Lazzaroni, 1883
Lazzaroni, Michele. *Osservazioni sopra alcuni monumenti principali di Roma ... dipinti a fresco da Benozzo Gozzoli*. Rome, 1883.

Lehmann-Brockhaus, 1960
Lehmann-Brockhaus, Otto. "Albertis 'Descriptio urbis Romae'." *Kunstchronik* 13 (1960), pp. 345–348.

Lenkeith, 1952
Lenkeith, Nancy. *Dante and the Legend of Rome*. Warburg Institute Mediaeval and Renaissance Studies, supplement 2. London, 1952.

Lewine, 1965
Lewine, Milton. "Vignola's Church of Sant'Anna de' Palafrenieri in Rome." *The Art Bulletin* 47 (1965), pp. 199–229.

Lewine, 1969
Lewine, Milton. "Nanni, Vignola, and S. Martino degli Svizzeri in Rome." *JSAH* 28 (1969), pp. 27–40.

Liber Pontificalis
Liber Pontificalis. Edited by L. Duchesne. 3 vols. Paris, 1886, 1892, 1957.

Libro di Antonio Billi: Fabriczy, 1891
"Il Libro di Antonio Billi e le sue copie nella Biblioteca Nazionale di Firenze." Edited by Cornelius von Fabriczy. *Archivio Storico Italiano*, s. 5, 7 (1891), pp. 299–368. Reprinted London, 1969.

Loomis, 1919
Loomis, Roger Sherman. "The Allegorical Siege in the Art of the Middle Ages." *American Journal of Archaeology*, s. 2, 23 (1919), pp. 255–269.

Loomis, 1967
Loomis, Roger Sherman. "The Heraldry of Hector, or Confusion Worse Confounded." *Speculum* 42 (1967), pp. 32–35.

Lotz, 1968
Lotz, Wolfgang. "Italienische Plätze des 16. Jahrhunderts." *Jahrbuch 1968 der Max-Planck-Gesellschaft zur Förderung der Wissenschaften e.V.*, pp. 41–60. Göttingen, 1968.

Maccari, 1873
Maccari, Enrico. *Graffiti e chiaroscuri*. Rome, n.d. [1873].

MacDougall, 1962
MacDougall, Elisabeth. Review of T. Magnuson, *Studies in Roman Quattrocento Architecture*. *The Art Bulletin* 44 (1962), pp. 67–75.

Magnuson, 1954
Magnuson, Torgil. "The Project of Nicholas V for Rebuilding the Borgo Leonino in Rome." *The Art Bulletin* 36 (1954), pp. 89–115.

Magnuson, 1958
Magnuson, Torgil. *Studies in Roman Quattrocento Architecture*. Rome, 1958.

Mallè, 1956
Mallè, Luigi. "Elementi di cultura francese nella pittura gotica tarda in Piemonte." *Scritti di storia dell'arte in onore di Lionello Venturi*, 1, pp. 139–174. Rome, 1956.

Mancini, 1967
Mancini, Claudio. *S. Apollinare*. Rome, 1967.

Mancini, 1911
Mancini, Girolamo. *Vita di Leon Battista Alberti*. 2nd ed. Florence, 1911.

Manetti
[See Manetti, *RIS*, and the information in chapter 6, note 1.]

Manetti: Battisti
Manetti, Giannozzo. "De secularibus et pontificalibus pompis." Edited by E. Battisti. In *Umanesimo e esoterismo: Atti del V convengo internazionale di studi umanistici*, edited by E. Castelli, pp. 310–320. Padua, 1960.

Manetti, "De pompis"
Manetti, Giannozzo. "De saecularibus et pontificalibus pompis ad dominum Angelum Asarolum." Urb. Lat. 387, fols. 261ʳ–266ᵛ.

Manetti, "Vita et moribus trium . . . poetarum"
Manetti, Giannozzo. "Vita et moribus trium illustrium poetarum florentinorum." Edited by A. Solerti. In *Le Vite di Dante, Petrarcha e Boccaccio scritte fino al secolo decimosesto*, pp. 108–151. Milan, n.d. [1904].

Manetti, *RIS*
Manetti, Giannozzo. *Vita Nicolai V*. In *RIS*, 1734, 3, part 2.

Manetti, 1970
Manetti, Antonio di Tuccio. *The Life of Brunelleschi*. Critical edition by Howard Saalman. Translated by Catherine Enggass. University Park and London, 1970.

Marchetti-Longhi, 1920
Marchetti-Longhi, Giuseppe. "Il Palazzo di Bonifacio VIII in Anagni." *ASRSP* 43 (1920), pp. 379–410.

Marchini, 1962
Marchini, Giuseppe, and Rodolico, Niccolò. *I Palazzi del popolo nei comuni toscani del medio evo*. Milan, 1962.

Martines, 1963
Martines, Lauro. *The Social World of the Florentine Humanists, 1390–1460*. Princeton, 1963.

Martini, 1965
Martini, Antonio. "Le corporazioni: Loro sede e chiese." In *Il Campidoglio*, pp. 87–95. Rome, 1965.

Mazzeo, 1956
Mazzeo, Joseph Anthony. "The Augustinian Conception of Beauty and Dante's *Convivio*." *Journal of Aesthetics and Art Criticism* 15 (1956–57), pp. 435–448.

Michel, 1930
Michel, Paul-Henri. *Un Idéal humain au XVᵉ siècle: La pensée de L. B. Alberti*. Paris, 1930.

Miglio, 1971
Miglio, Massimo. "Una Vocazione in progresso: Michele Canensi, biografo papale."
Studi Medievali, s. 3,12 (1971), pp. 463–524.

Miniature del Rinascimento, 1950
Miniature del Rinascimento: Catalogo della mostra, Quinta centenario della Biblioteca Vaticana. Vatican City, 1950.

Mitchell, 1951
Mitchell, Charles. "The Lateran Fresco of Boniface VIII." *JWC* 14 (1951), pp. 1–6.

Mitchell, 1961
Mitchell, Charles. *A Fifteenth Century Italian Plutarch (British Museum Add. MS. 22318).* London, 1961.

Mode, 1970
Mode, Robert L. "The Monte Giordano Famous Men Cycle of Cardinal Giordano Orsini and the *Uomini Famosi* Tradition in Fifteenth-Century Italian Art." Ph.D. dissertation, University of Michigan, Ann Arbor, Michigan, 1970.

Mollat, 1963
Mollat, G. *The Popes at Avignon, 1305–1378.* Translated from the 9th ed. (1949) by J. Love. London, 1963.

Mommsen, 1959
Mommsen, Theodor E. "Petrarch and the Decoration of the *Sala Virorum Illustrium* in Padua." *The Art Bulletin* 34 (1952), pp. 95–116. Reprinted in *Medieval and Renaissance Studies of T.E.M.,* edited by E. Rice, Jr., pp. 130–174. Ithaca, 1959.

Moroni
Moroni, Gaetano. *Dizionario di erudizione storico-ecclesiastica.* 109 vols. Venice, 1840—.

Muffel, 1953
Muffel, Nicholas. "Beschreibung der Stadt Rom." In *Codice topografico della città di Roma,* edited by R. Valentini and G. Zucchetti, 4, pp. 351–373. Rome, 1953.

Mühlmann, 1969
Mühlmann, Heiner. "Albertis St.-Andrea-Kirche und das Erhabene." *Zeitschrift für Kunstgeschichte* 32 (1969), pp. 153–157.

Münter, 1929
Münter, Georg. "Die Geschichte der Idealstädte." *Städtebau* 24 (1929), pp. 249–256; 317–340. Revised and reissued as *Idealstädte, ihre Geschichte vom 15.–17. Jahrhundert,* Berlin, 1957.

Müntz, *ACP*
Müntz, Eugène. *Les Arts à la cour des papes pendant le XVe et le XVIe siècle: Recueil de documents inédits.* Bibliothèque des Écoles françaises d'Athènes et de Rome, 4, 9, 28. 3 vols. Paris, 1878–82.

Müntz, 1885
Müntz, Eugène. "Les Arts à la cour des papes, nouvelles recherches." *Mélanges d'archéologie et d'histoire* 5 (1885), pp. 321–337.

Müntz, 1889
Müntz, Eugène. "Les Arts à la cour des papes, nouvelles recherches." *Mélanges d'archéologie et d'histoire* 9 (1889), pp. 134–173.

Müntz and Fabre, 1887
Müntz, Eugène, and Fabre, Paul. *La Bibliothèque du Vatican au XVᵉ siècle.* Paris, 1887.

Nash, 1961
Nash, Ernest. *Bilderlexikon zur Topographie des antiken Rom.* 2 vols. Tübingen, 1961–62.

Nolhac, 1907
Nolhac, Pierre de. *Pétrarque et l'humanisme.* 2 vols. 2nd ed. Paris, 1907.

Orlandi, 1968
Orlandi, Giovanni. "Nota sul testo della 'Descriptio urbis Romae' di L. B. Alberti." *Quaderno,* Università degli Studi di Genova, Facoltà di Architettura, 1 (1968), pp. 81–88.

Orlandi, 1964
Orlandi, Stefano. *Beato Angelico.* Florence, 1964.

Pagliucchi, 1906
Pagliucchi, Pio. *I Castellani del Castel S. Angelo.* Part 1: *I Castellani militari, 1367–1464.* Rome, 1906.

Pagnotti, 1891
Pagnotti, Francesco. "La Vita di Niccolò V scritta da Giannozzo Manetti: Studio preparatorio alla nuova edizione critica." *ASRSP* 14 (1891), pp. 411–436.

Palmieri, 1748
Palmieri, Matthiae. "De temporibus suis." Edited by Joseph Tartinius. In *Rerum Italicarum Scriptores . . . ex Florentinarum bibliothecarum codicibus* (series: Muratori), 1, cols. 239–278. Florence, 1748.

Paltroni, 1966
Paltroni, Pierantonio. *Commentari della vita et gesti dell'illustrissimo Federico Duca d'Urbino.* Edited by Walter Tommasoli. Urbino, 1966.

Panofsky, 1962
Panofsky, Erwin. *Studies in Iconology.* Harper Torchbooks. New York and Evanston, 1962. 1st ed., 1939.

Panofsky, 1970
Panofsky, Erwin. *Renaissance and Renascences in Western Art.* Norwich, 1970. Reprint of Stockholm edition, 1960.

Partner, 1958
Partner, Peter. *The Papal State under Martin V.* London, 1958.

Partner, 1960
Partner, Peter. "The 'Budget' of the Roman Church in the Renaissance Period." In *Italian Renaissance Studies,* edited by E. F. Jacob, pp. 256–278. London, 1960.

Paschini, 1940
Paschini, P. *Roma nel Rinascimento.* Istituto di Studi Romani: Storia di Roma, 12. Bologna, 1940.

Pastor, 1925
Pastor, Ludwig von. *Storia dei papi,* vol. 2 (Pius II through Sixtus IV). Edited by Angelo Mercati. Rome, 1925.

Pastor, 1938
Pastor, Ludwig von. *The History of the Popes,* vol. 1 (through Eugenius IV.) Edited by F. I. Antrobus. 6th ed. London, 1938.

Pastor, 1949
Pastor, Ludwig von. *The History of the Popes,* vol. 2 (Nicholas V and Calixtus III). Edited by F. I. Antrobus. 7th ed. London, 1949.

Patch, 1927
Patch, Howard R. *The Goddess Fortuna in Mediaeval Literature.* Cambridge, Mass., 1927.

Patch, 1950
Patch, Howard R. *The Other World According to Descriptions in Medieval Literature.* Cambridge, Mass., 1950.

Paul, 1963
Paul, Jürgen. "Die mittelalterlichen Kommunalpaläste in Italien." Ph.D. dissertation, University of Freiburg i.Br. Cologne, 1963.

Pernièr, 1929
Pernièr, Adolfo. "La Casina del Cardinale Bessarione." *Annuario dell'Associazione Artistica fra i Cultori di Architettura* (1925-28 [1929]), pp. 62-64.

Pernièr, 1934
Pernièr, Adolfo. "La Storia e il ripristino di una villa per primo Rinascimento sull'Appia." *Capitolium* 10 (1934), pp. 3-18.

Petrarch, *Ignorance,* 1948
Petrarch, Francesco. "On His Own Ignorance and that of Many Others." Translated by Hans Nachod. In *The Renaissance Philosophy of Man,* edited by E. Cassirer, P.O. Kristeller, and J. H. Randall, Jr., pp. 47-133. Chicago, 1948.

Petrarch, *Secret,* 1911
Petrarch, Francesco. *Petrarch's Secret, or the Soul's Conflict with Passion.* Translated by W. H. Draper. London, 1911.

Petrarch, *Solitude,* 1924
Petrarch, Francesco. *The Life of Solitude (De vita solitaria).* Translated by J. Zeitlin. University of Illinois Press, 1924.

Pietrangeli, 1948
Pietrangeli, Carlo. "Iscrizioni inedite o poco note dei palazzi Capitolini." *ASRSP* 71 (1948), pp. 123-137.

Pietrangeli, 1957
Pietrangeli, Carlo. "Campane e orologi sul Campidoglio." *Capitolium* 32, no. 4 (1957), pp. 1-8.

Pietrangeli, 1960
Pietrangeli, Carlo. "Il Palazzo senatorio nel medioevo." *Capitolium* 35, no. 1 (1960), pp. 3–19.

Pietrangeli, 1964
Pietrangeli, Carlo. "I Palazzi Capitolini nel medioevo; I palazzi Capitolini nel Rinascimento." *Capitolium* 39, no. 4 (1964), pp. 191–198. Reprinted in *Il Campidoglio,* Rome, 1965, pp. 21–28.

Pitti, 1967
Two Memoirs of Renaissance Florence: The Diaries of Buonaccorso Pitti and Gregorio Dati. Translated by J. Martines. Edited by G. Brucker. New York, Evanston, London, 1967.

Pius II, "De morte Eugenii IV"
Pius II (Aeneas Sylvius). "De morte Eugenii IV creationeque et coronatione Nicolai V . . . 1447." In *RIS* 3, part 2, cols. 878–898.

Pius II, 1959
Pius II (Aeneas Sylvius). *Memoirs of a Renaissance Pope: The Commentaries of Pius II.* Translated by F. L. Gragg. Edited by L. C. Gabel. New York, 1959. Capricorn Books Edition, 1962.

Platina
Platina, Bartolomeo. *Le Vite de' pontefici.* Venice, 1685.

Poggio, "De avaricia"
Poggio Bracciolini. "De avaricia." In *Prosatori Latini del quattrocento,* edited by E. Garin, La letteratura italiana, storia e testi, pp. 248–301. Milan and Naples, 1952.

Poggio, "Var. fortu.," 1953
Poggio Bracciolini. "De varietate fortunae." In *Codice topografico della città di Roma,* edited by R. Valentini and G. Zucchetti, 4, pp. 230–245. Rome, 1953.

Pope-Hennessy, 1952
Pope-Hennessy, John. *Fra Angelico.* London, 1952.

Potthast, 1874
Potthast, Augustus, ed. *Regesta pontificum romanorum.* 2 vols. Berlin, 1874–75. Reprinted Graz, 1957.

Ptolemy of Lucca, *Vita*
Ptolemy of Lucca. *Vita Martino V. RIS* 3, part 2, cols. 859–867. Also in *Liber pontificalis,* edited by L. Duchesne, 2, pp. 515–523, Paris, 1892. (Actual author is the continuer of the *Vitae.*)

Randall, 1966
Randall, Lilian M. C. *Images in the Margins of Gothic Manuscripts.* Berkeley and Los Angeles, 1966.

Raynaldus
Raynaldus, Odoricus. *Annales ecclesiastici . . . .* vol. 18. Rome, 1659.

Re, 1880
Re, Camillo, ed. *Statuti della città di Roma.* Rome, 1880.

Re, 1882
Re, Camillo. "Il Campidoglio e le sue adiacenze." *Bollettino della Commissione Archeologica Comunale di Roma*, s. 2, 10 (1882), pp. 3–38 in the offprint.

Re, 1920
Re, Emilio. "Maestri di strada." *ASRSP* 43 (1920), pp. 5–102.

Re, 1922
Re, Emilio. "Varietà: Maestri delle strade del 1452." *ASRSP* 46 (1922), pp. 407–409.

Re, 1952
Re, Niccolò del. *La Curia romana*. 2nd ed. Rome, 1952.

Re, 1954
Re, Niccolò del. *La Curia capitolina*. Rome, 1954.

Redig de Campos, 1941–42
Redig de Campos, D. "Di alcune tracce del palazzo di Niccolò III nuovamente tornate alla luce." *Pontificia Accademia Romana di Archeologia: Rendiconti* 18 (1941–42), pp. 71–84.

Redig de Campos, 1947–49
Redig de Campos, D. "Relazione." *Pontificia Accademia Romana di Archeologia: Rendiconti* 23–24 (1947–49), pp. 380–405.

Redig de Campos, 1959
Redig de Campos, D. "Les Constructions d'Innocent III et de Nicholas III sur la colline Vaticane." *Mélanges d'archéologie et d'histoire* 71 (1959), pp. 359–376.

Redig de Campos, 1960
Redig de Campos, D. "Die Bauten Innozenz' III. und Nikolaus' III. auf dem vatikanischen Hügel." *Römische Quartalschrift* 60 (1960), pp. 235–246.

Redig de Campos, 1967
Redig de Campos, D. *I Palazzi vaticani*. Bologna, 1967.

Redig de Campos, Bibliotheca Graeca, 1967
Redig de Campos, D. "Testimonianze del primo nucleo edilizio dei palazzi vaticani e restauro delle pitture delle stanze della 'Bibliotheca Latina' e della 'Bibliotheca Graeca'." In *Il Restauro delle aule Niccolò V e di Sisto IV nel palazzo apostolico vaticano*. Edited by the Direzione Generale dei Servizi Tecnici del Governatorato Vaticano. Vatican City, October, 1967 (unpaginated).

Redig de Campos, 1969
Redig de Campos, D. "Affreschi pisanelliani in Vaticano." *Strenna dei Romanisti* 30 (1969), pp. 125–128.

Redig de Campos, 1971
Redig de Campos, D. "Bramante e il palazzo apostolico vaticano." *Pontificia Accademia Romana di Archeologia: Rendiconti* 43 (1970–71), pp. 283–299.

Richental, 1961
Richental, Ulrich. *Chronicle of the Council of Constance*. Translated by Louise Ropes Loomis. In *The Council of Constance*, edited by J. H. Mundy and K. M. Woody, Columbia University Records of Civilization series, no. 63, pp. 84–199. New York and London, 1961.

Ringbom, 1965
Ringbom, Sixten. *Icon to Narrative: The Rise of the Dramatic Close-up in Fifteenth-century Devotional Painting*. Åbo, 1965.

Robathan, 1970
Robathan, Dorothy M. "Flavio Biondo's *Roma Instaurata*." *Medievalia et Humanistica*, n.s. 1 (1970), pp. 203–216.

Robertson, 1951
Robertson, D. W., Jr. "The Doctrine of Charity in Mediaeval Literary Gardens: A Topical Approach through Symbolism and Allegory." *Speculum* 26 (1951), pp. 24–49.

Robertson, 1962
Robertson, D. W., Jr. *A Preface to Chaucer: Studies in Medieval Perspectives*. Princeton, 1962.

Rodocanachi, 1901
Rodocanachi, E. *Les Institutions communales de Rome sous la Papauté*. Paris, 1901.

Rodocanachi, 1922
Rodocanachi, E. *Histoire de Rome de 1354 à 1471: L'antagonisme entre les romains et le Saint-siège*. Paris, 1922.

Roeder, 1947
Roeder, Helen. "The Borders of Filarete's Bronze Doors to St. Peter's." *JWC* 10 (1947), pp. 150–153.

Rogers, 1962
Rogers, Francis M. *The Quest for Eastern Christians: Travels and Rumor in the Age of Discovery*. Minneapolis, 1962.

Roma cento anni fa, 1970
Roma cento anni fa nelle fotografie del tempo. (Exhibition catalogue. Assessorato antichità belle arti e problemi della cultura; Associazione "Amici dei musei di Roma," Palazzo Braschi, Rome. 17 December 1970–17 March 1971). Rome, n.d.

Rosenau, 1959
Rosenau, Helen. *The Ideal City in its Architectural Evolution*. London, 1959.

Ross, 1948
Ross, David J. A. "Allegory and Romance on a Mediaeval French Marriage Casket." *JWC* 11 (1948), pp. 112–142.

Ross, 1963
Ross, David J. A. *Alexander Historiatus*. London, 1963.

Rotondi, 1950
Rotondi, Pasquale. *Il Palazzo ducale in Urbino*. 2 vols. Urbino, 1950.

Rotondi, 1969
Rotondi, Pasquale. *The Ducal Palace of Urbino*. London, 1969.

Rubinstein, 1958
Rubinstein, Nicolai. "Political Ideas in Sienese Art: The Frescoes by Ambrogio Lorenzetti and Taddeo di Bartolo in the Palazzo Pubblico." *JWC* 21 (1958), pp. 179–207.

Rubinstein, 1967
Rubinstein, Ruth Olitsky. "Pius II's Piazza S. Pietro and St. Andrew's Head." In *Essays in the History of Architecture Presented to Rudolf Wittkower*, edited by D. Fraser, H. Hibbard, and M. Lewine, pp. 22–33. London, 1967.

Rucellai, 1960
Rucellai, Giovanni. *Giovanni Rucellai ed il suo zibaldone;* 1: *"Il zibaldone quaresimale."* Edited by Alessandro Perosa. London, 1960.

Ruggieri, 1962
Ruggieri, Ruggero M. *L'Umanesimo cavalleresco italiano*. Rome, 1962.

Ruysschaert, 1969
Ruysschaert, José. "Sixte IV, Fondateur de la Bibliothèque Vaticane (15 Juin 1475)." *Archivium historiae pontificiae* 7 (1969), pp. 513–524.

Saalman, 1971
Saalman, Howard. Review of Pasquale Rotondi, *The Ducal Palace in Urbino* (English edition, London, 1969). *The Burlington Magazine* 113 (1971), pp. 46–51.

Salimei, 1930–32
Salimei, A. "Serie cronologica dei senatori di Roma dal 1431 al 1447." *ASRSP* 52–55 (1930–32), pp. 41–176.

Salimei, 1935
Salimei, A. *Senatori e statuti di Roma nel medioevo: I senatori, cronologia e bibliografia dal 1144 al 1447*. Rome, 1935.

Salmi, 1919
Salmi, Mario. "Gli Affreschi del palazzo Trenci a Foligno." *Bollettino d'Arte*, s. 1, 13 (1919), pp. 139–180.

Salmi, 1950
Salmi, Mario. "Gli Affreschi di Andrea del Castagno ritrovati." *Bollettino d'Arte*, s. 4. 35 (1950), pp. 295–308.

Salmi, 1954
Salmi, Mario. *Italian Miniatures*. Translated by E. Borgese-Mann. New York, 1954.

Salutati, "To . . . Dominici"
Salutati, Coluccio. "To His Venerable Father in Christ, Brother John Dominici, O.P." Translated in E. Emerton, *Humanism and Tyranny*, pp. 346–377. Cambridge, Mass., 1925.

Saxl, 1942
Saxl, Fritz. "A Spiritual Encyclopaedia of the Later Middle Ages." *JWC* 5 (1942), pp. 82–134.

Scaccia-Scarafoni, 1927
Scaccia-Scarafoni, Camillo. "L'Antico statuto dei 'magistri stratarum' e altri documenti relativi a quella magistratura." *ASRSP* 50 (1927), pp. 239–308.

Scaccia-Scarafoni, 1939
Scaccia-Scarafoni, Camillo. *Le Piante di Roma*. Rome, 1939.

Scaglia, 1964
Scaglia, Gustina. "The Origin of an Archaeological Plan of Rome by Alessandro Strozzi." *JWC* 27 (1964), pp. 137–163.

Scavizzi, 1969
Scavizzi, C. Paola. "Le Condizioni per lo sviluppo dell'attività edilizia a Roma nel sec. XVII: La legislazione." *Studi Romani* 17 (1969), pp. 160–171.

Scheller, 1962
Scheller, R. W. "'Uomini Famosi'." *Bulletin van het Rijksmuseum* 10 (1962), pp. 56–67.

Schiaparelli, 1902
Schiaparelli, L. "Alcuni documenti dei Magistri Aedificorum Urbis (sec. XIII e XIV)." *ASRSP* 25 (1902), pp. 5–60.

Schlosser (1895) 1965
Schlosser, Julius von. *L'arte di corte nel secolo decimoquarto* (originally: "Ein veronesisches Bilderbuch und die höfische Kunst des XIV Jahrhunderts." *Jahrbuch der kunsthistorischen Sammlungen des allerhöchsten Kaiserhauses* 16 [1895]). Translated by G. L. Mellini. Raccolta pisana di saggi e studi: Istituto di Storia dell'Arte dell'Università di Pisa. N.p., 1965.

Seigel, 1968
Seigel, Jerrold E. *Rhetoric and Philosophy in Renaissance Humanism.* Princeton, 1968.

Sella, 1934
Sella, Pietro. *Le Bolle d'oro dell'archivio vaticano.* Vatican City, 1934.

Sella, 1937
Sella, Pietro, and Laurent, M.-H. *I Sigilli dell'archivio vaticano.* 2 vols. Vatican City, 1937.

Serafini, 1910
Serafini, Camillo. *Le Monete e le bolle plumbee pontificie del medagliere vaticano.* 4 vols. Milan, 1910–28.

Seymour, 1966
Seymour, Charles, Jr. *Sculpture in Italy, 1400–1500.* Harmondsworth, 1966.

Siebenhüner, 1954
Siebenhüner, Herbert. *Das Kapitol in Rom: Idee und Gestalt.* Munich, 1954.

Signorili, 1953
Signorili, Niccolò. "Descriptio urbis Romae." In *Codice topografico della città di Roma,* edited by R. Valentini and G. Zucchetti, 4, pp. 151–208. Rome, 1953.

Simpson, 1966
Simpson, W. A. "Cardinal Giordano Orsini (d. 1438) as a Prince of the Church and a Patron of the Arts: A Contemporary Panegyric and Two Descriptions of the Lost Frescoes in Monte Giordano." *JWC* 29 (1966), pp. 135–159.

Simson, 1962
Simson, Otto von. *The Gothic Cathedral.* Harper Torchbooks. New York and Evanston, 1964 (1st ed., 1956; rev. ed., 1962).

Soranzo, 1924
Soranzo, Giovanni. *La Lega italica (1454–1455).* Milan, n.d. [1924].

Spencer, 1957
Spencer, John. *"Ut rhetorica pictura,* A Study in Quattrocento Theory of Painting." *JWC* 20 (1957), pp. 26–44.

Squarciapino, 1962
Squarciapino, Maria Floriani. "L'Obelisco di San Pietro a Roma e una pittura di San Pietro in Grado." *Studi Romani* 10 (1962), pp. 167–170.

Statuti di Lucca, 1960
Statuti urbanistici medievali di Lucca. Edited by Domenico Corsi. Venice, 1960.

Stevenson, 1881
Stevenson, Henry. "Di una pianta di Roma dipinta da Taddeo di Bartolo nella cappella interna del Palazzo del Comune di Siena (a.1413–1414)." *Bollettino della Commissione Archeologica Comunale di Roma,* s. 2, 9 (1881), pp. 74–105.

Storoni Mazzolani, 1970
Storoni Mazzolani, Lidia. *The Idea of the City in Roman Thought: From Walled City to Spiritual Commonwealth.* Translated by S. O'Donnell. Bloomington and London, 1970.

Suger, 1946
Suger, Abbot. *Abbot Suger on the Abbey Church of St.-Denis and Its Art Treasures.* Translated and edited by Erwin Panofsky. Princeton, 1946.

Symeonides, 1965
Symeonides, Sibilla. *Taddeo di Bartolo.* Siena, 1965.

Theiner, *Cod. dip.*
Theiner, Augustin. *Codex diplomaticus domini temporalis S. Sedis.* 3 vols. Rome, 1861–62.

Thelen, 1963
Thelen, Heinrich. Review of A. Frutaz, *Le Piante di Roma. The Art Bulletin* 45 (1963), pp. 283–286.

Thiem and Thiem, 1964
Thiem, Gunther and Christel. *Toskanische Fassaden-Dekoration in Sgraffito und Fresko.* Munich, 1964.

Thoenes, 1963
Thoenes, Christof. "Studien zur Geschichte des Petersplatzes." *Zeitschrift für Kunstgeschichte* 26 (1963), pp. 97–145.

Thurston, 1900
Thurston, Herbert, S.J. *The Holy Year of Jubilee.* London, 1900.

Tierney, 1955
Tierney, Brian. *Foundations of the Conciliar Theory.* Cambridge, 1955.

Toesca, 1958
Toesca, Elena Berti. *Benozzo Gozzoli: Gli affreschi della Cappella Medicea.* 2nd ed. Milan, 1958.

Toesca, 1952
Toesca, Ilaria. "Gli Uomini famosi della Cronaca Cockerell." *Paragone* 3, no. 25 (1952), pp. 16–20.

Tomasetti, 1897
Tomasetti, G. "Del sale e focatico del Comune di Roma nel medio evo." *ASRSP* 20 (1897), pp. 313–368.

Tomei, 1938
Tomei, Piero. "Le Case in serie nell'edilizia romana del '400 al '700." *Palladio,* n.s. 2 (1938), pp. 83–92.

Tomei, 1939
Tomei, Piero. "Un Elenco dei palazzi di Roma del tempo di Clemente VIII." *Palladio,* n.s. 3 (1939), pp. 163–174; 219–230.

Tomei, 1942
Tomei, Piero. *L'Architettura a Roma nel quattrocento.* Rome, 1942.

Tommasini, 1887
Tommasini, O. "Il Registro degli ufficiali del Comune di Roma esemplato dallo scribasenato Marco Guidi." *Atti della R. Accademia dei Lincei, Classe di Scienze morali, storiche e filologiche,* s. 4, 3 (1887), pp. 169–222.

Torquemada, *Consecratione*
Turre Cremata, Ioannis à. *In tractatum de consecratione commentarii.* Lyon, 1555.

Torquemada, *Poenitentia*
Turre Cremata, Ioannis à. *In tractatum de poenitentia commentarii.* Lyon, 1555.

Toynbee and Ward Perkins, 1956
Toynbee, Jocelyn, and Ward Perkins, John. *The Shrine of St. Peter and the Vatican Excavations.* London, et al., 1956.

Trinkaus, 1970
Trinkaus, Charles. *In Our Image and Likeness: Humanity and Divinity in Humanist Thought.* 2 vols. London, 1970.

Tuve, 1966
Tuve, Rosemond. *Allegorical Imagery: Some Mediaeval Books and their Posterity.* Princeton, 1966.

Ullmann, 1949
Ullmann, Walter. *Medieval Papalism.* London, 1949.

Ullmann, 1955
Ullmann, Walter. *The Growth of Papal Government in the Middle Ages.* London, 1955.

Urban, 1961–62
Urban, Günter. "Die Kirchenbaukunst des Quattrocento in Rom." *Römisches Jahrbuch für Kunstgeschichte* 9–10 (1961–62), pp. 73–297.

Urban, 1963
Urban, Günter. "Zum Neubau-Projekt von St. Peter unter Papst Nikolaus V." In *Festschrift für Harald Keller,* pp. 131–173. Darmstadt, 1963.

Vagnetti, 1968
Vagnetti, Luigi. "La 'Descriptio urbis Romae', uno scritto poco noto di Leon Battista Alberti." *Quaderno,* Università degli Studi di Genova, Facoltà di Architettura, 1 (1968), pp. 25–78 [includes a critical edition].

Valla, "Oratio"
Valla, Lorenzo. "Oratio clarissimi viri D. Laurentii Vallae habita in principio sui studii die xviii octobris mcccclv." Edited by M. J. Vahlen. In *Sitzungsberichte der philosophisch-historischen Classe der k. Akademie der Wissenschaft* 62 (1869), pp. 93–98.

Valla, 1922
Valla, Lorenzo. *The Treatise of Lorenzo Valla on the Donation of Constantine.* Translated and edited by Christopher B. Coleman. New Haven, 1922.

Vallone, 1955
Vallone, Aldo. *Cortesia e nobiltà nel Rinascimento.* Asti, 1955.

Vasari
Vasari, Giorgio. *Le Vite de' più eccellenti pittori scultori ed architettori.* Edited by G. Milanesi. 5 vols. and index. Florence, 1878–85.

Vegio, 1953
Vegio, Maffeo. "De rebus antiquis memorabilibus basilicae S. Petri Romae." In *Codice topografico della città di Roma,* edited by R. Valentini and G. Zucchetti, 4, pp. 375–398. Rome, 1953.

Vergerio, 1953
Vergerio, Pier Paolo. "Epistolo LXXXVI." In *Codice topografico della città di Roma,* edited by R. Valentini and G. Zucchetti, 4, pp. 89–100. Rome, 1953.

Vesco, 1919
Vesco, Giacomo. "Leon Battista Alberti e la critica d'arte in sul principio del Rinascimento." *L'Arte* 22 (1919), pp. 57–71; 95–104; 136–148.

Vespasiano, 1963
Vespasiano da Bisticci. *Renaissance Princes, Popes, and Prelates.* Translated by W. George and E. Waters. New York, Evanston, and London, 1963.

Vita di Cola, 1928
La Vita di Cola di Rienzo. Edited by A. M. Ghisalberti. Florence, 1928.

Vitruvius
Vitruvius. *De architectura.* Translated and edited by F. Granger. 2 vols. London and New York: Loeb Classical Library, 1934.

Weil, 1968
Weil, Mark S. "The History and Decoration of the Ponte S. Angelo." Ph.D. dissertation, Columbia University, New York, 1968.

Weiss, 1969
Weiss, Roberto. *The Renaissance Discovery of Classical Antiquity.* Oxford, 1969.

Westfall, *JHI,* 1969
Westfall, Carroll William. "Painting and the Liberal Arts: Alberti's View." *Journal of the History of Ideas* 30 (1969), pp. 487–506.

Westfall, *SR*, 1969
Westfall, Carroll William. "Society, Beauty, and the Humanist Architect in Alberti's *De re aedificatoria.*" *Studies in the Renaissance* 16 (1969), pp. 61–79.

Westfall, 1971
Westfall, Carroll William. "Biblical Typology in the *Vita Nicolai V* by Giannozzo Manetti." *Acta Conventus Neolatini Lovaniensis* (Proceedings of the First International Congress for Neo-Latin Studies), August 23–28, 1971. Edited by J. IJsewijn and E. Kessler. Munich (in course of publication).

Whitfield, 1965
Whitfield, J. H. *Petrarch and the Renascence.* New York, 1965 (1st ed. 1943).

Wilks, 1963
Wilks, Michael. *The Problem of Sovreignty in the Later Middle Ages.* Cambridge, 1963.

Wind, 1937–38
Wind, Edgar. "Charity." *JWC* 1 (1937–38), pp. 322–330.

Wittkower, 1962
Wittkower, Rudolf. *Architectural Principles in the Age of Humanism.* 3rd ed. London, 1962.

Wolff Metternich, 1967
Wolff Metternich, Franz Graf. "Über die Massgrundlagen des Kuppelentwurfes Bramantes für die Peterskirche in Rom." In *Essays in the History of Architecture Presented to Rudolf Wittkower,* edited by D. Fraser, H. Hibbard, and M. Lewine, pp. 40–52. London, 1967.

Wyss, 1957
Wyss, R. L. "Die neun Helden." *Zeitschrift für schweizerische Archaeologie und Kunstgeschichte* 17 (1957), pp. 73–106.

Yuen, 1970
Yuen, Toby. "The 'Bibliotheca Graeca': Castagno, Alberti, and Ancient Sources." *The Burlington Magazine* 112 (1970), pp. 725–736.

Zippel, 1907
Zippel, Giuseppe. "Per la storia del Palazzo di Venezia." *Ausonia* 2 (1907), pp. 114–136.

Zippel, 1911
Zippel, Giuseppe. "Paolo II e l'arte, note e documenti: IV: Gli edifici di San Pietro." *L'Arte* 14 (1911), pp. 181–197.

Zippel, 1919
Zippel, Giuseppe. "Piero della Francesca a Roma." *Rassegna d'arte* 19 (1919), pp. 81–94.

Zoubov, 1958
Zoubov, Vassili. "Leon Battista Alberti et les auteurs du moyen-Age." In *Medieval and Renaissance Studies,* edited by R. Hunt, R. Klibansky, L. Labowsky, 4, pp. 245–266. London: Warburg Institute, 1958.

List of Illustrations

Figures in the Text

A.   Map of Rome at the middle of the fifteenth century, indicating the major streets, palaces, and places of interest in Nicholas V's program, and other items of importance (after Touring Club Italiano and Magnuson)

B.   Schematic map of the Borgo, Rome, in the middle of the fifteenth century, indicating possible interpretations of Nicholas V's program (after Magnuson)

C.   General plan of the Vatican Palace grounds in the middle of the fifteenth century (after Magnuson and Redig de Campos)

D.   General, schematic plan of the Vatican Palace, locating the areas renovated by Nicholas V (after Magnuson and Redig de Campos)

Plates

1.   Filarete, Porta Argentea. St. Peter's, Rome, dated 1445 (Hertziana, C 7887)

2.   Filarete, *Eugenius IV Receiving the Keys from St. Peter*. Porta Argentea. St. Peter's, Rome, dated 1445 (Vat., XXXII 123.73)

3.   Filarete, *Martyrdom of St. Peter*. Porta Argentea. St. Peter's, Rome, dated 1445 (Alinari, 7030)

4.   Filarete, *Embarkation of the Greeks from Constantinople and Reception of the Eastern Emperor by the Pope at Ferrara*. Porta Argentea. St. Peter's, Rome, dated 1445 (Vat., XXXII 127.56)

5.   Filarete, *Council of Ferrara and the Embarkation of the Greeks for Constantinople*. Porta Argentea. St. Peter's, Rome, dated 1445 (Vat., XXXII 127.57)

6.   Filarete, *Coronation of Sigismund and his Reception by the Castellan of the Castel Sant'Angelo*. Porta Argentea. St. Peter's, Rome, dated 1445 (Vat., XXXII 123.55)

7.   Detail of fig. 6 (Hertziana, C 7923)

8.   Filarete, *Transfer of the Council from Florence to the Lateran, and the Assembly of the Church at Rome*. Porta Argentea. St. Peter's, Rome, dated 1445 (Vat., XXXII 127.54)

9.   Detail of fig. 8 (Hertziana, D 11672)

10.   Detail of fig. 8 (Hertziana, D 11673)

11.   Detail of fig. 8 (Hertziana, D 11674)

12.   Andrea del Castagno, *Uomini e donne famosi: Niccolò Acciaiuoli, Cumaean Sibyl, Queen Esther, Queen Tomyris, Dante.* Museo Andrea del Castagno, Florence; formerly Villa Pandolfini-Carducci, Legnaia, Florence (now detached), 1449–51 (Alinari, 30675a)

13.   Andrea del Castagno, sinopia: *Farinata degli Uberti.* In situ, Villa Pandolfini-Carducci, Legnaia, Florence, 1449–51 (G.F.S.G., Florence, 144245)

14.   Andrea del Castagno, *Eve, Madonna and Child, Adam.* End wall, in situ, Villa Pandolfini-Carducci, Legnaia, Florence, 1449–51 (G.F.S.G., Florence, 144241)

15.   Detail of fig. 14 (G.F.S.G., Florence, 144243)

16.   Andrea del Castagno, *Putto.* In situ, Villa Pandolfini-Carducci, Legnaia, Florence, 1449–51 (note area on left, which is next to one of the truss footings) (G.F.S.G., Florence, 71862)

17.   Taddeo di Bartolo, *Cicero, M. Porcius Cato,* and *P. Scipio Nasica.* Antechamber to the chapel, Palazzo Pubblico, Siena, dated 1413–14 (Foto Grassi, Siena, 114)

18.   Taddeo di Bartolo, *Aristotle.* Antechamber to the chapel, Palazzo Pubblico, Siena, dated 1413–14 (Foto Grassi, Siena, 118)

19.   Taddeo di Bartolo, *M. Junius Brutus.* Antechamber to the chapel, Palazzo Pubblico, Siena, dated 1413–14 (Foto Grassi, Siena, 113)

20.   *Golden Bull of Louis of Bavaria,* attributed to Leonardo da Venezia, dated 1328–40 (Hertziana, D 2808)

21.   Giacomo da Fabriano, *Rome. De civitate Dei.* Biblioteca Vaticana, Rome, Cod. Reg. Lat. 1882, fol. 2^r, dated 1456 (Bibl. Apos. Vat.)

22.   Niccolò Polani, *Rome. De civitate Dei.* Bibliothèque Ste.-Geneviève, Paris, Cod. 218, fol. 2^r, dated 1459 (Photographie Giraudon, Paris, LAC 45.341)

23.   Shop of Apollonio di Giovanni, cassone, *Rome.* Yale University Art Gallery, New Haven, Conn., J. J. Jarvis Collection, ca. 1460–65? (Yale University Art Gallery)

24.   Workshop of Cosimo Rosselli? *View of Florence with a Chain.* Staatliche Museen, Berlin, Kupferstichkabinett, ca. 1485 (Alinari, 50432)

25.   Taddeo di Bartolo, *Rome.* Antechamber to the chapel, Palazzo Pubblico, Siena, dated 1413–14 (G.F.N., Rome, C 11240)

26.   Masolino, *Rome.* Collegiate Church, Castiglione Olona (Varese), Baptistry, dated 1435 (Anderson, 32254)

27.   Anonymous, *Rome.* Biblioteca Reale, Turin, Ms. Varia 102, fol. 28^r, after 1432 (Istituto di Studi Romani)

28.   Anonymous, *Rome.* The Metropolitan Museum of Art, New York, Harris Brisbane Dick Fund 1958 (58.105) (Metropolitan Museum of Art, 198032)

29.   Alessandro Strozzi, *Rome.* Biblioteca Medicea-Laurenziana, Florence, Cod. Redi 77, fols. vii^v–viii^r, dated 1474 (Biblioteca Medicea-Laurenziana)

30.   Piero del Massaio, *Rome.* Bibliothèque Nationale, Paris, Ms. Lat. 4802, fol. 133^r, probably either 1453 or 1456 (Bibl. Nat., Paris, A 69/64)

31.   Piero del Massaio, *Rome.* Biblioteca Vaticana, Rome, Cod. Vat. Lat. 5699, fol. 127^r, dated 1469 (Bibl. Apos. Vat.)

54. *Putto.* North wall (see also fig. 55), Sala Vecchia degli Svizzeri, Vatican Palace, between 1447 and 1455 (Vat., XXXII 126.39)

55. *Putto and Butterflies.* North wall (see also fig. 54), Sala Vecchia degli Svizzeri, Vatican Palace, between 1447 and 1455 (Vat., XXXII 126.38)

56. *Putto Riding a Swan (?).* East wall, Sala Vecchia degli Svizzeri, Vatican Palace, between 1447 and 1455 (Vat., XXXII 127.5)

57. *Putto Shooting a Bow.* East wall, Sala Vecchia degli Svizzeri, Vatican Palace, between 1447 and 1455 (Vat., XXXII 126.32)

58. *Tiara and Keys.* East(?) or west(?) wall, Sala Vecchia degli Svizzeri, Vatican Palace, between 1447 and 1455 (Vat., XXXII 127.4)

59. *Putto and Bagpipe.* East wall, Sala Vecchia degli Svizzeri, Vatican Palace, between 1447 and 1455 (Vat., XXXII 126.34)

60. *Fortitude.* West wall, Sala Vecchia degli Svizzeri, Vatican Palace, between 1447 and 1455 (Vat., XXXII 127.1)

61. *Justice.* West wall, Sala Vecchia degli Svizzeri, Vatican Palace, between 1447 and 1455 (Vat., XXXII 126.36)

62. *Prudence.* West wall, Sala Vecchia degli Svizzeri, Vatican Palace, between 1447 and 1455 (Vat., XXXII 126.35)

63. *Tarquin's Attack on Lucretia.* Palazzo Vitelleschi, Tarquinia, dated 1437–40 (G.F.N., Rome, E 4827)

64. Stemma of Eugenius IV and decorative frieze. Palazzo Vitelleschi, Tarquinia, dated 1437–40 (G.F.N., Rome, E 23640)

65. *St. Luke.* Palazzo Vitelleschi, Tarquinia, dated 1437–40 (G.F.N., Rome, E 23642)

66. Wing of Nicholas V, Vatican, dated 1447–55 (with later additions) (Vat., XXXI 6.19)

67. Northwest corner, Sala Graeca, Vatican Palace, between 1447 and 1455 (G.F.N., Rome, C 8772)

68. South wall (with southeast corner), Sala Graeca, Vatican Palace, between 1447 and 1455 (G.F.N., Rome C 8771)

69. North vault boss, Sala Graeca, Vatican Palace, between 1447 and 1455 (G.F.N., Rome, C 8770)

70. North lunette of west wall, Sala Graeca, Vatican Palace, between 1447 and 1455 (Vat., III 10.12)

71. Piero del Massaio, *Borgo* (detail of fig. 30). Bibliothèque Nationale, Paris, Ms. Lat. 4802, fol. 133ʳ, probably either 1453 or 1456 (Bibl. Nat., Paris, A 69/64)

72. Piero del Massaio, *Borgo* (detail of fig. 32). Biblioteca Vaticana, Rome, Urb. Lat. 277, fol. 131ʳ, dated 1472 (Bibl. Apos. Vat.)

73. Alessandro Strozzi, *Borgo* (detail of fig. 29). Biblioteca Medicea-Laurenziana, Florence, Cod. Redi 77, fols. viiᵛ–viiiʳ, dated 1474 (Hertziana)

74. Piero del Massaio, *Borgo* (detail of fig. 31). Biblioteca Vaticana, Rome, Cod. Vat. Lat. 5699, fol. 127ʳ, dated 1469 (Bibl. Apos. Vat.)

75. Anonymous, *Borgo* (detail of fig. 34). Palazzo Ducale, Mantua, early 16th century (Alinari, 48209; detail)

Abbreviations for sources of photographs:

Bibl. Apos. Vat.: Biblioteca Apostolica Vaticana
Bibl. Nat., Paris: Bibliothèque Nationale, Paris
G.F.N., Rome: Gabinetto Fotografico Nazionale, Rome
G.F.S.G., Florence: Soprintendenze alle Gallerie, Firenze, Gabinetto Fotografico
Hertziana: Fototeca of the Bibliotheca Hertziana, Rome
Vat.: Archivio Fotografico dei Gallerie e Musei Vaticani

The plans in the text were executed by Allen D. Ho.

Index

In the case of paintings and sculpture, except for anonymous works, full citations appear only under the name of the artist. A citation to the location appears only for the first mention in the text.

Manuscript illustrations, drawings, and panel paintings (Except for anonymous works, only the first mention in the text is cited. Full citations appear under the name of the artist.)

1. Filarete, Porta Argentea. St. Peter's, Rome, dated 1445

2. Filarete, *Eugenius IV Receiving the Keys from St. Peter*. Porta Argentea. St. Peter's, Rome, dated 1445

3. Filarete, *Martyrdom of St. Peter*. Porta Argentea. St. Peter's, Rome, dated 1445

4. Filarete, *Embarkation of the Greeks from Constantinople and Reception of the Eastern Emperor by the Pope at Ferrara.* Porta Argentea. St. Peter's, Rome, dated 1445

5. Filarete, *Council of Ferrara and the Embarkation of the Greeks for Constantinople.* Porta Argentea. St. Peter's, Rome, dated 1445

6. Filarete, *Coronation of Sigismund and his Reception by the Castellan of the Castel Sant'Angelo.* Porta Argentea. St. Peter's, Rome, dated 1445

7. Detail of fig. 6

8. Filarete, *Transfer of the Council from Florence to the Lateran, and the Assembly of the Church at Rome.* Porta Argentea. St. Peter's, Rome, dated 1445

9. Detail of fig. 8

10. Detail of fig. 8

11. Detail of fig. 8

12. Andrea del Castagno, *Uomini e donne famosi: Niccolò Acciaiuoli, Cumaean Sibyl, Queen Esther, Queen Tomyris, Dante*. Museo Andrea del Castagno, Florence; formerly Villa Pandolfini-Carducci, Legnaia, Florence (now detached), 1449–51

13. Andrea del Castagno, sinopia: *Farinata degli Uberti*. In situ, Villa Pandolfini-Carducci, Legnaia, Florence, 1449–51

14. Andrea del Castagno, *Eve, Madonna and Child, Adam*. End wall, in situ, Villa Pandolfini-Carducci, Legnaia, Florence, 1449–51

15. Detail of fig. 14

16. Andrea del Castagno, *Putto*. In situ, Villa Pandolfini-Carducci, Legnaia, Florence, 1449–51 (note area on left, which is next to one of the truss footings)

17. Taddeo di Bartolo, *Cicero, M. Porcius Cato,* and *P. Scipio Nasica.* Antechamber to the chapel, Palazzo Pubblico, Siena, dated 1413–14

18. Taddeo di Bartolo, *Aristotle*. Antechamber to the chapel, Palazzo Pubblico, Siena, dated 1413–14

19. Taddeo di Bartolo, *M. Junius Brutus*. Antechamber to the chapel, Palazzo Pubblico, Siena, dated 1413–14

20. *Golden Bull of Louis of Bavaria*, attributed to Leonardo da Venezia, dated 1328–40

NTEREA.
GOTHORV
one agentium se
impetu magne
us euersionem
torumq: cultore
paganos uocam
gionem referre c
us & amarus de
re ceperunt. Vr
z elo domus de
phemias uel erro
dei scribere institu . Quod opus per aliquot annos

21. Giacomo da Fabriano, *Rome*. *De civitate Dei*. Biblioteca Vaticana, Rome, Cod. Reg. Lat. 1882, fol. 2ʳ, dated 1456

22. Niccolò Polani, *Rome.* *De civitate Dei.* Bibliothèque Ste.-Geneviève, Paris, Cod. 218, fol. 2^r, dated 1459

23. Shop of Apollonio di Giovanni, cassone, *Rome*. Yale University Art Gallery, New Haven, Conn.,
J. J. Jarvis Collection, ca. 1460–65?

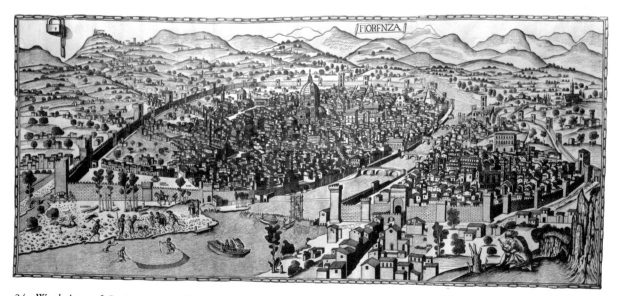

24. Workshop of Cosimo Rosselli? *View of Florence with a Chain*. Staatliche Museen, Berlin, Kupferstichkabinett,
ca. 1485

25. Taddeo di Bartolo, *Rome*. Antechamber to the chapel, Palazzo Pubblico, Siena, dated 1413–14

26. Masolino, *Rome*. Collegiate Church, Castiglione Olona (Varese), Baptistry, dated 1435

27. Anonymous, *Rome*. Biblioteca Reale, Turin, Ms. Varia 102, fol. 28ʳ, after 1432

28. Anonymous, *Rome*. The Metropolitan Museum of Art, New York, Harris Brisbane Dick Fund 1958 (58.105)

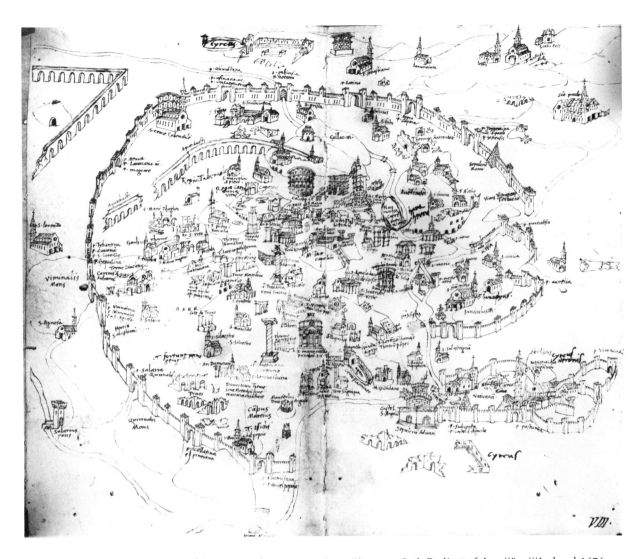

29. Alessandro Strozzi, *Rome*. Biblioteca Medicea-Laurenziana, Florence, Cod. Redi 77, fols. vii^v–viii^r, dated 1474

30. Piero del Massaio, *Rome*. Bibliothèque Nationale, Paris, Ms. Lat. 4802, fol. 133ʳ, probably either 1453 or 1456

31. Piero del Massaio, *Rome*. Biblioteca Vaticana, Rome, Cod. Vat. Lat. 5699, fol. 127ʳ, dated 1469

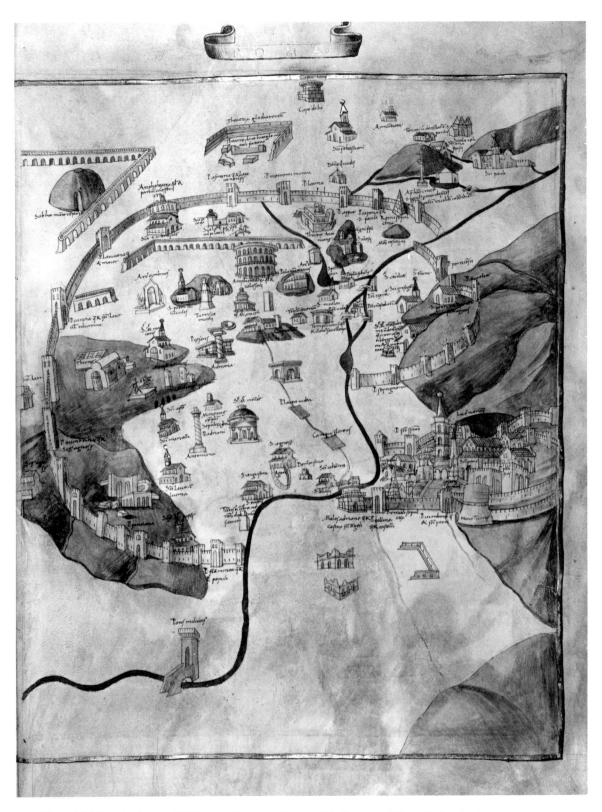

32. Piero del Massaio, *Rome*. Biblioteca Vaticana, Rome, Urb. Lat. 277, fol. 131ʳ, dated 1472

33. Benozzo Gozzoli, *St. Augustine Leaving Rome*. Sant'Agostino, San Gimignano, dated 1465

34. Anonymous, *Rome*. Palazzo Ducale, Mantua, early 16th century

35. Tentative reconstruction of the Palazzo del Senatore, Rome, just after 1303; after C. Pietrangeli

36. Anonymous, *Capitol, Rome.* Louvre, Paris, Cabinet des Dessins, no. 11028, ca. 1554–60

37. Palazzo del Senatore, Rome; façade toward the Forum

38. Palazzo del Senatore, Rome; façade toward the Forum

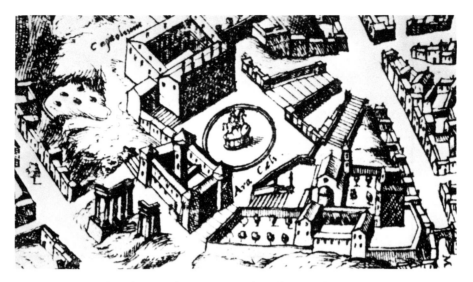

39. Etienne DuPérac (designer), Antonio Lafreri (engraver), *View of Rome* (detail). Single example, British Museum, London, Map Room, dated 1577

40. Anonymous copy from Marten van Heemskerck, *Rome from Monte Caprino* (detail). Staatliche Museen, Berlin, Kupferstich-kabinett, after 1534

41. Marten van Heemskerck, *Capitol, Rome*. Staatliche Museen, Berlin, Kupferstichkabinett, ca. 1535–36

42. Castel di San Giorgio, Mantua, late 14th century?

43. Palazzo Comunale, Viterbo, dated 1448–1503 ff.

44. Palazzo Comunale, Narni, 13th century and ca. 1460?

45. School of Domenico Ghirlandaio, *Ponte and Castel Sant'Angelo, Rome, in 1455(?).*
From Egger, *Codex Escurialensis*

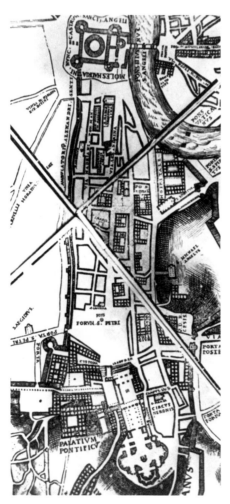

46. Leonardo Bufalini, *Borgo.*
Detail from map of Rome, dated 1551, reprinted 1560

47. Anonymous, *Ponte and Castel Sant'Angelo, Rome*. Biblioteca Estense, Modena, Marcanova Ms., fol. xiv^r, between 1453 and 1465

48. Decorative frieze. South wall, Sala dei Chiaroscuri, Vatican Palace, 12th century and between 1447 and 1455

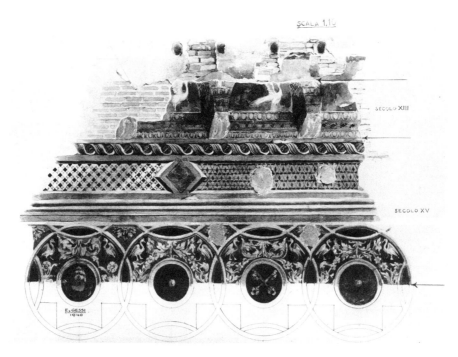

49. Decorative frieze. Sala dei Chiaroscuri, Vatican Palace, 12th century and between 1447 and 1455, reconstruction by E. Gessi

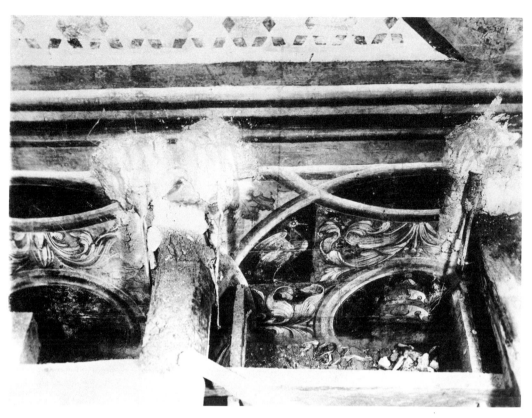

50. Decorative frieze. East wall, Sala dei Chiaroscuri, Vatican Palace, between 1447 and 1455

51. Decorative frieze. East wall, Sala dei Chiaroscuri, Vatican Palace, between 1447 and 1455

52. Decorative frieze. Southeast corner, Sala dei Chiaroscuri, Vatican Palace, between 1447 and 1455

53. Decorative frieze. South wall, Sala Vecchia degli Svizzeri, Vatican Palace, mid 13th century

54. *Putto*. North wall, Sala Vecchia degli Svizzeri,
Vatican Palace, between 1447 and 1455

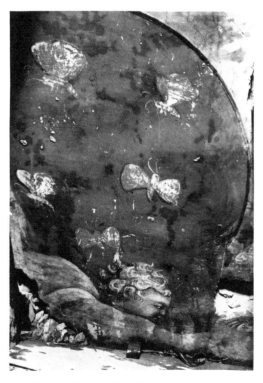

55. *Putto and Butterflies*. North wall

56. *Putto Riding a Swan (?)*. East wall, Sala Vecchia degli Svizzeri, Vatican Palace, between 1447 and 1455

57. *Putto Shooting a Bow*. East wall, Sala Vecchia degli Svizzeri, Vatican Palace, between 1447 and 1455

58. *Tiara and Keys*. East(?) or west(?) wall, Sala Vecchia degli Svizzeri, Vatican Palace, between 1447 and 1455

59. *Putto and Bagpipe.* East wall, Sala Vecchia degli Svizzeri, Vatican Palace, between 1447 and 1455

60. *Fortitude.* West wall, Sala Vecchia degli Svizzeri, Vatican Palace, between 1447 and 1455

61. *Justice*. West wall, Sala Vecchia degli Svizzeri, Vatican Palace, between 1447 and 1455

62. *Prudence*. West wall, Sala Vecchia degli Svizzeri, Vatican Palace, between 1447 and 1455

63. *Tarquin's Attack on Lucretia*. Palazzo Vitelleschi, Tarquinia, dated 1437–40

64. Stemma of Eugenius IV and decorative frieze. Palazzo Vitelleschi, Tarquinia, dated 1437–40

65. *St. Luke.* Palazzo Vitelleschi, Tarquinia, dated 1437–40

66. Wing of Nicholas V, Vatican, dated 1447–55 (with later additions)

67. Northwest corner, Sala Graeca, Vatican Palace, between 1447 and 1455

68. South wall (with southeast corner), Sala Graeca, Vatican Palace, between 1447 and 1455

69. North vault boss, Sala Graeca, Vatican Palace, between 1447 and 1455

70. North lunette of west wall, Sala Graeca, Vatican Palace, between 1447 and 1455

71. Piero del Massaio, *Borgo* (detail of fig. 30).
Bibliothèque Nationale, Paris, Ms. Lat. 4802, fol. 133ʳ,
probably either 1453 or 1456

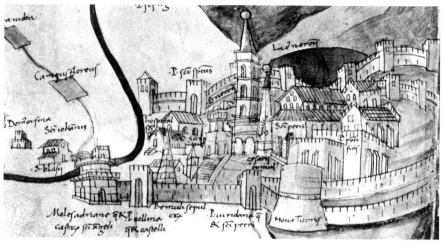

72. Piero del Massaio, *Borgo* (detail of fig. 32). Biblioteca Vaticana, Rome,
Urb. Lat. 277, fol. 131ʳ, dated 1472

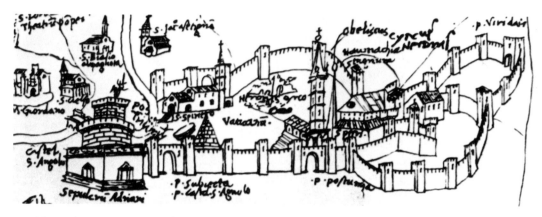

73. Alessandro Strozzi, *Borgo* (detail of fig. 29). Biblioteca Medicea-Laurenziana, Florence,
Cod. Redi 77, fols. viiᵛ–viiiʳ, dated 1474

74. Piero del Massaio, *Borgo* (detail of fig. 31).
Biblioteca Vaticana, Rome,
Cod. Vat. Lat. 5699, fol. 127ʳ, dated 1469

75. Anonymous, *Borgo* (detail of fig. 34). Palazzo Ducale, Mantua, early 16th century

76. *Arch of Alfonso I*. Castel Nuovo, Naples, mid 15th century

77. *Libro di matematica di Giuliano de'Medici.* Biblioteca
Riccardiana, Florence, Ricc. 2669, fol. 110ᵛ, between
1450 and 1500

78. Apollonio di Giovanni, *Dido Receiving the Ambassadors of Aeneas.* Biblioteca Riccardiana, Florence, Ricc. 492, fol. 74ᵛ, ca. 1460–65

79. Anonymous illustrator, *The Author Presenting his
Work to Eugenius IV*. Antonio da Rho (Antonii Rau-
densis), *Dialogi tres in Firmianum Lactantium*. Biblioteca Vaticana, Rome, Vat. Lat. 227, fol. 4ᵛ, between 1431 and 1447

80. Anonymous illustrator, *Miracle of the Poisoned Bread*. Gregorius I, *Dialogorium Liber
II Vita S. Benedicti*. The Pierpont Morgan Library, New York, M. 184, fol. 14ᵛ, ca. 1450

81. Taddeo Crivelli?, *King Solomon and his Court*. *Bible of Borso d'Este*. Biblioteca Estense, Modena, Ms. V.G. 12, vol. I, fol. 280ᵛ, dated 1455–61

82. Anonymous illustrator, *Neufs Preux*. Bibliothèque Nationale, Paris, Fr. 12559, fol. 125ʳ, late 14th century

83. Anonymous illustrator, *Neufes Preuses*. Bibliothèque Nationale, Paris,
Fr. 12559, fol. 125ᵛ, late 14th century

84. Giacomo Jaquerio, *Neufs Preux*. Portion of the left half of a wall in the great hall, Castello della Manta (Piedmont), first half of the 15th century

85. Giacomo Jaquerio, *Neufes Preuses*. Portion of the right half of a wall in the great hall, Castello della Manta (Piedmont), first half of the 15th century

86. Giotto, *Charity*. Arena Chapel, Padua, dated 1303

87. Giacomo da Fabriano, *Putti*. *De civitate Dei*. Biblioteca Vaticana, Rome, Cod. Reg. Lat. 1882, fol. 2ʳ, dated 1456